Pests of the West *Revised*

Prevention and Control for Today's Garden and Small Farm

Check out these bugs!
Whitney Cranshaw

WHITNEY CRANSHAW

FULCRUM PUBLISHING
GOLDEN, COLORADO

I would like to dedicate this book to Sue Ballou, my best friend and wife.

*I would also like to acknowledge the entire class of animals known as Insects,
which, although they sometimes wreak havoc in the garden,
are endlessly fascinating to observe.*

Copyright © 1998 Whitney Cranshaw
Cover design by Alyssa Pumphrey
Book design by Alyssa Pumphrey and Sarah Read
Cover image courtesy Animals Animals/Earth Scenes © 1998 Breck P. Kent
All photographs copyright © 1998 Whitney Cranshaw, except where otherwise noted.

Library of Congress Cataloging-in-Publication Data
Cranshaw, Whitney.
      Pests of the West : prevention and control for today's garden and
small farm / Whitney Cranshaw. —Rev. ed.
        p.   cm.
      Includes index.
      ISBN 1-55591-401-2 (pbk.)
      1. Garden pests—West (U.S.)—Control. 2. Plant diseases—West (U.S.).
I. Title.
SB605.U5C73   1998
635'.049'0978—dc21   98-29636
                                     CIP

Printed in Canada
0 9 8 7 6 5 4 3 2 1

Fulcrum Publishing
350 Indiana Street, Suite 350
Golden, Colorado 80401-5093
(800) 992-2908 • (303) 277-1623
website: www.fulcrum-gardening.com • e-mail: fulcrum@fulcrum-gardening.com

Table of Contents

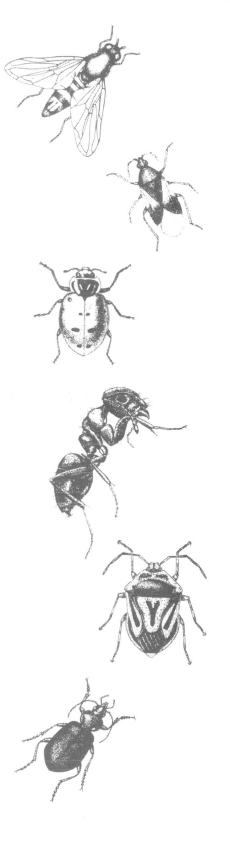

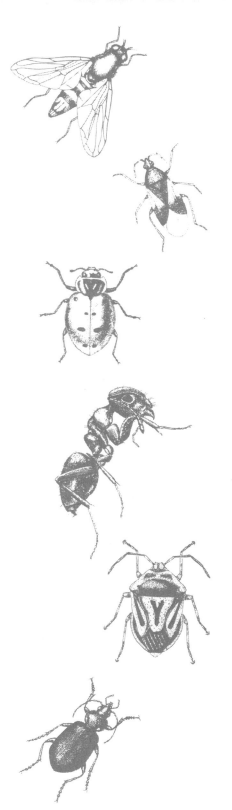

Notes on the Revised Edition

Much of a decade has passed since the first edition of *Pests of the West* was published in 1992. During that time it has frequently been my pleasure to discuss with fellow gardeners their experiences with common garden problems of this region. The Master Gardener program, which I immensely enjoy being associated with, has been a particularly rich source, bringing to my attention new pest problems, novel management ideas, and a good dose of reality to any ideas I have dared set forth on various gardening subjects.

In this newest version I have tried to include information that I have learned in the interim to update this book, to expand areas that could benefit from better treatment, and to correct a few errors or poorly stated sections. I also hope that the new format, improved graphics, and index will make this a more usable reference for gardeners of the Intermountain West and High Plains regions.

—Whitney Cranshaw
June 1998

Acknowledgments

Many have helped create this book.

Perhaps what has been most important is the system of cooperatively shared research information that has been developed through the state Agricultural Experiment Stations and Cooperative Extension via the Land Grant educational system. I have drawn heavily from the previously published efforts of my colleagues at Colorado State University and across the country, tempering these with my own observations and experience.

Several of these publications are worthy of particular note, including *Prevention and Control of Wildlife Damage*, produced cooperatively by Extension wildlife specialists in coordination with the University of Nebraska; *Weeds of the West* and *Weeds of Colorado;* and *Insects and Related Pests of Vegetables,* published by the University of North Carolina. These have been supplemented by scores of USDA technical bulletins and information fact sheets produced by the states that are within the scope of this book. In addition, I have found that the old standards, such as *Destructive and Useful Insects* and *Insects of Western North America,* continue to be outstanding references for information on insects. *Vegetable Diseases and Their Control* served as a very useful starting point for information on plant diseases. And I must further acknowledge the writings of Howard Ensign Evans, including *Life on a Little Known Planet,* as a source of fascinating information and inspiration for any bug-watcher.

Most of the artwork used in this book has also been developed for use in USDA or state Cooperative Extension publications. In addition, many illustrations have been borrowed from the California Department of Food and Agriculture Publication 518, *Stone Fruit Orchard Pests: Identification and Control,* and from the pest management publication series developed by the University of Illinois. There is also original artwork by several friends and associates, including Beth Brozo, Tom Weissling, Matt Leatherman, and Tess Henn.

Several individuals also helped me by reviewing sections as they were prepared. Laura Pickett-Pottorff, Barbara Hyde, Curt Swift, Ken Barbarick, and George Beck have all helped straighten me out when I ventured into areas on the fringe of my experience. Boris Kondratieff, Bill Brown, Howard Schwartz, Jim Feucht, and Bob Hammon have all provided invaluable technical assistance in developing sections of this book. Dave Leatherman, Frank Peairs, and John Capinera have helped not only in providing content, but also by supplying photographs and by simply being great people with whom I have had the pleasure to associate.

Finally, I must recognize all those at Fulcrum Publishing who have made this book possible. The original impetus behind this book came from Bob Baron, who also created the title. Jay Staten held my hand through the first edition and Sarah Read rose to the occasion in this current version.

I thank you all.

Introduction

HOW TO USE THIS BOOK

Western North America is a unique area in which to garden. Most areas are blessed by abundant sunshine, but rainfall is typically scarce and all too often is followed by hail. Soils are often less than ideal, a bit on the heavy side, high in clay, and tend toward the alkaline range. Salts can also pose a severe problem.

One difficulty in gardening anywhere is dealing with the occasional pest problem. In the West, we have our share of pests, although fortunately we are often spared many of the problems common to the warmer and wetter areas of the country.

Pests are organisms that cross human interests—or just rub us the wrong way. This is not a natural distinction; "good" bug versus "bad" bug means nothing in nature. What we choose to call a pest varies with the situation. For example, honey bees are more than welcome while pollinating fruit trees, but should they choose to nest in the wall of your home, they become pests. On the other hand, most people have trouble giving earwigs the time of day, but when they are not resting in your sweet corn, they are probably eating aphids, caterpillars, and other pests.

In the West, gardeners are faced with many pest problems unique to this area. Coyotes stealing melons and an elk napping in the cabbage patch are situations not typically encountered in most of North America, but they do occasionally occur in the West. California has its fruit flies,

harlequin bugs and root-knot nematodes roam the South, and Japanese beetles and gypsy moths often plague the eastern seaboard. None of these constitute major problems in the West, where soil diseases, grasshoppers, and potato psyllids may be the gardener's biggest headache.

Pests of the West emphasizes the common garden problems of the High Plains, Rocky Mountain, and intermontane regions of the United States and southern Canada. It covers the major insect pests, plant diseases, and weeds most often encountered in this area of tremendous diversity. The focus of this book is limited to commonly grown vegetables, fruits, flowers, and herbs. Lawns and landscape plants are not included.

This book has been organized into four major sections. Chapter 1 focuses on soils, fundamental to any garden. Common soil problems and how to correct them are discussed.

Chapters 2, 3, and 4 cover techniques for controlling garden pests. Natural and biological controls, which provide a tremendous amount of often unrecognized "background" plant protection, are examined first, as is appropriate. Cultural and mechanical controls follow, and the section concludes with chemical controls—pesticides (a subject that is also discussed further in Appendix IV).

The first step in managing pests is to properly identify the problem. To this aim, Chapter 5 provides an index of common afflictions of vegetables, fruit crops, herbs, and flowers grown in the West. Since cultural and environmental conditions are often at the root of garden problems, each crop is preceded by a brief discussion of the plant's growth requirements.

Finally, it is important to learn something about the habits, damage, and control of pests. Armed with this information, you can more effectively manage the whole picture. Chapter 6 describes "bugs" (insects, mites, slugs) familiar to the area. Chapter 7 deals with diseases caused by microorganisms (fungi, bacteria, viruses) and environmental stresses. Chapter 8 focuses on weed control for the vegetable and flower gar-

den, and, finally, Chapter 9 highlights everyday run-ins with mammals and birds.

Warning: Reading this book may be hazardous to your gardening enjoyment. *Pests of the West* will help you better understand what and whom you're dealing with so that you are less likely to butt heads. However, because the entire text is dedicated to this rather sordid subject, you may feel at times overwhelmed. You will likely begin to notice a few more pests around the garden after reading the book. But you may also discover that those bugs you thought were foes are actually your friends.

Sam Cranshaw checking out a parsleyworm

Pests of
the West

Chapter 1

Soils—The Foundation of a Healthy Garden

When planning a garden to resist damage by pests, focusing attention on the soil is fundamental. The condition of our garden soils is one of the basic determinants of the health of the plants we grow. Good garden soils nurture plants to grow vigorously, with minimal stress, as well as arming them to avoid or outgrow many disease and insect pest problems.

The soils of the West have formed as the result of constant but slowly evolving changes over the course of millions of years. Unfortunately, one of the forces at work in making your garden soil could be a recent one: the contractor who built your home. During house construction, topsoils are often stripped and poor-quality subsoils are brought to the surface. Machinery compacts soils and construction debris may be left behind. A gardener may start work with a soil plot that is far from ideal.

Several factors are involved in developing good garden soils. Soil texture affects how water and roots move through the soil. Soil chemistry determines how the nutrients necessary for growth are made available to the plant. A discussion of soil problems unique to the West is therefore the place to start toward building and maintaining a healthy garden.

SOIL TEXTURE AND STRUCTURE

Soils consist primarily of a blend of *minerals* from weathered rock and *organic matter* from plant ma-terials. The minerals form small particles that are classified by size. Extremely fine soil particles are known as *clay* and coarse particles as *sand*, and those that are intermediate are called *silt*. The soil's proportions of sand, silt, and clay determine the *soil texture*.

Soil texture is one of the most important characteristics of any soil, and problems with poor soil texture are common in the West. Soils high in clay are "heavy soils," consisting of small soil particles that make it difficult for roots to push through. This causes particular problems with root crops such as carrots.

Clay soils do help hold water—a definite plus in the arid West. However, they also tend to drain poorly and are easily waterlogged. This results in oxygen starvation as the water drives out soil oxygen required by roots to breathe and grow. Such conditions reduce the ability of the plant to absorb needed nutrients such as iron, resulting in critical deficiencies. Waterlogged soils also favor many fungi and bacteria, such as phytophthora wilt, which propagates serious garden diseases.

Sandy soils are less prevalent in this region, but do occur locally. Roots move easily through these soils and water drains rapidly. However, drought and loss of nutrients can really plague a sandy soil.

You can get a fairly good idea of your soil's texture by rolling some *slightly* moistened soil between your fingers. If it forms a firm ball, feels smooth, and becomes sticky when moistened, it is too high in clay. If you cannot form a ball, the soil won't stay together, and it feels somewhat grainy, the soil is of better texture. If, on the other hand, the soil feels very coarse, it may be too sandy and will not hold an adequate amount of water.

Subsoil Drainage

Poor drainage is one of the problems hindering plant growth in the West. This is a soil texture problem, usually occurring in the subsoil, below the level where most plant roots grow. Drainage convolutions, because they occur belowground, often go unnoticed by the gardener.

A simple test of soil drainage is conducted by digging a small hole about 12 inches deep and filling it with water. Return the next day and fill it again, this time taking note of how long it takes for the water to soak into the soil. If the water takes more than one hour to be absorbed, this indicates that your subsoil drainage might be poor. Water will tend to "pond" in your garden, increasing the accumulation of salts and favoring root rot. Alternatively, if the water soaks in within a few minutes, the subsoil drainage may be *too* good. Such soils do not hold water well and will tend to succumb to drought if not carefully tended. These soils will also easily lose some of the water-soluble plant nutrients, such as nitrogen, through leaching. If the water soaks in within 10 to 30 minutes, your subsoil drainage is probably pretty good. Get to work on the other aspects of your soil-building program.

Correcting Soil Texture Problems

One common reaction to the discovery of heavy clay soils is to consider adding sand. On the face of it, this seems logical—an attempt to balance the mixture of clay and sand particles. However, attempting to correct clay soil in this way does little to increase the amount of air spaces in the soil (soil pores) and provides little improvement. ("Sand on clay, money thrown away.") Unless *at*

least one-third, and often more, of the soil volume is altered, there will be few effects on the texture of clay soils common to this region. In other words, a layer of 3 inches of coarse sand might be needed to successfully improve the texture of the top 6 inches of garden soil. Small amounts of sand may even worsen drainage, creating "adobe" soils.

The situation is totally different where sandy soils are present. In this case, there can be some improvement in soil texture by amending soils with clay. ("Clay to sand, money in hand.") However, the added clay needs to be mixed thoroughly into the soil—a difficult chore to do well.

The addition of *organic matter* is the key to improving both clay and sandy soils. In clay soils, decomposition products of organic matter (polysaccharides) help to "glue" fine soil particles, creating secondary soil particles and enabling larger pores to form in the soil. Organic matter acts like a sponge to hold water in sandy soils. Although *soil texture* (the proportion of clay, silt, and sand) is little affected by the addition of organic matter, *soil structure* is improved.

Other practices that are sometimes recommended for improving soil structure but provide little benefit are gypsum and liquid amendments. Gypsum (calcium sulfate) provides amounts of calcium that are already in excess in most area soils. The only soils that can benefit by the addition of gypsum are certain uncommon types of salt-affected soils that are also high in sodium (sodic soils).

Various liquid products are also marketed to improve soils. These typically make claims to "break up clay soils" or to "condition the soil." However, most merely reduce the surface tension of the soil particles (as do detergents), facilitating deeper water penetration. Modest amounts of organic acids may be added, but these have little effect on increasing the size of soil pores, which is fundamental to improving soil structure. The

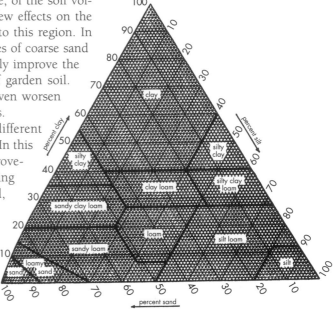

pH
4.0 4.5 5.0 5.5 6.0 6.5 7.0 7.5 8.0 8.5 9.0

strongly acid | neutral → | strongly alkaline

NITROGEN
PHOSPHORUS
POTASSIUM
SULFUR
CALCIUM
MAGNESIUM
IRON
MANGANESE
BORON
COPPER
ZINC
MOLYBDENUM

Courtesy of Kentucky Agricultural Experiment Station

Theoretical relationship between soil pH and relative plant nutrient availability.

short-term benefit of such products is rarely worth their high cost.

When correcting soil texture problems, work the soil deeply with the addition of organic matter. Problem subsoils also deserve attention. Light spading or a once-over with the rototiller doesn't reach these lower areas, which require mixing the soil at least a foot deep. Several gardening practices, such as double-digging and raised bed designs, provide a more thorough tilling of the soil.

SOIL ACIDITY (PH)

One of the most fundamental properties of any soil is how *acidic* or *basic* it is. This is determined by the ratio of two types of charged particles in the soil: hydrogen ions (or H^+) and hydroxyl ions (OH^-). The hydrogen power (*pouvoir hydrogene* in French) is measured as *pH*. The pH scale runs from 0 to 14, with neutral soil in the middle measured as pH 7.0. Acidic soils have higher levels of "hydrogen power" and a pH below 7.0; basic soils have lower numbers of hydrogen ions comprising a pH above 7.0. Basic soils are also known as alkaline soils. (However, they should not be confused with *alkali* soils, which result from an excess of soil salts.)

Soil pH affects the chemistry of soils, thereby affecting the availability of plant nutrients. Some pH conditions cause plant nutrients to chemically bind with other particles, making them unavailable for the plant to use. Alternatively, other nutrients may be released with changes in soil pH, allowing them to be picked up in the soil water around plant roots.

In areas of high rainfall, soils tend to be acidic—the result of leaching action by water, which removes the hydrogen ions. In the arid West, the opposite scenario is the general rule. Also, the high level of calcium common to regional soils acts to maintain (buffer) the basic nature of our soils and bind certain minerals, such as iron, in a form that plants cannot use.

Most plants do best with a pH that is fairly neutral or slightly acidic. Within the mid-range of pH 6.0–8.0, there is often little difference in plant growth. Troubles arise with extremes of acidity or alkalinity. Soils of pH 8.5 and higher can occur in parts of the region and they seriously affect plant growth. Garden plants have a range of tolerance to these highly basic (alkaline) soils. Plants that are alkaline-sensitive are often a challenge to grow in these soils.

TABLE 1-1: SENSITIVITY OF SOME GARDEN PLANTS TO SOIL ALKALINITY

Alkaline-tolerant

Snap Beans	Broccoli	Carrots	Cauliflower
Onions	Peaches	Nectarines	Rutabaga

Mid-range

Apricots	Basil	Cherries	Chives
Melons	Parsley	Peas	

Alkaline-sensitive

Brussels Sprouts	Beets	Cabbage	Corn
Cucumbers	Dill	Eggplant	Horseradish
Lettuce	Peppers	Pumpkins	Radishes
Raspberries	Tomatoes	Turnips	Watermelons

Extremely Alkaline-sensitive

Blueberries	Rhododendrons	Azaleas

Correcting Problems with Soil Acidity

Acidic soils are easily altered by the addition of materials that contain calcium. This includes limestone (calcium carbonate), gypsum (calcium sulfate), or dolomitic limestone. Wood ashes and the ground shells of shellfish can also be beneficial and serve to "sweeten the soil," making it less acidic. Newspaper or magazine gardening columns or books may recommend these practices, and limestone and gypsum are even sold in some local nurseries. These materials are suitable for many areas in the United States and Canada, but in the West, the already alkaline soils can be further impaired by adding these products.

Reducing the pH in the typically basic (alkaline) soils of the region is considerably more difficult. Sulfur, either alone or in combination with acidic fertilizers such as ammonium sulfate, can decrease the pH of soils. However, sulfur added to the soil combines readily with calcium to form gypsum—a slightly basic (pH 7.4) compound. The high level of calcium already present in most soils negates most of the positive effects of this treatment. Very high levels of sulfur may ultimately overcome this problem, but it should only be added in small amounts over several seasons to prevent plant damage.

The addition of organic matter is the only consistently effective means of lowering the pH of basic soils when high calcium levels are present. The decomposition of organic matter produces acids as a by-product. Some of these organic materials may be highly acidic, such as sphagnum peat moss. Manures or compost tend to be more neutral but they are also very successful in lowering pH. Each year, mix about 1 inch of organic matter into the vegetable or flower garden (a cubic yard covers about 350 square feet), preferably in the fall so it can begin to decompose and build the soil before spring planting.

SALT-AFFECTED SOILS

Salt is a stock kitchen condiment and also an essential nutrient. However, a high intake of salts can trigger human ailments, such as high blood pressure. Similarly, high levels of salts can be devastating to plants, as demonstrated by a brief visit to one of the western salt flat areas, which are largely devoid of plant life.

Salts affect plants by "pulling" water from the roots, making it difficult for the plants to take up enough water or nutrients. Young plants and germinating seeds are particularly susceptible to injury by salts, but all plants and plant varieties vary in their sensitivity to salt-affected soils.

Salts are commonplace in arid areas throughout the world. When moisture is lost through evaporation faster than it is replaced, salts move upward and concentrate in the root zone. When drainage is poor, salts cannot be flushed (leached) out of the root zone. Salty soils have seriously damaged agriculture, sometimes forcing crop production to be abandoned.

Sodium and/or water-soluble salts, such as sulfates or chlorides, are the most widespread. These become very obvious once they are drawn to the soil surface by evaporation, forming white crusts on the soil surface. However, even when such soil crusts are not present, plant growth and seed germination can be greatly reduced.

Salts can also be introduced into a garden through fertilizers or manures. Many nitrogen fertilizers, such as ammonium nitrate, are high in salts. Cattle manure from feedlots and poultry manure can be high in salts, causing "fertilizer burn." Aging these manures, by storing them outdoors for a year or more, often allows the salts to leach out so that the manure can be more safely used. A soil test is recommended before large amounts of manure of suspect quality are added to the garden.

Sodium salts also cause other problems. High-sodium soils (*sodic soils* or *black alkali*) affect how soil particles clump, changing the soil structure. Sodic soils are cloddy, drain poorly, and tend to crust.

Treatment of Salt-Affected Soils

Salt-affected garden soils are tricky to correct. Attention should first be given to improving

TABLE 1-2: RELATIVE SALT TOLERANCE OF VEGETABLE AND FRUIT CROPS

Most Tolerant

Asparagus	Beets	Broccoli	Tomatoes
Cantaloupe	Spinach	Cabbage	Grapes

Intermediate Tolerance

Cucumbers	Peppers	Potatoes	Sweet Corn
Lettuce	Sweetpotatoes	Apples	Pears

Least Tolerant

Peaches	Plums	Onions	Carrots
Apricots	Beans	Raspberries	Strawberries

drainage conditions. This is best achieved by fixing the soil structure (discussed earlier), usually with the addition of organic matter. However, one important caution regarding fresh animal manures is needed. Since manures are often high in salts, especially those from feedlot cattle operations, manures should always be aged for at least a year or more. Where precipitation is adequate, this allows some of the salts in the manure to be leached by rains and snow.

In compacted or very heavy clay soils, you may need to further work the soil to improve drainage. Using raised beds can facilitate this extra drainage. Deep tillage, such as double-digging, also improves drainage—once the addition of organic matter has improved the soil structure. Deep tilling is particularly crucial in gardens where heavy equipment (such as large rototillers) or other practices have compacted the lower soil layers, creating a *hardpan* layer that prevents drainage.

Salts can also be leached out of soils by watering. About 6 inches of water will normally reduce the amount of salt in the soil by about 50 percent; 12 inches of water reduces the salts in the root zone by approximately 80 percent. However, some local water sources are already very high in salts and will not be suitable for this leaching process. Also, if soil drainage problems have not yet been corrected, salts will likely again accumulate in the root zone.

Where raised beds are used, salts tend to accumulate at the top of the hills as they are drawn up during evaporation. Planting off-center on the hills will lower salt levels in the root zone.

Excess sodium can be minimized by applying soil amendments that increase the amount of calcium in the soil. Calcium replaces the sodium in the soil, allowing it to be more easily leached out of the root area. However, most soils in this region already have high amounts of calcium. In these instances, the goal is to release the existing calcium, usually by lowering the alkalinity (pH). This can usually be achieved by adding acidifying materials, such as sphagnum peat or other types of organic matter.

In those rare soils where calcium is deficient, calcium supplements can be a useful remedy. These act to convert sodium that is insoluble in water to forms that can be leached. Gypsum (calcium sulfate) is the standard calcium supplement, typically applied at rates of 5 to 10 pounds per 100 square feet. Calcium chloride is a faster-acting, but more expensive, calcium supplement. The use of these materials should be followed by leaching to remove the sodium. However, since calcium can also occur naturally in lower soil layers, a soil test for calcium (or gypsum) should be performed before any calcium amendments are added. If such a calcium layer is detected, tilling the soil to mix it through the topsoil solves this problem.

TABLE 1-3: SUMMARY OF COMMON PLANT NUTRIENTS AND DEFICIENCY SYMPTOMS

PLANT NUTRIENT	PLANT USE	DEFICIENCY SYMPTOMS
Nitrogen	Constituent in chlorophyll, proteins, and nucleic acids	Retarded plant growth and overall yield, yellow color (chlorosis) most pronounced on older leaves, very common
Phosphorus	Involved in energy storage and transfer, part of cell nuclei	Retarded growth, purple color of leaves, reduction in fruit production, commonly deficient in many soils
Potassium	Used in enzyme action and cell permeability, involved in cell division	Bronzing and brittleness of leaves, rarely deficient in regional soils
Sulfur	Constituent of proteins, found in several vitamins and plant oils	Reduced yield, rarely deficient in regional soils
Calcium	Important in production of cell walls. Also involved in formation of nucleus and mitochondria	Very rarely deficient in regional soils, although sometimes inadequately distributed within the plant. New growth may be retarded. Also blossom-end rot symptoms appear
Manganese	Involved in many enzyme systems	Speckling or spotting of younger leaves, infrequently occurs in region
Chlorine	Affects root growth	Rarely observed except experimentally
Boron	Needed for growth of new cells	Plant terminal stops growing and may die, restricts flowering and fruit development, rarely observed
Copper	Involved in many enzyme systems	Yellowing, "off" colors or small spotting, very uncommon in region
Iron	Involved in many chemical reactions (oxidation-reduction reactions, electron transfer)	General yellowing, concentrated on younger leaves, very common in region
Zinc	Involved in many enzyme systems	Areas between veins of younger leaves become yellow (chlorotic) and may die, leaves often smaller and thicker, very common in region
Molybdenum	Used in small amounts in certain nitrogen reactions	Reduced growth, very uncommon in regional soils

SOIL NUTRIENTS

Garden and landscape plants, like the gardener, require many different nutrients to grow and remain healthy. Some of these, such as carbon, hydrogen, and oxygen, the plant acquires from air and water through the miracle of photosynthesis. The other remaining thirteen-plus nutrients needed by the plant must be gleaned from the soil.

Nitrogen, phosphorus, and potassium are the three nutrients most heavily drawn from the soil. These are found in almost all fertilizers and are called *macronutrients*. Another group of nutrients used for many plant processes is composed of calcium, sulfur, and magnesium. These secondary nutrients tend to already exist in soils and are less commonly found in fertilizers. Small amounts of other nutrients needed by plants include iron, chlorine, boron, manganese, zinc, copper, and molybdenum—these are called *micronutrients* or *trace elements*.

Some soils are deficient in levels of one or more critical nutrients, restricting plant growth. For example, nitrogen is often deficient in native soils and is usually the nutrient that most limits plant growth. Garden soils can also become depleted of nutrients as we harvest plants and do not replace the nutrients that are removed.

Other nutrients occur in adequate levels in soils, but not in a form that plants can use. Soil nutrients must be carried in water to be picked up in plant roots. Under various conditions, they become insoluble in water and, hence, unavailable. For example, our high-pH soils render most of the iron, zinc, and copper unusable to the plants. These are released more readily when soils are more acidic.

Organic matter in the soil also affects the availability of soil nutrients. Nutrients in manures and plant matter cannot be utilized by plants until they have decomposed and are then released by soil microbes. When decomposition is slowed, as in cool soils, nutrients may be temporarily deficient. Phosphorus and nitrogen deficiencies are most often associated with cool soil temperatures.

Bacteria and other microbes that decompose organic matter also have "first grabs" on other soil nutrients, notably nitrogen. Adding to the garden plant materials that are high in carbon but low in nitrogen, such as leaves or straw, causes the microbes to withdraw nitrogen from the soil for their own growth. This can lead to a temporary shortage of nitrogen to the plants. Ultimately the nitrogen is again released to the plant as decomposition progresses, but this may take months or even years. Organic matter also forms strong chemical bonds with copper, reducing the available copper in the soil.

Finally, the proportion of various nutrients in the soil is important, since they compete for uptake by plant roots. For example, calcium, potassium, and magnesium are all brought into the plant using the same chemical process. Excess levels of any one can produce plant deficiencies of the other nutrients. Problems with a molybdenum deficiency in plants may be caused by high levels of competing manganese or copper. High levels of bicarbonates and phosphates lower iron availability. In addition, efforts to relieve iron deficiencies by using too much chelated iron can induce a zinc deficiency.

Soil Sampling

Fundamental to any plan to correct soil problems is a soil test. Several laboratories throughout the region perform soil tests and can be reached through county offices of the Cooperative Extension system or state universities. The test results describe soil texture, pH, and salt levels as well as various plant nutrients. Most soil testing labs also point out deficiencies or other problems and suggest methods of correcting them. Testing your garden soils as you start, and every few years thereafter, can identify your shortfalls and mark your progress.

The key to an effective soil test of your garden is providing a proper soil sample to the testing lab. The sample must be representative of the garden area that you are developing so that you can receive a comprehensive soil analysis and

Taking a sample for soil test

correct the problems. Soil testing labs usually provide guidelines for taking a soil sample, but general practices include testing sample areas that are fairly uniform. Often, garden soils around the yard have a checkered history due to past gardening practices or construction activities. Approach such different sites individually, sampling various areas separately. Otherwise the sample provided will constitute an average that does not truly represent any one garden area.

Within the sample area, take several samples. A minimum of ten subsamples is often requested. These should be thoroughly mixed together and a portion (usually about 1 to 2 pints) submitted to the soil testing lab. Sampling should take cores of soil of uniform thickness to a depth of at least 6 inches.

When submitting soil samples, indicate what tests you would like to have run. Although in the beginning it may be useful to go for the works, later testing can be more selective. For example, the amounts of many soil nutrients, such as micronutrients, are removed very slowly from soils. If earlier tests indicated that these were in adequate quantities, you can spare the extra expense of retesting for these later.

Treating Soil Nutrient Deficiencies

Changing the pH is one of the best ways to increase soil nutrients, particularly in alkaline soils. As soils become more acidic, many of the nutrients, such as iron, are released by chemical changes so that they can be used by the plant.

Adding fertilizer is the most obvious way to add nutrients that are deficient in the soil. Most garden fertilizers contain various concentrations of the macronutrients nitrogen (N), phosphorus (P), and potassium (K), often marked boldly on the bag in a 3-number shorthand (e.g., 10-10-10 or 20-10-5). Try to select the fertilizer blend that best matches your soil needs.

Peat moss is a useful amendment for lowering pH and improving soil structure

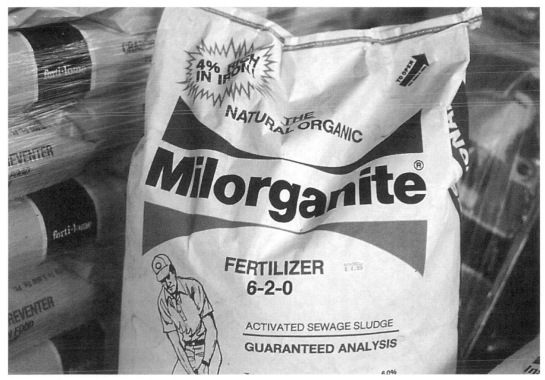

Milorganite® is an organic fertilizer used for flower beds

Caution: Never use "weed and feed" types of lawn fertilizers in the vegetable or flower garden. These contain herbicides that kill garden plants.

Micronutrients also are available, usually in some of the smaller (and much more expensive) containers of fertilizer designed to be mixed with water. In alkaline soils, however, the application of nutrients such as iron may do little good because they are rapidly changed into forms that plants cannot absorb. Using special forms of these nutrients, called *chelates,* which resist these actions of the soil, can circumvent this roadblock.

Plants may also be treated with fertilizers that can be absorbed through the leaves, a process called *foliar feeding.*

Organic matter is an excellent source of nutrients and it helps to improve soil texture and reduce pH. Plant and animal materials contain these nutrients in different proportions. As they are decomposed, the nutrients are released. This process is much slower than the release of nutrients found in most garden fertilizers. However, the steady release provides nutrients to the plant more consistently and prevents imbalances.

TABLE 1-4: APPROXIMATE CARBON/NITROGEN (C/N) RATIO AND LEVELS OF NITROGEN (N), PHOSPHORUS (P), AND POTASSIUM (K) IN SOME ORGANIC MATERIALS

Organic Fertilizer	C/N ratio*	% N	% P	% K
Sewage sludge				
(activated)	5/1–10/1	2–6	2–7	0–1
(digested)		1–3	0.5–4	0–0.5
Alfalfa	13/1			
Compost		1.5–3.5	0.5–1.0	1–2
Sheep manure	17/1	0.6–4	0.3–2.5	0.75–3
Beef cattle manure	17/1			

Organic Fertilizer	C/N ratio*	% N	% P	% K
Dairy cattle manure	25/1	0.25–2	0.15–0.9	0.25–1.5
Swine manure	17/1	0.3	0.3	0.3
Poultry manure	18/1	1.1–2.8	0.5–2.8	0.5–1.5
Horse manure	50/1	0.3–2.5	0.15–2.5	0.5–3
Dried blood		12	1.5	0.6
Steamed bonemeal		0.7–4.0	18–34	
Small grain straw	80/1			
Wood chips	400/1			
Sawdust		0.2	0.1	2
Wood ashes		0	1–2	3–7

*Carbon/nitrogen ratios of 20/1 or higher can induce soil nitrogen deficiencies due to the competing needs of soil microbes involved in decomposition for supplemental nitrogen.

Chapter 2

Natural and Biological Controls

When hornworms are eating your tomatoes and spider mites are sapping your roses, it may seem that garden pests are faring very well indeed. But pause for a minute and think about the normal, sorry lot of any insect.

For example, a mated female insect typically may lay 100 eggs. On average, 98 of these usually fail to reach the adult stage and reproduce—a miserable percentage by any measure. The rest suffer from starvation, lose bouts with severe weather, or end up as breakfast for some other animal.

All garden pests suffer tremendous mortality, with populations greatly affected by *natural controls*. Natural controls, or "the balance of nature," often prevent pest species from causing loss. Since small shifts in this balance can determine whether a pest becomes abundant enough to damage crops, it is important for the gardener to recognize and work with existing natural controls.

ABIOTIC (ENVIRONMENTAL) CONTROLS

Many of the most significant natural controls are *abiotic controls*. These include the effects of weather, such as temperature, moisture, and wind. For example, rainfall, though not often abundant in the West, is quite destructive to small insects and spider mites. Raindrops that we barely notice can bash a small aphid or mite, washing it from the plant to a certain death. Insects commonly drown in puddled water on plant leaves. Wetting the soil also determines when weed seeds germinate, and water on leaves is needed for the spread of most fungal and bacterial diseases. Improving airflow and drainage are effective disease-preventive practices precisely because they kill or inhibit the growth of many pathogens.

Strong winds, routine in the West, are also very destructive to insects and mites. Leaves brushing against each other crush or dislodge small insects. Weak flying insects, including disease vectors such as aphids, are carried and often destroyed by strong winds (or at least blown down the road, where you don't need to worry about them). Keeping things in perspective, the sand grains picked up on winds are flying like boulders to a hapless spider mite.

Temperature extremes are the most important control of overwintering insects. Several garden pests in this region, such as the corn earworm and aster leafhopper, cannot survive western winters and must migrate each year to milder areas in Mexico and the southern United States. Very cold weather may kill some insects that are only marginally adapted to survive in the area, such as the tobacco budworm (geranium budworm). Fungi and bacteria also suffer from temperature extremes. Each has its own optimal temperature for development. Overly cool temperatures prevent fungal spores from germinating and halt the growth of bacteria. Conversely, excessively high temperatures may kill these organisms.

BIOLOGICAL CONTROLS

Perhaps more familiar to the gardener, and a lot more fun to watch, are the various types of biological (or *biotic*) controls of garden pests. In particular, one can almost always see, with a little patience, some action in the garden involving natural enemies of insects and mites—their *predators, parasites,* and *diseases.*

Sevenspotted lady beetle, an insect recently introduced to the West (Photo by Frank Peairs)

Predators of insects and mites are organisms that move about and hunt, feeding on several prey before they become full-grown. Lady beetles (ladybugs), green lacewings, ground beetles, damsel bugs, and garter snakes are but a few well-known predators of insects.

The term *predator* is also used to describe certain natural enemies of weeds. Insects and mites that feed upon the plant and the seeds produced by the weed are described as predators, although they would be classified as pest insects if they fed on desirable plants. For example, the Colorado potato beetle is welcome when it cleans up the nightshade weeds in the garden, but becomes a different animal when your eggplant and potatoes are threatened.

There are also several groups of insect parasites comprising mostly wasps or flies of specialized habit. Most of these develop by growing within the host insect, consuming it internally. The host insect is almost always killed by these parasites, and it is not unusual for several parasites, sometimes even hundreds, to develop and emerge from a single parasitized host.

Insects and mites often fall victim to diseases caused by infection with fungi, bacteria, viruses, protozoa, and nematodes. Other fungi, viruses, and nematodes may attack weeds; some even kill or displace bacteria and fungi that cause plant disease.

Nor are the pathogens that produce plant diseases spared the effects of biological controls. Myriad microbes thrive on the surfaces of plants and in the root zone that may be antagonistic to pathogenic fungi and bacteria. Several fungi are *mycoparasites,* capable of invading other fungi and destroying them. Fungi and bacteria may also secrete antibiotic substances that inhibit pest microbes. Other microorganisms prevent these disease-producing organisms from becoming established by outcompeting them for space and nutrients.

Applied Biological Controls

Sometimes we may wish to get a little more help from biological controls than is provided by *laissez-faire* gardening. The term *applied biological control* is used to describe this manipulation of biotic controls for pest management. These applied biological controls can take many approaches, including:

- introducing natural enemies of pests into an area where the natural enemies did not previously exist;
- periodically releasing additional natural enemies to increase their numbers and effectiveness;

- conserving existing natural enemies of pests; and
- improving the effectiveness of pests' natural enemies by creating favorable environmental conditions for them.

The utilization of applied biological controls has primarily involved the management of insect and mite pests. However, some plant disease organisms and weeds have been controlled by biological means as well. In recent years, the study of biological controls has received increasing attention from researchers in many countries—with future benefits to the gardener.

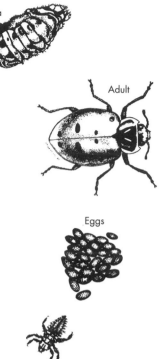

Recognizing Common Biological Control Organisms

Although there are many biological control organisms at work in our yards and gardens whose daily activities often escape our attention, the garden patch is a constant war zone for garden insects. (It's a jungle out there!) It is important that we recognize and appreciate these organisms so that we can better use them in pest management. Plus, their activities add an interesting dimension to garden enjoyment.

Although some are easily recognized, such as the adult stage of the lady beetle, others are frequently overlooked, such as the parasitic wasps and tachinid flies. Furthermore, as developing insects dramatically "morph" (undergo metamorphosis), all of the stages of these beneficial organisms often go unrecognized.

Life cycle of a lady beetle

Common Predators of Insects and Mites

Lady Beetles

Often called ladybugs or ladybird beetles, lady beetles (Coccinellidae family) are the most familiar insect predator to most gardeners. Although scores of species exist, they are all typically a round or oval shape, boldly patterned and brightly colored.

Typical garden lady beetles periodically lay masses of orange-yellow eggs that hatch in about five days. The immature or larval stages look very different from the garden variety and often are overlooked or misidentified. Lady beetle larvae are elongated, usually dark-colored and flecked with orange or yellow. Actively crawling about, they search for their insect prey—a behavior typical of insect predators.

Adult and larval lady beetles feed on large numbers of small, soft-bodied insects such as aphids. Lady beetles also eat the eggs of many insects. However, others specialize in their feeding habits. One group of very small, black lady beetles (species of *Stethorus*), aptly dubbed "spider mite destroyers," are instrumental in controlling spider mites, while another specialist group (species of *Coccidophilus*) concentrates on scale insects. Excepting some of these specialists, most lady beetles reproduce rapidly during the summer, completing a generation in less than four

Lady beetle larva (Photo by Frank Peairs)

Lady beetle feeding at flower

weeks and producing multiple generations during the year. Unfortunately, lady beetles tend to be fair-weather insects that are slow to arrive in the spring and often leave the garden by late summer. When calling it quits for the year, lady beetles typically scatter to winter shelters, sometimes aggregating under building siding, mulch, or other protective cover. (*Hippodamia convergens*, known as the convergent lady beetle, even "heads for the hills," migrating to the higher elevations in summer or early fall as aphid prey become scarce and beetles seek sites for winter shelter.)

More than eighty species of lady beetles inhabit the West. All are beneficial in that they feed on other insects and mites, with one exception. The lady beetle known as the Mexican bean beetle is the "bad apple" of the group, and has developed a fondness for bean leaves. Similar in shape but slightly larger in size than the insect-feeding lady beetles, the Mexican bean beetle is light brown and profusely spotted. Larvae of the Mexican bean beetle are yellow and spiny.

Ground Beetles

Ground beetles (Carabidae family) are well-known around the yard and garden. They are general feeders with powerful jaws that prowl the soil and soil surface at night. Almost any garden insect that spends part of its life on the soil surface is considered fair game for these insects.

Ground beetles rule the soil surface at night

Adult ground beetles are usually black or a dark metallic color, measuring $\frac{1}{2}$ to 1 inch long. Most are poor climbers, although some crawl effortlessly onto plants. The immature stages of ground beetles are seldom seen since they remain underground. Immature ground beetles are wormlike in shape, but boast a pair of powerful jaws that allow them to feed on many soil insects.

Rove Beetles

Rove beetles (Staphylinidae family) share the soil surface with ground beetles. The adult beetles are elongate with short wing covers, resembling an earwig without the pincers. Most rove beetles feed on small insects (e.g., springtails) that in turn feed on decaying organic matter. They are often spotted prowling around compost piles and manure. Some rove beetles have more specialized habits and can be critical controls for fly larvae, such as seedcorn maggot and onion maggot.

Green Lacewings

Several species of green lacewings (Chrysopidae family) are prevalent in gardens, particularly on shrubbery and fruit trees. The adult stage is a pale green insect with large, clear, highly veined wings that are held over the body when at rest. They are delicate and attractive insects and feed primarily on nectar. The females lay distinctive stalked eggs, approximately $\frac{1}{2}$ inch in height, in small groups or singly on leaves of plants throughout the yard.

Lacewing larvae emerge from the egg in about a week. These larvae, sometimes called "aphid lions," are voracious predators capable of feeding on small caterpillars and beetles as well as aphids and other insects. In general shape and size, lacewing larvae appear similar to lady beetle larvae. However, immature lacewings usually are light brown and have a large pair of viciously hooked jaws projecting

Larva of a green lacewing

*Green lacewing adult
(Photo by Frank Peairs)*

Syrphid fly larva

from the front of the head. Whereas lady beetles often limit their feeding to smaller insects such as aphids, green lacewings are capable hunters that make short work of slaying insects larger than themselves. Several generations of lacewings are produced during the summer.

Syrphid Flies

Syrphid flies (Syrphidae family), also called "flower flies" or "hover flies," are brightly colored. Typically marked with yellow or orange with black, they are excellent mimics of stinging insects such as bees or yellowjackets. Like bees, they generally feed on flowers. However, syrphid flies are harmless to humans and the adults feed simply on nectar and pollen.

It is the larval stage of the syrphid fly that is an insect predator—a connoisseur of aphids. Variously colored, the tapered maggots traverse foli-age, consuming dozens of aphids daily. Syrphid flies are particularly essential to controlling aphid infestations early in the season when it's still too cool for lady beetles and other predators to be of much help.

Not all members of the syrphid fly family are beneficial to gardeners. A notable exception are the "bulb flies," such as the narcissus bulb fly, that develop by feeding on and tunneling into plant tissues. These plant-feeding syrphid flies develop into large, stout-bodied flies that are frequently mistaken for bumblebees.

Predatory Bugs (Hemiptera Order)

Several "bugs" are predators of insects and mites. All feed by piercing prey with their very narrow mouthparts and sucking out the body fluids. A few may also give the unsuspecting gardener a little nip if they are mishandled or get trapped in clothing.

It's a Bee, It's a Wasp—It's a Syrphid Fly!

One of the most beneficial groups of insects in the average yard and garden is the syrphid fly (pronounced sir'fid). Adult stages of these insects are usually colored bright orange or yellow and black. Most resemble bees and wasps, and some even carry this act to convincing extremes by buzzing. However, adult syrphid flies (sometimes called "flower flies" or "hover flies") are harmless, feeding on nectar and pollen. Although not as efficient as bees, adult syrphid flies are valuable garden pollinators.

The immature larva is the beneficial stage, as it feeds readily on aphids and other soft-bodied insects. It is a tapered, usually green or gray maggot that crawls over plants in search of prey.

Perhaps it is their appearance (it *is* hard to find good press about any maggot), but syrphid flies are widely underrecognized, although they are superior natural controls against aphids in the garden. Many syrphid flies show up early in the season and then retire late, sustaining their existence even after the more highly touted predators, such as lady beetles, have vacated the yard. Syrphid flies can also squirm into tightly curled leaves and confound the bowlegged lady beetles and lacewings, thus providing biological control of leaf-curling aphids.

Syrphid fly maggots also, fortunately, are not harassed by ants, which routinely drive off other predators that threaten aphids. Syrphid maggots feed undisturbed on aphid prey, perhaps because they often cover their body with disposed aphid carcasses. These "sheep in wolves' clothing" elude the defenses that ants erect against other more conspicuous predators, such as lady beetles.

Adult syrphid fly, also known as a flower fly

Stink bugs (Pentatomidae family) are the largest of the predatory bugs and are characterized by their distinctive, shieldlike body and their ability to emit an unpleasant odor when disturbed. A regular customer common in the vegetable garden is the twospotted stink bug—a red and black species with a distinctive horseshoe band on its back—a predator of beetle larvae such as the Colorado potato beetle. Several other species of stink bugs residing in the region also feed on insects, although a few others feed on plants and are occasional pests.

Assassin bugs (Reduviidae family) are capable predators that subdue large insects such as caterpillars and beetles. Most assassin bugs are elongate and spiny, and have a pronounced snout in front, which is the base for their stylet mouthparts. Despite their prodigious ability to dispatch most garden pests, they rarely abound in a garden because they have too many enemies of their own (mostly egg parasites).

Big-eyed bugs (species of *Geocoris*) are the "good guys" in the seed bug family (Lygaeidae), which primarily includes crop pests. Big-eyed bugs get their name from the large, prominent eyes that overlap the sides of the head. They are general predators, well-known as the valued natural enemies of caterpillars and aphids.

Damsel bugs (Nabidae family) are fairly common but less frequently observed insect predators. The damsel bugs (also called "nabid bugs") are light brown and may reach a size of 3/8 inch. Damsel bugs can be spotted on the foliage

Damsel bug

Minute pirate bug

of all plants, where they seek out aphids, insect eggs, and small insect larvae.

Minute pirate bugs (Anthocoridae family), the most plebeian of the predatory bugs, are very small (less than 1/8 inch). The adult stage is marked by black and white, but the pale orange nymphs resemble hyperactive aphids. Minute pirate bugs can be observed in flowers or in the crevices of a green plant, where they feed on thrips, spider mites, and insect eggs.

Hunting Wasps

Many wasps prey on insect pests and feed them to their young. These hunting wasps build nests out of mud or paper. Other hunting wasps construct nests by tunneling into soil or pithy plant stems, such as rose or raspberry. The adult wasps then capture insect prey and take them back to the nest, whole or in pieces, to feed to their immature offspring.

Most hunting wasps are *solitary wasps*. The female constructs the entire nest, excavating it out of the center of pithy plants, in rotten wood, or digging it in the soil. (Meanwhile the male hangs out on plants waiting for "action.") The female then searches for prey, which it immobilizes with a paralyzing sting and carries back to the nest. The young wasps develop by dining on the fare provided. The solitary hunting wasps (Sphecidae family) have very discriminating tastes that motivate them to search only for selective types of prey. For example, some develop on leafhoppers, others attack caterpillars, and beetles are also prey for some hunting wasps. The largest hunting wasp is the cicada killer, which resembles a giant yellowjacket and kills the dog-day cicada. Despite their often fearsome appearance, solitary hunting wasps rarely sting and do not possess the potent venom of the social wasps.

Other hunting wasps, such as paper wasps and yellowjackets (Vespidae family), are social species in which many individuals work together in a colony of specialized *castes* (queen, drone,

Nymph of a twospotted stink bug feeding on Colorado potato beetle larva

and worker). These wasps construct their nests of a papery material formed by chewing wood, cardboard, or other materials. The nests are built under eaves, in trees, or underground in holes around building foundations or abandoned rodent burrows. Every year these *social wasps* create new colonies, which are often aggressively defended by stinging guard wasps, much to the dismay of the unwary gardener. However, most social wasps rear their young on a diet of caterpillar paste or other insects and are competent in the control of garden pests. At the end of the season, the nests of the social wasps are abandoned.

Hunting wasp with caterpillar prey

Predatory Mites
Many types of mites are predators of plant-feeding spider mites. Typically, these predatory mites (pri-

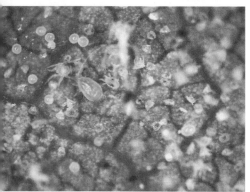
Predatory mite eating spider mite

marily members of the Phytoseiidae family) are a little larger than spider mites and faster moving than their prey. Predatory mites provide much-appreciated control of spider mites, but most are slowed down by dry weather—they like it hot and humid. Predatory mites are also more susceptible to insecticides than are the plant-feeding species.

Spiders
Although hardly a favorite of most gardeners, spiders (Araneida order) are actually our best allies. All spiders feed only on living insects or other small arthropods, protecting garden plants.

The web-making spiders, such as the silvery colored banded argiope, are the most common, yet there are a great many spiders that do not build webs—wolf spiders, crab spiders, and jumping

Artisans of the Garden—The Orb-Web Spiders

Few spiders garner as much attention as do the orb-weaving spiders (Araneidae family). These tend to be large spiders that make elaborate and often beautifully patterned webs—although not as sophisticated as those fashioned by the most famous orb-weaver of all, the star of *Charlotte's Web*.

In much of western North America, the banded argiope (*Argiope trifacsciatus*) is the most striking species residing in the late summer garden. Webs may stretch several feet between plants and are formed with concentric patternings. Running up and down the middle is a dense zig-zag pattern of silk, "the stabilamentum," which is thought to advertise the web sufficiently so as to escape accidental damage by a passing bird. The spider itself may rest splayed in the middle of the web or along one corner, measuring over an inch in length with a glistening silver-banded back. The banded argiope produces sacks of eggs late in the summer that will hatch the following spring.

These spiders are harmless to humans and add interest to the garden.

Another common orb-weaver is the "monkey-face" or "catface" spider (*Araneus gemma*). These large spiders sometimes reach the diameter of a quarter. Brownish gray with bizarre humps on their backs, they like to set up webs near evening light that attracts prey. Common nesting areas are under the eaves near porch lights or around a kitchen window. Webs manufactured by the catface spider don't even approach the artistic quality of the argiope spiders, being irregularly patterned and constantly refashioned in different arrangements as they sustain the normal wear and tear that comes with entrapping passing bugs.

Banded garden spider

spiders. These less conspicuous spiders move about plants and hunt for their prey on soil or plants. They can be more reliable than their flashier, web-spinning relatives in controlling insect pests such as beetles, caterpillars, leafhoppers, and aphids.

Common Parasites of Insects
Tachinid Flies

Tachinid flies (Tachinidae family) develop as parasites inside other insects. They are about the size of a housefly, generally gray or brown, and are covered with dark bristles. They are rarely seen but often leave a "calling card": a white egg laid on various caterpillars, beetles, and bugs, usually near the head. The eggs hatch within one day and the young fly maggots tunnel into their host. There they feed for a week or two (carefully avoiding the vital organs until the end), eventually killing the host insect.

Braconid and Ichneumonid Wasps

The parasitic wasps, including the braconid and ichneumonid wasps (Braconidae and Ichneu-

Parasitic wasp larvae emerging from caterpillar host (Photo by John Capinera)

monidae families), are a diverse group that develop as insect parasites. Some are very small and elusive, attacking small insects such as aphids. Others even live in the eggs of various pest insects. Larger parasitic wasps attack caterpillars or wood-boring beetles.

There is usually little evidence of parasitic wasps in the garden because the young wasps develop inside the host insect from eggs that were inserted by the mother wasp. However, parasitized insects may differ somewhat in form. For example, aphids that are parasitized by these wasps are typically small and discolored and are called "aphid mummies." Other common braconid wasp species spin distinctive yellow or white pupal cocoons after emerging from a host.

Chalcid Wasps

There are hundreds of species of chalcid wasps (Chalcidoidea superfamily), which attack and kill other insects. However, most chalcid wasps are very small and are rarely visible to the gardener. Like the braconid and ichneumonid wasps, chalcid wasps do not sting and are harmless to humans.

Some of the more notable chalcid wasps attack aphids and the caterpillar stages of cutworms, fall webworms, and cabbage loopers. Some chalcid wasps are also available from suppliers of biological control organisms. For example, the trichogramma wasps, which develop within the eggs of various caterpillar pests, are offered in many garden catalogs. A parasite of the greenhouse whitefly, *Encarsia formosa*, is also available from several commercial outlets. (See "Commercially Available Biological Controls," later in this chapter, for more details.)

Insect Diseases

Although not readily apparent to the casual observer, insects and mites can suffer from disease. Periodically, waves of disease caused by fungi, bacteria, protozoa, or viruses may sweep through a population, making the Black Death of the Middle Ages (bubonic plague, a bacterial disease

Tachinid fly eggs on hornworms (Photo by John Capinera)

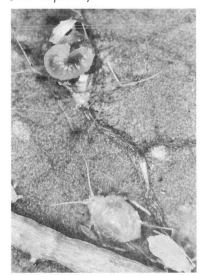

Parasitic wasp larva exposed in aphid mummy

of humans spread by fleas) seem like a mild head cold. Although the classes of organisms that inflict human disease are the same for many other animals and plants (e.g., viruses, bacteria, and fungi), it is important to keep in mind that insect diseases are very specific in their effects. They do not infect mammals or birds, restricting their effects to the arthropods. Furthermore, most insect diseases are so specific in their effects that they can infect only a few insect species.

Viruses are prominent among the caterpillars and sawflies. One particularly gruesome group of these viruses (nuclear polyhedrosis viruses) cause the "wilt disease." Caterpillars infected by these visuses succumb rapidly, their virus-filled bodies hanging limply by their hind prolegs. At the slightest touch, the insects rupture, spilling the virus particles on the leaves below to infect subsequently more insects.

Other types of viruses provoke less spectacular infections. Most are slower-acting than the wilt viruses. External evidence of these viruses includes a chalky color and general listlessness of the insect. (Of course, making observations on the relative listlessness of insects is not of great interest to most gardeners.)

Although viral diseases of insects are widespread in nature, rarely have they been adapted for applied biological control. Much of this is due to problems associated with registering them as insecticides. Regulatory agencies have disagreed on how to ensure the safety of such mysterious particles as viruses. Manufacturers have also been leery of developing viruses due to production complications (they need live cells to develop), and because the selectivity of viruses renders them effective against only a few insects, limiting their marketability.

Bacteria have received more attention, due almost entirely to the successful adaptation of *Bacillus thuringiensis* (Bt). Several manufacturers have produced and marketed various strains of this famous bacteria. Many other types of bacterial disease occur naturally among insects as well, often producing similar symptoms.

One of the outstanding success stories for biological insect control, *Bacillus thuringiensis,* or Bt, works by disrupting the gut lining of susceptible insects, ultimately killing them by a type of starvation or blood poisoning. Infected insects shrivel and darken. This naturally occurring bacteria was first identified as a disease of insects some eighty years ago. Bt is now manufactured by several companies and used as a biological insecticide. It is sold under a variety of trade names, such as Dipel®, Thuricide®, Biobit®, MVP®, and Caterpillar Attack®.

The outstanding advantages of Bt are its highly specific action and associated safety. Individual strains of Bt affect only limited groups of insects, and must be ingested to provide control. Hazards to other desirable species, such as humans, pets, or beneficial insects, are negligible or nonexistent. This safety factor is why Bt is particularly valuable for use on garden crops, and it fits in well with Integrated Pest Management programs because it spares naturally occurring biological controls.

Bt can be very toxic to some insects, however. The disease kills by producing a toxic protein crystal that is activated in the digestive tract of susceptible species. Almost immediately it paralyzes the gut of the insect, causing it to cease feeding, though it may take several days for it to die. In a sense, insects succumb to a sort of terminal "Montezuma's revenge," often complicated by blood poisoning.

Bt has generated tremendous interest for decades, which has accelerated recently with developments in biotechnology. Dozens of different strains have been identified, each effective against specific types of insects. Some of the older and most widely used strains (such as *kurstaki* and *thuringiensis*) are popular for garden use and can control several caterpillars that damage the garden, including the following:

- Imported cabbageworm
- Diamondback moth
- Looper

Bt crystalline toxin

Bt spore

Normal gut bacteria

Course of infection by *Bacillus thuringiensis*

- Hornworm
- Parsleyworm
- Leafroller
- Climbing cutworm
- Tomato fruitworm
- European corn borer (in corn whorl)

More recently, commercial development has focused on the *israelensis* strain that kills immature stages of mosquitoes and related flies such as fungus gnats. It is fast becoming the standard for community mosquito control programs.

About a decade ago, a strain capable of controlling leaf beetles such as the Colorado potato beetle (*tenebrionis* or *san diego* strain) joined the market. Bt products that target leaf beetle control can now be found in many garden catalogs, sold under trade names such as Novodor®, M-One®, M-Trak®, and Trident®.

Fungi are responsible for some of the more spectacular diseases of insects. A wide variety of insects succumb to fungal disease around the yard and garden. Fungus-stricken insects and mites stiffen and are often firmly attached to a leaf or stem. When conditions are right, they become encased in a white, light green, or pink fuzz—the spores of the fungus.

Perhaps the most commonly observed fungal diseases involve species of *Entomophthora*. These induce an interesting behavior in the infected insect, causing it to crawl to the top of a high object before it dies. This is a useful characteristic for the fungus, since it facilitates the dissemination of spores. How the invading fungus elicits this behavior in the hapless insect is another intriguing question. In any case, be on the lookout for mass epidemics of fungus-killed root maggot flies following wet weather in the spring. Also watch for the all-too-rare outbreak of fungal disease among grasshoppers, which causes them to wave in the wind—still and dead—and to stick to the grasses they ordinarily would be eating.

Infections by fungi were the earliest insect diseases observed, and for over a century attempts have been made to use them for applied insect control. Unfortunately, they have proved difficult to use, resisting most human efforts to manipulate them consistently. Sensitivity to environmental conditions, notably a need for high moisture, has usually foiled their use. In recent years, however, development of fungi for biological control has resurged and at least one organism is now marketed, *Beauveria bassiana* (BotaniGard®, Naturalis®). *B. bassiana* is capable of infesting a wide range of insects, but current products seem to be particularly useful for control of whiteflies.

Conserving and Enhancing Biological Controls

The fundamental need of any insect predator or parasite is procuring enough food to sustain reproduction and development. This means that there must always be some pest insects in the vicinity to maintain a population balance with their natural enemies. Biological controls struggle to survive and cannot thrive in a garden in which all the pest insects have been eliminated.

Sometimes alternative hosts of other species of insects are necessary for biological control organisms to thrive. For example, many predators, such as lady beetles, are general feeders of a wide variety of small insects. Nondamaging aphid populations on one plant may provide food that nourishes lady beetles, which move on and later control aphids on another type of plant. Minute pirate bugs, a primary predator of spider mites, may use thrips as an alternative host and thus build up their populations. Mixed plantings help provide a constant source of alternative hosts on which beneficial insects can feed.

Other types of food are also used by insect predators and parasites. Many adult stages of the wasps and flies that develop inside pest insects feed upon nectar as a source of sugar-rich energy. Although many flowers contain nectar, most are not usable by small insects, since their mouthparts cannot reach deep into the flower. Shallow flowers of plants in the parsley family (Apiaceae), such as dill and cilantro, are ideal food plants for these beneficial insects. The well-fed wasps live

Fungus-killed flies

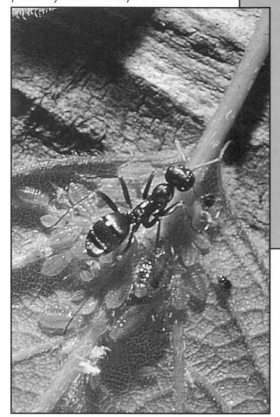

Ant tending an aphid colony (Photo by Frank Peairs)

Ants and Aphids—A Benevolent Sisterhood

Insects are not generally esteemed for their friendly, cooperative behavior. Certainly there are examples of truly social insects, such as honeybees, paper wasps, and termites, that develop elaborate caste systems with different members of the colony given separate tasks. These are insects that truly cannot survive except as a colony. However, even these insects rarely cooperate with other insect species.

Ants are an exception. Several of the ants common in the West seek out sweet materials as a major food source. Honeydew, the sugary byproduct of aphids (and many other related insects, such as leafhoppers, soft scales, and whiteflies), provides this favored food. Ants collect honeydew from leaves or prod the insects to excrete honeydew for immediate collection. Later, the honeydew is returned to the colony to feed the developing ants.

Ants that find rich sources of honeydew will often provide a "guard detail" that effectively protects their food provider. Ants usually associate with developing colonies of aphids and other honeydew producers. In return for the steady food source, the ants drive away the aphids' potential natural enemies, such as lady beetles and parasitic wasps. The result is a temporary ant-induced disruption of biological controls. This benevolent sisterhood (males are rare among both aphids and ants) undermines insect control. In many cases, the best control of aphids is the control of their ant protectors.

longer, lay more eggs, and do a better job of insect control in the garden.

Providing artificial foods for beneficial insects is a way to increase their performance. Applications of sugar water or various sugar/yeast mixtures entice lacewings and lady beetles to linger in a garden. Often applied as a paste or thick spray to plants, these mixtures apparently simulate the honeydew produced by insects that are common prey, such as aphids. Sugar/yeast sprays can also help adult predatory insects to live longer and to mature more eggs.

Shelter requirements may limit the effectiveness of other natural enemies of insect pests. Ground beetles can be important predators of cutworms and other insects found in the soil. But ground beetles need shelter during the day. Mulches or other ground covers aid the performance of ground beetles. Earwigs commonly feed on pest insects and require specific shelter. Earwigs seek out cool, dark areas in which to hide during the day. Banding fruit trees with burlap provides suitable shelter and enables earwigs to better search the trees at night for common prey such as aphids. For the hunting wasps, suitable nest sites may be limited. Small holes drilled in wood or plant canes pruned to expose the pith provide nesting for wasps that attack aphids and leafhoppers.

Biological controls are best protected by using chemical and cultural control practices that minimize damage to them. Insecticides vary widely in their ability to kill natural enemies of pest insects. Selective insecticides can preserve the effectiveness of these natural enemies. Pesticide applications may also be timed in such a manner as to make them more selective; for example, using dormant oils on fruit trees to kill eggs of pest insects spares insect predators and parasites that do not overwinter on trees. The use of pesticides is discussed further in Chapter 4.

Cultural practices that promote biological control include reducing the amount of soil and dust on plants. Spider mites can wreak havoc in dusty areas, because the dust particles stick in the webbing and protect them from predators. Dust is also destructive to the small parasitic wasps.

Introducing Biological Controls to the Yard and Garden

Several natural enemies of insect pests have been introduced into this region and are now permanently established. For example, one of the most common natural enemies of the cabbageworm inhabiting area gardens is the small parasitic wasp, *Cotesia (Apanteles) glomeratus,* which was introduced into the United States in 1872. Even more significant (and effective) was the introduction of the Vedalia lady beetle in 1888 to control the cottony cushion scale in California. The seven-spotted lady beetle, *Coccinella septempunctata,* is a much more recent immigrant but it, too, is now well established throughout the region.

This branch of biological control—introduction and permanent establishment of natural insect enemies—is called *classic biological control.* Over the past century, this technique has repeatedly proved successful in the United States, and it continues to be developed by the USDA and many state agencies. Newly established natural enemies can provide ongoing control and greatly reduce the damage caused by pest insects. Recent projects to establish natural enemies of the Russian wheat aphid and alfalfa weevil have been getting much attention.

Insects have also been introduced to help control weeds, particularly introduced rangeland or pasture weeds. For example, nearly a half dozen species of flea beetles, a stemboring beetle, and a leaf-feeding caterpillar have been introduced into this region in attempts to manage leafy spurge. Knapweed, thistles, puncture vine, and purple loosestrife are additional weeds that government agencies have targeted for biological control in the Rocky Mountain region.

Commercially Available Biological Controls

Some natural enemies of pests can be mass-produced or collected in large numbers, and these are then released in a yard or garden as a biological pesticide. These types of biological controls typically have to be released either annually or repeatedly during a season to achieve optimum pest control. Several companies produce biological control organisms that are sold through mail-order catalogs or at garden centers.

The effectiveness of these "bugs for hire" is variable. Some appear to provide highly effective control under proper conditions. The track record of others is more mixed, while a few, such as the praying mantid, are probably best considered "recreational pest controls." Some of the biological control organisms that are available from commercial suppliers are listed as follows.

"Bugs for Hire"

Lady beetles—Lady beetles (ladybugs) are some of the most plentiful and beneficial insects found in the yard and garden. Commercially available lady beetles (*Hippodamia convergens*) are also conveniently accessible from many mail-order outlets and some area nurseries. They are collected from foothill and mountainous areas in California where lady beetles mass in large concentrations to survive periods when aphid prey are scarce. (Similar aggregations occur during winter in the Black Hills and the Rocky Mountains, particularly east of the Continental Divide.) Lady beetles collected from these overwintering aggregations are in a state of arrested development and do not readily produce eggs. Furthermore, the field-collected lady beetles almost invariably disperse after they become active and rarely remain in the release area for more than a few hours.

Convergent lady beetle (Photo by Frank Peairs)

The Use of Flowering Plants by Beneficial Insects

Many insects essential to the biological control of plant pests have special food needs during their adult stage. An example is syrphid (flower) flies, which must feed on pollen or nectar to mature eggs. Many other insects use pollen and nectar (and honeydew) to sustain them, often prolonging their survival, enabling them to produce more progeny and, hence, provide an overall higher level of biological control. Lady beetles, green lacewings, and parasitic wasps are some natural insect enemies that utilize nectar and pollen in this manner.

Numerous studies have shown that the availability of the flowering plants that provide these supplementary foods can increase the beneficial activities of these natural enemies. However, it is also clear that there is a very wide range in how useful specific flowering plants are for this purpose. The majority of plants are not available to the insects' mouthparts, which are much shorter than other, better known nectar feeders such as bees and butterflies.

Releasing them during cool periods, especially near existing aphid colonies, improves their retention prospects. In most cases, however, there is little benefit realized from the introduction of these purchased lady beetles, and the practice of their purchase and release is generally discouraged by entomologists.

Green lacewings—Several species of green lacewings are native to this region, all general predators that feed on a wide variety of insect pests. In addition, green lacewings are usually reared by insectaries and are available through catalogs, typically in the form of eggs. Distributing these eggs in a planting can provide some control of pest insects as the developing lacewing larvae (aka "aphid lions") feed and develop. Because of the wide host range of green lacewings and because the larvae cannot disperse until they become fully grown, green lacewings are useful as general-purpose predators. After lacewings reach the winged adult stage, however, they will disperse from an area unless large numbers of aphids and similar plant pests remain.

Mantids—Mantids are some of the largest insects that might colonize the garden and become an entertaining addition. However, their ability to control pest insects is highly overrated, for several reasons. Their choice of foods is by no means restricted to pest insects, being composed primarily of noninjurious flies and bees. Furthermore, they limit the bulk of their feeding to only those insects that are relatively fast-moving, not the sessile aphids, caterpillars, and beetle larvae that munch leisurely on plants. Mantids also produce only a single generation per season, preventing them from increasing in their ranks' response to increasing populations of pest insects.

A few species of mantids are native to this region. Small, inch-long ground mantids can be found in the shortgrass prairies. Moderate-sized species (species of *Stigmomantis*) may also be present. Often supplementing these are European mantids (*Mantis religiosa*)—the praying mantid—green or brown insects that measure about 3 inches and are marked with a characteristic bull's-eye pattern in the "armpit." However, the mantid of commerce, sold in the form of egg cases, is the Chinese mantid (*Tenodera aridifolia sinensis*). This is the largest mantid in North America—4 inches or greater in length. Not very well adapted to harsh winters, it generally dies out at the end of each season.

Spined soldier bugs—A type of predatory stink bug, the spined soldier bug (*Podisius maculiventris*) has recently been advertised as an insect predator. These large insects feed on caterpillars and beetles and can be useful predators. However, they are also native insects in western gardens and the value of supplemental releases is unproven—and expensive. In addition, spined soldier bugs may be manipulated by using a pheromone that the males produce to attract females.

Green lacewing eggs

European mantid

Predatory stink bug

Sold as Soldier Bug Attractant®, it may help to increase local populations in a specific area of the garden by luring them from nearby locations.

Predatory mites—Several species of mites that develop as spider mite predators are commercially available, including *Neoseiulus californicus,* *Phytoseiulus persimilis, Mesoseiulus longipes,* and *Galendromus occidentalis.* In addition, *Amblyseius cucumeris* is marketed for the control of thrips. All of these are promoted for the control of greenhouse pests; use on outdoor crops is limited and should be considered experimental. Each species has an optimal range of temperature and relative

---

Dealing with the Decline of Honeybees

Much of North America, including the Rocky Mountain states, saw dramatic declines in honeybee populations beginning in the mid-1990s. Several reasons for this have been proposed, including the use of certain agricultural insecticides. However, the general consensus is that two accidentally introduced mite pests have had the greatest impact on honeybee populations.

The tracheal mite (*Acarapis woodi*) is of European origin, as are most strains of the common honeybee found in North America. Minute in size, it has been present in the region since the mid-1980s. Tracheal mites feed within the main breathing openings (tracheae) of honeybees and seem to act as a general stressor. The greatest effect they seem to have is that they cause colonies to die out during winter. The varroa mite (*Varroa jacobsoni*) is a much newer associate of honeybees, having first jumped to it from an Asian relative in the 1950s, and since then has spread worldwide. It has only been known in western North America for less than a decade but is potentially very injurious. Varroa mites are large external parasites that suck the blood of developing young bees, seriously crippling and sometimes killing them.

Beekeepers have adapted to these new threats by using various treatments that manage the parasitic mites reasonably well. However, most untreated hives have been decimated, including those honeybees that nest outside an apiary (feral or "wild honeybees") in sites such as hollow trees or wall voids. The upshot has been a dearth of pollinators in many areas where active beekeepers are not close—a typical scenario in larger communities. The effect in the garden can be greatest on those plants that are largely dependent on insects for pollination and flower early in the season—apples, pears, and all the stone fruits.

Yet honeybees are not the only bees that pollinate in the garden, and there has been speculation that some of the native "wild bees" will eventually fill some of the gap that honeybees have left. There are already scores of native bees in regional gardens and, in some cases, steps can be taken to both encourage and enhance their activities. Unlike honeybees, most are "solitary bees" that do not live in colonies, the individual female instead constructing her own nest for rearing young. Unobtrusive of habit, nonaggressive, and very unlikely to sting, solitary bees typically nest in rotten wood, existing holes and crevices, or in belowground tunnels that they dig. Leafcutter bees (page 115) are probably the most familiar of the solitary bees. Small carpenter bees, too, sometimes set up shop in the center of a pruned rose or raspberry (page 81). Ground-nesting bees often take advantage of undeveloped land. This latter group includes some that have specialized foraging habits, such as concentrating their activities on the blossoms of squash and related plants. Among the native bees, only the bumblebees are social insects that form a colony. However, unlike the honeybee, bumblebees set up an annual colony, in which only the large female "queens" survive the winter and initiate new colonies every spring.

Honeybee and varroa mite

How to Encourage Pollinators in the Yard and Garden

Support your local beekeepers. Few gardeners have the inclination or resources to keep their own honeybees, but many benefit from the pollination activity of those that local beekeepers maintain and protect.

Provide nesting sites for native bees. This is probably the most fundamental way to increase local populations of pollinators. Often a limiting factor to their success is the absence of suitable nesting sites, and sometimes gardeners can assist in this regard. For example, many bees (and some beneficial hunting wasps) nest in cavities. Taking advantage of this, certain leafcutter bees that have proved useful in the pollination of alfalfa are often provided predrilled "bee boards" by growers as inviting way stations. A large block of wood similarly drilled (about 3/8-inch diameter is about right) or even bundled soda straws set out in the yard may encourage these bees to take up local residence. Equip the nests with some sheltering cover from the elements, as well as protection from marauding varmints, and you will do much toward enhancing the local populations of mason bees and leafcutter bees.

The nesting needs of some other wild bees are a little more challenging to meet. Bumblebees traditionally nest in abandoned rodent burrows and digger bees favor certain banks of clay. If you have the opportunity to observe such nesting areas, take precautions to protect them.

Protect bees from pesticides, because many garden insecticides can kill them. Those that are particularly insidious are relatively slow acting and allow the bees to return to the nest, poisoning other members with contaminated pollen and nectar. (Carbaryl, aka Sevin®, is a notorious culprit.) Bee poisonings are most likely to occur when insecticides are applied to blooming plants, a practice that is strongly discouraged and usually prohibited by label directions.

---

humidity within which they can be expected to be most effective. For most, the humidity requirements may be too high for regional conditions (e.g., 60 to 90 percent RH for *Phytoseiulus persimilus*). I recommend working with suppliers to identify the species most likely to be effective. Also, predatory mites are more perishable than most commercially available biological controls, and careful attention given to shipping will help to ensure intact deliveries.

Aphid predator midge—A tiny midge, *Aphidoletes aphidimyza,* develops into a predator of aphids. This insect is native to this region and the orange maggots usually fraternize with aphid colonies during the latter half of the growing season. Aphids are rendered immobile by a paralyzing toxin that the maggots inject and which quickly dissolves their body contents. Each predator midge may feed on between 10 to 100 aphids during its development, leaving behind aphid shells that have been sucked dry. This insect is sold by several biological suppliers to control aphids in greenhouses, but goes dormant without the aid of supplemental lighting between early autumn and early spring.

Trichogramma wasps—Several species of trichogramma wasps are sold. All of these tiny wasps attack and kill insect eggs, specifically the eggs of caterpillar pests, such as cabbage loopers and corn earworms. Insect larvae that have already hatched are not susceptible to trichogramma attacks.

Commercially available trichogramma wasps are generally sold as a form of biological insecticide, and they are expected to eliminate most of the developing eggs of the pests shortly after release. Multiple releases of trichogramma wasps are recommended, since the persistence of the parasites may be short-term. The many trichogramma species differ in terms of the environments in which they are most effective. Some are better used in orchards, while others are more adapted for home garden conditions.

Whitefly parasites—A small wasp, *Encarsia formosa,* attacks and develops within immature whitefly nymphs. Introduction of this parasitic wasp has proven useful for managing the greenhouse whitefly in greenhouses where average (day and night) temperatures remain at 72°F or above. Under cooler temperatures, this parasite will not be effective for whitefly control as it reproduces too slowly. Sticky yellow traps, which are also used to control whiteflies, catch few of the parasites and can be added for increased whitefly control. *E. formosa* is not very effective for managing sweet potato whitefly.

More recently, another parasite of whiteflies has emerged on the scene—*Eretmocerus californicus.* More adapted to sweetpotato whitefly, it also has proved to be effective for managing greenhouse whitefly under favorable conditions. This wasp attacks and develops within whitefly nymphs, but the adult wasps also kill quite a few of them as they sting to draw blood for a blood meal.

Aphid parasites—Tiny parasitic wasps in the genus *Aphidius* are a common resident of yards and gardens. The adults lay eggs in young aphids, which the developing wasps then voraciously consume. Such parasitized aphids, harboring a young parasitic wasp, become bloated, discolored, and stuck to the leaf wasps—aphid "mummies" as they are termed. *Aphidius matricariae* is also sold for control of aphids in greenhouses. More difficult to come by is *Aphidius colemani,* purported to be more effective against the cotton/melon aphid.

Mexican bean beetle parasite—*Pediobius foveolatus* is a small parasitic wasp that develops within the immature stages of the Mexican bean beetle. This parasite can control the Mexican bean beetle if it is released when the beetle larvae are first observed. Releases of the parasite must be made annually, since it cannot survive winter conditions in the West.

Bacillus thuringiensis—*Bacillus thuringiensis* (Bt) is a bacterial disease organism that has been formulated into a number of microbial insecticides. Most Bt products are highly effective for control of leaf-feeding Lepidoptera (webworms, cabbageworms, leafrollers, tussock moths, cutworms, etc.). Trade names include Dipel®, Thuricide®, Caterpillar Attack®, and Biological Worm Spray®. The exceptional safety of Bt products and their specific activity, which conserves beneficial organisms, make them ideal for the control of many insect pests.

Several strains of Bt have been identified and developed, each with the ability to control specific pest insects. The *israelensis* strain is effective against the larvae of certain flies. Sold under trade names such as Gnatrol®, it controls fungus gnats in soil; other formulations control mosquito larvae in water. The *tenebrionis* (aka *san diego*) strain is used against leaf beetles such as the Colorado potato beetle and the elm leaf beetle.

Pseudomonas fluorescens **A506**—The A506 strain of *Pseudomonas fluorescens,* sold as BlightBan®, is sold both to manage fire blight and for frost protection. It is a naturally occurring bacteria, well adapted to living on plant surfaces. Applications of the bacteria enable it to colonize a plant and displace the fire blight bacteria. Similarly, the *P. fluorescens* strain A506 may outcompete the "ice-nucleating bacteria" that possess surface proteins which promote frost formation and contribute to freezing injuries.

"Biofungicides"—Beginning in 1997, several fungi and bacteria antagonistic to plant disease-producing fungi began to be marketed. The majority of these are currently touted to help control root and seedling diseases including the bacteria *Streptomyces griseoviridis* K61 strain (Mycostop®), *Burkholderia cepacia* type Wisconsin (Deny®), and the fungus *Gliocladium virens* (GlioCad®). All of these have successfully suppressed organisms that contribute to damping-off diseases and some also indicate effectiveness against Fusarium and Phytophthora. The effectiveness of these

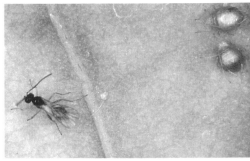

Aphid parasite and mummies

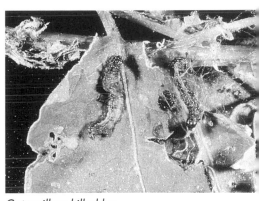

Caterpillars killed by Bacillus thuringiensis (Photo by John Capinera)

"biofungicides" has been documented almost entirely with container-grown plants grown by nurseries and greenhouses. Use in established gardens is more experimental.

Powdery mildew is another target of these new biological controls. The bacteria *Ampelomyces quisqualis* isolate M-10 (AQ10®) secretes antibiotic compounds that inhibit powdery mildew and has succeeded on field-grown cucurbits, fruit crops, and ornamentals.

Beauveria bassiana—*Beauveria bassiana* is a naturally occurring, common fungus that infects insects. Germinated spores of the fungus penetrate the bodies of susceptible insects, killing them rapidly. Newly killed insects appear slightly reddish brown and, when humid conditions persist, a flush of white spores will cover the infected insect. A wide variety of insects are susceptible to *B. bassiana*, but commercial formulations (Naturalis®, BotaniGard®) are used primarily to control whiteflies and aphids. Fairly high humidity at the time of application improves control significantly.

Nosema locustae—*Nosema locustae* is a protozoan disease that can infect many species of grasshoppers. Common trade names include NoLo Bait®, Grasshopper Spore®, and Semaspore®. As a typical protozoan disease, infection tends to debilitate rather than kill most insects. Young grasshoppers are more likely to succumb than older grasshoppers. Frequently, the symptoms of infection are sluggishness, reduced appetite, and reduced egg laying. In rangeland areas, where the immediate suppression of grasshoppers is of less critical concern, *N. locustae* has had greater effect.

N. locustae also occurs naturally and can be spread via the eggs or by the cannibalization of infected insects. However, different species of grasshoppers exhibit varying degrees of susceptibility to infection. Although most of the common pest species of grasshoppers are fairly susceptible to the disease, some are not.

Proper timing and use of quality strains of the disease organism are crucial to the successful application of *N. locustae*. Much higher infection rates occur when younger stages of grasshoppers are exposed to the disease organism. Fresh, well-stored preparations are also determinant in maintaining maximum viability of the spore. *N. locustae* is perishable, so poorly prepared or improperly stored formulations may result in ineffective control.

Parasitic (predator) nematodes—Several species of nematodes develop within insects and then kill them. These insect-parasitic (or predator) nematodes have become commercially available in the past few years and are now offered in many garden catalogs under such trade names as Predator Nematodes®, BioVector®, and ScanMask®. Because they require a high degree of moisture, insect-parasitic nematodes can be utilized for controlling insects that occur on or in the soil, such as white grubs, root weevils, sod webworms, cutworms, and raspberry crown borer.

The most widely available species of parasitic nematode, *Steinernema carpocapsae*, is particularly effective against Lepidoptera (e.g., crown borers, sod webworms, and cutworms). *S. carpocapsae* also has the advantage of being fairly easy to sustain and store. Recently, techniques have been developed that allow nematodes to be stored for longer periods, so they are increasingly publicized in garden catalogs and nurseries. A related species, *Steinernema feltiae*, is sold to control fly larvae, notably fungus gnats in greenhouses.

Species of *Heterorhabditis* (most commonly, *H. bacteriophora*) have proved to be the most effective parasitic nematodes for control of beetle grubs in soil, such as root weevils and white grubs. *Heterorhabditis* nematodes are capable of directly penetrating the body of an insect, rather than being limited to entering through natural openings. However, they are more perishable than *S. carpocapsae* and require warmer soil temperatures.

Parasitic nematodes typically kill insects within a few days following infection. Reproduction of the nematodes occurs within a majority of the infected insects, and sometimes thousands of nematodes emerge from a parasitized caterpillar or grub. These in turn may infect other susceptible insects in the soil, although persistence extending between seasons does not seem to occur. Numerous natural enemies of these nematodes also reside in the soil, and the effects of temperature extremes and soil drying take a toll.

TABLE 2-1: PLANTS OBSERVED TO BE VISITED MOST OFTEN AS SOURCES OF ALTERNATIVE FOODS BY COMMON SPECIES THAT ASSIST IN BIOLOGICAL INSECT CONTROL IN EASTERN COLORADO, 1993—1994

Scientific Name ('Cultivar')	Common Name
Achillea filipendulina 'Coronation Gold'	Common Yarrow
Achillea millefolium 'Summer Pastel,' 'Moonshine'	Fern-leaf Yarrow
Ajuga reptans 'Bronze Beauty'	Carpet Bugleweed
Allium tanguticum	Lavender Globe Lily
Anethum graveolens	Dill
Anthemis tinctoria 'Kelwayi'	Dyer's Chamomile
Aquilegia x *hybrida* 'Bluebird'	Columbine
Astrantia major 'Margery Fish'	Masterwort
Aster alpinus	Dwarf Alpine Aster
Aurinia saxatilis	Basket-of-Gold
Atriplex canenscens	Four-wing Saltbush
Callirhoe involucrata	Purple Poppy Mallow
Chrysanthemum parthenium	
Coriandrum sativum	Coriander
Foeniculum vulgare	Fennel
Lavandula angustifolia	English Lavender
Linaria vulgaris	Butter-and-Eggs
Limonium latifolium	Sea Lavender
Lobelia erinus	Edging Lobelia
Lobularia maritima	Sweet Alyssum
Mentha x *piperita*	
Monarda fistulosa	Wild Bergamot
Penstemon strictus	Rocky Mountain Penstemon
Potentilla recta 'Warrenii'	Sulfur Cinquefoil
Potentilla verna	
Sedum album	White Stonecrop
Sedum kamtschaticum	Orange Stonecrop
Sedum spurium 'Dragon's Blood'	Two-row Stonecrop
Solidago virgaurea 'Peter Pan'	European Goldenrod
Stachys officinalis	Wild Betony
Thymus serphyllum coccineus	Crimson Thyme
Veronica spicata 'Blue Fox,' 'Red Fox'	Spike Speedwell

Chapter 3

Cultural and Mechanical Controls

Aside from natural and biological controls, gardeners enjoy a wide variety of options for managing garden pests. Gardeners can manipulate the garden environment to avoid problems by creating conditions that are unfavorable for pest species. Other practices can be employed specifically to destroy garden pests, such as using traps, sprays, or mulches. Pest problems are typically managed most effectively when several techniques are combined.

CULTURAL CONTROLS

The techniques we use to grow plants dictate many of the problems we may have with insects, diseases, and other pests. What we plant, where we put it in the garden, when it gets planted, and just how we go about putting together the garden all may greatly affect susceptibility to pest problems. When consciously employed, these *cultural controls* are among the safest and most practical means of managing pest problems in the garden.

Promotion of Healthy Plant Growth

Fundamental to garden pest management is employing cultural practices that promote healthy

plant growth. Favorable growing conditions can greatly influence plant tolerance to injuries, enabling plants to "outgrow" attacks. Healthy plants also discourage many pest populations from reaching damaging levels.

Plants stressed by poor nutrition or inadequate water are more susceptible to several of the leaf-spotting fungal diseases, such as early blight. Many "weak" pathogens, such as cytospora canker, are more damaging to weakened plants. Some insects also prefer to feed on plants that are deficient in certain nutrients. For example, the squash bug has shown a preference for squash plants that are deficient in sulfur, magnesium, and potassium, since these plants also contain higher

Secondary pest problems can develop from overwatering

levels of the amino acids desired by squash bugs. Shothole borers, wood borers, and spider mites all thrive on plants stressed by drought or poor growing conditions.

On the other hand, many insects, such as some aphids, thrive on healthy plants that produce vigorous new growth. However, even with these pest problems, healthy plant growth makes it easier for plants to outgrow the damage. Furthermore, many seedling problems, such as injury by flea beetles or slugs, can be avoided if the plants can simply grow past the susceptible seedling stage. Healthy growth thus enables plants to better tolerate damage that does occur, reducing the need for other control measures.

Proper plant nutrition and culture generally require providing for plant growth needs throughout the season. Fertilization and watering should be moderate but consistent, thereby avoiding sudden changes in growing conditions.

Use of Pest-Free Planting Materials

Sometimes you get more than you pay for when making garden purchases. Many pests are inadvertently brought into the garden through infested soil or plants. Later problems with these pests are avoided by purchasing uninfected, healthy plants.

For example, one of the easiest garden insect problems to avoid is the greenhouse whitefly. In areas of the West that sustain freezing temperatures, all whiteflies die outdoors during the winter, although they may survive perfectly well indoors on infested houseplants and in greenhouses. Using of whitefly-free transplants during the spring prevents more serious outbreaks during the summer. Always be careful to look under leaves for the pale, scalelike, immature stages of whiteflies. (Just say "No!" to whitefly problems by purchasing insect-free plants.)

Several viral diseases may be introduced into the yard and garden that can then spread to healthy plants. Viral diseases usually occur on plants that have been reproduced by cuttings,

tubers, or other vegetative plant parts, such as potatoes, strawberries, and raspberries. Another problem in recent years has been the tomato spotted wilt virus, which flourishes in transplants of greenhouse-grown tomatoes, peppers, and various garden flowers. Prevent these problems by buying plants from a reputable nursery and carefully checking plants before placing them in the garden.

It is particularly important to avoid introducing pests that can become permanently established in a garden. Slugs often sneak in a yard in the form of clusters of pearl-like eggs carried within the containers of nursery or bedding plants. Fungal diseases such as fusarium wilt of tomatoes, verticillium wilt, or white mold can become severe and permanent once they enter a garden on infested soil or plant parts. Cheap deals on nursery plants often are no bargain. (I learned this lesson the hard way after unintentionally purchasing narcissus bulb flies via some inexpensive mail-order bulbs. Annual replacement of daffodils and hyacinths has since become a major garden expense.)

Weeds also enter a yard unannounced, often as stowaways. Animal manures and straw mulches are habitually infested with weeds. Soil or borrowed garden equipment may spread weed seeds.

Inspect all plants carefully prior to purchase. Discard or return plants that appear diseased or infested with insects. Soil sterilization or high-temperature composting can minimize the transference of weed seeds.

Check transplants before purchase to avoid introducing pest problems

Adapted, Pest-Resistant Varieties

Some plants have been bred specifically to resist plant diseases (and occasionally insects). Most common are the many VFN or VFTN tomato varieties, which are resistant to such diseases as verticillium wilt (V), fusarium wilt (F or FF), tobacco mosaic virus (T), and root-knot nematodes (N). Garden catalogs also frequently feature

*Many disease resistant plants are
available*

varieties of peppers, cucumbers, and melons that
are resistant to various fungi and viruses.

Plants may also be bred to better tolerate the
effects of weather or garden conditions. For example, some varieties of broccoli and spinach
resist premature flowering (bolting) under hot
conditions—an important characteristic for the
warmer areas of the West. Similarly, cold tolerance and shortened maturity are characteristics
of other plant varieties, which make them ideal
for gardening in the high country.

Always choose types of plants that are
adapted to local conditions. In the West, problems such as soils high in salts or pH and late
spring frosts often damage plants that are poorly
adapted to these conditions, leaving them more
susceptible to pests. Unfortunately, most garden plants were developed in areas of the country with very different growing conditions, and
seed companies often distribute standard product lines to nurseries. As a result, plants offered
for sale may not be locally adapted. Consult local gardeners and your county Extension office
and also draw from your own experience to
find the best plants to grow in your yard and
garden.

Planting Site Preparation

Proper site preparation is fundamental to limiting pest problems. In vegetable and flower gardens, good soil preparation promotes rapid, uniform germination and emergence. This minimizes
injury by such seedling pests as damping-off fungi,
seedcorn maggots, cutworms, and flea beetles. Be
sure that the soil is adequately warm before planting, particularly when growing warm-season plants
such as beans, corn, and squash, which require soil
temperatures of at least 50°F to 60°F to germinate.
You may need to break up soil crusts and keep the
soil moist to allow small seeded plants like onions,
carrots, and many flowers to emerge.

Preparing for proper planting is particularly
advisable for perennial plants, such as fruit trees
and berries, that will remain in the same place
for many years. Poor preparation often prevents
plantings from ever becoming well established
and thriving.

Fruit trees and shrubs should be planted in
holes wide enough to encourage future root
growth. Amending the existing soil with about
one-third quality topsoil or peat moss is useful
where heavy clay predominates. Scoring or cutting into the sides of the planting hole facilitates

---

TABLE 3-1: PLANTS COMMONLY FOUND IN
REGIONAL GARDENS, ARRANGED BY FAMILY

Chenopodiaceae (Goosefoot family)

Beets	Lambsquarters	Spinach	Swiss chard

Amaranthaceae

Amaranth	Redroot pigweed

Rosaceae (Rose family)

Apple	Apricot	Cherries	Hawthorn
Peach	Pear	Plum	Potentilla
Raspberry	Rose		

Saxifragaceae

Currants	Gooseberry	Strawberry

Cucurbitaceae (Gourd family)

Cantaloupe	Cucumber	Gourd	Muskmelon
Pumpkin	Summer squash	Watermelon	Winter squash

Asteraceae (Compositae) (Sunflower family)

Aster	Canada thistle	Chrysanthemum	Coneflower
Cosmos	Dahlia	Daisy	Dandelion
Globe artichoke	Jerusalem artichoke	Lettuce	Marigold
Sowthistle	Strawflower	Sunflower	Tarragon
Zinnia			

Convolvulaceae (Morning glory family)

Bindweed	Morning glory	Sweetpotato

Brassicaceae *(Cruciferae)* (Mustard family)

Arugula	Bok choy	Broccoli	Brussels sprouts
Cabbage	Cauliflower	Chinese cabbage	Collard
Horseradish	Kale	Kohlrabi	Mustard
Parsnip	Pepper	Radicchio	Radish
Rutabaga	Turnip	Watercress	

Poaceae (Gramineae) (Grass family)

Barnyardgrass	Foxtails	Kentucky bluegrass	Quackgrass
Perennial ryegrass	Popcorn	Sweet corn	

Lamiaceae (Labiatae) (Mint family)

Basil	Catnip	Lavender	Mint
Oregano	Rosemary	Sage	Thyme

Fabaceae (Leguminosae) (Pea family)

Alfalfa	Broad beans	Clover	Dry beans
Lima beans	Lupines	Peas	Snap beans
Soybeans	Sweet pea		

Lilliaceae (Lily family)

Asparagus	Chives	Daylily	Garlic
Hyacinth	Leeks	Onion	Scallion
Shallot	Tulip		

Malvaceae (Mallow family)

Hibiscus	Hollyhock	Mallow	Okra

Portulacaceae (Purslane family)

Moss rose (Portulaca)	Purslane

Solanaceae (Nightshade family)

Nicotiana	Nightshade	Potato	Tomato
Tomatillo	Pepper	Petunia	Eggplant

Apiaceae (Umbelliferae) (Parsley family)

Carrot	Celery	Chervil	Coriander/Cilantro
Dill	Fennel	Parsley	

later root penetration and growth of the plants. Plantings also must be made at the proper depth. Planting too deeply is a very common shortfall and causes suffocation of the roots and, consequently, a slow decline of the plant. Overly shallow plantings expose roots to drying and dieback. Also, containers, bags, string, and wire that come with the plant from the nursery should all be removed at planting. Guy wires used to stabilize an establishing tree or shrub need to be removed as soon as possible, within the next year or two at the latest; otherwise they can eventually grow into, girdle, and even kill the plant they were designed to support.

Fertilization

Many pest problems are minimized in more vigorously growing plantings, and the proper balance of available nutrients is essential for healthy growth. As the garden is developed, have the soil tested periodically to detect deficiencies or excesses. Correct soil problems by increasing organic matter, adjusting pH, or adding deficient nutrients. (Soils and soil testing are discussed in Chapter 1.)

Some pest infestations may actually worsen with excess nutrients. For example, excess nitrogen produces succulent growth, which is favorable to many leaf diseases and some insects. Overly stimulated top growth can produce imbalances because it is at the expense of healthy root growth that sustains a healthy plant. Common root diseases of vegetables, such as fusarium wilt, are aggravated when plants are excessively fertilized.

Fruit trees may need to be fertilized if characteristic annual growth is lagging. Nitrogen fertilizers should not be used during the first year of a planting since they may stimulate excessive top growth. Late-season nitrogen applications during any season should be avoided to prevent succulent growth that may not be frost-hardy.

Crop Rotation

Crop rotation is a basic step in managing many of the more critical diseases of the vegetable garden, such as verticillium and fusarium wilt. Disease problems tend to intensify when related plants are repeatedly planted in the same soil, allowing disease organisms to thrive there. These organisms survive in the plant debris, and some produce resistant stages that persist for years in the soil. Rotation to nonsusceptible crops can stop the development of the disease organism and, ultimately, allow it to die out. Crop rotation also aids the control of insects that overwinter in gardens in egg stages, such as the corn rootworm.

When possible, set up a garden plan that includes the annual movement of related plants to different areas. This can include rotations between plants of the most common families:

- Gourd family (cucumbers, squash, melons, pumpkins)
- Nightshade family (tomatoes, peppers, potatoes, eggplant)
- Sweet corn
- Lily family (onions, garlic, leeks, shallots)
- Carrot family (carrots, parsley, dill, fennel, cilantro)
- Mustard family (broccoli, cauliflower, Brussels sprouts, cabbage, turnips, radishes, kohlrabi, kale, etc.)
- Pea family (beans, peas)

Plants from other plant families, such as lettuce and beets, can also be incorporated into crop rotation plans. A rotation that allows at least three to four years between the replantings of a related crop adequately reduces most soil diseases. However, the benefits of crop rotation are not fully realized if infected soil is moved about the garden during tillage when weeds are common or when infected plants are introduced into the garden.

Sanitation

Many yard and garden pest problems are best alleviated by a good cleanup program. On perennial plants, pruning can interrupt pest life cycles and development. For example, removing diseased limbs (preferably during the dormant season) is an effective deterrent of stubborn fire blight. Cane borers in raspberries or roses can be arrested by removing the infected canes—as long as it is done before the insect has dispersed. As a general rule, pruning refuse should be disposed of promptly since many disease organisms and insects can continue to develop in the discarded material.

It is also a good idea to remove and dispose of infested plants that die out in the fall but still harbor pest species. Several of the fungal diseases common in gardens, such as alternaria leaf blight, survive on crop debris that has not yet decomposed. Some insects, such as aphids that attack asparagus and columbine, remain attached to the old growth of the previous season. The eradication of these pests can be achieved by removing old plant parts or tilling them into the soil so that they are physically covered and can later decompose.

"Off"-type plants that are discolored or show unusual growth changes may indicate infection with diseases produced by viruses or phytoplasma bacteria. Removing these plants ("rouging") as they are discovered can stave off the infection of other plants.

Sanitation is particularly crucial to managing weed problems in the yard and garden. A vigorous program of weed control, before weeds reseed, diminishes next year's troubles.

Many gardeners compost the organic materials they accumulate in the yard and garden and may even add kitchen scraps. The end result is an excellent soil amendment. Properly constructed and maintained, compost piles can be an important part of any garden operation and will destroy any associated garden pests. However, compost piles that are poorly maintained and decompose slowly, producing only low temperatures, allow weed seeds and disease organisms to survive. Furthermore, slugs, millipedes, and vinegar flies that thrive in the moist organic matter can quickly build to damaging proportions.

Tillage

Tillage in the flower border or vegetable garden, either by hand turning the soil or rototilling, usually serves to prepare a more uniform seedbed. But tillage can also limit many plant disease problems. By incorporating old plant materials, the soil cover prevents many fungi and bacteria from spreading. Crop residues and the disease organisms in them also decompose more rapidly in the soil. This is important because many fungi that cause plant disease survive in intact crop debris but are killed when it decomposes. In much of the region, this breakdown of plant matter occurs primarily in the following season, since the rapid soil cooling (and drying) in fall inhibits the activity of soil microorganisms.

Tillage also adversely affects some insect pests. Grasshopper eggs can be exposed and killed during tillage. Cutworms that overwinter in the garden can be exposed or crushed during tillage, along with the occasional white grub and wireworm. However, most garden insect pests are highly mobile and overwinter outside of the garden and thus resist the effects of tillage.

Watering

For control of many fungal and bacterial diseases of vegetables and flowers, plantings should be watered in such a way as to allow the leaves to remain wet for a short time. Several factors influence leaf wetting, especially *how* and *when* you water.

Some methods of watering the garden will reduce leaf wetting. These include drip irrigation, using soaker hoses, or constructing basins or furrows to hold the water. An additional benefit of spot watering systems, such as drip or basin irrigation and soaker hoses, is that water is conserved and weed germination is reduced in drier areas. However, these types of watering lose benefits in control of thrips, spider mites, and cabbageworms, which are decreased by hosing or overhead irrigation.

Watering during the day usually facilitates rapid drying, unless overcast or rainy conditions exist. Watering during midday, however, often results in substantial water loss through

Sam pruning the fruit tree

Guttation fluids may assist development of several plant pathogens

Cardboard collar to attract pupating codling moth (Photo by Rick Zimmerman)

Floating row cover

evaporation—an important consideration in the water-short West. Watering in early morning usually solves this problem.

Early watering also offers benefits for pest management. Dew formation on plants is often the result of *guttation fluids,* which plants exude as droplets from leaf pores. These beads of water, often seen in early morning along leaf edges, contain sugars and other nutrients that provide an ideal environment for fungus spores to germinate. Watering in early morning washes off these sugary droplets.

MECHANICAL AND PHYSICAL CONTROLS

Mechanical and physical controls are practices or devices used specifically to eradicate or exclude pests. Many of these controls are fairly labor-intensive but work well in small gardens. Furthermore, they can be immediately rewarding. While cultural controls work behind the scenes, you get an immediate sense of satisfaction as you pick off a potato beetle or watch a weed shrivel after hoeing.

Barriers

Several significant pests of vegetables and fruits can be detoured away from plantings by using barriers. *Collars* of cardboard around seedlings can prevent injury by cutworms and other insects that move to transplants from other areas of the garden.

Floating row covers, used to extend the growing season, also provide insect control. Row covers are particularly exclusive of insects that are highly mobile in the adult stage and do not spend the winter next to susceptible crop plants. Cabbage worms, Colorado potato beetles, most aphids, Mexican bean beetles, flea beetles, squash bugs, and tomato hornworms are some insects that can be excluded by row covers.

Sticky materials applied to plant stems prevent ants from climbing them and interfering with biological controls. Although not commonly found in area garden centers, specially designed sticky substances used to trap insects (Tangle-foot®, Stick'em Special®, etc.) are sold in many garden catalogs.

Some slug control is afforded by surrounding susceptible plants with abrasive materials, such as diatomaceous earth. Slugs also will not cross barriers of copper foil, which may be placed around new garden beds.

Mulching

Mulches are barriers placed on top of the soil and they have a variety of uses in gardens and landscape plantings. Weed control is the biggest reason for mulching, since weed seedlings are smothered by an effectively applied mulch. Organic mulches, such as straw or wood chips, have a long and proven record in gardens and landscape plantings. Straw also helps repel many insects. Recently, various fabric weed barriers have been marketed, particularly for weed control around shrubs and trees. (Further details on the uses of mulch for weed control can be found in Chapter 8.)

Mulching around the base of trees directs mowing and weed control activities away from the plant. This curtails trunk injuries by lawn mowers and "weed eaters," one of the biggest threats to new plantings.

Aluminum foil and similar *reflective mulches* can repel many flying insects. Aluminum foil has been demonstrated to prevent aphid transmission of viral diseases to vegetables such as squash and peppers.

Mulches also modify the growing environment of the plant. Plastic mulches warm the seedbed,

A homemade slug trap, sans beer bait

allowing warm-season plants such as peppers and tomatoes to grow more rapidly. Mulching reduces the evaporation of water as well, minimizing plant stress caused by fluctuating soil moisture.

One potentially serious problem associated with organic mulches, such as straw, is that weed seeds can be harbored in the mulch. If possible, buy straw from sources known to be free of weeds.

Solar Heating (Solarization)

The high temperatures and intense solar radiation experienced in some areas of the region can be maximized to kill garden pests. By intensifying soil heating by solar energy, a process known as *solarization* or *solar pasteurization,* many weeds, weed seeds, and disease-producing fungi can be exterminated. This technique is gaining favor as an alternative to soil fumigants for sterilizing growing areas that have a history of some persistent soil-borne pest problem.

Attaining soil temperatures that are lethal to weed seeds and soil fungi can be achieved by covering the soil surface with clear plastic sheeting. First, prepare the garden site by loosening the soil with a tiller or spade. Then moisten the soil thoroughly as wet soil better conducts heat and makes many fungi and weed seeds more susceptible to heating. Although a single deep watering may provide lasting moisture throughout a solarization treatment, consider installing soaker hoses or drip irrigation to maintain moisture levels. Cover the area with the thinnest polyethylene sheeting available, taking care to secure the edges and create a tight seal.

Solarization is most effective when solar radiation and temperatures are greatest, usually in early summer. The effects are also increased with increased length of treatment. A month-long treatment is considered the minimum in most areas; 6 weeks is more commonly recommended. Where the growing season is short, solarizing a garden bed will likely take it out of production for an entire season. Longer seasons may permit it to be squeezed in between spring and fall cool-season crops, such as spinach, lettuce, and mustard family plants.

Soil treated by solarization is very susceptible to reinfestation with weed seeds and fungal pathogens. Contaminated soil and running water are two ways in which garden soils can be reinfested. Take steps to avoid recontamination. The addition of beneficial microbes, such as those used for biological control of root diseases (see page 46), might be particularly useful in a solar-sterilized garden bed.

Hosing/Syringing

Many insect and mite pests can be controlled by forcefully hosing (*syringing*) plants with water. (Plus, it's fun!) Small, soft-bodied insects and mites can be destroyed by these sprays, including aphids, spider mites, thrips, and even small caterpillars feeding on leaves. The force of the water crushes some, flinging others from the plant where their future prospects are dim. Other pests may drown during a bout with the garden hose. Young cabbageworms are particularly susceptible, because the waxy leaves and structure of the plants they frequent cause small pools of water to collect at the base of the leaves.

Hosing plants also can control powdery mildew. This common fungus disease is vulnerable to management by a sharp jet of water every few days. The spores and mycelia that grow on the leaf surfaces are decimated by this simple treatment.

Handpicking

One-on-one, "hand-to-bug" combat is one of the easiest routes to take when managing insects in small plantings. Several vegetable garden insects, such as the Colorado potato beetle, spinach leafminer, and the Mexican bean beetle, produce conspicuous egg masses. Large beetles and caterpillars, particularly the hornworms, can be readily collected or killed by hand—a generally satisfying experience. Handpicking is most effective when done frequently—at least once a week—since the insects may develop rapidly and wreak havoc in a short period of time.

Hard scales, such as oystershell scale and San Jose scale, can be rubbed off the plants with a plastic

Sue knocking the aphids off the roses

Handpicking potato beetles

scrub pad. Eggs sheltered under the scale covering dry out and die soon after this treatment. A light rubbing is all it takes to rip the mouthparts of any feeding insect that has its stylets sunk into the plants. Aphids and other soft-bodied insects are also rubbed out by light scrubbing.

Most weevils can be knocked off of plants by sharply shaking them. Weevils—such as those that feed on hollyhocks, fruit trees, and roses—typically play dead in response to such a disturbance and readily drop to the ground, where they can then be collected on a plastic sheet or cardboard placed under the plant.

For the gadget-minded, *vacuuming* is an option as well. Most insects that are easily handpicked or easily shaken from a plant can be scooped up with a shop-vac or even a handheld mini-vac. (Although a good-sized hornworm would probably really plug things up!) Vacuuming also has advantages for picking up some of the smaller, more mobile insects such as plant bugs, thrips, and flea beetles.

Hoeing/Tilling

Hoeing, hand-pulling, or a well-timed pass with the rototiller are all central to managing weeds in an established garden.

Weeds are easiest to restrain when they are young. Hoeing early in the day allows the sun to dry and kill the plants rapidly. Irrigation should be suspended for at least a day following hoeing to prevent possible rerooting.

Large weeds are more resistant to hoeing or cultivation, since their underground root systems that allow regrowth may be in place. Even when pulled, these plants may continue to reroot, drawing on reserves of stored energy. Large plants that have been pulled, and succulent weeds such as purslane, should be removed from the garden area to prevent rerooting.

Well-established perennial weeds, such as bindweed and Canada thistle, can be difficult to eradicate. Repeated hoeing is necessary to eliminate these weeds. What is more effective is to hoe these plants within two weeks of their reemer-

Hoeing for weed control

gence, as the plants subsequently begin to store new food reserves in their roots.

Regardless of the type of weed, preventing the plants from setting seed will curb the establishment of future infestations. Flowering and seeding may take only a couple of weeks for some weeds, particularly late in the season. Periodic weeding is a necessary chore in all yards and gardens and should not be neglected just because the summer has ended.

Traps

A wide variety of traps aid in the control of insects and slugs. Typically, these traps involve visual or chemical attractants that lure the pest in and then destroy it.

Color traps attract many flying insects. Conventional yellow sticky traps capture whiteflies, thrips, psyllids, and some aphids. White is attractive to whiteflies and plant bugs; light blue is better for capturing flower thrips. Sticky coatings, such as Tanglefoot®, Stick'em Special®, or Tack-Trap®, cover the traps to ensnare insects. Heavy-grade oil or grease can also serve to trap insects, although these materials liquefy and drip in high temperatures. Several sticky traps are currently offered in garden catalogs, although homemade ones may be equally effective. (*Trapping tip:* If you make your own color traps, cover them with a plastic bag, applying the sticky adhesive to the inside of the bag and inverting it when covering

Yellow sticky trap

the trap. This reduces the mess of covering the traps with the adhesive and the covers are then easy to replace.)

Fermenting materials, such as beer or sugar water and yeast, are well-known attractants to slugs. Slugs will travel several feet to visit saucers containing these baits and then they drown. Millipedes and sow bugs also fall for this trap.

Molasses or molasses-and-vinegar baits have been used to lure many kinds of moths. Ferment-

Those Fantastic Pheromones

Insect vision is so poor it would be charitable to call them legally blind, and most are also mute (although some do produce sounds). As a result, insects often communicate instead by odors. Chemicals that animals of the same species secrete as their means of communication are called *pheromones*. These signals function in a number of ways. Ants lay down a *trail-marking pheromone* as they forage for food, allowing them to return to the nest and direct others to the food. Honeybees produce an *alarm pheromone* that enables them to launch a mass attack to defend their colony against an intruder. *Aggregation pheromones* are used by bark beetles to concentrate egg laying on a single tree and, in so doing, help overcome the plant's defenses.

It is the *sex pheromones*, used to attract and court mates, that have received the most attention. Use of sex pheromones appears to be widespread in the insect world; these are almost always chemicals produced by the female to attract a male. Among the moths, sex pheromones of incredible potency have been discovered. Often only a few molecules of the "eau de female" can be perceived by a receptive male moth, making insect pheromones among the most biologically active chemicals known. Over the past twenty-five years, tremendous progress has been made in our understanding of insect pheromones. A great deal of research has been conducted on how we might use these fantastic chemicals for taming insect pests.

A relatively new approach to the use of sex pheromones for insect control, the *male confusion method*, or *mating disruption*, has shown significant promise. This method entails dispersing numerous pheromone sources throughout the crop so as to permeate the air with the sex pheromone. To the male moths, the entire world smells like the object of their desire. In response they exhaust themselves visiting all the "false" females or simply become so tolerant to the artificially high pheromone levels that the pheromones produced by the female moths are no longer sufficiently attractive. (Female moths do not detect the sex pheromones they produce or at least do not respond or change their behavior because of them.)

Disrupting the mating process by mass-released pheromones has been successful for the control of many insects, particularly species that feed on only one kind of crop and don't migrate overly far. Early examples of insect control included the artichoke plume moth on artichokes, pink bollworms on cotton, and the grape berry moths on grapes. Over the past decade, progress has accelerated in the control of several orchard insects, including the arch-enemy of apples and pears—the codling moth. Mating disruption is now commonplace in large areas of western orchards, resulting in greatly reduced insecticide use and the conservation of the natural enemies of other pests. However, the technique does not work well at all sites, with effectiveness notable primarily in large block plantings (a 5-acre minimum is often considered the lower size limit) that are not located near heavily infested sites that could provide mated female migrants. Using pheromones on a few backyard trees in a residential area is not likely to produce similar results due to the continuous threat of nearby female moths— active outside the pheromone site and able to mate—moving to the fruit trees.

Pheromone trap

ing molasses baits are tried-and-true recipes for controlling adult stages of the codling moth, a common nemesis of apples.

Light traps, or variations on the ubiquitous "bug zappers," are widely sold for insect control. Light traps can help control some insects in confined situations. Fly control in dairy barns is one such use of these traps. However, light traps have repeatedly proved to be ineffective for controlling garden pests. Moreover, some studies show *increases* in some pest problems, such as white grubs, in the vicinity of light traps. Although many insects are killed by light traps, most are nonpest insects or are beneficial species, such as lacewings. (Sometimes there are fewer insects 100 feet or so from a light trap, at the periphery of its attraction zone. Therefore, the best application for a "bug zapper" that will protect *your* yard may be to give it to your neighbor to use.)

Other traps offer shelter sought by insects. Dark, tight-fitting, moist areas are favored by earwigs and slugs. Moistened, rolled-up newspaper creates the ideal environment for these types of pests to collect. They can then be destroyed in the early morning.

The caterpillars of several insect pests, such as the codling moth and the tent caterpillar, search for protected locations to pupate and will congregate under burlap bands or corrugated cardboard placed around the trees on which they feed. The insect pupae can then be collected and destroyed.

Trap crops involve the purposeful use of certain types of plants that are particularly favored by the pest. By cultivating these plants, you can divert some of the feeding damage from the desired main crop. For example, radishes and Chinese cabbage are highly preferred by the western cabbage flea beetle, which may then spare the cabbage or broccoli. Squash bugs prefer winter squash, pumpkins, and melons, and when you're trying to nurture a new seeding past the slugs, lettuce or beans are their favored trap crops. Weeds may even constitue a suitable trap crop, as Colorado potato beetles head first to the hairy nightshade, passing the eggplant and potatoes by.

TABLE 3-2: SOME REGIONAL GARDEN PESTS NATIVE TO WESTERN NORTH AMERICA

Cabbage looper	Corn earworm/tomato fruitworm	Colorado potato beetle
Migratory grasshopper	Mexican bean beetle	Western corn rootworm
Tomato/tobacco hornworms	Redlegged grasshopper	Potato (tomato) psyllid
Western cabbage flea beetle	Aster leafhopper	White grubs
Wireworms	Peach tree borer	Raspberry crown borer
Lygus bugs	Hairy nightshade	

TABLE 3-3: SOME REGIONAL GARDEN PESTS INTRODUCED INTO WESTERN NORTH AMERICA

Imported cabbageworm	Green peach aphid	European earwig
Diamondback moth	European corn borer	Asparagus beetle
Asparagus aphid	Gray garden slug	Codling moth
Pear psylla	Bronze cane borer	Pillbug (roly-poly)
San Jose scale	Fusarium wilt	Tomato spotted wilt
Beet curly top	Redroot pigweed	Lambsquarters
Purslane	Field bindweed	Canada thistle
Dandelion	Starling	Imported currantworm

The Scoop on "Companion Planting"

Although receiving less press in garden publications, companion planting is still sometimes promoted as a means to avert pest problems in a garden. Basically this idea suggests that interplanting with certain "companion" plants will repel and prevent attacks on nearby plants by some pest insect. For example, nasturtiums may be reputed to repel flea beetles; garlic, the Colorado potato beetle; and marigolds, almost everything. Many aromatic herbs are also commonly hyped as having pest-averting properties in a garden.

Almost all plants produce some defensive chemicals, *allelochemicals*, to help protect them when attacked. However, there is essentially no evidence that interplanted "companion plants" deter insect attacks on nearby plants by chemical repellency. Nor should one expect that they could. Although most of the listed "repellent plants" appear to have been selected because they have a strong odor to us, this reflects a very anthropocentric perspective. Insects detect chemicals in a very different manner than we do, through the sense organs on their antennae. Rather than having the broad sense of smell we possess, insects are only are capable of detecting a few odors—although those that do have special importance to them may be detected with fantastic ability. Also, the specific odors of their favorite food plants may be repellent or distasteful to us. The western cabbage flea beetle, a destructive pest in many western gardens, is highly attracted to mustard gas, which it pursues in search of the radishes, cabbage, and related plants that it prefers to dine on. Sweet perfume to the hungry flea beetle, this is the same mustard gas that is so toxic to humans that it has been used in chemical warfare! Conversely, the strong scents we perceive from a marigold or garlic are most likely not detected at all by a passing insect.

This is not to say that interplantings with purported companion plants—or many other plants—are without pest management benefit. However, the positive effects are achieved as a result of diversifying the garden environment, rather than by introducing some repellent chemical. One of the big pluses is that interplanting unrelated plants makes it more difficult for a migrating insect to find its hosts through the physical barriers the interplanting provides. Also, by breaking up a planting, attractive odors are disseminated, rather than condensed.

Diversified plantings also come to the aid of a pest insect's natural enemies. Some flowering plants provide nectar and pollen that are the supplementary nourishment of beneficial insects such as lady beetles, syrphid flies, and parasitic wasps. Low-growing plants may form a surface to protect ground beetles and rove beetles. Also, since different insects will be found feeding on different garden plants, a diverse planting can provide natural enemies with a more steady supply of insect prey. This can be very useful to support general predators, such as lacewings, minute pirate bugs, damsel bugs, lady beetles, and spiders, allowing these biological controls to act more effectively throughout the garden.

Marigolds as interplanted "companion crop"

Chapter 4

Chemical Controls in the Garden

Chemical controls are considered by most gardeners as a backup control for garden pests. They are usually employed when other·types of controls have not been sufficient or have been too slow-acting to solve an imminent problem. Chemical controls, however, should not be used if there are good garden cultural practices that can prevent development of serious pest problems from developing.

PESTICIDES

Managing pest problems can involve use of chemical controls, or *pesticides*.

Proper use of pesticides is more complex and involves hazards not associated with other pest management techniques. It is very important to understand their characteristics and how they should be used. A wide variety of different chemicals are used for the control of weeds, insects, disease organisms, or other pests. Based on their use, garden pesticides fall into one of the following classes.

- *Herbicide*—a chemical substance sold to kill undesirable plants (also known as weed killers)
- *Insecticide*—a chemical substance sold to kill undesirable insects
- *Fungicide*—a chemical substance sold to kill undesirable fungi

- *Miticide* (or *Acaricide*)—a chemical substance sold to kill mites or ticks
- *Bactericide*—a chemical substance sold to kill bacteria (includes many antibiotics)
- *Molluscicide*—a chemical substance sold to kill pest mollusks such as slugs and snails
- *Nematicide*—a chemical substance sold to kill nematodes

Some pesticides may be categorized or classified in a number of ways, based on their chemistry, origin, or mode of action and use. (Characteristics of specific garden pesticides are discussed in Appendix IV.)

Botanical Pesticides

Some pesticides, particularly insecticides, are described by how their source or method of production. This is because several insecticides are obtained from natural sources, often derived from plants. Pyrethrum, neem, and sabadilla are examples of naturally derived insecticides. Other examples of pesticides having a plant origin are hot pepper (capsaicin), which is a fairly effective deterrent to deer browsing, and corn gluten meal, which can suppress germinating weeds.

Spraying to control insects

Mineral-Based or Inorganic Pesticides

Other pesticides are derived from minerals, such as sulfur and copper. These include the oldest pesticides in use. For example, Homer of ancient Greece extolled "pest-averting sulfur," and sulfur remains the basic ingredient in several fungicides and miticides. Frequently, these mineral-based pesticides are combined with other materials to produce a *Bordeaux mixture* (a mixture of lime, copper sulfate, and water) or *lime sulfur* (sulfur salts produced by boiling water, lime, and sulfur).

Flower of the pyrethrum daisy

TABLE 4-1: SOURCES OF BOTANICAL INSECTICIDES

Insecticide	Active ingredient	Source
Neem	Azadirachtin, certain neem seed oils	Extracted from seed pods of the tree, grown primarily in southern Asia.
Pyrethrum	Several compounds known as pyrethrins	Crushed flowers (pyrethrum) or extracts of active ingredients (pyrethrins) of the young flowers of the daisy *Chrysanthemum cinaeriofolium,* grown primarily in West Africa.
Garlic	Unknown	Generally sold as partially purified crude extracts of crushed garlic.
Rotenone	Rotenone and other resinous rotenoids	Found in dozens of species of leguminous plants. Commercially produced rotenone is derived from either species of *Derris,* found in Malaysia and the East Indies, or *Lonchocarpus* (cubé), from South America. Rotenone registration has been allowed to lapse in the United States because of inability to meet current pesticide registration standards. Existing stocks can be sold and used as labeled.
Ryania	Ryanodine	Ryania is the powdered extract from the roots and stems of the plant *Ryania speciosa,* native to South America. Ryania is sold primarily as a minimally processed extract from ground stems, formulated in a wettable powder.
Sabadilla	Veratrine alkaloids	Ground seeds of a South and Central American plant in the lily family, sabadilla (*Schoenocaulon officinale*).
Nicotine sulfate	Nicotine	Extract from leaves of tobacco and related species of *Nicotiana.* Nicotine-based insecticides (e.g., Black Leaf 40®) are no longer registered for use in the United States, although previously existing stocks are still allowed for sale and use as labeled.

Another pesticide that is mined is *diatomaceous earth*. It occurs as large deposits of the glasslike shells of diatoms (golden-brown algae) and is effective as an insecticide. The shells are very abrasive and it generally is thought that diatomaceous earth kills insects by abrading their exterior cuticle, causing excessive water loss. Recent evidence suggests that the actual mode of action is somewhat different, that as diatomaceous earth collects and mats on the body of the insect, it wicks up their protective waxy coat. Regardless, diatomaceous earth is considered an example of a *desiccant dust*, killing insects by drying.

"Organic" Pesticides

The term "organic" is widely used in reference to various gardening practices, including the use of certain pesticides. Because this term has various scientific, popular, and legal definitions, however, its meaning has become muddled.

Technically, all chemical compounds are classified as having *inorganic* or *organic* chemistry. According to this definition, organic compounds are those that contain molecules of carbon. Inorganic substances do not contain carbon. Under the strictly chemical definition, inorganic pesticides would include most of the older pesticides, such as Bordeaux mixture, sulfur, lime sulfur, copper fungicides, and boric acid (now used for cockroach and ant control in homes). Since essentially all widely used pesticides have a carbon chemistry, most are technically organic.

However, the use of the term "organic" in reference to garden pesticides more often refers to the pesticide source or history of use. Materials derived from natural sources, such as the botanical insecticides pyrethrum, sabadilla, and rotenone, as well as certain mineral-based pesticides, such as sulfur and Bordeaux mixture, are among the pesticides commonly considered to be acceptable for organic gardening. Selective insecticides, such as *Bacillus thuringiensis* (Bt) and soaps, may also be included in this category. The underlying assumption for pesticides described as organic in this manner is that they are naturally derived, have a long history of use, and/or involve minimal environmental hazards.

Because of the tremendous interest in the commercial cultivation of organic produce, several states and growers' organizations have recently established legal systems to certify produce as having been grown organically. This required defining what materials are acceptable in the production of "Certified Organic" fruits or vegetables. Although regulations among individual states vary, most define pesticides by their source. Naturally derived pesticides are generally acceptable; materials that have involved some synthetic alteration are usually prohibited. National requirements for organic food production are currently pending (1998), following nearly a decade of debate of the original legislation passed to set uniform standards.

Insecticidal Soaps and Horticultural Oils

These types of insecticides are receiving increased attention by gardeners because of their safety, effectiveness, and selective action. The advantages, as well as their associated limitations, are based on their action as short-residual *contact insecticides*. Both soaps and oils must be applied directly to the body of the insect, and effects are of very short duration. With these materials, "what you spray is what you can get," and they are not forgiving of poor coverage. However, soaps and oils usually cause little harm to desirable organisms such as birds, pets, beneficial insects—and you.

The soaps being touted for insect control are *just* soaps. (Chemically, most insecticidal soaps are the product of oleic or linoleic fatty acids that have undergone reaction with potassium hydroxide to form a water-soluble potassium salt. Some alcohol is often added to commercial products as an inert ingredient.) The insecticidal activity of some soaps has been known and exploited for over 200 years. However, their use has always been limited by their potential for damaging plants, a problem further exacerbated by inconsistent manufacture. In recent years, several companies have developed these products (and the price!) by more carefully select-

Insecticidal soap

TABLE 4-2: SOAPS AND OILS—THE PROS AND CONS OF PEST CONTROL

Insecticidal Soaps	Horticultural Oils
Advantages	*Advantages*
Safety to humans	Safety to humans
Safety to wildlife, pets	Safety to wildlife, pets
Conserves insect natural enemies	Conserves insect natural enemies
Effective against many small insects	Effective against some difficult insects to control with other methods (e.g., leafcurling aphids, scales)
Limitations	*Limitations*
No residual activity	No residual activity
Purely contact action/high coverage requirement	Purely contact action/high coverage requirement
Effective only against small soft-bodied insects, mites	Limited range of effectiveness
Some potential plant injury (phytotoxicity)	Some potential plant injury (phytotoxicity)
Works best when environment allows slow drying	
Effectiveness reduced by minerals in hard water	

ing the soaps that both kill insects and are safe for plants. During this process, specific plant-destructive soaps were also developed, some of which are being sold as herbicidal soaps.

Similarly, soft hand soaps and household dish detergents exhibit insecticidal action. Many of these over-the-counter products are effective insecticides when used as a dilute spray (1 to 2 percent concentration or about 3 to 5 tablespoons per gallon), and are safe for most plants. As would be expected, they are also much cheaper. However, the use of any such household cleaner is strictly "caveat emptor" when it is selected to control pests on plants. Many of these products make poor insecticides. Many also are too harsh to apply to plants without causing unacceptable injury. Furthermore, such products can be of inconsistent manufacture—particularly since they are always "New and Improved"—which gives one no hint of their relative utility as a garden pest management tool from one case lot to the next.

Oils used for insect and mite control are highly refined specialty oils designed for use on plants. They generally distill at low temperatures (412°F to 438°F) and have many of the sulfur-containing impurities (aromatic compounds) removed to decrease their risk to plants. Oils are usually sold for application as dormant oils to fruit trees and other woody plants before buds break in the spring. Scales and spider mite eggs, which winter on such trees and plants, are the most common targets of these treatments. However, many of the newer spray oils have been sufficiently refined so that they can be safely used on plants even after leaves emerge. Recently, their spectrum has been expanded to include the control of whiteflies and other small insects on vegetable and greenhouse crops as well as summer use on trees. Spray oils also contain a small amount of emulsifier, which enables them to be mixed with water. (Some vegetable oils, notably cottonseed and soybean oils, can also kill many insects. Used at about a 2 percent dilution, homemade mixtures of oils need to be mixed with a little soap or detergent to act as an emulsifier.)

Both soaps and oils are designed to be used as sprays, diluted to a concentration of around 1 to 3 percent. Soaps apparently work by disrupting the cell membranes of susceptible insects, mites, or plants. They are fast-acting, usually showing results within a few hours. Oils are generally regarded to act as suffocants that plug the small spiracles through which insects breathe. They can also kill insect eggs. Both oil and soap sprays are primarily effective against small, soft-bodied insects or mites. Larger insects (and other animals) are rarely affected by these treatments.

Other types of soaps control different garden pests. Some soaps have been formulated to be highly damaging to plants and these herbicidal soaps are sold to control weeds, acting as a non-residual "burn-down" type of herbicide. Some soaps also serve as repellents to deer browsing.

Microbial Insecticides

A few pesticides are derived from microorganisms. The most common of these *microbial* pesticides contain naturally occurring microbes that kill specific types of susceptible insects. Although microbial diseases of pests are widespread in nature and are already naturally occurring controls, relatively few are manufactured and sold for pest management. Most important are the *Bacillus thuringiensis* products (see page 20). Several strains of these bacteria have been developed specifically to control caterpillars (Thuricide®, Biobit®, Dipel®, MVP®, and Caterpillar Attack®). Newer strains have recently appeared on the market for the control of leaf beetles and mosquito larvae in water.

Similarly, a protozoan disease of grasshoppers, *Nosema locustae,* is sold under various trade names such as NoLo Bait® or Semaspore®. This is a slow-acting disease in infected grasshoppers that tends to debilitate rather than kill. More recently, products containing fungi that produce insect disease (primarily *Beauveria bassiana*) have begun to be marketed for control of certain insect pests of greenhouse-grown plants.

Insect parasitic nematodes (species of *Steinernema* or *Heterorhabditis*), also called "predator" or more appropriately "entomopathogenic" nematodes, are among the newer microbial insecticides available for garden use. Entomopathogenic nematodes have been most effective for the control of soil insects, such as cutworms, crown borers, and root weevils, since the nematodes require moist conditions and protection from sunlight to effectively infect insects.

Microbes Used to Control Plant Diseases

Recently, several microbes have come on the market targeting the control of plant pathogens. Some of these act by colonizing leaf surfaces and thus displacing potential pathogens. For example, the strain of the bacteria *Pseudomonas fluorescens,* sold as Blight Ban®, assists in this manner to control fire blight–producing bacteria. Other fungi and bacteria sold as biological controls perform by parasitizing pathogens or by producing antibiotic substances that inhibit their growth. At present such products can only be purchased through specialty catalogs primarily for commercial uses such as greenhouses, nurseries, and orchards.

Synthetic Organic Pesticides

Currently almost all pesticides are synthetically produced compounds with a carbon-based chemistry. Synthetic organic pesticides include such compounds as carbaryl (Sevin®), diazinon, malathion, glyphosate (Roundup®), and triforine (Funginex®). Some of these are based on naturally occurring chemicals. For example, the insecticides known as pyrethrins derived from the pyrethrum daisy are the chemical godparents of the popular class of insecticides known as the *pyrethroids.* Some pyrethroids have made their way to the garden shelf in the form of permethrin (for control of most garden insects) and allethrin (for control of nuisance flying insects such as wasps and mosquitoes). A discussion of the characteristics and uses of common garden pesticides is included in Appendix IV.

Systemic Pesticides

Pesticides may also be classified as being either *systemic* or *nonsystemic* compounds. Systemic pesticides comprise those that can be picked up through the leaves and/or roots of plants and then move within the plant. Systemic pesticides vary as to how mobile they are within the plant with some only moving locally, while others are more generally distributed in plant tissues. Systemic pesticides do tend to move in specific directions within a plant. For example, the herbicide glyphosate (Roundup®, Kleenup®), when applied to leaves, may move into and kill the plant's roots. Alternatively, the insecticide disulfoton (DiSyston®), applied to roots, moves upward in the plant and concentrates in actively growing foliage.

Systemic activity often improves the effectiveness of a pesticide by providing better plant coverage. However, the systemic pesticides often come with some special hazards. For example, most systemic insecticides, such as Orthene®, should not be used on food crops. Accidental treatment of these plants results in pesticide residues that are not only illegal but also potentially unsafe. Several systemic insecticides are also fairly toxic to humans and other mammals, particularly DiSyston®, the active ingredient found in various systemic rose and flower care products. Systemic herbicides such as glyphosate (Roundup®, Kleenup®) have a great potential for damaging desirable plants that they may accidentally contact.

Eradicant Versus Protectant Fungicides

Fungicides are often classified as either *protectants* or *eradicants*. Protectants, such as maneb and chlorothalonil (Daconil 2787®), must be in place on the surface of the plant before fungal infection of the plant occurs. Eradicants, such as benomyl (Benlate®, Tersan 1991®), can move within the plant and kill developing fungi.

Preemergent and Postemergent Herbicides

Many herbicides that are appropriate for use in vegetable and flower gardens are the *preemergent* *herbicides*. These must be applied before seeds germinate, since they act to prevent early seedling development. Dacthal® (DCPA®) and Treflan® are examples. After seeds have germinated and the weeds have grown a supporting root system, these herbicides are no longer effective for weed control. Conversely, other herbicides are applied to plants after they emerge. These *postemergent* herbicides include 2,4-D, glutosinate, and glyphosate. (For more discussion on herbicides, see Chapter 8.)

Mode of Entry

Special terms are used to describe insecticides according to the means through which they enter the insect. *Stomach poisons,* such as *B. thuringiensis,* must be ingested by the insect to be effective. *Contact insecticides* can penetrate through the external skeleton (cuticle) of the insect. (This term is also used to describe herbicides that kill plant cells at the point of contact, such as herbicidal soaps.) Insecticides that enter through the breathing openings (spiracles) of insects as a gas are known as *fumigants.*

Pesticide Selectivity

Pesticides are further described as being *selective* or *nonselective*. Selective herbicides are those that can be used to control one type of plant but cause little or no injury to another. For example, fluazifop-butyl (Grass-B-Gon®) is generally considered to be selective, since it is much more effective against grasses than against broadleaf plants. Several selective insecticides are also available. For example, B. *thuringiensis* only kills caterpillars that eat the pesticide; beneficial insects such as lady beetles—and nonsusceptible pests such as aphids—are not affected by B. *thuringiensis*. Insecticidal soaps are fairly selective because they primarily control small, soft-bodied insects and mites that are contacted with the soap spray during application. Many larger insects are not susceptible to soap sprays, and insects that visit the plant after the soap has dried suffer no ill effects.

Selectivity is also determined by how a pesticide is used. Glyphosate is a nonselective herbicide that can be used selectively to kill a thistle in the flower garden if it is carefully placed on the weed. A spot treatment of Sevin® may be useful for controlling a patch of blister beetles on a potato plant, and is increasingly selective in its effects as the treated area is more limited. Horticultural oils applied during the dormant season could kill beneficial insects on a fruit tree, but they are selective, since these insects are not often on the tree at the time oils are sprayed. If used at the improper time or mixed in high concentrations, all pesticides can become nonselective and can injure plants, insects, or other organisms that otherwise could tolerate the treatment.

Nonselective herbicides are compounds that are toxic to both crop and weed species of plants. Glyphosate (Roundup®, Kleenup®) and glufinosate (Finale®) are examples of nonselective herbicides that will kill or weaken almost any sprayed plant. Because of their potential to cause injury, nonselective herbicides must be used with extreme care around desirable plants.

Often the term *broad spectrum* is applied to nonselective insecticides. This indicates that a wide variety of insects—and sometimes other organisms—are susceptible to their effects. For example, chlorpyrifos (Dursban®) and diazinon are insecticides that can kill most species of insects as well as many mites. In some situations, such as when several pests commonly attack the plant, broad-spectrum activity in an insecticide can be useful. However, broad-spectrum insecticides also commonly kill beneficial insects, such as the natural enemies of insects and mites, and thus do not integrate well with existing biological controls.

Soil sterilants are nonselective herbicides applied to soil that can kill actively growing plants and prevent growth of new plants for as long as the compound remains active, often several years. Soil sterilants are used primarily for maintaining rights-of-way or in areas where no vegetation is desired, such as driveways and sidewalks. Serious inadvertent injuries to desirable plants, including trees and shrubs, have resulted from us-

ing soil sterilants such as pramitol (Triox®) near landscape plantings. Soil sterilants have no place in or around garden areas. Some states have even moved to make these products "Restricted Use Pesticides," available only to certified pesticide applicators who have passed an exam administered by the state Department of Agriculture or the Environmental Protection Agency.

INTEGRATED PEST MANAGEMENT (IPM)

A variety of control techniques may be required to effectively manage pest problems. For example, managing cutworms in a garden can include rototilling to kill overwintering larvae (cultural control), the use of cardboard collars to protect plants (mechanical control), and selective use of insecticides (chemical control). None of these techniques alone may be sufficiently effective.

Care must be taken to coordinate these various control techniques so that their effects don't conflict in overall pest management. For example, certain insecticides can seriously reduce the effectiveness of biological insect controls. Mulching for weed control can increase slug populations, particularly with high-moisture conditions. Tillage and harvest practices may have an impact on beneficial biological control organisms as well as pests.

Maintaining effective pest management is also often a problem in areas where single control approaches are repeatedly used. This has been most often documented with the use of pesticides. Many insects, mites, fungi, and even a few weeds have become resistant to pesticides that formerly were effective. Pesticide use may also cause shifts in pest problems. For example, nightshade weed problems proliferate in fields following the application of several common herbicides that were ineffective against nightshade. Mite problems in fruits and field corn are often aggravated by early-season insecticide use directed against other pests.

Finally, other serious nontargeted effects may result from pest management practices. Many pesticides are highly toxic to the applicator or to wildlife within or around the treated area. Pesticides may move into and pollute ground or surface waters. Pesticide residues can contaminate food or feed, and plants may be inadvertently damaged by pesticides. These hidden costs from pest control practices are not always fully considered during pest control decision-making.

Integrated Pest Management (IPM) is a system for optimizing pest management decisions based on both ecological and economic considerations. It is not a particularly new idea, since sound pest management practices have always involved IPM approaches.

Fundamental to Integrated Pest Management are a number of assumptions:

- Optimal pest management is achieved by employing a variety of techniques.
- Pest management techniques should be used in a coordinated (integrated) manner so that their effects complement each other.
- Since eradication of many pests is not often achievable or desirable, controls should be applied only when pest populations are so dissruptive as to justify their action. Monitoring pest populations is usually necessary to achieve this goal.
- Pest management techniques should consider the long-term costs of the practice, including their effects on beneficial organisms, health, and the environment.
- The performance of any pest management practice should be continually reevaluated to determine whether it is achieving the desired result in the most effective manner.

COMMON MISTAKES USING YARD AND GARDEN PESTICIDES

"Spray First, Read Labels Later (If at All)"

The information that appears on a pesticide label is the result of extensive research and experience and includes both the benefits and the potential hazards of the pesticide. Although often difficult to read, the label's information is essential to safe and proper use of the pesticide. Furthermore, the label instructions are a legal document, so using the pesticide in a manner that is not indicated is a violation of federal law. Failure to thoroughly read label instructions can result in several problems:

- Plants that are sensitive to the effects of the pesticide may be injured.
- The pesticide may be applied to a food crop for which its use is not permitted. This results in illegal residues appearing on the food and subsequent health risks.
- Preharvest intervals required between the time of application and harvest may be neglected, resulting in excessive pesticide residues on food.
- Pesticides may be applied in a manner that poses a high risk to wildlife, pets, or humans.
- The applicator may receive excessive exposure to the pesticide.
- The applicator will be legally liable for any damage resulting from an illegal pesticide application.

"Got a Problem? Spray It!"

No single pesticide can control every pest problem. In addition, few yard and garden problems are simple enough to be solved simply by spraying pesticides. It is necessary to first diagnose the problem so that the most effective controls are used. The inappropriate use of pesticides as a first-line defense may result in the treatment being ineffective. The underlying problem may persist and cause further damage. Pesticide treatments may even aggravate the problem. For example, problems with spider mites increase with the application of insecticides that kill their natural enemies. In either case, the money and effort involved in controlling the pest are wasted.

Checking Out New Garden Products—
The Backyard Experiment

As growing a western garden provides many unique challenges, it is only through trial and error that most gardeners discover the practices that work best for them. This also includes finding effective pest management practices, such as evaluating the performance of some insecticide or home-concocted spray. One shortcut in this ongoing process, a means of conclusively determining what does or does not work, is to establish some simple garden trials along the lines of a designed experiment.

Paging through a garden catalog, one finds it sprinkled with testimonials from satisfied product users. For example, in the sections selling pest management products a typical quote might be: "Last year I had problems with squash bugs. This year I tried your product and had no squash bugs. Your product really works!"

What's wrong with this statement? Well, basically, it failed to have a *control* (or check). The control of the experiment is similar in all ways, except for the treatment you are testing. The reason this is needed is that insect populations often vary greatly from year to year and even during short periods within the growing season. Without a control, you have nothing with which to compare the effectiveness of the experimental treatment. It may have worked, or the insects may naturally not have been as abundant.

Populations of insects and incidences of plant diseases fluctuate dramatically between seasons. Only with a control that provides a reference point can the effectiveness of garden practices be quantified. For example, you might be able to state, with a high degree of confidence, that something you did "controlled 80 percent of the squash bugs in my garden."

Furthermore, it is a very good idea to *replicate* your results. Insects are rarely distributed uniformly in an area, often being more abundant on certain plants or along edges of fields. Typical field experiments usually require at least three or four replications for the researcher to begin to feel confident that the results are real and repeatable. So, for example, if you were to test the effects of a soap spray on a garden insect, you might want to first divide the area into eight areas, four of which would receive the soap spray and four areas that would serve as the untreated control for comparison.

Then you are ready to "reap your results" and see how things turned out. For insect control trials, this will require taking some measurement of how well the treatments worked. For example, you may observe how many insects are left on a leaf or how much damage was done to the plant. Through careful measurements, and a well-designed experiment, you can come up with results that you will have confidence in and can share with others.

"If a Little Is Good, More Is Better"

Using pesticides casually may pose many problems. One popular tendency is to use a stronger dilution of pesticide for "insurance." If pesticides are used at rates exceeding those recommended in the instructions, they can injure various plants. The rates of pesticide dilution and application listed on the label were established, in part, to avoid plant injury, and even insecticides and selective herbicides, such as 2,4-D, can injure normally tolerant plants when applied inappropriately. The pesticide label also serves as a legal document. Using any pesticide in a manner that is not specified on the label is illegal.

The rates of pesticides described on the label are also designed to ensure that pesticide residues on harvested crops do not exceed safe levels. Using higher rates of pesticides can result in amounts of residues that exceed known safety levels, and can also increase the risk of injuring beneficial insects, wildlife, and other "nontarget" organisms.

Using too much of a pesticide is usually the result of "guesstimating" the amount needed. Typically, these estimates are off by 25 to 50 percent or more. Always read and follow the label directions. *Measure* the amount of pesticide to be used—*never* guess.

"Protective Clothing Is for 'the Other Guy'"

The use of pesticides assumes that basic protective measures will be followed by the applicator. It cannot compensate for the "worst case" applicator who may expose himself or herself to very high rates of the pesticide by handling it carelessly. The potential for exposure to pesticides is especially great during mixing, since concentrated pesticides are being handled. Exposure to the pesticide through inhalation or skin contact is common during application. All pesticides, from insecticidal soaps to the most toxic agricultural pesticides, will carry directions for protective equipment.

Gloves are the single most important piece of protective equipment because the great majority of pesticide exposures occur to the hands. Gloves used for mixing and applying pesticides should be made of neoprene rubber or some other material that is not absorbent. Cloth or leather gloves are not recommended because they are absorbent and can concentrate pesticides next to the skin.

A dust mask also affords protection when applying pesticides. The fine droplets produced by sprayers are easily inhaled. Pesticides in dust form present even greater risks of being inhaled. Dust masks also help to prevent irritation from materials such as diatomaceous earth or sabadilla.

Finally, some sort of eye protection is always a good idea. Several pesticides, such as sulfur, can be very painful if they get into the eyes. Drift into eyes is also very common when spraying upward into a fruit tree. A pair of goggles or safety glasses protect eyes from pesticides at these times.

"Herbicides Only Kill Weeds"

Herbicides are pesticides designed to kill plants. Most herbicides have a particular action that makes them more lethal to certain plants than to others—the basis of their selectivity. However, used inappropriately, no herbicide can distinguish between "good plants" and weeds. The proper use of herbicides is primarily up to the applicator.

One of the most devastating injuries caused by herbicides around the yard involves the soil sterilant herbicides. These are used to control weeds in driveways, sidewalks, and waste areas for long periods of time. Unfortunately, they often cause unwanted effects as tree roots grow under the driveway or water carries the herbicides downhill. Established trees may be killed by the careless use of soil sterilant herbicides.

Herbicides used in gardens, such as Dacthal® or trifluralin (Treflan®), are usually designed to prevent the germination of weed seeds. However, some weeds are close relatives of our cultivated plants, and careful reading of the label instructions will indicate that many of these are also susceptible.

The nonselective herbicides glyphosate (Roundup®, Kleenup®) and glufinosate (Finale®) have also gained acceptance in gardens. Most plants are susceptible to these herbicides, as gardeners are generally aware. However, unless used with great care, fine droplets may drift or sprayer nozzles may drip so that desirable plants are accidentally treated. They must also be used carefully around the base of trees and shrubs to avoid absorption by green wood.

Most injuries resulting from herbicides and other pesticides can be prevented by reading the label instructions. "The label is the law," but the label is also your best guide to using pesticides safely.

Roundup®, a common systemic herbicide

Chapter 5

Common Disorders of Garden Plants

Asparagus field

This chapter will help you troubleshoot and diagnose the causes of your own garden problems. Under each crop, a list of common disorders will refer you to subsequent chapters and sections detailing the control of specific problems. Since the cultural requirements of the crop may also be important for diagnosis, a brief description prefaces each section. Vegetables are discussed first, followed by fruit crops, flowers and, finally, roses.

VEGETABLE CROPS

Asparagus

Asparagus is one of the few perennial vegetable plants common in the vegetable gardens of the West. The delicious shoots, which emerge each spring from the crown of the plant, are one of the first ready to harvest. If the shoots are not harvested, they become ferns that produce energy for the next season's crop.

Asparagus is generally planted as roots that are one to two years old; seeds are also usually available through catalogs. Because the plants are not moved after planting, extra care needs to be taken to prepare the site before planting. Asparagus is very tolerant of salts, but high levels of organic matter and a soil that drains well are prerequisites for asparagus culture. The plants also require phosphorus and potassium, which are best applied before planting. Attention to weed control and protection from frost should also be considerations when planning an asparagus bed.

Because asparagus plants need to build root reserves, they are typically not harvested for two to three years after planting. Peak production usually follows five to ten years later. Application of a nitrogen-containing fertilizer is required to maintain plant growth.

Asparagus produces either male or seed-bearing female plants. Yields from female plants are lower because of energy used in seed production. Recently, high-yield, all-male varieties have been introduced.

Asparagus is vulnerable to some serious pest problems. Asparagus beetles and asparagus aphids damage plants in some areas, and asparagus rust is an occasional problem. Removing old ferns helps reduce problems with aphids and rust.

COMMON DISORDERS OF ASPARAGUS
Affecting spears
New spears die back, shrivel
    Frost injury (184)
New spears chewed
    Asparagus beetle (90)
    Spotted asparagus beetle (90)
    Cutworms (108–109)
Black eggs on spears
    Asparagus beetle (90)
Spears tough, pithy

Spears too old
Lack of fertility

Affecting ferns
Ferns chewed, appear bleached
    Asparagus beetle (90)
Stunted, bushy ferns
    Asparagus aphid (140)
Fern growth slow
    Excessive picking during establishment
    Cultural problems (e.g., poor fertility or water-
    ing, insufficient sunlight, overcrowding)
Fern growth slow, yellow/reddish/black areas on
ferns
    Asparagus rust
Dieback of ferns, crown death
    Fusarium wilt (164)
    Phytophthora root rot (162)

Beans

Beans are an herbaceous annual plant grown for seeds (dry beans) or immature pods (snap beans). Several different species of beans can be cultivated, but most are varieties of the common bean, *Phaseolus vulgaris.*

Bean seeds require warm temperatures and sufficient soil moisture to germinate and grow. The minimum soil temperature for seedling emergence is 60°F. The plants are susceptible to frost and optimal temperatures for growth are in the 70°–80°F range.

Maturity of most garden beans is not affected by day length. Numerous varieties of beans are available, with bush types generally maturing more rapidly than vine varieties. Other types of beans, such as limas, chickpeas, black-eyed peas, and asparagus beans, require warmer temperatures and a longer growing season than snap beans.

Beans are legumes, capable of extracting nitrogen from the air through bacteria that grow on root nodules. As such, they do not need additional nitrogen but can require moderately high levels of potassium and phosphorus for optimum growth. Beans are also susceptible to iron and zinc deficiencies related to high-pH conditions in many regional soils.

Garden-grown beans generally suffer few problems with pests, although the overeager gardener risks run-ins with seedcorn maggot and damping off when planting too early in cool, wet soils. The Mexican bean beetle, the "bad apple" of the lady beetle family, can be quite damaging in some locations.

COMMON DISORDERS OF BEANS
Seedling problems
Poor seedling emergence
    Cool soil temperatures
    Uneven watering
    Seedcorn maggot (120)
    Damping-off disease (173)
Seedlings chewed irregularly, slime trails may be
present
    Slugs (153)
Seedlings emerge but growing point killed
("snakehead" beans)
    Seedcorn maggot (120)
New leaves curled
    Wind injury
    Onion thrips (127)
Seedlings appear cut
    Rabbits (209)
    Cutworms (108–109)

Affecting foliage
New leaves curled
    Wind injury
    Onion thrips (127)
    Herbicide (2,4-D, etc.) injury (189)
    Bean aphid (146)
Aphids
    Bean aphid (146)
Small pits chewed in upper leaf surface
    Palestriped flea beetle (98)
Leaves clipped from stems, cut at sharp angle
    Rabbits (209)
Leaves chewed, ragged
    Grasshoppers (129)
    Slugs (153)
    Mexican bean beetle (87)
    Western bean cutworms (108–109)
    Blister beetles (97)

Pole beans

Leaves with small veins remaining, lacy
appearance
    Mexican bean beetle (87)
    Slugs (153)
Upper leaf surface with dark or yellow spotting
    Halo blight (178)
    Common bacterial blight
    Bacterial brown spot
    Bean rust (177)
Leaves with meandering tunnels
    Vegetable leafminer (123)
Leaves with yellow, green or blue-green mosaic
patterning
    Common bean mosaic virus
Leaves yellowed and puckered, plants stunted
    Beet curly top (160)
Leaves yellowing between veins
    Iron deficiency (iron chlorosis) (191)
    Zinc deficiency (191)
Leaves with small, white flecks, retarded growth
    Spider mites (150)
    Onion thrips (127)
Top leaves "scorched" along edges
    Wind damage during hot, dry weather

Affecting pods, seeds
Flowers fail to "set," abort
    High temperatures
    Western flower thrips (128)
    Plant bugs (135)
Tunneling into pods
    European corn borer
    Mexican bean beetle (87)
    Western bean cutworms (108–109)
    Slugs (153)
Twisted bean pods
    Herbicide injury (189)
Poor seed set
    Drought stress during blossom set
    Plant bug injury (135)
Seeds hard
    Overmaturity

Broccoli and Cauliflower

The edible broccoli head or cauliflower curd is
actually a tightly packed mass of flower buds. In
typical varieties, all the flower heads have merged
to form a single head. Sprouting types of broccoli,
such as Romanesco, can form several distinct heads.
Intermediate types exist, such as the purple cauli-
flowers, which are classified as broccoli. Broccoli
and cauliflower are biennial plants grown as annuals. However, many broccoli varieties can flower
during a single season, particularly when extended cold weather follows transplanting.

Like all members of the cabbage family, broccoli and cauliflower are cool-season plants, with
optimal temperatures for growth around 60°F
to 70°F. High temperatures can produce a variety of growth disorders, such as poor head quality and off flavors. Heading is also delayed by
high temperatures.

Although they can be seeded, transplants are
most commonly used. Broccoli can easily be transplanted. However, cauliflower is more sensitive
to checks on growth, and transplanting is more
difficult. Plants with about four true leaves that
do not show the blue coloration associated with
stress are best for transplanting.

Both broccoli and cauliflower require good
soil fertility and structure for best production.
However, watering is usually the most critical
cultural practice since both crops are heavy drink-
ers. The quality of broccoli and cauliflower can
be greatly affected by periods of drought stress,
so watering should be even and consistent
throughout growth.

Early-maturing "snowball" types of cauliflower
usually require blanching of the head by tying the
inner wrapper leaves. Many later-season varieties
have infolding leaves that self-blanch the head.

Broccoli and cauliflower may be attacked by
several insect pests, including western cabbage
flea beetles and various cabbageworms.

COMMON DISORDERS OF BROCCOLI AND
CAULIFLOWER
Affecting whole plant
Plant growth slow, stem shriveled at soil line
    Wirestem (Rhizoctonia) (175)
    Wind injury
    Root pruning (cultivator blight)

Broccoli

Seedlings cut
    Cutworms (108–109)

Affecting leaves
Small, circular holes or pits in leaves
    Western cabbage flea beetle (87)
Larger, irregular holes chewed in leaves
    Imported cabbageworm/southern cabbage-
    worm (99)
    Cabbage looper (102)
    Grasshoppers (129)
    Diamondback moth (112)
    Zebra caterpillar (100)
    Slugs (153)
Leaves with warty, brown lumps (cauliflower)
    Edema (184)
Leaves with meandering tunnels
    Vegetable leafminer (123)
White spotting on leaves, often distorted
    Harlequin bug (134)
Yellow, angular spots progressing inward from leaf
edges, wounds
    Black rot (167)
Dieback of leaves from edges, wilting, and rot of
roots (cauliflower)
    Phytophthora root rot (162)

Affecting stem
Hollow stem
    Hollow stem disorder (resulting from fertili-
    zation with high rates of nitrogen
    and overstimulated growth)

Affecting head
Premature setting of heads, head size very small
    Exposure of transplants to shifting warm/cool
    temperatures
Bolting (flowering) of broccoli
    Excessive maturity
    Poorly adapted variety
    High-temperature stress
Curd of cauliflower appears uneven and fuzzy
(riceyness)
    Warm temperatures during curd development
Flower buds of broccoli turn brown
    Brown bud disorder (physiological problem
    associated with rapid growth)

Cauliflower head yellow
    Exposure of head to direct sun

Cabbage, Brussels Sprouts, Collards, and Kale

Cabbage, Brussels sprouts, collards, and kale are closely related members of the cabbage family, the latter two being in the headless group that most closely resemble their wild ancestors. Cabbage produces a single large head of densely packed leaves, which develop after the plants have produced a rosette of outside wrapper leaves. Brussels sprouts produce a large stalk that supports numerous smaller heads at the base of the leaves. Cabbage, Brussels sprouts, collards, and kale are all biennial plants that generate a flower stalk in their second season.

Like all members of the cabbage family, they are cool-season plants, with optimal temperatures for growth around 60°F to 70°F. They are also frost-tolerant and usually survive early fall freezes that kill most other garden plants. Freezing temperatures can actually improve the flavor of these plants, particularly Brussels sprouts. High temperatures slow growth and reduce the quality and flavor of the leaves. Kale and collards are more tolerant of high temperatures than cabbage.

All cabbage family members can be grown by directly seeding in the garden, and seeds germinate with soil temperatures above 40°F. However, transplants are more popular, particularly for cabbage. Young cabbage exhibits good frost tolerance and is easily transplanted. Plants with about four true leaves that do not show the blue coloration associated with stress are the best specimens for transplanting.

All the cole crops are heavy users of water due to their large leaf surface area. Therefore, they grow best in heavier soils, which better retain water. They do not tolerate poor drainage, however. Cabbage and Brussels sprouts are among the vegetables that demonstrate the best growth response to fertilization. Kale and collards are more tolerant of poor growing conditions.

Cabbage

Disease problems with these vegetables are few in the West. Cabbage is plagued by several insect pests, particularly the western cabbage flea beetles and various cabbageworms. Brussels sprouts often develop large populations of cabbage aphids late in the season. Collards and kale are relatively pest-free.

COMMON DISORDERS OF CABBAGE, BRUSSELS SPROUTS, COLLARDS, AND KALE
Seedling problems
Seedlings wilt, die
  Damping-off/seedling blights (173)
  Wirestem (Rhizoctonia) (175)
Seedlings cut
  Cutworms (108–109)
  Rabbits (209)

Affecting whole plant
Plant growth slow, stem shriveled near soil line
  Wirestem (Rhizoctonia) (175)
  Wind injury
Plant growth slow, roots chewed and tunneled
  Cabbage maggot (120)

Affecting leaves
Small, circular holes or pits in leaves
(*Note:* a small purple halo often develops around these wounds on mustard greens)
  Flea beetles (87–89)
Large holes chewed in leaves
  Imported cabbageworm/Southern cabbageworm (99)
  Zebra caterpillar (100)
  Cabbage looper (102)
  Diamondback moth (112)
  Grasshoppers (129)
  Slugs (153)
White spotting on leaves, some distortion
  Harlequin bug (134)
Yellow, angular spots moving inward from wounds and leaf margin
  Black rot (167)
Rot progressing from lower leaves
  Bottom rot (Rhizoctonia) (175)

Dieback of outer leaves from edges, wilting and root rot
  Phytophthora root rot (162)

Affecting head
Head distorted, aphids present
  Cabbage aphid, turnip aphid (143)
Raised, brown warts on inner leaves
  Edema (184)
  Onion thrips (127)
Dieback of inner leaves (cabbage, Brussels sprouts)
  Tip burn (183)
Head size small
  Overcrowding
  Poor culture (fertility, water)
Cracking of cabbage heads
  Excess water following dry period
  Overmaturity
Bitter, off flavors
  Irregular watering during heading

Carrots and Parsley

Biennial plants grown as annuals, carrots and parsley tolerate cool temperatures well and can overwinter in the garden if given some winter protection. If left in the garden over winter, they produce a flower stalk the following season.

Carrots and parsley prefer moderately warm soil temperatures. Germination can occur in soils as low as 40°F, but optimal sprouting is more likely at 60°F to 65°F. The seeds are small and should be planted shallowly and kept moist. Seedlings are weak and may have difficulty growing through crusted soils. Carrots are almost never transplanted because the taproot and subsequent growth are so sensitive and easily distorted. However, parsley transplants readily.

Additionally, carrots require deep, loose soils, since soil compaction inhibits root growth. In heavy soils, varieties that develop short taproots are most adapted. Carrots respond well to nitrogen fertilization, but are less demanding of phosphorus and potassium.

Parsley

These plants have few pest problems. East of the Rockies, aster yellows is the most common disease of carrots. Parsleyworm, the larva of the black swallowtail butterfly, is common on parsley and related plants, such as dill and fennel.

COMMON DISORDERS OF CARROTS AND PARSLEY
Seedling problems
Poor seedling emergence
    Crusted soil
    Slugs (153)
    Millipedes (153)
    High temperatures

Affecting leaves
Top growth chewed
    Rabbits (209)
    Climbing cutworm (108–109)
    Alfalfa webworm
    Parsleyworm (100)
    Slugs (153)
Leaves show bronze discoloration, bushy top growth
    Aster yellows (181)
    Carrot aphid (146–147)

Affecting flowering
Flower stalk is produced
    Normal flowering by two-year-old plant

Affecting roots
Roots hairy, top growth excessively bunchy
    Aster yellows (181)
Forked roots
    Damage to root tip
    Stony or heavy clay soils
Twisted roots
    Overcrowding
Roots chewed
    Carrot rust fly (126)
    Millipedes (153)
    Slugs (153)
    Lesser bulb fly (127)

Roots cracked
    Overmaturity
Roots rotted
    Phytophthora root rot (162)

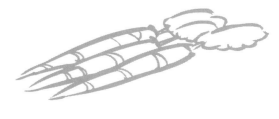

Cucumbers

As warm-weather plants, cucumbers do not tolerate frost. Germination requires minimum soil temperatures of 60°F with optimal temperatures somewhat higher. Optimal average temperatures for growth are in the 70°F to 75°F range. Many varieties mature 50 to 60 days after germination.

Cucumbers require pollination by bees or other insects. All garden cucumbers bear both male and female flowers on the same plant. Unlike many other squash family plants, most of the flowers are female, capable of producing fruit.

Cucumbers demand large amounts of water, and the fruits boast the highest water content of all garden vegetables. Some wilting during midday is normal and unavoidable during high temperatures. However, wilting during early morning indicates drought stress. Inadequate water contributes to problems such as poor fruit development and off flavors. Cucumbers are among the vegetables that respond well to fertilization.

In much of the region, cucumbers have few insect problems. Angular leaf spot and other fungal diseases can be a problem where leaf wetting encourages infection.

COMMON DISORDERS OF CUCUMBERS
Seedling problems
Poor seedling emergence
    Seedcorn maggot (120)
    Damping-off disease (173)
    Cool soil
Small pits chewed in seedlings
    Striped cucumber beetle (91)
    Palestriped flea beetle (88)
New leaves curled
    Wind injury
    Onion thrips (127)
    Herbicide (2,4-D, etc.) injury (189)

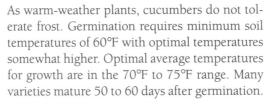

Affecting whole plant
Sudden wilting of plant
Fusarium wilt (164)

Affecting leaves
Leaves with small, white flecks, retarded growth
Spider mites (150)
Onion thrips (127)
Mottling/yellowing of leaves
Cucumber mosaic (159)
Watermelon mosaic (160)
Squash mosaic
Greenhouse whitefly (139)
Dark spotting and death of tissues between veins
Angular leaf spot (177)
Anthracnose (164)
Phytophthora wilt (162)
Meandering tunnels in leaves
Vegetable leafminer (123)
White covering on leaves
Powdery mildew (167)
New leaves puckered, distorted
Herbicide injury (189)
Viral disease (various mosaic viruses) (162)
Onion thrips (127)

Affecting fruit
Failure to set fruit
Lack of female flowers
Excessive heat, rain during flowering
Poor pollination (186)
Knobby or misshapen fruit
Lack of pollination (186)
Water stress during fruit development
Cucumber mosaic (159)
Watermelon mosaic (160)
Fruit with blackened end
Blossom-end rot (183)
Fruit pitted
Angular leaf spot (177)
Anthracnose (164)
Cold damage (184)
Off flavor
Water stress
Temperature fluctuations

Eggplant

Eggplant

Eggplant is a warm-weather plant that grows best with optimal temperatures of 70°F to 85°F. Seed germination requires a minimum of 60°F. Because it needs an extended growing season, eggplant is almost always grown from transplants started six to ten weeks before the last expected frost. Eggplant is highly susceptible to frost injury and grows poorly during periods of cool temperatures (below 50°F). Fruit will not set when temperatures drop below 60°F to 65°F.

Plants transplant with some difficulty. Short, stocky transplants with a large root mass do much better than spindly plants. Transplants are also susceptible to wind injury and drying.

A fairly heavy feeder of soil nutrients, eggplant needs a regular supply of nitrogen and water for best growth. During heavy fruit set, plants are susceptible to breakage in high winds.

The Colorado potato beetle is the most notorious pest of eggplant east of the Rockies. Fusarium wilt can be a problem in soils where it becomes established.

COMMON DISORDERS OF EGGPLANT
Affecting whole plant
Plants wilt, roots appear brown, dark streaks inside stem
Fusarium wilt (164)
Plants wilt, dead areas on stem around soil line
Phytophthora wilt (162)

Affecting leaves
Small holes chewed in leaves
Flea beetles (87–89)
Large areas chewed in newer leaves
Colorado potato beetle (92)
Edges of leaves chewed
Grasshoppers (129)
Colorado potato beetle (92)
Leaves with small white flecks, retarded growth
Spider mites (150)
Leaves die back, yellow from margins, dark streaks inside stem
Verticillium wilt (163)

Affecting fruit
Pitting, discoloration of fruit
    Cold damage (184)
    Verticillium wilt (163)
Poor fruit set
    Low light
    Cool night temperatures

Lettuce

Lettuce prefers cool weather and, unlike many other vegetables, it thrives in partial shade. It requires moist conditions during growth and may produce bitter flavors if grown in hot, dry weather. The plants tend to produce a seed stalk (bolt) when temperatures are too high, although heat-tolerant varieties are available. Spring and fall crops are commonly grown in the region, with summer plantings restricted to the cooler, high-altitude gardens.

Lettuce is almost always grown from seed. During germination, moisture must be fairly high and temperatures must be favorable. Germination can occur in cool soils as low as 35°F, although the optimal temperature is somewhat higher. However, germination is inhibited by temperatures above 85°F.

Easily transplanted, lettuce is quite cold-tolerant and can usually be grown as long as temperatures stay above 25°F.

Slugs show a particular fondness for lettuce and are often the bane of this crop. Aphids may be abundant, particularly in fall, and aster yellows is often damaging to varieties that form heads.

COMMON DISORDERS OF LETTUCE
Seedling problems
Poor emergence
    High temperatures during planting
    Planting too deep
    Soil crusting
    Slugs (153)

Affecting whole plant
Formation of seed stalk (bolting)
    High temperatures
    Cold weather during seedling stage

Wilting
    Tomato spotted wilt (161)
    Lettuce root aphid (149)

Affecting leaves
Twisting of head, yellowing, dark latex spots
    Aster yellows (181)
Yellowing of foliage, no twisting or latex spotting
    Beet western yellows viruses
    Cucumber mosaic (primarily older leaves) (159)
Foliage chewed
    Cabbage looper/celery looper (102)
    Slugs (153)
    Palestriped flea beetle (88)
Aphids on leaves
    Lettuce aphid (146)
    Potato aphid (144)
    Green peach aphid (142)
Dieback of inner leaves
    Tip burn (physiological problem related to high temperature and rapid growth) (183)

Affecting roots
White, cottony insects on roots
    Lettuce root aphid (145)

Affecting heads
Soft heads
    Immaturity
Head decay
    Bottom rot (Rhizoctonia) (175)
    Tomato spotted wilt (161)
Bitter taste
    Hot, dry weather

Muskmelons (Cantaloupe) and Watermelons

Muskmelons and watermelons are long-season, warm-weather plants that do not tolerate frost. The growth, yield, and quality of these crops are best where warm, sunny weather prevails; melons are difficult to grow at higher elevations. Optimal temperatures are 70°F to 85°F for watermelon, somewhat lower for muskmelons. Varieties vary in maturity, ranging from 75 to 100 days.

Muskmelon plant

The seeds of muskmelon and watermelon require a minimum of 60°F to germinate but are very tolerant of dry soil conditions during sprouting. To force in the garden, plants can be started early. However, like all cucurbits, they do not tolerate disruption of the root system, so transplanting must be done with extra care to avoid breaking roots.

Because they are dioecious (have separate male and female flowers), muskmelons and watermelons require pollination. New seedless watermelon varieties require interplanting with a fertile pollinator.

Both muskmelon and watermelon require fairly high levels of watering, particularly during emergence and pollination. However, the root system of muskmelon does not go as deep as that of watermelon and thus needs more frequent applications of moisture. Plants should not be moist during the harvest period or the sugar content will decrease.

Developing watermelons and muskmelons pose few pest problems, primarily wilt and mosaic diseases. However, as fruits ripen, coyotes—and neighborhood children—develop a particular fondness for these garden favorites.

COMMON DISORDERS OF MUSKMELON AND WATERMELON
Seedling problems
Poor seedling emergence
    Cool temperatures
    Seedcorn maggot (120)
    Damping-off disease (173)
    Uneven watering
New leaves cupped
    Wind injury
    Onion thrips (127)
Small pits chewed in seedlings
    Striped cucumber beetle (91)
    Palestriped flea beetle (88)

Affecting whole plant
Sudden wilting of plant
    Bacterial wilt (muskmelon only) (191)
    Fusarium wilt (164)
    Phytophthora wilt (162)

Affecting leaves
Leaves with small, white flecks, retarded growth
    Spider mites (150)
    Onion thrips (127)
New leaves curled, distorted
    Wind injury
    Onion thrips (127)
    Herbicide (2,4-D, etc.) injury (189)
Meandering tunnels in leaves
    Vegetable leafminer (123)
White covering on leaves
    Powdery mildew (167)
Mottling/yellowing of leaves
    Watermelon mosaic (160)
    Cucumber mosaic (159)
    Greenhouse whitefly (139)
Irregular dead areas on leaves
    Anthracnose (164)
    Phytophthora wilt (162)

Affecting fruit
Failure to mature fruit
    Cool temperatures (184)
Worms scarring bottom of fruit
    Striped cucumber beetle (larvae) (91)
Fruit pitting
    Anthracnose (164)
    Cold injury (184)
Fruits chewed by large animal
    Coyote
    Raccoon (208)

Onions, Leeks, and Garlic

Onions and related species of *Allium*, such as garlic, shallots and leeks, are biennial plants generally grown as annuals. Some *Allium*, such as bunching onions and chives, are also cultivated as spreading perennials.

Seeding should take place early. Germination requires a minimum of about 35°F, but optimal temperatures are above 50°F. They do not want large amounts of soil moisture to germinate, but the seedlings are weak and have difficulty penetrating soil crusts. The onset of bulbing is determined by day length and soil temperature, so crops planted late may bulb early and be small.

Grown from bulbs, onions generally produce larger, earlier crops. However, if cool weather after transplanting is followed by an early summer, many of the larger bulbs may prematurely bolt and produce a seed stalk. Early removal of these flowering spikes forces the plants to renew bulb growth.

Since onions are shallow rooted, they crave frequent watering, particularly in sandy soils. When grown for bulbs, onions should be allowed to mature naturally. Top growth will topple and the neck area will dry, reducing problems with diseases that might enter the bulb. As the plants mature, watering should be reduced.

Onions generally have few enemies in the home garden, except in areas where onion maggots have become established. Thrips, bulb rots, and leaf diseases are occasionally troublesome. Crop rotation is critical in limiting the development of many diseases, particularly fungi that produce root rotting.

COMMON DISORDERS OF ONIONS, LEEKS, AND GARLIC
Seedling problems
Poor emergence
    Soil crusting
Seedlings being plucked whole from ground
    Starling, house finch (212)

Affecting leaves
Leaves scarred, flecked with light areas
    Onion thrips (127)
Elongate, brown-purplish dead areas on foliage
    Purple blotch (166)
    Botrytis leaf blight (167)
    Downy mildew (174)

Affecting bulbs
Plants produce flowers (bolting), bulbs woody
    Biennial bearing (overwintered bulbs)
    Cool, wet weather following transplanting
Bulb size small
    Late planting
    Onion thrips (127)
    Poor culture (watering, fertilization, etc.)

Bulbs rot
    Fusarium basal rot (164)
    Pink root
Bulb tunneled
    Seedcorn maggot (121)
    Onion maggot (121)
    Lesser bulb fly (127)
    Millipedes (153)

Peas

Although areas with cool summer temperatures can sustain cropping throughout the summer, peas are a cool-season crop that is generally planted in early spring and again in late summer. Seed germination requires a minimum soil temperature of 40°F, and crop growth is optimal at 60°F to 65°F. Growth is slowed and plants become stressed by high temperatures, although there is a wide range in tolerance of high temperatures among varieties. Soil moisture should be fairly high while seeds germinate, but seeds should not be soaked before planting or they can crack and rot.

Moderate consumers of water during growth, peas are legumes that do not require supplemental nitrogen fertilization.

Though peas have few pest problems, powdery mildew commonly develops in early summer.

COMMON DISORDERS OF PEAS
Seedling problems
Poor seedling emergence
    Seedcorn maggot (121)
    Damping-off disease (173)
Seedlings chewed
    Slugs (153)
    Rabbits (209)
    Housefinch (212)

Affecting whole plant
Wilting
    Pea aphid (146–147)
    Fusarium wilt (164)
Retarded growth
    High temperatures

Affecting leaves
Entire leaves chewed, leaving stems
    Rabbits (209)

Onions

Peas

Leaves chewed, ragged
    Looper (102)
    Climbing cutworm (108–109)
    Grasshoppers (129)
    Slugs (153)
Leaves with small white flecks, retarded growth
    Spider mites (150)
White covering on leaves
    Powdery mildew (167)

Affecting pods, peas
Pods with scarring
    Flower thrips (128)
    Onion thrips (127)
Peas hard
    Overmaturity
    High temperatures

Peppers

A warm-weather vegetable, peppers cannot tolerate frost. In the West, the length of the growing season is rarely long enough to allow direct seeding in the garden, so peppers are grown from transplants started about six to eight weeks before planting. Germination requires a minimum soil temperature of 60°F.

Peppers perform best when daily temperatures average 70°F to 85°F, with somewhat cooler night temperatures. Hot pepper varieties tolerate and thrive at higher temperatures than sweet peppers. Pepper growth and ripening cease and blossoms may drop when night temperatures fall below 55°F. Peppers also need even watering, particularly when flowers are being pollinated and fruits begin to form.

Most garden problems with peppers are related to culture, such as uneven watering, or temperature and excess sunlight, as opposed to any serious pests.

COMMON DISORDERS OF PEPPERS
Affecting whole plant
Plants wilt, roots show browning, decay
    Verticillium wilt (163)
    Fusarium wilt (164)
    Phytophthora wilt (162)

Plants wilt, roots appear healthy
    Tomato spotted wilt (161)
Growth retarded
    Cool temperatures (184)
    Viral disease (potato virus Y, common mosaic) (162)

Affecting leaves
Small holes chewed in leaves
    Flea beetles (87–89)
Large areas chewed in leaves
    Tomato/tobacco hornworm (104)
New growth small, discolored
    Beet curly top (160)
    Tomato spotted wilt (161)
    Viral disease (potato virus Y, common mosaic) (162)
    Herbicide (2,4-D, etc.) injury (189)
Leaves thick, leathery
    Viral disease (potato virus Y, common mosaic) (162)
Leaves with irregular, dead areas
    Phytophthora wilt (162)
Sticky honeydew present
    Green peach aphid (142)
    Greenhouse whitefly (139)

Affecting fruit
Fruit tunneled
    Corn earworm (tomato fruitworm) (102)
    European corn borer
Fruit shows discoloring in ring pattern
    Tomato spotted wilt (161)
Fruit shows blotchy, dead patches
    Sunscald (184)
    Phytophthora wilt (162)
Blossom end of fruit dead
    Blossom-end rot (183)
Ripe fruit shows circular, slightly sunken patches
    Anthracnose (164)
Fruit color dull
    Cold injury (184)
Fruit fails to ripen
    Cool temperatures (184)
Poor fruit set
    Low nighttime temperatures
    Low light

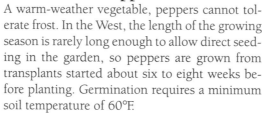

Green pepper

Fruit distorted
    Uneven growing conditions (temperature, water)
    Low temperature during blossoming

Potatoes

Unlike most garden vegetables, potatoes are not grown from true seeds. Instead, they are vegetatively propagated using seed pieces of cut or whole potatoes, and sprouts develop from the dormant eyes. Because true seeds are not used, potatoes are much more likely to carry over diseases between seasons. As a result, a highly recommended practice is to plant certified seed potatoes, which are grown to meet strict standards of disease control.

Potatoes prefer moderately cool weather, with optimal growth at 60°–65°F. However, the plants are very sensitive to frost and generally should not be planted earlier than two to three weeks prior to the last spring frost. Healthy tuber growth is dependent on even water and fertilization conditions, particularly when the vines are growing most vigorously.

The base of the cultivated plant should be covered with soil (hilling) to protect the tubers from light, which causes tuber greening. Because the plants grow shallow, spreading roots, weeding within 6 to 8 inches of the plants should be done carefully early in the season to avoid root damage.

COMMON DISORDERS OF POTATOES
Stand establishment problems
Poor germination
    "Blind" seed pieces (no eyes)
    Seed piece decay (Fusarium) (178)
    Blackleg (soft rot/Erwinia) (195)

Affecting whole plant
Plants wilt frequently
    Lack of water
    Roots pruned by cultivation
Plants wilt, roots appear brown
    Verticillium wilt (177)
Plants wilt, stems black and soft
    Blackleg (soft rot/Erwinia) (195)

Affecting leaves
Small holes chewed in leaves
    Flea beetles (87–89)
Large areas chewed in leaves
    Colorado potato beetle (92)
    Grasshoppers (129)
    Blister beetles (97)
    Cabbage looper (102)
    Climbing cutworm (108–109)
White flecking of leaves
    Garden leafhopper (139)
New growth small, discolored, curled
    Potato (tomato) psyllid (149)
    Aster yellows (181)
    Viral disease (potato leaf roll, potato virus Y) (162)
New growth may die back
    Frost injury (184)
    Lygus bug (135)
    False chinch bug (134)

Affecting tubers
Tubers chewed
    Cutworms (108–109)
    Field mouse
    Slugs (153)
Tubers with dark streaking
    Tuber flea beetle (tunnels irregular) (89)
    Potato leaf roll virus (phloem areas of tuber dark)
    Verticillium (on stem end of tuber only) (163)
Tubers appear punctured
    Quackgrass (rhizomes) (199)
    Wireworm
Tubers with hollow center
    Hollow heart (physiological problem related to uneven growth)
Tuber size small, tuber skin rough
    Potato (tomato) psyllid (149)
Knobby tubers
    Potato (tomato) psyllid (149)
    Uneven growing conditions during tuber set
Tubers show greening (virescence)
    Exposure to light
Tubers sprout prematurely
    Potato (tomato) psyllid (149)

Tuber skin with dark spotting ("dirt" won't wash off)

    Rhizoctonia (175)

Tuber skin with small light, scabby patches

    Enlarged lenticels (related to cool, wet soils)

Tubers form on stem above ground

    Potato (tomato) psyllid (149)

    Aster yellows (181)

    Rhizoctonia (175)

Radishes, Turnips, and Rutabagas

Radishes, turnips, and rutabagas—root crops of the cabbage family (Cruciferae)—thrive when temperatures are cool, and seeds can germinate in soils with a temperature as low as 40°F. Optimal growth occurs at 60°F to 65°F, and slows when temperatures exceed 75°F. They can tolerate frosts; the flavor of turnips and rutabagas is actually enhanced by a light frost.

Planted in early spring and late summer, these vegetables are more adaptable to varying growing conditions than are other members of the cabbage family. Turnips and rutabagas are biennials, flowering the second year after planting. Radishes will often set a seed stalk a few months after sprouting. Turnips and radishes should be picked when small or they will develop a strong flavor and poor texture.

Radishes, turnips, and rutabagas attract relatively few pests. The western cabbage flea beetle infestation can become severe in some areas, killing seedlings. The cabbage maggot tunnels roots in localized areas of the West.

COMMON DISORDERS OF RADISHES, TURNIPS, AND RUTABAGAS

Seedling problems

Seedlings die

    Damping-off fungi (Rhizoctonia, others) (175)

Affecting leaves

Small shotholes in leaves

    Western cabbage flea beetle (88)

Ragged holes in leaves

    Diamondback moth (112)

    Imported cabbageworm (99)

Affecting roots

Tunneling of root

    Cabbage maggot (120)

    Slugs (153)

Roots fibrous, with strong flavor (turnips, radishes)

    Overmaturity

Spinach, Swiss Chard, and Beets

A cool-season crop, spinach gives its best performance when temperatures average 60°F to 65°F. Plants produce seed stalks (bolt) during long, sunny days—a process accelerated by high temperatures. Bolt-resistant varieties are being increasingly refined. Spinach is usually grown as a spring and fall crop. It is extremely cold-tolerant and can overwinter in the garden. Seed germination can occur in cool soils (about 40°F) and is inhibited in warm soils. Spinach should be planted as early as possible to deter bolting.

Swiss chard is related to spinach, another member of the Chenopodiaceae family. Originally cultivated for its root (now grown as a separate vegetable—the garden beet), the outer leaves and petioles can be used in cooking. Chard resists bolting as temperatures rise, a distinct advantage for many gardeners. If stressed by high temperatures and drought, it may produce a seed stalk. By pinching this off as soon as possible, leaf growth will again be stimulated. Like spinach, chard is grown from seed and tolerates a fairly wide range of garden conditions.

New Zealand spinach, sometimes sold as a heat-tolerant spinach, is actually a very different species in a different plant family (Tetragoniaceae).

Beet seeds usually come in clusters of four or five seeds. As a result, some thinning may be needed. Beets generally require less nitrogen and more phosphorus than do nonroot crops. They also prefer lighter, looser soils, and can tolerate highly alkaline soils as well.

Spinach, beets, and chard are all attacked primarily by the spinach leafminer, which produces dark blotches in the older leaves.

COMMON DISORDERS OF SPINACH, SWISS CHARD, AND BEETS

Seedling problems
Poor seed germination
    High soil temperatures

Affecting whole plant
Formation of flower stalk (bolting)
    Long day length (accelerated by high temperatures)
Roots rot
    Rhizoctonia (175)
Plant wilts, roots tunneled
    Sugarbeet root maggot (121)
Plants stunted, may die
    Blue mold (downy mildew) (174)
    Sugarbeet root maggot (121)
Beets fail to bulb
    Overcrowding

Affecting leaves
Dark, hollowed blotches in leaves
    Spinach leafminer (123)
Holes in leaves
    Flea beetles (87–89)
    Webworm
Aphids on leaves
    Green peach aphid (142)
    Lettuce aphid (146)
White or red blisters on lower leaf surface
    White rust (176)
    Red rust (spinach)
Leaves yellow, often rotted
    Blue mold (downy mildew) (174)
Red spotting of leaves
    Leafhopper (beets) (139)
Small leaves, growth slow
    High temperatures

Summer Squash and Zucchini

Summer squash are prized for their immature fruit. Almost all summer squashes have been bred for bush-type growth, unlike the vining growth of most hard or winter squashes. They require a relatively short growing season, producing fruit about 40 to 50 days after planting.

Summer squash are *dioecious,* producing separate male and female flowers. Generally, far more male flowers occur, which do not produce fruit, and they require cross-pollination by bees or other insects.

Warm-weather plants, these squash are fairly difficult to transplant and are usually seeded in the garden. Seed germination requires a minimum soil temperature of 60°F and growing plants prefer temperatures in the 65°F to 80°F range. Summer squash cannot tolerate near-freezing conditions, and growth ceases below 50°F.

The plants form an extensive but shallow root system and demand plenty of water. However, they are satisfied with less fertilization than most other vegetable crops.

Pest problems are few, though plantings in cool soils are frequently bothered by seedcorn maggots. Viral diseases transmitted by aphids are a threat in some areas.

Spinach

COMMON DISORDERS OF SUMMER SQUASH AND ZUCCHINI

Seedling problems
Poor seedling emergence
    Seedcorn maggot (121)
    Damping-off (173)
    Cool soils
Small pits chewed in seedlings
    Striped cucumber beetle (91)
New leaves cupped
    Wind injury
    Onion thrips (127)

Affecting whole plant
Sudden wilting and death of plant
    Bacterial wilt (91)
    Fusarium wilt (164)
    Squash bug (133)
    Squash vine borer (134)

Plants wilt frequently
>Salt injury
>Root pruning

Affecting leaves
New leaves curled
>Wind injury
>Onion thrips (127)
>Herbicide (2,4-D, etc.) injury (189)
Leaves with small white flecks, retarded growth
>Spider mites (150)
>Garden leafhopper (139)
>Onion thrips (127)
Mottling/yellowing of leaves
>Mosaic (cucumber, watermelon) viruses (159–160)
>Angular leaf spot (177)
>Varietal character of some yellow squash
>Greenhouse whitefly (139)
White covering on leaves
>Powdery mildew (167)
Small, gray bugs on leaves
>Squash bug (133)
Dead areas on leaves
>Angular leaf spot (177)
>Squash bug (133)
Dark spots on leaves, often with concentric pattern
>Early blight (166)

Affecting flowers
Insects feeding on flowers, pollen
>Western corn rootworm (90)
>Striped cucumber beetle (91)
>Spotted cucumber beetle (91)
Plants flower but don't set fruit
>Male flowers only

Affecting fruit
Gray-brown bugs on fruit
>Squash bug (133)
Fruit mottled, misshapen
>Cucumber mosaic (159)
>Watermelon mosaic (160)
>Poor pollination (186)

Fruit chewed
>Western corn rootworm (90)
>Striped cucumber beetle (91)
Skin tough, thick
>Overmaturity
Dark pitting of fruit
>Cold damage (184)
Fruit bitter tasting
>Irregular watering during fruiting

Sweet Corn

Sweet corn cannot withstand freezing temperatures. In order for seeds to germinate the soil must attain a minimum temperature of 50°F, with the optimum topping 60°F. Germinating the new "supersweet" varieties is more difficult.

Since it is wind-pollinated, sweet corn should be planted in blocks to facilitate optimal pollination. Plantings should be isolated from field corn, since cross-pollination will produce kernels that lack sweetness.

Sweet corn has a hearty appetite for nitrogen and water, and watering is particularly critical during pollination.

Raccoons constitute the biggest threat in the sweet corn patch. Corn earworms also cause trouble in southern areas of the West. East of the Rockies, the western corn rootworm often clips the silk of later plantings, hampering pollination.

COMMON DISORDERS OF SWEET CORN
Seedling problems
Poor seedling emergence
>Seedling blights (Penicillium, damping-off) (173)
>Seedcorn maggot (121)
Seedlings chewed at soil line
>Cutworms (108–109)
Seedlings purple
>Phosphorus deficiency
>Cool soil

Affecting leaves
Lower leaves die back and yellow
>Nitrogen deficiency (190)

Spider mites (Banks grass mite, Twospotted spider mite) (150–151)
Lower leaves with streaks of chewing
    Slugs (153)
Leaves with regular rows of holes as they emerge
    European corn borer
Leaves in midsummer with streaks of chewing
    Western corn rootworm (90)
Small, red-brown, raised area on leaves
    Rust (176)

Affecting roots
Roots chewed
    Western corn rootworm (90)

Affecting tassels
Aphids covering tassel
    Corn leaf aphid (146)
Tassels chewed
    House finch (212)

Affecting silk
Silk clipped
    Western corn rootworm (90)
    European earwig (131)

Affecting ear
Poor kernel set
    Western corn rootworm (90)
    Poor pollination (drought, adverse weather during pollen shed)
Ear husks discolor and dry
    Banks grass mite (151)
Kernels lack sweetness
    Overmaturity
    Cross-pollination with field corn
Enlarged, gray growths on stems, tassels or ears
    Common smut (171)
Insects in ear
    Corn earworm (102)
    Western bean cutworm (109)
    Dusky sap beetle (98)
    European corn borer
    Bumble flower beetle (98)
    Western corn rootworm (90)
    European earwig (131)

Worms tunneling into ear, stalk
    European corn borer
    Dusky sap beetle (98)
Ear tips chewed off by large animal
    Deer (210)
Ear pulled from plant and chewed with husk removed
    Raccoon (208)

Tomatoes

Perhaps the most popular garden vegetable, tomatoes challenge the gardener more than most other vegetables. Warm-season plants that require a long growing season to produce, tomatoes almost always begin life in the garden as transplants, started six to ten weeks before planting. Transplanting should take place in warm soils after frost. Growth slows considerably in cool soils, and plants are vuluerable to frost injury.

Most tomatoes offered for sale are hybrids, although open-pollinated varieties, such as Rutgers, Beefsteak, and Roma, are also widely available. The many tomato varieties cover a broad spectrum of maturation times, with many newer varieties continually being developed for more rapid growth.

Tomatoes exhibit either a *determinate* or *indeterminate* growing habit. Determinate varieties stop growing at a certain point, are compact, and usually bear early. Indeterminate varieties continue to grow as long as conditions permit. They display a more sprawling growth and benefit more from staking.

Pollination can be disrupted by either excessively warm or cool temperatures. Warm nighttime temperatures also aid fruit ripening.

Tomatoes require high fertility. However, excessive nitrogen accelerates top growth at the expense of flowering. Consistent and steady watering curbs their susceptibility to blossom-end rot.

Tomatoes are also susceptible to hornworms and potato (tomato) psyllids throughout most of the West. Common diseases include the leaf-spotting fungi, such as early blight, and fusarium wilt.

COMMON DISORDERS OF TOMATOES

Seedling problems

Seedlings cut near soil line
　　Cutworms (108–109)
　　Blowing soil

Affecting whole plant

Growth retarded; leaves thick, leathery
　　Common mosaic virus (162)
Growth retarded; new leaves small and discolored
　　Potato (tomato) psyllid (149)
　　Beet curly top (160)
Plants wilt, roots appear brown
　　Fusarium wilt (note browning of vascular system) (164)
　　Phytophthora wilt (162)
Plants wilt and may die, roots appear healthy
　　Tomato spotted wilt (161)

Affecting leaves

Small holes chewed in leaves
　　Flea beetles (87–89)
Large areas chewed in leaves
　　Tomato and tobacco hornworm (104)
Spotting, dieback of leaves
　　Early blight (164)
　　Septoria leaf spot
Lower leaves first yellow, then die
　　Fusarium wilt (164)
Leaves with brown, warty lumps
　　Edema (184)
Leaves thickened, curled
　　Beet curly top (160)
　　Potato leaf roll virus
　　Common mosaic (162)
　　Physiological leaf curl
　　Potato (tomato) psyllid (little thickening) (149)
New growth small, discolored
　　Potato (tomato) psyllid (149)
　　Beet curly top (160)
　　Cucumber mosaic (159)
　　Tomato spotted wilt (161)
　　Herbicide (2,4-D, etc.) injury (189)

Sticky honeydew present on leaves
　　Potato aphid (144)
　　Greenhouse whitefly (139)
White, sugarlike pellets on leaves and soil
　　Potato (tomato) psyllid (149)

Affecting fruit

Fruit chewed
　　Tomato and tobacco hornworm (104)
　　Corn earworm (tomato fruitworm) (102)
　　Slugs (153)
Fruit shows discoloring in ring pattern
　　Tomato spotted wilt (161)
Fruit with brown spots
　　Early blight (166)
Green "shoulders"
　　Genetic condition of many heirloom varieties
Overripe fruit with circular, sunken spots
　　Anthracnose (164)
Fruit with yellow spots
　　Plant bugs (135)
Blotchy, white area on upper surface of fruit
　　Sunscald (184)
Blossom end of fruit dies
　　Blossom-end rot (183)
Blossom end of fruit distorted (catfacing)
　　Cool temperatures during early fruit development
Fruit cracks
　　Irregular growth due to alternating wet/dry conditions
　　Excessive nitrogen
Fruit size unusually small
　　Drought, poor growing conditions
　　Potato (tomato) psyllid (149)
"Puffy"-textured fruit
　　Potato (tomato) psyllid (149)
　　Poor pollination (186)
Flowering delayed
　　Long-season variety
　　Excessive nitrogen fertilization
Fruit fails to set
　　Excessive heat (at least 90°F) during pollination
　　Cool temperatures (nighttime temperatures below 50°F)

Fruit fails to ripen
    Short growing season
    Cool night temperatures
Skin becomes discolored, russeted
    Cold injury (184)
Mealy texture
    Potato/tomato psyllid (149)
    Poor pollination (186)

Winter Squash, Pumpkins, and Gourds

Winter (or hard) squash and pumpkins are grown as long-season annuals, the fruit picked when mature. Typical varieties take 90 to 110 days, sometimes more, to mature.

A minimum of 60°F is necessary for the seeds of winter squash and pumpkins to germinate. However, seeds are rarely affected by dry soil conditions during sprouting. Because the plants do not easily recover from any disturbance of their roots, transplanting may be difficult. These warm season crops display optimal growth in the 70°F to 95°F range.

The plants build extensive, yet shallow root systems. Their sprawling growth habit makes them ideal candidates for training. Bush varieties are also available for smaller gardens, although the fruit quality is not as good.

For optimum growth, pumpkins and squash, as heavy users of water, favor a soil texture that can distribute water more evenly.

As with other cucurbits, the plants depend on pollination. Cross-pollination between different types of squash will work but will produce fruit with intermediate characteristics if seeds are planted the following year.

Pest problems can be severe in some areas, especially in the warmer regions of the West. Squash bugs can be a particularly difficult insect to control, and striped cucumber beetles have a penchant for seedlings. Root-rotting fungi, such as *Phytophthora*, can cause serious problems in heavy soils.

COMMON DISORDERS OF WINTER SQUASH, PUMPKINS, AND GOURDS
Seedling problems
Poor seedling emergence
    Seedcorn maggot (121)
    Damping-off disease (173)
    Cool soil
Small pits chewed in seedlings
    Striped cucumber beetle (91)
    Palestriped flea beetle (88)

Affecting whole plant
Sudden wilting and death of plant
    Squash bug (133)
    Squash vine borer (134)
    Bacterial wilt (91)
    Fusarium wilt (164)
    Phytophthora root rot (162)
    Verticillium wilt (163)
Periodic wilting, recovery
    Lack of water
    Root pruning

Affecting leaves
New leaves cupped
    Wind injury
    Onion thrips (127)
    Herbicide (2,4-D, etc.) injury (189)
Leaves with small, white flecks, retarded growth
    Spider mites (150)
    Garden leafhopper (139)
    Onion thrips (127)
Leaves with irregular dead areas
    Phytophthora wilt (162)
Leaves covered with white powder
    Powdery mildew (167)
Mottling/yellowing of leaves
    Cucumber mosaic (159)
    Watermelon mosaic (160)
    Angular leaf spot (177)
    Varietal character of some yellow fruited varieties
Browning, dieback of leaves
    Squash bug (133)

Pumpkin

Garden leafhopper (139)
Angular leaf spot (177)

Affecting fruit
Pitting of fruit
Squash bug (133)
Striped cucumber beetle (91)
Western corn rootworm (90)
Gummy stem blight/black spot
Cold injury (184)
Irregular shape of fruit
Poor pollination (186)
Cucumber mosaic (159)
Irregular watering
Watermelon mosaic (160)
Russeting of fruit
Cold injury (184)

FRUIT CROPS

Apples

Apples are the most widely adapted tree fruit in the West. However, as with most tree fruits, cold, dry, desiccating winds, sunscald, and late spring frosts can take a toll. Thus, they are best cultivated in more sheltered areas.

Commercially available apples are not grown from seed, which makes for highly variable plant types. Instead, they are propagated by grafting from desirable varieties. Most apple trees sold are dwarf or semidwarf varieties, produced by grafting the fruit-bearing variety atop special rootstocks that dictate a dwarfing growth. Since these rootstocks vary in winter-hardiness and anchorage in the soil, the choice of rootstock can be almost as important as the fruit-bearing variety in determining suitability. At higher elevations and in northern areas, only the most winter-hardy and early-maturing varieties are adapted.

Apples require pollination by insects to set fruit. Many varieties are not self-fruitful and must be further cross-pollinated, involving the transfer of pollen from a separate variety, known as a pollinizer or pollinator. Fruit develops on short fruiting spurs. The rosette of leaves sur-rounding the fruit determines fruit quality. Thinning fruit to one per cluster to increase fruit size and to prevent alternate-year, or biennial, bearing is recommended.

Some pruning to remove dead or diseased wood and nonfruit-bearing sucker growth is necessary. Pruning also trains the growth of the tree. The most common training involves production of a central leader and strong, lower scaffold limbs. It is best to prune in early spring, before growth starts, to avoid spreading fire blight.

The codling moth (appleworm) is an apple tree's most formidable enemy throughout the West. Fire blight is the most important disease problem that can kill trees.

COMMON DISORDERS OF APPLES
Affecting twigs, branches
Twigs or branches die back, leaves wilt suddenly and do not fall
Fire blight (179)
White woolly material on branches, trunk
Woolly apple aphid (145)
Branches covered with small circular scales
San Jose scale (148)
Twigs with series of splinter wounds, often dying back
Cicada, treehopper egg-laying damage
Small holes in bark
Shothole borer (96)

Affecting lower trunk, roots
Trees decline in vigor, trunk tunneled
Flatheaded apple tree borer/Pacific flathead borer (101)
Roundheaded apple tree borer
Trees decline in vigor, root and crown areas show decay
Phytophthora root and crown rot (162)

Affecting leaves
White speckling or streaking of leaves
White apple leafhopper (136)
Tentiform leafminer (123)
Leaves covered with white powder
Powdery mildew (169)

Leaves bronze-colored, may drop prematurely
    Twospotted spider mite, McDaniel spider
    mite (150)
Leaves with brown, scabby patches
    Appleleaf blister mite (151)
    Cedar-apple rust (176)
Leaves chewed
    Tent caterpillar (109)
    Red-humped caterpillar
    Speckled green fruitworm (109)
    Apple flea beetle
Leaves curled
    Rosy apple aphid, green apple aphid (144)
    Leafroller (111)

Affecting fruit
Fruit tunneled
    Codling moth (110)
    Apple maggot/western cherry fruit fly (124)
    European earwig (enters previous wounds)
    (131)
Fruit deformed, with scabby wounds on surface
    Leafroller (111)
    Oriental fruit moth
    Speckled green fruitworm (109)
    Apple scab (172)
    Hail injury
Fruit deformed, dimpled
    Plant bugs (135)
    Stink bugs
    Apple curculio
    Rosy apple aphid (149)
    Hail injury
Fruit deformed, no obvious external injury
    Poor pollination (186)
Light spotting of fruit
    San Jose scale (148)
    Flower thrips (128)
Dark spotting of fruit
    White apple leafhopper (136)
    Hail injury
Fruit surface with general brown coloring
(russeting)
    Spray injury
    Powdery mildew (169)

Cherries

Typical backyard cherries are either sweet cherries (*Prunus avium*) or sour (pie) cherries (*Prunus cerasus*). The latter are much more winter-hardy and widely adapted in the West. Hardiness is also related to the rootstock on which the plants are grafted. Mehalab rootstocks tend to be hardier and earlier bearing, but shorter-lived trees than cherries grafted to Mazzard rootstock. A recent addition are the G.M. series dwarfing rootstocks, which have the advantage of tolerating heavy clay soils.

Like winter freezing injury, blossom damage by spring frosts is a common weather-related problem with cherries. To delay blossoming, trees should be located in shaded areas of the yard, which warm later.

Cherries generally need less pruning and training than other tree fruits. Prune to remove dead or damaged branches and crossing limbs, and to allow additional light into the tree.

Moderate watering should suffice, though sweet cherries are much more sensitive to drought than sour cherries, and fertilization needs are modest for most sites. Cherries must be pollinated by insects. Sour cherries are self-fruitful, but most sweet cherries rely on a nearby pollinizer for cross-pollination.

Fruit damage by birds is usually the most conspicuous pest injury to cherries. Cherries, like all stone fruits, are susceptible to the peach tree borer. As trees age, they tend to succumb to Cytospora cankers.

COMMON DISORDERS OF CHERRIES
Affecting whole plant
Trees decline in vigor
    Peach tree borer (113)
    Stem-pitting virus
    Phytophthora root rot (162)
    X-disease (182)
    Cytospora canker (173)

Affecting leaves
Leaves curled, undersides often with dark aphids
    Black cherry aphid (143)

Leaves yellow
        Iron chlorosis (191)
        X-disease (182)
Upper surface of leaves chewed, often leaving main veins
        Pearslug (118)
Leaves chewed and tent of webbing produced
        Eastern tent caterpillar (109)
        Fall webworm (109)
White powdery covering on leaves
        Powdery mildew (169)
Small holes in leaves
        Shothole fungus (172)

Affecting branches, twigs
Clear, amber ooze from bark
        Cytospora canker (173)
Branches die back
        Cytospora canker (173)
        Shothole borer (96)
Small holes in bark of twigs, branches
        Shothole borer (96)
Tips of twigs die back, twigs tunneled
        Peach twig borer

Affecting lower trunk
Clear, amber ooze from bark
        Cytospora canker (173)
Amber ooze mixed with sawdust, often near or below soil line
        Peach tree (crown) borer (113)
Pitting at graft union
        Stem-pitting virus
Roots discolored and rotted
        Phytophthora root rot (162)

Affecting fruit
Fruit eaten but not tunneled
        Bird damage (212)
        Cherry curculio (94)
Fruit small and conical with pebbly skin (sweet cherry only)
        X-disease (buckskin) (182)
Fruit burst, but not eaten (fruit cracking)
        Heavy rainfall prior to harvest

Fruit pit infested
        Cherry curculio (94)
Fruit infested with white worms
        Western cherry fruit fly (124)
Fruit swollen and hollow (chokecherry only)
        Chokecherry gall midge

Currants and Gooseberries

Two of the most easily grown fruit crops in a regional garden are currants and gooseberries. Although they require continuous moisture for optimum production, they can better adapt to drier and more exposed sites than can other fruits. They may be planted in spring or fall and bear moderately alkaline soils but will continually battle with iron chlorosis in high-pH soils.

Regular pruning translates to superior fruit production, since most fruit is borne on young, year-old wood. Currants and gooseberries are self-fruitful and do not require cross-pollination with a separate pollinizer.

Several insects favor currants, including the imported currantworm, currant borer, and currant aphid. Gooseberries experience less damage by these insects, although the gooseberry maggot is locally a problem on later-maturing varieties in some areas of the West.

COMMON DISORDERS OF CURRANTS AND GOOSEBERRIES
Affecting leaves
Leaves pucker and may show reddening
        Currant aphid (146)
Leaves lightly speckled or bronze-colored
        Twospotted spider mite (150)
New growth generally yellow
        Iron chlorosis (191)
White flecking on leaves
        Leafhopper (139)
White powdery coating on leaves
        Powdery mildew (169)
Dark spotting on leaves
        Leaf spot (anthracnose) (164)
        Rust (176)

Currants

Leaves chewed
    Imported currantworm (117)
    Currant spanworm (117)
    Currant flea beetle
    Gooseberry fruitworm
Center of leaves dry out
    Drought injury
    Currant borer (114)
    Bronze cane borer (96)
    Spider mites (150)

Affecting canes
Canes die back during midsummer
    Currant borer (114)
    Bronze cane borer (96)

Affecting fruit
Fruit soft, with pale spotting
    Sunscald (184)
Maggots in berries, berries discolored
    Currant fruit fly (gooseberry maggot)

Grapes

The two species of grapes most often cultivated regionally are the European wine grape (*Vinis vinifera*) and the native North American species (*Vinis labrusca*). The native types, and the many hybrids between the two species, are far more winter-hardy and adapted to the West. Wine grapes are usually limited to only the mildest locations.

Grapes should be planted where they will receive full sun and no extreme frosts. Since they consume less water and fertilization than most plants, including turf, they should be planted accordingly. The winter survival rate is improved by watering to promote early-season growth, but then allowing the soil to dry late in the season. Vines should be planted deep, about 1 foot, to promote rooting and limit winter kill.

Fruit forms on shoots that develop from buds produced during the previous season. Pruning and vine training are critical in grape culture to maintain productive buds.

Native grapes present few pest problems—other than raccoons and neighborhood children.

However, wine grapes habitually suffer from powdery mildew, grape leafhoppers, and mites.

COMMON DISORDERS OF GRAPES
Affecting vines
Irregular woody growth on stem, usually at soil line
    Crown gall (178)
Insect tunneling of canes
    Apple twig borer

Affecting leaves
Buds tunneled
    Apple flea beetle
    Climbing cutworm (108–109)
Powdery covering on leaves, stems
    Powdery mildew (171)
Leaves with white spotting
    Grape leafhopper, Zic-zac leafhopper (137)
Leaves with grayish color, may drop prematurely
    Twospotted spider mite (150)
Leaves with meandering pale streaks
    Leafminer (123)
New leaf growth distorted, small
    Herbicide injury (189)
    Eriophyid mite (151)
Large areas of leaves chewed
    Western grape leaf skeletonizer (112)
    Eightspotted forester
    Achemon sphinx
    Apple flea beetle

Affecting berries
Berries shrunken, rotten
    Sour rot
    Botrytis (167)
Berries split
    Powdery mildew (169)
Berries covered with small, dark spots
    Grape leafhopper (137)
Berries chewed, damaged
    Bird injury (212)
    Grape berry moth
Berries eaten rapidly (overnight)
    Raccoon (208)
    Fox squirrel (207)

Grapes

Peaches

One of the more difficult fruit trees to grow in the West is the peach. Spring frosts mercilessly kill blossoms, and freeze damage often damages branches or twigs. Relatively few varieties or rootstocks are well adapted to this region. Trees need to be situated in slowly warming, well-protected areas of the yard to minimize this cool-season injury, although they also need full sun during the growing season.

Peaches are most often pruned using the "open vase" method. This involves cutting out much of the center of the tree to promote spreading growth of the lower scaffold limbs. The open center affords more light and air circulation. The trees can be pruned in summer as well as during the dormant season.

Though peaches are pollinated by insects, most varieties are self-fruitful and do not depend on a pollinizer variety for cross-pollination. If fruit set is very heavy, they should be thinned by hand or fruit size will be reduced.

Responding well to fertilization, particularly with nitrogen, peach trees also need regular watering or the plant will drain water from the developing fruit. However, watering and fertilization should be curtailed after harvest to allow the trees to harden off for optimum winter protection.

Pests are a moderately severe problem on peaches. The peach tree borer tunnels the lower trunk, and the green peach aphid can curl and distort new growth in the spring. Coryneum (shothole) blight is the most serious disease, and cytospora canker is readily established in weakened or damaged trees.

COMMON DISORDERS OF PEACHES
Affecting leaves
Leaves curled
    Green peach aphid (142)
White powdery covering on leaves
    Powdery mildew (169)
Small holes in leaves
    Coryneum (shothole) blight (172)
Trees decline in vigor, leaves yellow
    X-disease (182)

Leaves yellow with veins darker green
    Iron chlorosis (191)

Affecting twigs, branches
Clear, amber ooze from bark
    Cytospora canker (173)
Branches die back
    Cytospora canker (173)
    Peach tree (crown) borer (113)
    Shothole borer (96)
Small holes in bark of twigs, branches
    Shothole borer (96)
Tips of twigs die back, twigs tunneled
    Peach twig borer
    Oriental fruit moth

Affecting lower trunk
Amber ooze from bark
    Cytospora canker (173)
Clear ooze from bark
    Freeze injury
Amber ooze mixed with sawdust, often near or below soil line
    Peach tree (crown) borer (113)

Affecting fruit
Fruit blemished, but not tunneled
    Coryneum blight (172)
    Powdery mildew (rusty spot) (169)
    San Jose scale (148)
    Plant bugs (135)
    Flower thrips (128)
    Hail injury
    Bird damage (212)
Fruit swollen at flower end
    X-disease (182)
Amber ooze from fruit (gummosis)
    Cytospora canker (173)
    Coryneum blight (172)
Mealy textured fruit
    Overmaturity
    Drought during fruit development
Fruit tunneled
    Oriental fruit moth
    Peach twig borer
    Walnut husk fly (124)
    European earwig (131)

Pears

Pears are not as well adapted to western conditions as apples are, due primarily to their sensitivity to spring frost damage and fire blight. The careful selection of adapted varieties is essential for achieving success with pears in the region. Rootstocks have been developed that provide some dwarfing of pears, producing trees that will grow to 15 or 20 feet tall.

Some training of plant growth is necessary for pears. Shoots tend to grow upward, which will produce weak crotches susceptible to breakage if not corrected. Pears also send up numerous non-fruit-bearing vegetative shoots, particularly in response to pruning. However, the fruit forms on slow-growing fruiting spurs, and their development is inhibited by the vegetative shoots. Larger fruit will originate on younger spurs. Spur development is encouraged by selectively pruning the actively growing vegetative branches. All pruning should occur during the dormant season to limit the spread of fire blight.

Pears require pollination by insects to set fruit. They are not self-fruitful, and the pollen must be from a compatible variety to achieve successful pollination. Because the flowering period is short and pear flowers contain relatively low quantities of attractive sugars in their nectar, pollination can sometimes be poor. If the fruit has set well, it is useful to thin it to one per cluster to increase fruit size and prevent alternate year, or biennial, bearing.

Fire blight is the most serious pest problem threatening pears. Developing multiple leaders early in its growth can better protect the tree. The infected branches can then be cut away and disposed of. The codling moth is also a common concern throughout the region, and pear psylla thrive west of the Rockies.

COMMON DISORDERS OF PEARS
Affecting leaves
Leaves bronze-colored, may drop prematurely
    Twospotted spider mite, McDaniel spider
    mite (150)

Leaves with brown, scabby patches
    Pear leaf blister mite (eriophyid mite) (151)
Upper surface of leaves chewed, leaving veins
    Pearslug (118)
Leaves curled and chewed
    Leafrollers (111)
Leaves yellow and drop prematurely
    Psylla shock (pear psylla injury) (148)
    Iron chlorosis (191)
Sticky material (honeydew) on leaves, fruit
    Pear psylla (148)

Affecting fruit
Fruit tunneled
    Codling moth (110)
Fruit deformed, old wounds with scarring
    Leafroller (111)
    Oriental fruit moth
    Climbing cutworm (108–109)
    Hail injury
Fruit deformed, old wounds form dimples
    Plant bugs (135)
    Stink bug
Fruit deformed, no external injuries
    Poor pollination (186)
Spotting of fruit
    San Jose scale (148)
    Hail injury
Fruit surface with brown coloring
    Russet mite (eriophyid mite) (151)
    Sooty mold growing on pear psylla honey-
    dew (148)
    Damage from oil-based sprays
Fruit crop heavy one year, light the next
    Alternate year (biennial) bearing

Pears

Plums

Although a number of native plum species grow in the region, plums cultivated for eating are almost always either European plums (*Prunus domestica*) or Japanese plums (*Prunus salicina*). European plums tend to be more winter-hardy than the Japanese variety, approximating apples in this regard. European plums also bloom later, escaping damage by

spring frosts that can damage the Japanese plum crop in the West.

The European plum is fairly easy to grow and tolerates heavy soils. However, the rootstock on which the plum variety is grafted determines its hardiness. Dwarfing rootstocks are available.

Plums require only moderate fertilization for best production. However, regular watering is critical or fruit will be aborted. Pollinated by insects, primarily bees, most varieties are not self-fruitful and require a second pollinizer variety for cross-pollination.

Though in need of little pruning, plums are produced on one-year-old wood, and periodic pruning may be needed to stimulate production. Pruning is best done in early spring.

Few pest problems bother plums in the West. Cytospora canker moves readily into weakened and damaged limbs, and the peach tree borer is well-known for damage in much of the region.

COMMON DISORDERS OF PLUMS

Affecting leaves
Leaves curled, undersides often with aphids
    Green peach aphid (142)
    Leaf curl plum aphid (146)
    Rusty plum aphid
Upper surface of leaves chewed, often leaving main veins
    Pearslug (118)
Leaves chewed, silken tent produced
    Tent caterpillar (109)
    Fall webworm (109)
White powdery covering on leaves
    Powdery mildew (169)
Small finger galls on leaves
    Eriophyid mite (151)

Affecting trunk or branches
Clear, amber ooze from bark
    Cytospora canker (173)
Amber ooze mixed with sawdust, often near soil line
    Peach tree (crown) borer (113)
Branches die back, trees decline in vigor

    Cytospora canker (173)
    Peach tree (crown) borer (113)
Branches with circular scales
    San Jose scale (148)
Small holes in bark of twigs, branches
    Shothole borer (96)
Tips of twigs die back, twigs tunneled
    Peach twig borer

Affecting fruit
Fruit drops prematurely
    Insufficient water during fruit set
Fruit pit infested by insect
    Plum gouger (94)
    European earwig (131)
    Apple maggot (124)
    Western cherry fruit fly (124)
Gum oozing from fruit
    Plum gouger (94)
    Cytospora canker (gummosis) (173)

Raspberries

Several types of raspberries can be successfully grown in the region, although weather conditions often cause extensive winter injury. More marginally adapted types of brambles (blackberries, black or purple raspberries, and loganberries) are quite difficult to establish and require special winter protection.

Bearing of raspberries occurs either in the summer or fall. Fall-bearing varieties, which form the fruiting cane during the growing season, are the easiest to care for. (A small, second crop is produced if the canes of fall-bearing varieties are overwintered.) Summer-bearing varieties, which form a biennial cane that does not fruit until the second season, are more susceptible to winter injury. Mulching the summer-bearing types for winter protection is a necessity in most areas.

Regular pruning is also a must with raspberries, both to remove the old canes and to get rid of cane-boring insect pests. Fall-bearing types can simply be mowed at the end of the season, since they produce new suckers in the spring.

Raspberries can be damaged by several insect pests. Most important is the raspberry crown borer, which tunnels the base of the plants. Cane borers, such as the stemboring sawfly, cause trouble.

COMMON DISORDERS OF RASPBERRIES
Affecting canes
Canes wilt progressively from the bottom
    Verticillium wilt (163)
    Raspberry crown borer (114)
Entire canes wilt and die
    Phytophthora root and crown rot (162)
    Raspberry crown borer (114)
    Rose stem girdler/bronze cane borer (96)
Wilting of cane restricted to top of plant
    Spur blight/cane blight
    Stemboring sawfly (116)

Affecting leaves
Leaves puckered and/or mottled yellow
    Viral disease
    Iron chlorosis (191)
New leaves form tight cluster (rosette)
    Viral disease
Leaves flecked with small light spots
    Twospotted spider mite (150)
Leaves chewed
    Rose slugs and other sawflies (118)
    Leafroller (111)

Affecting fruit
White spotting of fruit
    Sunscald (184)
Fruit gouged by chewing
    Grasshoppers (129)
    Yellowjackets (118)
Fruit soft, rotted
    Botrytis (167)

Strawberries

Strawberries are the most widely planted garden fruit and are easily grown. They are perennial, with plants usually persisting for about three years before they stop bearing fruit. The time of bearing tends to follow one of three patterns: June-bearing types produce a single large crop in late spring; ever-bearing varieties produce two main crops in spring and early fall, with scant production in between; and day-neutral varieties bear more consistently throughout the season. The performance of all strawberry varieties can differ depending on variations in altitude and light intensity.

Strawberries are almost always started from rooted runners, although seeds of some types are available. Strawberries require at least 8 hours of full sun, so plantings should be located in an open area, preferably with a south-facing exposure. They are fairly tolerant of various soils, but heavy, poorly drained soils can promote root decay.

Although fairly cold-tolerant, strawberries should be protected from winter injury due to drying and freeze/thaw cycles. After soils have cooled in late fall, a mulch of straw or other nonmatting material should cover the plants. Early blossoms, particularly those of June-bearing varieties, are susceptible to freezing injury. Delaying the removal of mulch until new growth has started affords the plants maximum protection.

Old crowns decline in vigor and it is recommended that strawberries either be replanted at 2- to 3-year intervals or "renovated" annually. Renovation entails mowing all the plants shortly after harvest and then fertilizing with nitrogen to promote regrowth.

Few diseases or insect pests afflict strawberries. However, the ripe fruits are attractive to millipedes and slugs—and the occasional two-legged visitor.

COMMON DISORDERS OF STRAWBERRIES
Whole plant affected
Plants die back, cottony masses on roots
    Root aphid (145)
Plants die back, roots appear chewed and/or decayed
    Strawberry root weevil (95)
    Red stele root rot
    Black root rot
Plants fail to survive winter
    Winter drying
    Frost heaving (freeze/thaw) injury to roots

Affecting leaves
Small, dark spots on leaves
    Leaf spot fungi (166)
Leaves with powdery white covering
    Powdery mildew (169)
Leaves with yellow and green mottling
    Viral disease
New growth small, crown area with tunneled streaks
    Strawberry crown miner
Leaves chewed and curled
    Leafroller (111)
New leaves curled, not crinkled
    Cyclamen mite

Affecting fruit
Fruit with small areas of tightly packed seeds
    Cold injury (184)
    Plant bugs (135)
Fruit rotten
    Botrytis (167)
Fruit tastes moldy
    Botrytis (167)
Fruit with large areas chewed
    Slugs (153)
    Rabbits (209)
Black beetles in ripe fruit
    Sap beetle (98)
White worms in fruit
    Millipedes (153)

ANNUAL FLOWERS AND HERBS

Common Disorders of Flowers and Herbs

Whole plant affected
Wilting
    Fusarium wilt (164)
    Cutworms (108–109)
    Slugs (153)

Affecting roots
    Root aphids (145)
    Fusarium wilt (164)
    Root weevils (95)

Affecting leaves
New leaves curled
    Cold injury (184)
    Onion thrips (127)
    Herbicide (2,4-D, etc.) injury (189)
    Aphids (140–147)
Leaves chewed
    Grasshoppers (129)
    Slugs (153)
    Cutworms (108–109)
    Hollyhock weevil (hollyhock only) (95)
    Parsleyworm (parsley, dill, fennel only) (100)
    Thistle caterpillar, variegated fritillary (101)
    Flea beetles (87–89)
Leaves with dark spotting
    Leafminer (123)
    Anthracnose (164)
    Rust (176)
    Early blight (alternaria) (166)
Orange-red patches on lower leaf surface
    Rust (176)
Leaves with white coating
    Powdery mildew (167–170)
Leaves generally yellow
    Nitrogen deficiency (190)
    Iron deficiency (191)
    Aster yellows (181)
    Greenhouse whitefly (139)
    Aphids (140–147)
Leaves with white flecks
    Leafhoppers (139)
    Spider mites (150)
    Gladiolus thrips (gladiolus only) (128)
    Onion thrips (127)
Leaves distorted, puckered
    Aphids (140–147)
    Aster yellows (181)

Affecting flowers
Flower head distorted
    Aphids (140–147)
    Aster yellows (181)
Flower buds chewed
    Tobacco (geranium) budworm (103)
    Hollyhock weevil (hollyhock only) (95)

Flower petals chewed
    Tobacco (geranium) budworm (103)
    Earwigs (131)
    Grasshoppers (129)
    Blister beetles (97)
    Bumble flower beetle (98)
    Hollyhock weevil (hollyhock only) (95)
Flowers speckled, deformed
    Flower thrips (128)
    Onion thrips (127)
Flower buds, petals soft and rotted
    Botrytis (167)

BULBS AND IRISES

Common Disorders of Bulbs and Irises

Affecting flowers
Flower shoots emerge but fail to flower
    Cold injury (184)
Plantings produce small plants, flowers
    Narcissus bulb fly (126)
    Overcrowding
Flowers scarred and/or deformed
    Gladiolus thrips (gladiolus only) (128)
    Flower thrips (128)

Affecting bulb or corm
Bulbs/corms decay, die out
    Narcissus bulb fly (126)
    Fusarium wilt (164)
    Freezing damage (184)
    Iris borer (iris only)
Base of iris leaves infested with aphids
    Bulb aphid (145)
Bulbs dug up from soil
    Fox squirrel (207)
    Vole (206)

ROSES

Roses are the most popular garden flower, and a tremendous number of types are offered through the nursery trade. Hybrid tea, miniature, floribunda, grandiflora, climber, polyantha, and shrub classes are among those most adapted to the West.

Roses are best planted in sunny locations in early spring. Plantings should have good air circulation to reduce disease problems, but also offer protection from winds, which can damage and dry out plants. Almost all roses are grafted onto a rootstock, and the bud union should be placed at, or slightly below, the soil surface.

For optimum flower production, roses demand regular pruning. Spent blossoms should be removed to encourage the formation of new flowers. Pruning also serves to remove dead or diseased wood and helps to shape the plant so that it gets good light penetration into the interior. Typically, the canes of hybrid teas, grandifloras, and floribundas suffer substantial winter injury and should be pruned back to living wood in early spring. (Living wood has green inner bark and a white center pith.)

Fertilization maintains flower production. Fertilizer blends should contain fairly balanced amounts of phosphorus in relation to nitrogen. The best times to fertilize are early and mid-season. Late-season fertilization should be avoided to prevent succulent new growth, which is not winter-hardy, from forming.

Winter protection and care are critical, particularly for the less hardy hybrid teas and grandifloras. Most crucial is the protection of the bud union, since plants that die back to this point will produce canes from the rootstock rather than from the grafted variety. During winter, the bud union should be covered with insulating material,

Rose

such as loose soil or straw. Periodic watering during winter also helps to prevent drying.

Roses typically are pest-intensive, with spider mites and powdery mildew the most common maladies.

Common Disorders of Roses

Affecting leaves
Powdery covering on leaves
    Powdery mildew (169)
Leaves with white spotting
    Rose leafhopper (136)
    Twospotted spider mite (150)
    Rust (176)
Small, ball-like growths on leaves, usually reddish
    Gall wasp (116)
Leaves with yellow or mottled colors
    Viral diseases
Orange-red patches on lower leaf surface
    Rust
Angular, brown spots on leaves
    Spot anthracnose (164)
Interior areas of leaves chewed
    Rose slugs and other sawflies (118)
Even, semicircular cuts in leaf edge
    Leafcutter bee (115)
Leaves curled
    Powdery mildew (169)

Affecting canes
Aphids
    Rose aphids (144)

Insects tunneling into pith of cane
    Hunting wasps (81)
    Small carpenter bees (81)
    Leafcutter bees (115)
Exterior area of cane girdled, sometimes with associated dieback
    Stemboring sawfly (116)
    Bronze cane borer/rose stem girdler (96)
Mossy or ball-like growths on stem
    Gall wasps (116)
Woody, tumorlike growth, usually on lower stem
    Crown gall (178)
Swellings in canes, often with associated vertical cracking
    Bronze cane borer/rose stem girdler (96)

Affecting flowers
Flower buds killed, fail to emerge ("blind" shoots)
    Rose midge (125)
    Fluctuating, cool temperatures
    Rose curculio (93)
Flower petals scarred
    Flower thrips (128)
Flower petals chewed or tunneled
    Earwigs (131)
    Rose curculio (93)
    Tobacco budworm (103)
    Speckled green fruitworm (109)
Flowers produced are "off-type" after winter (grandiflora and hybrid tea roses)
    Dieback to the grafted rootstock

Life in a Rose Cane

A pruning cut exposing the pith of rose, raspberry, elderberry, or other garden plant is an invitation to set up housekeeping for a number of insects. Such sites are ideal for nesting hunting wasps or solitary bees—highly beneficial insects that assist the gardener.

Among those taking up residence are tiny wasps (species of *Pemphredon*) that hunt aphids to feed their young. Female wasps establish their nests by excavating the pith from plants. (The wood of the canes is not tunneled and the plants suffer no injury by this activity.) In most plants, particularly those with a small-diameter pith, a series of individual nest cells are built sequentially on top of each other. In larger canes, a system of branching chambers may be constructed. This work complete, the female sets off to find aphids, which she dispatches with a paralyzing toxin and brings back to the nest cells. Again and again she forages until the nest cell is packed with about two dozen stunned aphids. The mother wasp then lays an egg and seals the cell. A few days later the wasp grub hatches and leisurely munches on the aphid snacks left for it. Later pupating and ultimately emerging as an adult wasp, the cycle is repeated, usually about twice a year. However, these wasps will only nest once in a cane, shunning those where the pith has been previously excavated.

Some solitary bees, notably the small carpenter bees (species of *Ceratina*), will nest in canes. These very beneficial insects are important native pollinators. A thin shellac-like coating covers the tunnel walls and the nest cells are packed with a blend of pollen and nectar for the developing young. Although plant damage is rare from small carpenter bee activity, occasionally their excavations can be more extensive as they may reuse and extend tunnels in subsequent generations.

The activity within a rose cane "condo" can get interesting. Other hunting wasps use canes for nests, all being species that hunt the smaller denizens of the garden, such as leafhoppers and aphids. Other bees may also seek pithy plants for residence, occasionally including leafcutter bees in the largest diameter ones. Furthermore, the well-provisioned residences attract many other species of bees and wasps, parasitic relatives living off the efforts of the original residents.

Hunting wasp exposed in old ash twig

Nest entrance for hunting wasp in old rose cane

What's Been Chewing in My Garden?

After returning from a short vacation or an overnight trip, you may find that your garden has taken a turn for the worse. Fruit may be harvested and plants damaged or even destroyed in a very short time. Although it may be of little solace, you can often determine the culprit.

Cutworms. Plants are damaged at night. Leaves or developing fruit may be chewed. Whole plants may disappear or be chewed near the soil line. The caterpillars are difficult to detect, because they spend the day under cover near the damaged plants. Damage occurs almost entirely in the spring.

Caterpillars (cabbageworms, hornworms, etc.). Irregular areas are chewed out of leaves and developing fruit. Often, feeding injuries are concentrated along leaf margins. Severe damage is preceded by "windowpane" feeding where upper leaf surface remains after lower leaf surface is chewed. Damage can occur on many types of plants during the growing season and in sporadic bursts as the caterpillars grow larger and feed more. The caterpillars often feed during the day and these insects, or their droppings, may be readily detected.

Colorado potato beetle. Leaves of potatoes, eggplant, nicotiana, nightshade, and related plants are irregular along the edge. New growth is favored by the immature stages of the insects, which leave dark, smeary droppings on the leaves. Adult beetles chew notches along the leaf edge. Feeding takes place during the day and the insect may be detected simply upon plant inspection.

Root weevils. Many weevils create very characteristic notching injuries along the margins of leaves. Most are active at night and so are difficult to observe, but the wounds are more rectangular than those produced by grasshoppers or caterpillars, and they rarely originate in the center of the leaf.

Grasshoppers. Irregular chewing occurs along leaf edges. The bark of twigs may also be chewed, causing dieback. Damage is most severe in late summer. Often, a wide variety of plants are affected and the grasshoppers are easy to detect.

Flea beetles. Small pits or shothole wounds are chewed in the leaves. Small seedlings can be killed when severely damaged. Damage is usually limited to a few types of closely related plants. The beetles are active and present on the plants during the day but jump readily when disturbed. The most severe damage is caused during May and June but can occur later.

Mexican bean beetle. Bean leaves are skeletonized, leaving only the main veins. Feeding damage is concentrated on the underside of the leaf. Small yellow specks are frequently left behind. Adult or larval stages of the insect can usually be found on the leaves.

Slug sawflies (pearslugs, rose slugs). Leaves are skeletonized, leaving the main veins. The destruction resulting from feeding is usually concentrated on the upper surface of the leaf, but sometimes a rose slug will feed on the lower leaf surface, leaving the upper leaf surface as a "window." Damage occurs during the day, peaking in mid to late summer, and the insects can be found on site.

Slugs. Leaves are irregularly skeletonized, fruit may be chewed or tunneled, and small seedlings can be destroyed. The presence of mucous slime trails is distinctive of slug infestation. Slugs do their damage at night and are difficult to detect during the day. Peak injury occurs in spring and early fall.

Earwigs. Soft plant parts are eaten, with preference given to materials such as flower petals and corn silk, which are also earwigs' favored hiding places. Feeding is concentrated along the edge of leaves or flowers and is usually shallower than that of grasshoppers or caterpillars. Damage occurs at night, while the earwigs hide in tight, dark places during the day.

Raccoons. Ripening fruit is particularly appealing to raccoons, especially sweet corn, melons, cherries, and grapes. Plant injury due to ripping claws (shredded corn husks, scooped-out fruit) is characteristic. Digging injuries may also be apparent. However, feeding on small fruit may show little evidence of actual plant injury. Damage occurs at night, sometimes extensively.

Rabbits. Green plants cut at an oblique (about 45-degree) angle and the sudden onset of damage are the work of rabbits. In winter, lower branches or trunks may be gnawed in the region at or just above snow cover. Damage usually occurs at night.

Birds. Bird damage to seedling vegetables often is marked by V-shaped cuts along the leaf margins of plants such as radishes or lettuce. Some birds, such as starlings, will also pull out the whole plant to feed on. In addition, ripening fruit is enticing to birds, with characteristic pecking injuries often sustained by some of the remaining fruit. Damage occurs during the day but may appear suddenly when migrating flocks make a pit stop in the garden.

Deer. Chewing injuries are extensive and plants often suffer distinctive shredding when deer invade a garden. During the growing season, tender tips of sweet corn, heads of broccoli and cauliflower, and other garden plants may be deer's first choice. In winter, twigs are browsed up to a height of about 5 feet. Feeding occurs mainly after dusk, but tracks are almost always visible even if the animals are not.

Chapter 6

Management of
Common Garden "Bugs"

Bugs in the garden, bugging the plants. Although the word *bug* shares its origins with the bogeyman, the scarecrow, and the bugbear, the twentieth-century bug has come to have many different definitions. Technically the word best applies to a group of insects, the Hemiptera or "true bugs," such as box elder bugs, squash bugs, or bedbugs. (The idea that "all bugs are insects but not all insects are bugs" is commonly taught, with little permanent effect, in any introductory entomology class.) However, "bug" is more popularly used to describe any "wee little creature," such as the arthropods.

Arthropods (aka the "jointed-foot" animals) are distinguished by their unique set of characteristics. For example, only among the arthropods will you find animals possessing a segmented body, an external skeleton (exoskeleton) that is periodically shed (molted) as they develop, and jointed appendages (legs, antennae, feet). Arthropods also have distinctive internal structures, such as a tubelike heart that runs down the back and a nerve cord that runs along the lower body.

In terms of numbers and diversity, the arthropods dominate. Over 80 percent of all animals are arthropods (about 1.1 million species), with insects overwhelmingly the most abundant. (Mites, millipedes, pill bugs, lobsters, and crabs are some other noninsect arthropods.) Conser-

Not all arthropods are plant pests

vatively, it is estimated that there are about one million insect species described to science, with new species being reported at a rate of about 30 per day. Furthermore, only about one-eighth of all the insects that actually do exist have ever been described—much less is anything known about them.

While we don't have many problems with lobsters or crabs, several arthropods are serious pests. Some of these are the focus of this chapter. However, only a tiny fraction of all arthropods can be judged to rank as "pests." The great majority have highly beneficial roles in natural systems, such as pollinating plants, recycling nutrients, destroying pests, and serving as vital links in the food chain.

INSECTS

Insects comprise the largest group of arthropods and can be identified by certain additional characteristics that separate them from other arthropods. These include three body regions (head, thorax, abdomen), three pairs of legs, and, often, a winged adult stage.

Subgroups of insects (orders) are then recognized by such features as types of wings, mouthparts, and the changes they undergo during their life cycle (metamorphosis). More than thirty orders of insects exist, including the following common garden visitors:

- Moths and butterflies (Lepidoptera, the scale-winged insects)
- Beetles (Coleoptera, the hardened-winged insects)
- Flies (Diptera, the two-winged insects)
- Lacewings (Neuroptera, the nerve-winged insects)
- Bees, wasps, sawflies, and ants (Hymenoptera)
- Grasshoppers, crickets, and their kin (Orthoptera, the straight-winged insects)
- Earwigs (Dermaptera)
- Aphids, scales, whiteflies, and related insects (Homoptera)
- "True" bugs (Hemiptera, the half-winged insects)
- Thrips (Thysanoptera, the fringe-winged insects)

Metamorphosis—"Change in Form"

All arthropods, including insects, undergo changes in form as they grow. This process is called *metamorphosis*. The forms arthropods take may vary dramatically as they develop. Two patterns of metamorphosis predominate: *simple* (or gradual) metamorphosis and *complete* metamorphosis.

Aphids, leafhoppers, earwigs, grasshoppers, and true bugs are some of the insects that undergo *simple metamorphosis*. Emerging from eggs, the immature stages of these insects are called *nymphs*. As the nymphs feed and grow, they periodically shed their skins and transform to the next stage, a process known as *molting*. Typically, insects go through three to seven molts before they are fully grown. In the final molt they transform to the adult stage. Both nymphs and adults of insects that undergo simple metamorphosis feed in the same manner, are often found together, and also resemble each other.

However, adult insects are sexually mature and often winged.

Moths, butterflies, beetles, flies, ants, and lacewings are some insects that experience *complete metamorphosis*. Following egg hatch, they enter the immature stage as *larvae*. Frequently, it is the larval stage of these insects that causes the most injury to plants or animals, since they must feed heavily in order to develop. As they grow, the larvae molt and shed their skin repeatedly. After reaching full development, larvae shed their last larval skin and transform into a unique developmental stage, the *pupa*. Although insects in the pupal stage do not feed and appear to be inactive, dramatic changes in form occur that result in the adult stage. Among the insects with complete metamorphosis, larvae and adults may look strikingly different and maintain very different feeding and behavioral habits.

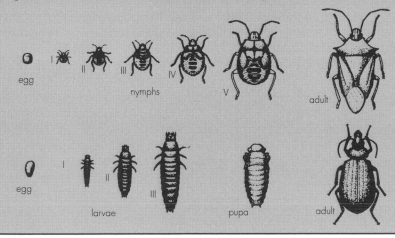

egg   I   II   III   IV   V   adult
nymphs

egg   I   II   III   pupa   adult
larvae

Wing types vary greatly among the insects. For example, beetles have a hardened pair of front wings, while moths and butterflies have wings covered with scales. Flies and mosquitoes have only a single pair of wings, in contrast to the two pairs of other insects. And some insects never produce wings at all. Mouthparts of insects are generally designed to either cut and chew or to suck fluids.

Grasshoppers, beetles, caterpillars, bees and wasps are typical of insects with chewing mouthparts. With these insects, a hardened pair of mandibles that work sideways is critical for grinding or cutting. A second set of mouthpart structures, the maxillae, also help to crush or handle food. In some insects, such as predatory green lacewings, the mouthparts form a sickle to pin and capture prey.

Insects with sucking mouthparts include aphids, leafhoppers, the true bugs, certain flies, moths, and thrips. In most of these insects, the mouthparts (mandibles and maxillae) are greatly elongated and form a tube. These mouthparts allow them to suck nectar or remove fluids such as sap. The thrips, however, have a rasping-sucking mouth that allows them to puncture and drink the contents of the top layers of cells. Many of the insects with sucking mouthparts are important pests since they can transmit disease organisms to plants or inject toxic substances during feeding.

ARACHNIDS

Coming across mites, ticks, spiders, and other "bugs," the gardener may consider them to be simply another type of insect. Actually, these are members of a separate group of arthropods, the *arachnids,* with very different forms and habits. The distinguishing feature of arachnids is their four pairs of legs. Most arachnids also have two distinctive body regions (cephalothorax and abdomen), although this is not apparent in the arachnids that are generally round in body shape, such as daddy longlegs.

The most damaging arachnids to have in a garden are the spider mites. Spider mites produce eggs. These hatch, often within a few days, and a very small larva with only three pairs of legs emerges. The larvae feed, later molt (to the nymph stage), and have the typical fourth pair of legs from that point on. The nymph feeds, grows, and molts repeatedly until it reaches the mature adult stage.

OTHER COMMON ARTHROPODS

Other types of arthropods occasionally appear as pests in the yard and garden. *Sowbugs* and *pillbugs* (roly-polies) are land-adapted crustaceans, related to shrimp and lobsters found in water. They feed primarily on decaying plant materials, but can also damage seedlings and soft plant materials, such as strawberries, that lie on the ground. *Millipedes* (diplopods), the "1,000-leggers" of the garden, make up another group of arthropods that feed on soft and decaying plant materials. *Centipedes* (chilopods), or "100-leggers," are also commonly found under rocks and debris. At night they actively hunt and feed on insects or other small arthropods.

SLUGS AND SNAILS

Most gardeners will sooner or later encounter a slug in their lettuce patch or gnawing on a precious tomato plant. Slugs, and the less common snails, are members of the class known as gastropods. As such, they are more similar to clams and mussels than to the other "bugs," such as insects and spider mites. Controls used for slugs and snails, including pesticides, are very different from those used for arthropods.

Slugs and most snails require moist conditions to survive and develop. Because of this limitation, problems with slugs and snails are relatively infrequent in this region, in contrast to the more humid areas of the country. However, populations can become severe in some environments, such as greenhouses or lush garden areas. Snails and slugs can easily move to new locations on infested plant materials, the means by which all western garden slugs have spread to gardens.

Snails and slugs reproduce by eggs, which are round and clear, laid in small masses in soil cracks and around the base of plants. Eggs hatch in a few weeks and the young snails and slugs begin to eat. Snails and slugs can live a year or more, but usually become semidormant when temperatures get too hot or cold.

COLEOPTERA (BEETLES)

Mexican Bean Beetle (Epilachna varivestis)

Damage: The Mexican bean beetle is the "bad apple" of the lady beetle family and the most important insect pest of beans. Both the adult beetles and the spiny, yellow grub stage feed on bean leaves. Typical damage is restricted to the soft tissues on the leaves' undersides. Larger veins are left intact, creating a distinctive skeletonizing injury. Throughout the growing season, the plants can tolerate some injury without yield losses. Beans are most sensitive to the effects of defoliation during flowering and when the pods are being set. Also, both adults and larvae will chew tender pods.

Life History and Habits: Mexican bean beetles overwinter in the adult stage in protected areas along the edges of plantings infested during the previous season. They straggle out from their overwintering sites over a period of several weeks in late spring. The beetles feed on the leaves, and the females begin to lay egg masses on the leaves' undersides. The orange-yellow larvae that subsequently emerge feed heavily for about a month before they are fully grown. They then pupate on the underside of the leaves, often in small groups. One or two generations occur annually, depending on temperatures during development. Peak populations typically occur in late July and August.

Natural and Biological Controls: Natural controls, such as predatory bugs, are important and may successfully reduce populations to nondamaging levels. These controls can then be supplemented by annual releases of the parasitic wasp *Pediobius faveolatus* (see page 216). This wasp kills bean beetle larvae and has proved to be an effective biological control in some areas. Since *P. faveolatus* releases should be timed to coincide with the occurrence of the first newly hatched larvae, place orders as soon as eggs are first detected. This usually occurs in July.

Cultural Controls: Most damage occurs in July and August, so early planting can avoid most injury. Short-season varieties may prevent the buildup of a large population. Thus, most bush beans are less susceptible to damage than pole beans. Also, there is a range in susceptibility among beans, with purple podded varieties being among those less damaged by Mexican bean beetles. After harvest, plants should be destroyed as soon as possible to kill the remaining insect stages on the plants.

Mechanical Controls: Handpick the adults and crush the eggs when discovered during plant inspections.

Chemical Controls: Adults and larvae can be controlled by most garden insecticides, including pyrethrins. However, many gardeners report that Mexican bean beetles have exhibited resistance to insecticides. Younger larvae are the easiest to control.

Miscellaneous Notes: The Mexican bean beetle is a true lady beetle (Coccinellidae family), the only species of lady beetle in the region that feeds on plants. The adults can be distinguished from the beneficial lady beetles by their large size, yellow-orange color, and numerous (fourteen) spots. Immature stages of the Mexican bean beetle are yellow and spiny, very different from the lady beetles that feed on insects. The best way to separate "good" from "bad" in the lady beetle clan is to note which plants they have settled on. If it is a bean plant, be suspicious. If not, the lady beetles are probably beneficial insect predators.

Western Cabbage Flea Beetle (Phyllotreta pusilla)

Damage: Adult beetles feed on the foliage of many kinds of garden plants, causing small shothole wounds. Mustard family plants are particularly favored, but damage can also occur to a variety

Mexican bean beetle (Photo courtesy of USDA)

of other plants, such as beets and lettuce. Seedlings are particularly susceptible, and flea beetles can kill or retard plantings during establishment. Later in the season, shothole feeding by flea beetles can blemish leafy vegetables, such as mustard and Chinese cabbage, prior to harvest. On some leafy vegetables, such as mustard, reddish-brown, circular areas develop around feeding wounds. Although flavor and nutritional value are not compromised by this injury, the damaged leaves may be considered unattractive.

Life History and Habits: Western cabbage flea beetles overwinter in the adult stage under protective debris around previously infested plants. They become active as temperatures warm in early spring and fly to feed on various host plants, first concentrating on wild mustards. Cabbage flea beetles are strong fliers, so infestations of garden plants can originate from a long distance away. Adults chew the characteristic pits in leaves, and females periodically lay eggs in soil cracks around the base of plants. The small, wormlike larvae feed on root hairs but do not appear to cause any serious damage to garden plants. However, they then pupate in the root area, later emerging as beetles, which repeat the cycle. There are typically three generations per year at approximately 45-day intervals.

Natural and Biological Controls: Although the number of western cabbage flea beetles varies significantly from season to season, little is known about the specific natural controls that affect these insects. A native species of nematode is one naturally occurring biological control. Parasitic wasps attack the adults.

Cultural Controls: Since seedlings are particularly vulnerable, using transplants or planting seeds in a well-prepared seedbed hastens seedling growth and helps them overcome insect injury. When possible, plantings in gardens may also dictate high seeding rates, later thinned after plants are established. Alternately, the deliberate planting of "trap crops," such as radish or daikon, can divert feeding during the seedling stages and

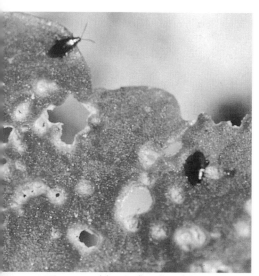

Western cabbage flea beetle

Palestriped flea beetle

ease the establishment of other crops that are less tolerant of flea beetle injury. (For example, radishes sown at 3-inch intervals around broccoli has been shown to effect a 60 to 80 percent reduction in the population of flea beetles on broccoli.) Also, weeds in the garden that appeal to flea beetles may be retained to further protect the crop. Of course, these weeds should be destroyed before they compete with garden plants or produce flowers. Because the adult beetles are so mobile, crop rotations have little effect on the control of this insect.

Mechanical and Physical Controls: Most flea beetles overwinter under debris outside the garden. During this period, floating row covers or other screening can exclude the beetles during seedling establishment. Flea beetles can be vacuumed off foliage, but this practice needs to be repeated frequently as reinvasion of plants can be rapid.

Chemical Controls: Control is usually necessary only during plant establishment for crops that produce edible heads, such as broccoli, cabbage, and cauliflower. Leafy brassicas—particularly mustard and Chinese cabbage—may require more extensive protection. Carbaryl (Sevin®) and permethrin can provide fairly good control for about a week. Horticultural oils, sulfur, and some neem insecticides have demonstrated some repellent effect on this insect.

Related Species: The horseradish flea beetle (*Phyllotreta armoraciae*) is associated with horseradish and is marked with broad light brown bands on the wing covers. In the southwestern states, a bronze-colored flea beetle, *Phyllotreta albionica*, can be a threat to mustard family plants.

Palestriped Flea Beetle (Systena blanda)

Damage: Adult beetles chew small pits in the upper surface of leaves of many garden vegetables. Beans, beets, melons, and sunflowers are among the plants most commonly damaged, but potatoes, squash, tomatoes, lettuce, and several common weeds (e.g., lambsquarters, redroot pigweed) also can serve as host plants. When they are numerous, palestriped flea beetles can decimate seedlings and retard the development of surviving plants. The larvae, which feed on plant roots, occasionally damage germinating seeds that have been planted late. They have also been reported to tunnel sweet potato tubers.

Life History and Habits: The life history of the palestriped flea beetle has been little studied. Overwintering stages probably consist of a mixture of nearly full-grown larvae, pupae, and perhaps some adult beetles. Development continues in the spring, and the beetles are most active in late spring. Adult beetles can fly and feed on leaves for several weeks. Eggs are laid in soil cracks during early summer and hatch in about 10 to 15 days. The larvae then feed on germinating seeds and plant roots, causing some injury to young plants. They pupate in the soil, and a second generation of adult beetles is active in late July and August.

Cultural Controls: Cultural conditions that promote vigorous seedling growth enable plants to outgrow adult palestriped flea beetle injuries. Higher seeding rates, followed by thinning, can dilute adult beetle attacks. Tillage can kill overwintering stages of the palestriped flea beetle in the soil. Keeping weeds under control also deters egg laying within a planting.

Chemical Controls: Palestriped flea beetles are difficult to control when abundant. They are susceptible to the garden insecticides carbaryl and permethrin but can continually reinfest plantings since their development is staggered. Neem and diatomaceous earth can provide some repellent effect.

"Potato/Tomato" Flea Beetles
Potato flea beetle
(Epitrix cucumeris)
Western potato flea beetle
(Epitrix subcrinita)
Tobacco flea beetle
(Epitrix hirtipennis)

Tuber flea beetle
(Epitrix tuberis)
Eggplant flea beetle
(Epitrix fuscula)
Epitrix parvula, and others

Damage: The majority of "potato/tomato" flea beetles are small, black or coppery brown beetles, which characteristically jump when disturbed. Primary damage is done by the adults, which chew pits in the leaves. These injuries may impede plant development and have also been credited with the increased incidence of some diseases that enter the wounded tissues. Most plants in the nightshade family (Solanaceae) suffer damage by these insects, particularly tomatoes, potatoes, eggplant, petunias, and nicotiana.

One species, known as the tuber flea beetle, also seriously damages the skin of potato tubers. The developing larvae burrow into the tubers, making shallow, dark tunnels. The resultant wounding produces a rough, scabby texture on the tuber surface.

Life History and Habits: Winter is spent in the adult stage, under protective cover in the vicinity of previously infested plantings. The beetles become active in the spring as temperatures warm above 50°F, and consequently will feed on a wide variety of plants. As nightshade hosts develop, they then move to these and begin to lay their eggs in soil cracks around the host plants. The larval flea beetles are tiny and worm-like, and thrive by feeding on the roots and stolons. With the exception of the tuber flea beetles, no serious damage is produced by the larvae; tuber flea beetles, on the other hand, will make shallow scars in potatoes. Pupation occurs in the soil, and adults from this first generation emerge in late June and July. A single generation is the rule for most species, with the adults moving to overwintering shelter by midsummer. However, a second generation can be produced and, with the tuber flea beetle, it is the most damaging.

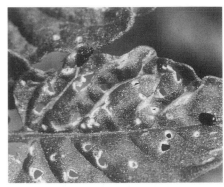
Potato flea beetle

Larval injury by the tuber flea beetle

Asparagus beetle larvae

Asparagus beetle

Spotted asparagus beetle

Cultural Controls: Vigorously growing plants can almost always outgrow flea beetle damage to leaves. For example, it is estimated that on potatoes more than 50 "shotholes" per leaflet are needed before any adverse effect on growth is realized. By providing cultural care for rapid plant establishment and growth, serious damage can almost always be avoided.

Mechanical Controls: Seedlings of transplanted tomatoes or eggplant may need some protection during establishment, which can be provided in the form of row covers. Adult insects can be vacuumed or swept with a net.

Chemical Controls: Insecticides that are effective against beetles (e.g., carbaryl, permethrin) can control potato flea beetles during outbreaks.

Asparagus Beetle (Crioceris asparagi)

Damage: As they chew pits in emerging asparagus spears, the adult beetles distort the plant's growth and lay large numbers of dark eggs on the spears. However, most injury is caused by the sluglike larvae, which chew the ferns, giving it a bleached appearance and reducing photosynthesis capability. Asparagus beetles are so abundant in some locations that these injuries can significantly reduce subsequent yields and sometimes even kill the plants. Moderate injury, more typical in regional gardens, is tolerated with little or no effect.

Life History and Habits: Asparagus beetles overwinter in the adult stage around asparagus plantings. As they become active in the spring, they fly to emerging spears and mate. The beetles chew on the spears and females lay upright, dark eggs on the plant. Eggs hatch in about 1 week and the gray, grublike larvae feed on the ferns. The larvae reach full growth in about 2 to 3 weeks and then drop to the soil to pupate. Adults emerge and repeat the cycle. Two or three generations are completed in a season with some larvae surviving into September.

Natural and Biological Controls: A tiny parasitic wasp (*Tetrastichus asparagi*) often kills large numbers of asparagus beetles. The adult wasps sting and feed on the blood of asparagus beetle eggs, killing them, while the immature wasps develop as parasites within asparagus beetle larvae. This wasp is common throughout much of the region and usually provides adequate control of asparagus beetles wherever it has become established.

Cultural Controls: Regularly pick asparagus spears in the spring to eliminate early-laid eggs. Actively growing plants are rarely seriously injured by this insect, even when feeding injuries are extensive, so proper crop culture can be pivotal in minimizing the effects of feeding that do occur.

Mechanical Controls: The dark eggs, attached to the spears and ferns, can easily be discovered during garden inspections and can then be crushed to prevent subsequent damage by larvae. Adults and some larvae can also be shaken off the plants for collection or vacuumed.

Chemical Controls: Adult beetles and larvae are destroyed by several insecticides, although few insecticides allow use on asparagus. Dilute sprays of liquid dishwashing detergent or insecticidal soaps can offer some control of larvae, particularly the younger stages. Pyrethrins and the recently registered synthetic pyrethrin insecticide, permethrin (BugStop®, Intercept®), are also effective. Neem-derived insecticides should also be effective against young larvae.

Related Insects: The spotted asparagus beetle, *Crioceris duodecimpunctata*, a bright-orange beetle with black spots, is also a familiar sight on asparagus plantings. Since the larvae of this beetle develop within asparagus berries and do not damage the fern, little actual injury is caused. Minor chewing on ferns is initiated by the adults.

Western Corn Rootworm (Diabrotica virgifera)

Damage: These adult beetles feed on and clip the silks of corn. Although the damage is usually of little consequence, heavy infestations can occur in later plantings because the beetles concentrate on these plants. Where silks are pruned severely during pollination, seed set can be poor. Beetles are also attracted to squash blossoms and can scar developing fruits. Larvae of the western corn rootworm feed on corn roots and weaken the plants, causing them to fall over.

Life History and Habits: Western corn rootworm beetles are present from late July through mid-September. Female beetles lay their eggs during this time near the base of corn plants. Adults of both sexes may be found feeding on corn silks, tender corn leaves, and squash blossoms. Eggs of the western corn rootworm hatch in June of the following year. The young, wormlike larvae require corn roots to develop and will soon starve if corn is not replanted within a few feet of where the eggs have been laid. If corn roots are found, the larvae feed on them, sometimes causing severe root pruning. Pupation takes place in the soil during July and adult beetles emerge later. There is one generation per year.

Natural and Biological Controls: Eggs of the western corn rootworm are preyed upon by a number of soil organisms, such as predatory soil mites. The addition of organic matter, which increases populations of organisms on which predatory mites feed, has been shown to reduce the survival of the western corn rootworm through increased egg predation. Several trials conducted with insect-parasitic nematodes and fungi for control of corn rootworm larvae have had mixed success.

Cultural Controls: Crop rotation is extremely effective for the control of the western corn rootworm since practically all the eggs are laid around the base of corn plants in late summer. The larvae that hatch the following June starve if they do not have ready access to corn.

Chemical Controls: Under most conditions, corn silks can outgrow corn rootworm feeding and pollination will occur even when some beetles are present. However, when high numbers of beetles are present (around five or more per ear tip), pollination can be disrupted, resulting in poor kernel set. Some insecticides (carbaryl, permethrin) are registered for control of adult corn rootworm beetles. One highly selective insecticide formulation used to control western corn rootworm combines an attractant and feeding stimulant with carbaryl to create a bait. Sold under the trade name Adios®, this bait contains far less insecticide and minimizes the effects on other insects more than conventional sprays. However, it is not generally available and marketed for garden use.

Miscellaneous Notes: The western corn rootworm is very similar in appearance to the striped cucumber beetle, so the two species are commonly mistaken for each other. However, their habits differ greatly. Striped cucumber beetles are pests of cucumbers, squash, and melons grown in the region.

Western corn rootworm feeding on corn silk

Striped Cucumber Beetle (Acalymma vittata)

Damage: Feeding on emergent seedlings, adult beetles can retard development or even kill young plants. Later they may amass in large numbers in flowers of squash or melons and may chew the pits in fruit. Larvae feed on the roots, causing little apparent injury, but may move into the rind of ripening melon fruit on the soil surface. Adult beetles transmit bacteria (*Erwinia tracheiphila*) that produce bacterial wilt in cucurbits and cucumber mosaic virus.

Life History and Habits: Adult beetles overwinter around field edges. (Beetles that have previously fed on plants infected with bacterial wilt harbor the bacteria in their digestive systems.) As temperatures warm in the spring, they become active and feed on the leaves and flowers of several different trees and shrubs. When squash plants emerge, the beetles move to the crop and chew seedlings. Seedling damage occurs at this time, and plants may become infected with the

Striped cucumber beetle larva on muskmelon rind

Striped cucumber beetles. There is one western corn rootworm at lower left, center

bacteria. Eggs are laid in cracks around the base of the plants, and the hatching larvae feed on the roots for about a month. They then pupate in the soil, later emerging as adult beetles. Typically, there are two generations per season.

Cultural and Mechanical Controls: Where problems with the cucumber beetle and bacterial wilt are severe, prepare a thick original planting, later thinning the surviving noninfected plants to the desired population. Row covers or mesh screening exclude beetles and protect seedlings. Injury to fruits by the tunneling of larvae is dependent on very moist soil as fruits ripen. Limit water during this period to prevent this damage. Mulches or some other barrier slipped under the fruit will also impede feeding by larvae migrating to fruit.

Chemical Controls: Striped cucumber beetles are readily controlled with sprays of carbaryl or permethrin. Special bait formulations (e.g., Adios®) that contain a powerful feeding stimulant (cucurbitacins) mixed with a small amount of carbaryl can be a very effective and selective chemical control. On melons where the primary injury is from larval tunneling of fruit rinds, control is facilitated by treating adults three to four weeks prior to harvest.

Miscellaneous Notes: The striped cucumber beetle is often confused with the western corn rootworm. In fact, they may be found feeding together in late summer on the blossoms of squash, melons, or cucumbers. The striped cucumber beetle has straight (rather than wavy) dark stripes, is brighter yellow, and has rows of small depressions on its wings. Another insect that is similar in appearance is the threelined potato beetle (*Lema trilineata*); the larvae of this insect feed on the leaves of tomatillo.

Colorado Potato Beetle (*Leptinotarsa decemlineata*)

Damage: Both the adult beetles and the larvae chew on the foliage of potatoes, eggplant, and tomatoes, reducing yield. Certain related flowers, such as nicotiana and occasionally petunia, are also damaged by this insect.

Life History and Habits: Colorado potato beetles overwinter in the adult stage undercover near plantings infested the previous season. They are capable of flying, and move back to fields in late spring as potatoes and other susceptible plants emerge. Eggs are laid during June, and the orangered larvae feed on leaves for several weeks. After becoming full-grown, they drop from the plant and pupate in the soil. In about 2 weeks, the adult beetles emerge and feed on plants. Beetles present early in the season may lay several egg masses, repeating the cycle. Later-emerging beetles feed for a few weeks and then disperse to overwintering shelters without producing any offspring during the season.

Natural and Biological Controls: During midseason, potato beetle eggs are often destroyed by lady beetles (particularly *Coleomegilla maculata*), and the surviving larvae are prey for the twospotted stink bug, *Perillus bioculatus*. A tachinid fly is also a common parasite of Colorado potato beetle larvae. The *tenebrionis* (aka *san diego*) strain of *Bacillus thuringiensis* can control young larvae.

Damage by the second generation of the beetle is dependent upon warm early-season temperatures; in cooler seasons, most beetles that

Adult Colorado potato beetle

Colorado potato beetle larva

develop during the first generation will not lay many eggs. Increasing numbers of beetles will lay eggs during the second generation if warm temperatures prevail early in the growing season.

Cultural Controls: Some hairy-leaved varieties of eggplant (e.g., Dusky Hybrid) are less preferred by the Colorado potato beetle. Planting early-maturing potato varieties can deter much of the damage. It is sometimes possible to use existing infestations of hairy nightshade, a common weed, as a trap crop because this plant is highly appealing to the beetles. Collect and destroy beetles that feed on these trap crops.

Mechanical Controls: In small plantings, hand-pick the adults and crush the eggs. Adults and some larvae can also be removed with a strong vacuum.

Chemical Controls: Plants can usually tolerate low levels of leaf loss (at least 25 percent) with little or no yield reduction. Protecting plants is most critical while new tubers are forming. Most insecticides registered for use on potatoes are effective for the control of the Colorado potato beetle in the West. However, this insect has developed a resistance to insecticides in the eastern United States.

Neem-based insecticides and some garlic sprays have also been shown to be effective for control of this insect.

Miscellaneous Notes: The infamous Colorado potato beetle is widespread and devastates crops throughout eastern North America and most of Europe. The name of a western state was attached to this species since it was native to the region and thought to have first been described in Colorado. However, it was actually first described a bit farther east during the course of the 1819–1820 expedition of Stephen Long to the Colorado Rockies and thus might be better dubbed the "Iowa" or "Missouri" potato beetle.

Related Insects: The threelined potato beetle (*Lema trilineata*) feeds on the leaves of tomatillo and occasionally other nightshade family plants. Adults are striped and resemble the striped cucumber beetle. Larvae are gray and cover themselves with excrement.

East of the Rockies a common insect that resembles the Colorado potato beetle is the sunflower beetle (*Zygogramma exclamationis*). Adults of both insects are very similar, although the sunflower beetle is a bit smaller and its side stripes are broken. Larvae of the sunflower beetle feed on the leaves of sunflowers and some related plants.

Colorado potato beetle injury to hairy nightshade

Rose Curculio
(*Merhynchites bicolor*)

Damage: The rose curculio damages roses by puncturing the flower buds while feeding, resulting in ragged flowers. Peak injury occurs during late spring and if buds are not common, feeding occurs on the tips of shoots, killing or distorting them. Most seriously damaged by this insect are the Rugosa roses, but other types may also succumb; the "bent neck" condition of hybrid tea roses can be caused by this insect.

Life History and Habits: The adult stage of the rose curculio is a red-snouted beetle (weevil) with a black beak. They become active in late spring and lay eggs in developing flowers. The larval

Rose curculio injury to petals

Rose curculio feeding on flower bud

Cherry curculio injury to pit

(grub) stage feeds on the reproductive parts of the flower. Blossoms on the plant, including those clipped off by the gardener, are suitable environments for the insect to develop. When full-grown, the grubs fall to the soil and dig a small hibernation chamber. They pupate the following spring with only a single generation produced annually.

Mechanical Controls: Regular handpicking and removal of spent blossoms will prevent larvae from completing their development. However, other brambles also serve as hosts for this insect. Adult weevils drop readily from plants and feign death when disturbed. Where plantings allow, shake plants over a container to facilitate hand collection of the rose curculio.

Chemical Controls: The rose curculio can be controlled with most rose insecticides, applied during late May and June when the adults are first observed.

Cherry Curculio
(*Anthonomus consors*)

Damage: Early in the season the adults chew small holes in the base of flowers and cause developing fruit to abort. The skins of older fruit are pitted as a result of this injury. Eggs are inserted into the fruit and larvae tunnel it, ultimately consuming the pit. Damage is limited to sour cherries and chokecherries.

Life History and Habits: The cherry curculio spends the winter as an adult snout beetle (weevil) around trees infested the previous season. They fly to the trees in spring as flower buds form, and they feed on its buds and flowers. After several weeks, the developing fruits emerge and the females insert eggs into them. The young larvae feed and hollow out the pit, then pupate within it, and leave just as the cherries ripen. There is only one generation per year.

Natural Controls: Several types of parasitic wasps commonly attack the cherry gouger. These suppress the insect below damaging numbers in most areas.

Mechanical Controls: Adult weevils can be shaken from trees and collected on sheets. However, they are difficult to see and they play dead when disturbed.

Cultural Controls: To prevent the insect from developing, damaged fruit should be picked and destroyed as soon as it is discovered.

Chemical Controls: Little work has been done on the chemical control of this insect. Effective insecticides, applied before flowering, should provide control.

Related Species: Several other species of small weevils (aka "curculios") can attack tree fruits but none are serious pests in this region. Controls are basically the same for all varieties.

The apple curculio, *Anthonomus quadrigibbus*, feeds on *Amelanchier* (serviceberry, shadbush) and apple trees. It is difficult to detect since it remains motionless, with beak raised up, when disturbed, and closely resembles bud scales or dried petals. The apple curculio bores small holes in the leaves and feeding punctures in the fruit. Fruit injured in late spring heals over, resulting in dry, sunken areas on the fruit. Similar to the cherry gouger, the females excavate holes in which eggs are laid. Larvae and pupae develop only within shed apples (growing apples kill them). Only some varieties of apples are susceptible, including Delicious. Cleaning up June drop apples keeps the insect at bay but will not eliminate spring feeding damage during the first year.

The plum gouger, *Coccotorus scutellaris*, feeds on hard types of plums. Adult weevils make numerous feeding punctures in the developing fruit, many of which result in a flow of clear ooze from the wound. Eggs are laid in some of the puncture holes, and the larvae develop within the pit. This species apparently spends the winter as an adult within the pit as well. Removing damaged fruit should help control this species.

Recently, isolated infestations of plum curculio (*Conotrachelus nenuphar*) have become established in parts of Utah and the Pacific states. This is a serious threat to tree fruits in eastern North America, with larvae commonly developing in apple, plum, and apricot. Damage is also caused by the adult stages, which cut crescent-shaped wounds into the fruit skins, inducing distorted growth.

Hollyhock Weevil (*Apion longirostre*)

Damage: The hollyhock weevil feeds on the seeds, buds, and leaves of hollyhocks. Small feeding punctures in developing leaves and petals give the plant a ragged appearance. The larvae consume the seeds of the plant.

Life History and Habits: Hollyhock weevils spend the winter in their adult stage, either in protected areas around hollyhock plantings or within the seeds. They move to hollyhock plants in late spring and feed by chewing small holes in the buds of the plants. During this time hollyhock weevils are commonly observed mating, the female being identifiable by her extremely long "beak." As flower buds form in June, the females chew deep pits in the buds and lay their eggs. The grub stage of the insect feeds on the developing embyro of the seed. Once feeding is completed, it pupates within the seed. Adults usually emerge in August and September, but some remain within the seeds, emerging the following spring. There is one generation per year.

Hollyhock weevil, mating pair

Cultural Controls: Seed pods should be removed as they develop to prevent the insects from maturing.

Mechanical Controls: Hollyhock weevils drop readily when disturbed and can be easily collected by shaking plants over a tray. The spring, when the weevils first move to the plant and before eggs are laid, is the best time to do this.

Chemical Controls: Recent information on the chemical control of this insect is lacking. Sprays are best timed for late spring before the flower buds develop and eggs are laid.

"Root Weevils" Black Vine Weevil (*Otiorhynchus sulcatus*) Strawberry Root Weevil (*Otiorhynchus ovatus*) and other species

Damage: The grublike larvae feed on the roots of ornamental shrubs, small fruit, and some flowering vines. In large populations, serious root pruning may occur, causing wilting or dieback of the plant. Adults feed on foliage, cutting rectangular notches into leaf edges. These injuries are most common on euonymus, lilac, and clematis. Root weevils also may become a nuisance when they wander into homes during the summer and early fall. Although root weevils do not fly, they are very common pests of nursery stock and have become widely distributed through the movement of infested plant materials.

Life History and Habits: Root weevils spend the winter in the larvae stage around the roots of plants on which it feeds. Adults emerge during late spring and early summer and feed for about two weeks before laying eggs. Feeding takes place at night with the insects moving to sheltering debris around the base of plants during the day. Eggs are laid throughout the summer in soil cracks around host plants and hatch soon after they are laid. Larvae begin to feed during the summer and

Black vine weevil leaf notching

Black vine weevil (Photo by John Capinera)

fall, but peak feeding occurs the following spring as they mature. They pupate in the soil and there is just one generation per year.

Cultural Controls: In strawberries, root weevils can be controlled by tilling plant beds after harvest, which kills developing larvae. As the insects crawl only limited distances, new plantings should be located as far as possible from previously infested ones.

Invading houses during early summer, the strawberry root weevil makes a nuisance of itself. Apparently attracted to the shade and humidity of homes, migrations are greatest during hot, dry summers and can be deterred, in part, by reducing watering around building foundations.

Mechanical Controls: Adult weevils seek daytime cover, so moistened burlap, boards, or other sheltering debris can be placed around plants to concentrate the insects for collection. Adults can be shaken off plants at night and collected in containers.

Biological Controls: Insect-parasitic nematodes can provide good control of root weevil larvae. Nematodes in the genus *Heterorhabditis* have been most effective and are applied as soil drenches watered into the root zone.

Chemical Controls: Root weevils are quite resistant to most insecticides. Best control has been achieved with acephate and permethrin.

Shothole Borer
(*Scolytus rugulosus*)

Damage: The grublike larval stage of the shothole borer tunnels under the bark of twigs and branches of peach, plum, and cherry trees. (Apple and pear are less common hosts.) This produces a girdling wound that can weaken, and sometimes kill, the plant. Trees already in poor health are much more susceptible to shothole borer damage. When the adult beetles emerge through the bark, they chew small exit holes—the familiar shotholes. The branches may ooze gummy sap where the beetles make entry tunnels.

Life History and Habits: Shothole borers spend the winter as grublike larvae under the bark of trees. They continue to develop, pupate, and metamorphose to the adult stage in late spring. The small ($^1/_{10}$ inch), brown adult beetles emerge in June and July. After mating, the females seek out unhealthy tree branches and chew out a 1- to 2-inch-long egg gallery under the bark. Eggs are laid along the gallery, and the newly hatched larvae later feed under the bark, making new galleries offshooting the central one. (The pattern formed by the egg and larval galleries is indicative of shothole borer infestation.) There are usually two generations per year. The larvae become full-grown by midsummer, and a second generation is then produced.

Cultural Controls: Shothole borers rarely attack, and cannot thrive, in trees that are growing robustly. Serious damage by shothole borers can be almost entirely avoided by cultivating trees under favorable conditions. Trees stressed by drought, winter injury, poor site conditions, wounding injuries, or other problems are at greater risk of shothole borer damage. Regularly prune dead or dying branches and limbs in which shothole borers breed. Since the insects can continue to develop in pruned wood, remove or destroy it before adult beetles emerge.

Chemical Controls: On nonbearing trees, some carbaryl and permethrin-containing insecticides are registered to control shothole borers (and other bark beetles). These need to be applied to the branches before the adult beetles have tunneled into the tree and laid eggs (early to mid-June).

Rose Stem Girdler/
Bronze Cane Borer
(*Agrilus aurichalceus*)

Damage: The flathead borer stage (larva) carves out meandering tunnels under the bark of rose, raspberry, and currants. Characteristically, a slightly swollen area develops around the wounded area of the stem. Canes often die back

Shothole borer exit holes (Photo courtesy USDA)

or break at these wounded sites, sometimes several weeks after the tunneling occurs.

Life History and Habits: The rose stem girdler overwinters as a partially developed borer under the bark of the canes. In spring it resumes feeding and pupates within the plant. The adult stage is a bronze-colored beetle, about 3/8-inch in length, that emerges in mid to late May and may be seen sunning on the leaves. Females lay eggs at this time, in cracks on the stem or at the base of leaves. Within a week the eggs hatch and the larvae burrow into the canes, creating meandering tunnels just under the bark surface. The tunnels of older larvae completely girdle the stems and they then cut a small chamber into the cane for pupation. There is one generation per year.

Cultural Controls: Canes that show evidence of injury should be pruned before mid-spring to destroy the insects before they emerge. Pruned canes must be disposed of or developing borers can complete their development in the pruned wood.

Chemical Controls: Effective chemical controls have not yet been demonstrated. If attempted, they are best applied in late spring to kill the adult beetles before they have laid eggs. Larvae within stems cannot be destroyed with insecticides.

Related Species: Several other species of *Agrilus* are also borers in caneberries and other woody plants. In addition to the bronze cane borer, *Agrilus rubricola* is occasionally a local problem and has a similar life history. *Agrilus polistas* is common in caneberries, currants, and other woody plants grown east of the Rockies. The rose stem girdler is also related to the rednecked cane borer, *Agrilus ruficollis,* an eastern species that is responsible for similar injury to caneberries. Other common borers that attack small fruits and roses in western North America include the stemboring sawfly, raspberry crown borer, and currant borer.

Blister Beetles
(species of Epicauta and Meloe)

Damage: Blister beetles appear during June and early July and feed on the leaves and flowers of plants, sometimes causing serious damage. Most often, injuries are sustained by potatoes or legumes (beans, peas, etc.), but many different garden plants fall prey to attack. Late in the season, flowers are particular favorites of blister beetles, and the petals are shredded by feeding. Blister beetles usually feed in groups, massing in a small area of the garden. They appear—and disappear—quite abruptly. An abundance of blister beetles often follows a year of high populations of grasshoppers, whose eggs are a primary food source for most blister beetle larvae.

Life History and Habits: Most blister beetles develop by feeding on grasshopper egg pods within the soil. The adult beetles lay groups of eggs in small soil depressions during midsummer. The newly hatched larvae are hyperactive and burrow through the soil, seeking grasshopper eggs. When eggs are found, the young blister beetles feed and develop rapidly. They then form a cell in the soil and pass the winter as a fully developed larva or pupa. Adults emerge in late spring the following season. Some blister beetles feed on other insects. For example, one group of large, fat, black blister beetles known as "oil beetles" (species of *Meloe*) feed on ground-nesting bees rather than grasshoppers.

Mechanical Controls: Blister beetles can be barred from susceptible plants by using shade cloth or floating row covers. The beetles can also be handpicked, but they produce a chemical that can injure tender skin—use gloves.

Chemical Controls: Blister beetles are easily controlled with several garden insecticides (e.g., Sevin®, permethrin).

Miscellaneous Notes: Blister beetles produce a protective toxic chemical, cantharidin, which is

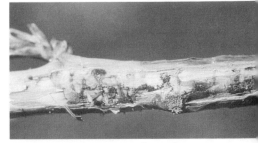

Bronze cane borer tunneling of raspberry cane

Bronze cane borer adult

Blister beetle

released when the insects are crushed. Cantharidin can cause blistering of tender human skin. Blister beetles are highly toxic to some livestock, notably horses, which sometimes eat them in alfalfa hay. Many different types of blister beetles inhabit this region, and the amount of cantharidin produced fluctuates among the various species.

Dusky Sap Beetle
(Carpophilus lugubris)

Damage: Dusky sap beetles feed on a wide variety of overripe fruit, but cause the most injury to sweet corn. The adult beetles feed on corn silk and some of the kernels at the ear tips. Eggs are also laid at this time and the small pale-colored larvae extensively tunnel the ear, although no external evidence of infestation is visible. Most often, the dusky sap beetle is found in ears that were previously damaged, usually by corn earworm, but they can also invade intact corn.

Life History and Habits: Dusky sap beetles breed in decaying organic matter, and overwintering populations may be found in piles of discarded fruit or partially buried vegetable debris. However, their favorite breeding sites are often in the "bacterial ooze" of elms, cottonwoods, and many other trees. Adult beetles are attracted to sweet corn shortly after pollen begins to be shed, about the same time that corn silk first begins to brown. Eggs are laid and larvae feed within the food source, while pupal stages occur nearby in the soil. A single generaton can be completed in as little as 3 weeks with numerous generations being produced during the season. Dusky sap beetle adults are present from early spring through November, with numbers peaking in late spring and midsummer.

Cultural Controls: Sap beetles may develop large local populations early in the season if abundant foods are available. Decaying plant materials should be eliminated by thoroughly composting or deeply burying them. However, the beetles are migratory and will readily move short distances throughout a neighborhood. Planting sweet corn varieties with tight, long husks will help exclude sap beetles as well as corn earworms. These are not readily available but include Victory Golden, Golden Security, Tender Joy, Stowell's Evergreen, Country Gentleman, Early Sunglo, and Trucker's Favorite. Planting later-maturing sweet corn also cuts down on beetle problems.

Dusky sap beetles are attracted to baits consisting of fermenting bread dough. A mixture of 4 parts flour:2 parts water:1 part sugar with some yeast constitutes an appealing bait that lasts for about a week. By placing the bread dough bait in a jar or other container with a funnel entry, large numbers of beetles can be trapped. However, it is not known if such trapping affects damage to nearby plants, since dusky sap beetles are often extremely abundant as well as highly mobile.

Chemical Controls: Some insecticides (e.g., Diazinon®, Sevin®/carbaryl) can control sap beetles before they enter ear tips. Treatments should be applied after silks start to brown, a somewhat later time than is appropriate for corn earworm. Control of corn earworms (see page 102), European corn borer, or other causes of ear injuries will prevent attacks on sweet corn by sap beetles.

Related Insects: Several other sap beetles are common in this region, primarily the shiny, black-spotted "picnic beetles" in the genus *Glischrochilus*. These scavengers are often seen around yards feeding on overripe strawberries, tree sap, or other fermented materials.

Bumble Flower Beetle
(Euphoria inda)

Damage: Bumble flower beetles rarely cause serious injury in gardens, but they do attract attention. Large masses of beetles can sometimes be found in late summer clustered on oozing sap or in damaged corn or melons. Earlier in the season, the grub-stage larvae often feed on manure, with a particular fondness for horse manure. The large, hairy beetles occasionally feed on flowers, including strawflower, sunflower, and daylily.

Dusky sap beetles

Bumble flower beetle

They may transmit bacterial diseases to some of these plants, which will produce wilting.

Life History and Habits: The overwintering state is the adult beetle. These are broadly oval, about $1/2$ to $5/8$ inch long, and densely covered with yellowish brown hairs. In the spring, the beetles usually lay eggs in fresh manure (particularly horse manure), rotten wood, or compost, and the C-shaped grubs thrive in the decaying organic matter. As they feed, they form small, packed chambers in which they later pupate. The grubs are often found in gardens that have been fertilized with manure or compost, but they do not feed on plant roots. The adults emerge in mid to late summer and dine on a wide variety of sweet or fermenting liquids. In late summer, they are usually attracted to the bacterial ooze of a tree that results from infection. They may also occasionally damage ripening corn, ripe apples, grapes, melons, and peaches. The pollen and nectar of flowers such as sunflowers, strawflowers, and daylilies serve as food sources. There is one generation per year.

Chemical Controls: No controls have been developed and would unlikely be of any benefit. Because the adults are so mobile, insecticides do not have much impact. Handpicking beetles as they are discovered is probably the best control. Larvae do not damage plants.

LEPIDOPTERA (MOTHS AND BUTTERFLIES)

Imported Cabbageworm (Pieris rapae)

Damage: The caterpillar stages of the imported cabbageworm chew on leaves of broccoli, cabbage, and related plants. Feeding injuries and the contamination of edible heads and leaves by the insects or their droppings can render the plants inedible. This is the most common and destructive of the "cabbageworms" in the garden.

Life History and Habits: The imported cabbageworm is widely distributed throughout the region, and it feeds on many mustard family plants (crucifers). The overwintering stage is the pupa, which often occurs in protected sites several yards away from the host plants. The adult insects (the familiar cabbage butterflies) emerge in mid-spring and females lay their yellow, bullet-shaped eggs on leaves. The larvae hatch in 3 to 5 days and begin feeding on the plants, initially concentrating on the outer leaves. Later, they tunnel into the head. Larvae reach their full growth in 2 to 3 weeks. Pupation takes place in the vicinity of the plant, often a few feet from where they were feeding earlier. Three generations typically occur per growing season.

Natural and Biological Controls: Several naturally occurring predators and parasites can greatly reduce cabbageworm infestations, including ground beetles, paper wasps, spiders, and parasitic wasps. One of the most common parasitic wasps is *Apanteles* (=*Cotesia*) *glomeratus,* which produces small masses of yellow cocoons after emerging from the caterpillar. Young caterpillars are also very susceptible to drowning following heavy rains or overhead irrigation. *Bacillus thuringiensis* is effective against larvae. Periodic releases of trichogramma wasps enable this insect to parasitize and destroy some cabbageworm eggs.

Cultural Controls: Caterpillar populations tend to increase later in the season, so early plantings can escape serious injury. Although no cabbages are resistant to imported cabbageworms, red cabbage varieties are less appealing than green varieties. Caterpillars are typically more damaging to cabbage and broccoli than other mustard family plants. Ground covers and straw mulches provide daytime cover, which improves the garden habitat for cabbageworm predators such as ground beetles. Interplantings of various herbs or flowers for control have been recommended in gardening publications for many years, but numerous experimental trials conducted throughout North America have repeatedly proved this recommendation to be without value.

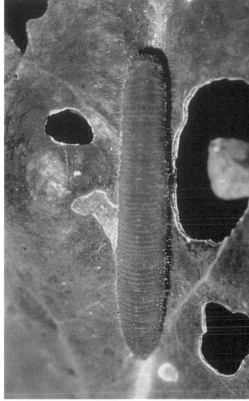

Imported cabbageworm

Cabbage butterfly, adult of the imported cabbageworm, laying an egg

Zebra caterpillar

Parsleyworm

Mechanical and Physical Controls: Overhead watering or periodic hosing of plants with a forceful jet of water gets rid of many small caterpillars. Handpicking also is feasible for small plantings. Insects may be excluded by using plant covers, such as floating row covers, which prevent the butterflies from laying eggs on plants.

Chemical Controls: After plants have become established, they tolerate considerable defoliation (up to 50 percent) with little or no loss in yield. However, as plants begin to produce heads, the possibility of injury increases, and damage to the edible heads is a serious threat. Several insecticides (including *Bacillus thuringiensis* products) are registered that can usually provide control on crucifers. Control is more challenging when older caterpillars are present since they tend to tunnel more deeply into the plant. Adequately covering the plants can be difficult when varieties have large leaves. Because the plants do have waxy leaves, the addition of a small amount of soap or detergent usually aids coverage.

Related Species: A closely related cabbageworm sometimes visiting gardens is the yellow and black-spotted southern cabbageworm (*Pontia protodice*). The adult stage of this insect is best known as the checkered white butterfly and exhibits more dark spotting on its white wings. Other common caterpillars that attack plants of the mustard family (Brassicaceae) are the cabbage looper, diamond-back moth, and zebra caterpillars.

Parsleyworm/ Black Swallowtail Butterfly (*Papilio polyxenes asterius*)

Damage: The parsleyworm is a brightly colored (black, white, and yellow) caterpillar that feeds on the leaves and flowers of parsley, dill, fennel, and occasionally celery, carrots, and parsnips. They may also clip the heads and feed on developing dill seeds.

Life History and Habits: The parsleyworm spends the winter as a pupa attached to tree bark, sides of buildings, or other protected locations. The adult, known as the black swallowtail butterfly, emerges during late May and early June and lays eggs on plants in the carrot family (Apiaceae). After hatching, the young parsleyworms start out as small, black caterpillars that resemble bird droppings. As they get older and larger, they undergo a dramatic color change, sporting conspicuous white, yellow, and black stripes. After they become full-grown, they wander away from the plant to find a place to pupate. They then form the pupa within a grayish chrysalid that blends into the background. Adult butterflies emerge after about 2 weeks and feed on nectar. They then mate, lay eggs, and produce a second generation beginning in early August. There are two generations per year.

Biological Controls: Several general predators, such as spiders, make off with the larvae. Parasitic wasps also take their share of the caterpillars, and tachinid flies attack the pupae. The parsleyworm is very susceptible to *Bacillus thuringiensis*.

Mechanical Controls: The caterpillars are brightly colored and are easy to spot and pick off plants if damage becomes objectionable. However, they do defend themselves by everting a pair of fleshy horns that emit an unusual and somewhat "interesting" odor.

Black swallowtail, adult of the parsleyworm

Parsleyworms

One of the more entertaining insects found within the yard and garden is the parsleyworm. As its name suggests, this caterpillar prefers to feed on parsley, but it can also be found on related plants such as dill, fennel, and carrots.

Parsleyworms start out as small, black caterpillars that resemble bird droppings. As they get older and larger, they undergo a dramatic color change, becoming conspicuously striped with white, yellow, and black. Perhaps most interesting, parsleyworm caterpillars display a Y-shaped horn from behind their head when disturbed. This is assumed to be a defense against predators, such as birds, since it has a powerful smell—

compared by some to rancid butter. However, this very behavior also renders them attractive for children to collect and observe.

Parsleyworm caterpillars save their best display for the adult stage. After pupating in a camouflaged corner of the garden, the black swallowtail emerges. This butterfly is one of the largest and most attractive species that graces our yards and gardens. It is closely related to the tiger swallowtails, whose larvae have similar behavioral habits but with appetites that favor chokecherry and ash instead.

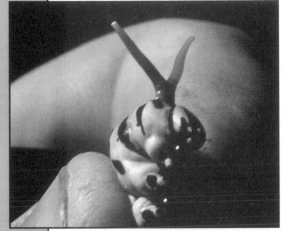
Parsleyworm everting its defensive "horns"

Painted Lady/Thistle Caterpillar (*Vanessa cardui*)

Damage: The thistle caterpillar will feed on a fairly wide range of plants, with more than 100 species from several plant families serving as hosts. By far the most common host is the Canada thistle, and this caterpillar is beneficial in controlling this serious weed. However, some other garden plants may also become caterpillar fare, including the sunflower, globe thistle, Jerusalem artichoke, globe artichoke, hollyhock, common mallow, lupins, soybean, basil, artemisia, and geranium.

Life History and Habits: The adult stage of the insect is known as the painted lady, *Vanessa cardui*. It is generally orange with irregular black and white spotting on the wings. This species is one of the most common butterflies found in the

Painted lady butterfly, adult of the thistle caterpillar

Rocky Mountain region. However, it is an annual migrant, spending the winter in more southerly areas, including Mexico. In spring, migrations head northward; in fall, to the south. The adult butterflies feed only on nectar and other fluids, sometimes drinking from damp spots on the ground. Females lay eggs on host plants. The Canada thistle leads the pack as by far the most preferred host, giving rise to its alternative name—the thistle caterpillar. The caterpillar stage is generally black with some lighter flecking and is rather spiny. The caterpillars feed on leaves and often produce a little webbing, using it to tie the leaves to form a protected pocket. When abundant thistle caterpillars extensively defoliate plants, and once the food plant is destroyed, the caterpillars will migrate. Pupation occurs in a silvery chrysalid, usually some distance from the food plant. Adults emerge about 1 week after pupation and usually disperse from the area. Several overlapping generations are produced annually with return, southward migrations observed in late summer.

Mechanical Controls: Individual larvae can be handpicked. Although covered with fleshy spines, they are harmless.

Thistle caterpillar

Natural and Biological Controls: Thistle caterpillars are usually heavily parasitized by wasps and tachinid flies, so outbreaks tend to be short-lived. In addition, since the butterflies are so dispersive, they typically move out of the area where earlier they developed. Thistle caterpillars are susceptible to *Bacillus thuringiensis*.

Related Insects: Another annual migrant is the variegated fritillary, *Euptoieta claudia*. The brightly colored larvae of this butterfly prefer to feed on pansies, but also munch on lobelia and petunia.

Cabbage Looper
(Trichoplusia ni)

Damage: The cabbage looper damages mustard family plants in a manner similar to that of the imported cabbageworm. In addition, it may feed on a wide range of other garden plants, including potatoes, peas, lettuce, spinach, nasturtiums, and carnations. Injury to these latter plants is usually minor. The highest numbers of insects are usually reached late in the growing season.

Life History and Habits: The cabbage looper overwinters as a pupa within a loose cocoon, located on plant debris around plantings of the previous year. The adult moths emerge in mid-spring. At night, the females glue their eggs singly to the leaves of plants. The caterpillars feed on the plants, becoming full-grown in about 3 to 4 weeks. Pupation occurs near the host plant. There are typically two to three generations per year.

Natural and Biological Controls: Cabbage loopers are preyed upon by several garden predators, such as damsel bugs, paper wasps, and spiders. Tachinid flies and parasitic wasps commonly kill the larvae and pupae, although not until after the insect has already fed extensively. A wilting viral disease is very destructive to the insect, and it tends to occur most frequently late in the season. Parasitism of eggs by trichogramma wasps occurs at low levels.

Trichogramma wasps can be introduced into a planting as a supplemental control. Cabbage loopers are also vulnerable to *Bacillus thurin-*

giensis. Caterpillars that are dead and dying from viral disease may be collected and sprayed on plants to capitalize on the disease as a form of control.

Mechanical Controls: Row covers or other materials exclude the moths from the plants and prevent egg laying. Tilling debris may kill some of the overwintering pupae, although the moths are migratory and come to infest plantings from great distances.

Chemical Controls: Several insecticides, including *Bacillus thuringiensis*, control cabbage loopers. However, treatments are most effective against small caterpillars. Older caterpillars possess a resistance to many insecticides and can also tunnel into plants, making their control difficult.

Miscellaneous Notes: The cabbage looper gets its name from its distinctive looping manner of walking, since it lacks a few pairs of the abdominal prolegs found on other cabbageworms. Although other related species of loopers also enjoy vegetables (e.g., celery looper, alfalfa looper), the cabbage looper is the only species that attacks crucifers (mustard family plants).

Corn Earworm/
Tomato Fruitworm
(Helicoverpa zea)

Damage: Corn earworm larvae feed on the ear tips of sweet corn, causing extensive damage. Pepper and tomato fruits may also be tunneled and destroyed. The corn earworm is considered one of the most destructive insects in the United States, attacking many of the most important field and vegetable crops.

Life History and Habits: The corn earworm is unable to survive western winters, except in some of the warmer southern areas of the region. (I-70 is often regarded as the dividing line at which some corn earworms may begin to successfully survive the winter.) Almost all infestations arise from the annual migrations of the adult moths from the southern United States and Mexico. The migration

Cabbage looper

Corn earworm larva

flights typically commence in June but additional migrations continue throughout the growing season when favorable weather patterns are present. The female moths fly at night, laying their eggs singly on suitable host plants. On sweet corn, eggs are laid on green silks; on tomatoes and peppers, the eggs are usually laid on the new leaves near the flowers of developing fruit. Eggs hatch in about 2 to 5 days, and the young caterpillars begin to tunnel into the plants. Corn earworm caterpillars usually feed for about 4 weeks before becoming full-grown. They vary in color from pale green, to pink, or even black. Since they are highly cannibalistic, it is fairly uncommon to find more than one within a single ear of corn. When full-grown, they drop from the plant, construct a small cell in the soil, and pupate. Adults emerge in 10 to 14 days. Once corn earworms have migrated into an area, the damage tends to cycle as peak numbers of eggs are laid around the time of the full moon.

Natural and Biological Controls: General predators, such as minute pirate bugs and damsel bugs, feed on the eggs. Corn earworm larvae are also highly cannibalistic and will readily eat each other. Caterpillars are susceptible to *Bacillus thuringiensis*, which can be an effective treatment on peppers and tomatoes. Its effectiveness on sweet corn is marginal, since the insects tunnel into untreated parts of the silk and ear tip soon after hatching. Insect-parasitic nematodes injected into the ear tips wipe out existing larvae, but their use as a preventive treatment has not been successful in areas where hot summer temperatures subdue or inactivate the nematodes. Releases of trichogramma wasps can kill some of the eggs and help suppress infestations when used repeatedly during periods of egg laying.

Cultural Controls: Varieties of sweet corn with husks that tightly cover the ear tip are more resistant to corn earworms. Since sweet corn is highly favored, it can be used as a trap crop to divert the egg-laying moths from less susceptible crops such as peppers and tomatoes.

Mechanical and Physical Controls: Injecting a small amount of mineral oil into the silks can control caterpillars. Because oil treatments can interfere with pollination, they should be applied after silks begin to brown to avoid injury. Some vegetable oils, such as soybean, also provide some earworm control, but they are less effective than mineral oil.

Chemical Controls: Sweet corn attracts egg-laying moths from the time silks first emerge from the plant until they turn brown. Eggs are laid on the silk at that time. Insecticide applications (e.g., permethrin, carbaryl) should correspond to this critical period of silking and be directed at the ear tip zone. Since the insect usually overwinters in southern states, its presence in much of the region is irregular. Pheromone traps or light traps can monitor flights and help determine if large numbers are moving into the area. Where pheromone traps are used, trap design is critical and "Heliothis" models should be used. However, corn earworm pheromones are chemically unstable and must be replaced frequently (at 1- to 2-week intervals) once removed from the refrigerator.

Miscellaneous Notes: The corn earworm is called the tomato fruitworm when it attacks tomatoes. On cotton, it is known as the cotton bollworm. Its wide range and destructive habits make it the number-one agricultural insect pest in the United States.

Corn earworm adult

Tobacco Budworm/ "Geranium Budworm" (Heliothis virescens)

Damage: Tobacco budworm damage consists primarily of the tunneling of flower buds, which subsequently prevents or shortens flowering. Young larvae tunnel primarily small buds, while larger caterpillars feed on flower petals, chewing the reproductive ovaries of the flowers. Geraniums and petunias are most commonly damaged, but a wide variety of other flowers (e.g., nicotiana, ageratum, dandelion, marigold) are also on the budworms' list. Although its accepted scientific name is the tobacco budworm, its fondness for geraniums and other flowers has earned it the

Geranium budworm feeding on buds

name "geranium budworm" when encountered in flower gardens.

Life History and Habits: The tobacco budworm overwinters as a pupa in an earthen cell buried a few inches beneath the soil surface. During late spring, the adults emerge. The adult stage is a pale green moth, which is active in the early evening. Migrations of moths into more northern areas are sometimes responsible for summer infestations outside of areas where the insect normally survives winter conditions. The moths glue eggs singly onto flower buds and leaves. The young caterpillars emerge and feed on buds, flowers and, rarely, leaves. They become full-grown in about 3 weeks, causing extensive injury. They then drop to the soil and pupate. There are probably two generations per season, with the caterpillar populations highest in August and early September. The damaging caterpillars are often visible on the plant. They are highly variable in color, ranging from pale brown or light green to red or black. The color of the flower on which they are feeding determines, in part, the caterpillar's color.

The tobacco budworm is a very serious pest of cotton and tobacco in more southern areas. It is generally considered to be a warm-weather, subtropical insect usually restricted to areas south of northern Texas and New Mexico. Although the overwintering pupae cannot survive temperatures below 20°F, local "microclimates" in and around homes and buildings may enable the insect to survive farther north (e.g., Denver, Grand Junction). In these areas, problems tend to be most serious following mild winters.

Natural and Biological Controls: Cold winter temperatures, which freeze the soil in which the pupae overwinter, are the most influential natural control of tobacco budworm in this region. Local populations of budworms can be wiped out by a severe freeze. During the summer, several biological controls come into play, including tachinid flies and general predators such as ground beetles, damsel bugs, and minute pirate bugs. The tobacco budworm is susceptible to *Bacillus thuringiensis* (Bt). However, since the caterpillars tend to tunnel plant buds, there is often little chance for the insect to eat enough to be killed by this treatment. Bt is more effective on plants on which the caterpillars eat the petals (e.g., petunias) than when they restrict their feeding to buds (e.g., geraniums).

Cultural Controls: Because the insects survive winters in the soil, potted geraniums should not be brought indoors. (However, taking cuttings is safe, since these should not be infested with the insect.) Tilling the garden bed in the fall will further expose pupae to freezing winter temperatures. Some plants appear to be resistant to tobacco budworm. For example, ivy geraniums are rarely injured, in contrast to standard geranium types.

Mechanical Controls: Handpicking the caterpillars is often the best control for small plantings.

Chemical Controls: The tobacco budworm is difficult to control with most insecticides because it has become insecticide-resistant. However, the younger caterpillars are more susceptible than the older ones.

Tomato Hornworm
(Manduca quinquemaculata)
Tobacco Hornworm
(Manduca sexta)

Damage: Two similar species of hornworm grace our gardens: the tobacco hornworm and the tomato hornworm. Caterpillars chew leaves and plants are rapidly defoliated. Fruits are also in danger. Tomatoes are particularly susceptible to injury, but other related plants, such as peppers and potatoes, are only occasionally infested.

Life History and Habits: Tomato and tobacco hornworms overwinter as pupae in the soil in the vicinity of gardens. The adult moths (a type of sphinx, hawk, or hummingbird moth) emerge in late spring. They are strong fliers and appear after

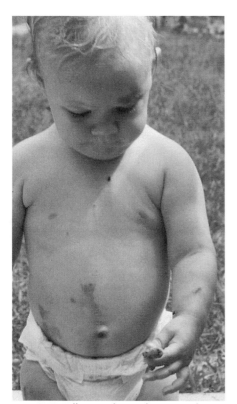

A young Bill Cranshaw playing with a hornworm

dusk to feed on nectar. The female moths lay large, pearly eggs on the upper surface of leaves. The young caterpillars hatch and feed on the plant for a month or more. They have tremendous appetites and consume large quantities as they grow older and larger. After feeding, they wander away from the plant and pupate in the soil. There is usually one generation per season, although a few moths will emerge and produce a second generation.

Natural and Biological Controls: Hornworm eggs and small larvae are killed by many general garden predators, such as spiders, predatory stink bugs, and damsel bugs. The most conspicuous natural hornworm enemy is a parasitic wasp that develops within the caterpillars. When the developing wasps emerge from the hornworm caterpillar, they remain attached to their host and spin distinctive pale-colored cocoons. Despite their large size, hornworms are extremely susceptible to *Bacillus thuringiensis*.

Mechanical and Physical Controls: Hornworms can be handpicked off plants or cut with scissors

during regular plant inspections. Larvae are easy to locate early in the morning, when they tend to graze on the exterior of the plant.

Chemical Controls: Hornworms are easily controlled with most insecticides registered for use on tomatoes.

Miscellaneous Notes: The tobacco hornworm frequents regional vegetable gardens more often than the tomato hornworm, but both may be found together, and they have similar habits. The tomato hornworm has a green horn with black sides, while the horn of the tobacco hornworm is red. The caterpillars can also be differentiated by the white striping along their sides. These form a series of Vs with tomato hornworms, while they are diagonal dashes on the tobacco hornworm. Occasionally, dark forms of the tomato hornworm occur that are much darker than the normal green, although the adult moths differ little in appearance.

Several other species of hornworms hang around the yard and garden but do not feed on

Tomato hornworm

Hornworms

Running across a hornworm in the vegetable patch is one of the more startling garden encounters. Hornworms are the largest common garden insect and reach a length of 3 to 4 inches when full-grown. They are also marked with a fearsome-looking horn on the hind end. (Its only known function is to scare gardeners.)

Diagnosing problems with the tomato hornworm is relatively easy: the rapid disappearance of leaves stripped to the stem, followed by the appearance of large, dark green droppings around the base of the plant. However, the caterpillars are remarkably difficult to find, being extremely well camouflaged to blend in with the foliage. Eggs and young caterpillars may be present in early summer, but most garden damage is observed during mid to late summer as the caterpillars rapidly increase in size—and appetite. Since the caterpillars eat most of their food at the very end of the caterpillar stage, gardens can be devastated

in short order (like when you are away for a 3-day vacation).

The tomato hornworm is only one member of the hornworm family of caterpillars (Sphingidae). Indeed, throughout most of the region, the tobacco hornworm is at least as common on tomatoes. Other common hornworms feed on trees (elm, ash, and poplar, particularly), grape, and Virginia creeper (a "hornless" hornworm, the Achemon sphinx) and weeds such as purslane (the common whitelined sphinx). The full-grown hornworms tend to wander away from the plant on which they develop and can usually be observed crossing the yard late in the season.

The adult stages of the hornworms are heavy-bodied, strong-flying insects known as sphinx, hawk, or hummingbird moths. The latter name comes from their resemblance to hummingbirds as they feed from deep-lobed flowers at dusk.

Whitelined sphinx, the most common "hummingbird moth," is the adult of a kind of hornworm

vegetable plants. The largest species is the giant poplar sphinx, which develops on cottonwoods and poplars. The whitelined sphinx is a particularly common species and feeds on a number of weeds such as purslane. A hornless hornworm, the larva of the Achemon sphinx moth, also resides in the West and feeds on grape and Virginia creeper.

TABLE 6-1: SOME COMMON HORNWORMS FOUND IN THE REGION

Common Name and Scientific Name	Host Plants; Notes
Whitelined sphinx (*Hyles lineata*)	Very wide host range that includes primrose, portulaca, apple, grape, four-o'clock, and peony. The adult is marked with strong white bands on the wing and is by far the most often encountered "hummingbird moth."
Achemon sphinx (*Eumorpha achemon*)	Grape, Virginia creeper, woodbine. These purplish-brown caterpillars are minus the characteristic "horn" and have in its place only a dark eyespot.
Tobacco hornworm (*Manduca sexta*)	Tomato, eggplant, and other nightshade family plants
Tomato hornworm (*Manduca quinquemaculata*)	Tomato, eggplant, and other nightshade family plants
Elm sphinx (*Ceratomia amyntor*)	Elm
Great ash sphinx (*Sphinx chersis*)	Ash, lilac, privet
Wildcherry sphinx (*Sphinx drupiferarum*)	Plum, cherry, chokecherry
Giant poplar sphinx (*Pachysphinx modesta*)	Poplars, willow. Along with the Columbia basin sphinx, this is the largest species.
Columbia basin sphinx (*Pachysphinx occidentalis*)	Poplars, willow. Along with the giant poplar sphinx, this is the largest species.
Twinspot sphinx (*Smerinthus jamaicensis*)	Poplar, birch, elm, willow, ash, apple
Common clearwing sphinx (*Hemaris thysbe*)	Honeysuckle, viburnum, hawthorn, snowberry, cherry, plum. Adults have clear wings and resemble oversized bumblebees.

Army Cutworm
(*Euxoa auxiliaris*)

Damage: Army cutworms cut and feed on seedlings of a wide variety of garden plants, including tomatoes, beans, and corn. They are the most common garden cutworms in the Rocky Mountain and High Plains region, as well as being an important pest of winter wheat and alfalfa. Their name is derived from their occasional habit of migrating in large bands during outbreaks. The adult stage of the army cutworm is the infamous miller moth of the High Plains and eastern Rockies.

Life History and Habits: The eggs of the army cutworm are laid in late summer and early fall, particularly in areas of dense growth. They hatch shortly after being laid, and the young caterpillars then feed on weeds and garden plants. Because of their small size, they are not capable of causing any injury during the fall. However, in the spring the developing caterpillars can seriously damage young plants that emerge or are transplanted in the garden. After feeding for several weeks, the caterpillars dig a small chamber underground and pupate. They emerge as "miller moths" in mid- to late May and early June. The adult moths then migrate to higher elevations and feed on the nectar of flowering plants. They do not lay eggs or reproduce during these flights, but can be a serious nuisance in homes and cars. Ultimately, the moths reach the mountains, where they spend the summer. By midsummer they begin to make a return migration to the plains, laying eggs to repeat the cycle. There is one generation per year.

Natural and Biological Controls: Cutworms are preyed upon by several garden insects, such as ground beetles, rove beetles, and spiders. Mulches and other ground covers that favor these beneficial species can help with cutworm control. Toads and snakes also devour cutworms. Parasites of cutworms include tachinid flies and various parasitic wasps. Although they are a type of caterpillar, most cutworms are relatively immune to *Bacillus thuringiensis*.

Insect-parasitic nematodes can be effective cutworm controls, provided soil temperatures are warm enough (about 50°F minimum) to allow their activity.

Cultural Controls: Weed control is fundamental to avoiding cutworm problems. Weedy gardens attract egg-laying moths during late summer. Tillage in the garden in the fall and spring can destroy many cutworms. Cultural practices that promote rapid seedling growth and using transplants can help plantings outgrow cutworm damage. Well-established plants are generally not bothered much by cutworms. In the spring, some weeds can be retained temporarily as an alternate

Army cutworm (Photo by John Capinera)

Cutworms

Caterpillars that cut and kill seedling plants around the soil line are usually described as cutworms. This habit is shared by many different caterpillar species within the cutworm family, Noctuidae, which also includes such garden pests as the cabbage looper and corn earworm. In addition, there are many species of "climbing cutworms" that do not restrict their feeding to the soil surface and climb plants and chew leaves. Cutworms typically feed at night and hide in soil cracks, under dirt clods, or other cover during the day.

A variety of habits characterize the many cutworm species. Most of the damaging cutworms in the region produce one generation per season and lay eggs during late summer among weeds and other dense vegetation. However, some cutworm moths do not survive area winters and annually migrate into the region. This includes the black

cutworm, beet armyworm, and "true" armyworm. Problems with these insects occur more sporadically than with cutworms that overwinter in the region.

Adult stages of cutworms are moderately large, gray or brown moths, usually with indistinct markings. Some cutworm moths are quite abundant at times and are popularly known as "millers." One species in particular, the army cutworm, is the *miller moth* of Colorado, New Mexico, and Wyoming, where it sometimes becomes an overwhelming nuisance in and around homes during its annual migration from the plains to the mountains. However, the term "miller moth" may be used to describe any type of nuisance moth that occurs in large numbers and is a reference to the scales of the moths, which may resemble the flour on the smock of a grain miller.

food for young cutworms. This will divert some of their feeding from garden plants. The weeds should be removed and destroyed before they compete with garden plants or produce seeds.

Mechanical and Physical Controls: Young transplants are protected by various barriers that prevent the cutworm from reaching the plant. These can be constructed from a variety of items such as cut milk jugs or paper cups. Outdoor lighting should be minimized during the egg-laying period since light attracts the adult moths.

Chemical Controls: Several garden insecticides sprayed on susceptible plants provide cutworm protection. Various baits are also available that can be spread around the base of plants. Baits generally afford a more selective type of treatment than sprays or dusts, since fewer beneficial organisms are likely to contact the insecticide.

TABLE 6-2: SOME COMMON CUTWORMS FOUND IN THE REGION

Common Name	Comments; Habits in the West
Army cutworm (*Euxoa auxiliaris*)	Winters as small larvae with peak injury in early spring. Adult stage is the common "miller" of Colorado and Wyoming. One generation per year.
Armyworm (*Pseudaletia unipuncta*)	Winters in southern United States and Mexico; an annual migrant. Climbing cutworm causes peak injury in mid to late summer. Primarily found in dense, grassy sites. Can have two generations per year.
Beet armyworm (*Spodoptera exigua*)	Winters in southern United States and Mexico; an annual migrant into the region. Climbing cutworm causes peak injury in mid-to-late summer and has a very wide host range. Probably two generations per year in the West.
Black cutworm (*Agrotis ipsilon*)	Winters in southern United States and Mexico; an annual migrant. Feeds at or just below the soil surface and is the most notorious species for cutting plants; although within the region, occurs most often as a pest of golf greens. Peak injury typically occurs in late spring. Probably two generations per year in the West.
Yellowstriped armyworm (*Spodoptera ornithogalli*)	Found west of the Rocky Mountains, primarily in California, Oregon, and Washington. A climbing cutworm with general feeding habits found on many fruit and vegetable crops. Multiple generations are produced with the insect overwintering as a pupa.
Clover cutworm (*Scotogramma trifolii*)	Winters as a pupa, emerging to lay eggs in late spring. Feeds as a climbing cutworm, primarily on legumes. Two generations per year.

Darksided cutworm (*Euxoa messoria*)	Winters as eggs, which hatch in spring, the caterpillars causing peak injury in late spring. Typically feeds around the soil surface. One generation per year.
Speckled green fruitworm (*Orthosia hibisci*)	Winters as a pupa, which lays eggs in early spring. A climbing cutworm causing peak injury in June. One generation per year.
Spotted cutworm (*Amanthes c-nigrum*)	Winters as a pupa, emerging and laying eggs in late spring. Mostly a climbing cutworm with very wide host range. Probably two generations per year.
Variegated cutworm (*Peridroma saucia*)	Winters as a pupa, emerging and laying eggs in late spring. Mostly a climbing cutworm with very wide host range. Probably three generations per year.
Western bean cutworm (*Loxagrotis albicosta*)	Overwinter as full-grown larvae but do not transform to adults until July. Peak injury in August. One generation per year. Restricted to east of Rockies.

Eastern Tent Caterpillar (*Malacosoma americanum*) Western Tent Caterpillar (*Malacosoma californicum*)

Damage: Tent caterpillars fashion a tight tent in the crotch of various trees and shrubs, particularly fruit trees such as cherry, plum, apricot, and apple. They tend to rest on or within the tent during the day, crawling away at night to chew on leaves. Developing fruit may also be chewed and damaged. When abundant, tent caterpillars can destroy a substantial number of leaves, thereby weakening the tree.

Life History and Habits: Tent caterpillars overwinter in shiny brown egg masses glued to twigs. The eggs typically hatch in late April or early May, about the time apple leaves begin to emerge. The caterpillars stay grouped together and spin a small tent in the fork of branches. As they feed and grow, the tent enlarges, becoming quite conspicuous after about 1 month. After becoming full-grown, the caterpillars wander off to find places to pupate. They spin a white cocoon on trunks or on other sheltering objects near the infested tree. The adult moths emerge about 2 weeks later and mate, and the females lay egg masses. There is one generation per season.

Natural and Biological Controls: Tent caterpillars fall prey to many insects, such as tachinid flies and parasitic wasps. Birds' fledging young also seek caterpillars as food, and a virus disease, producing "wilt" symptoms, can devastate their populations. These natural controls typically prevent outbreaks of tent caterpillars from persisting long enough to cause serious damage. Tent caterpillars are very susceptible to sprays of *Bacillus thuringiensis*.

Mechanical Controls: The caterpillars and tents can easily be dislodged from trees and destroyed.

Chemical Controls: Tent caterpillars are susceptible to most insecticides used for the control of codling moths and other

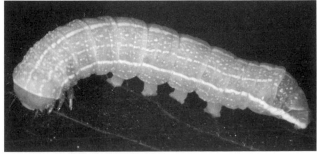

Speckled green fruitworm (Photo by Frank Peairs)

Western tent caterpillar colony

Codling moth damage

fruit pests. Dormant season sprays of horticultural oils can also destroy many of the overwintering eggs.

Associated Insects: The most common tent-making caterpillar in this region is the fall webworm (*Hyphantria cunea*). This insect constructs large, loose tents on the outer, sun-exposed branches of cottonwoods, poplars, chokecherry, and other trees in midsummer.

Codling Moth
(*Cydia pomonella*)

Damage: Larvae of the codling moth tunnel into the fruit of apple, pear, and crabapple trees. (It is almost always the worm in a wormy apple.) Less frequently, it may damage other fruits, including apricot and peach. It is the single most important insect pest of tree fruits in the western United States.

Life History and Habits: Codling moth larvae spend the winter inside a silken cocoon attached to rough bark or other protected locations around the tree. With warm spring weather, they pupate and later begin to emerge around blossom time as small (about $1/2$ inch), gray moths. The spring debut of this adult stage takes place over the course of 1 or 2 weeks, but can last much longer if the weather is cool. During periods when early evening temperatures are warm (above 60°F) and it is not windy, the moths lay small, white eggs on the leaves. The hatching larvae may first feed on the leaves, but then migrate to the fruit, usually entering the calyx (flower) end. They tunnel the fruit, feeding primarily on the developing seeds. After about 3 to 4 weeks, the full-grown larvae leave the fruit and crawl or drop down the tree to spin a cocoon in which to pupate. After about 2 weeks, most, but not all, of the pupae develop to produce a second generation of moths. Those that remain dormant emerge the following season. (For example, in western Colorado, only about two-thirds go on to produce a second generation, and fewer than 50 percent of their progeny go on to produce a third generation.) These moths lay their eggs directly on the fruit, and the damage by the larvae to the fruit is greatest at this time. Once fully grown, the larvae emerge from the fruit and seek protected areas to pupate. In the warmer, southern parts of the region, a small third generation is produced in late summer. This one generally incurs much less damage to apples and pears than the earlier generations.

Natural and Biological Controls: The codling moth has many natural enemies, although these biological controls often are not adequate. Birds, notably downy and hairy woodpeckers, will feed on the larvae and pupae in cocoons. Perhaps most significant, codling moth larvae and pupae are often killed by several types of parasitic wasps. The activity of these wasps has been improved in some areas by cultivating flowering plants that provide alternative foods. Codling moth larvae are also attacked by several general predators, such as ground beetles and earwigs. Some additional control is possible with repeated applications of *Bacillus thuringiensis*, timed for periods when the moths are laying eggs. However, since it acts as a stomach poison, it must be applied shortly before the larvae enter the fruit. Trichogramma wasps, available for mass release, can parasitize and destroy codling moth eggs.

Cultural Controls: Keeping loose bark scraped off trees and removing debris from around the tree eliminates shelter sought by the insects when they pupate. This leaves them more exposed to

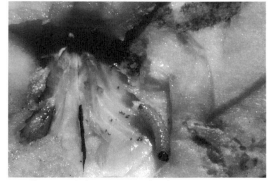

Codling moth larva in apple core

birds and other natural controls. Since young caterpillars often need some leverage to help them cut into the fruit, many of them enter at a point where two fruits are touching. Thinning apples to avoid this reduces the survival rate of the delicate young larvae and controls damage to remaining fruit.

Mechanical Controls: Adult moths can be attracted to baits and trapped. A typical design is a gallon jar baited with a pool of fermenting molasses and water (1:10 to 1:15 dilution is suggested). This attracts both male and female moths. (Pheromone traps capture only the male moths and provide no control.) Coarse screening can be added to exclude visiting honeybees. However, raccoons readily feed on this mixture and if present will often destroy the traps.

The pupal stages of the moth can be aggregated by placing bands of corrugated cardboard or burlap around the trunk. They can then be collected and destroyed.

Chemical Controls: Insecticides should be applied during periods of peak egg laying. Two damaging generations of codling moths are the norm—one in late spring (after petal fall) and the other in midsummer. Feeding by the second generation causes most of the fruit damage. Pheromone traps containing the sex attractant of the female moth can improve treatment timing. (See discussion of pheromone traps in Chapter 3.) Using this technique, insecticides are most effective 10 to 14 days after peak flights are detected in pheromone traps.

Experimental work indicates that pheromones may be effectively used in the "male confusion" method of control of codling moths in large block-planted orchards. This entails permeating the air with the sex attractant used by the females to attract males, reducing mating. In backyard settings, this would be most effective only if apple and pear trees are isolated from other sources of codling moths (including crabapple trees), which could otherwise migrate into the yard. These are not yet available to gardeners, as they are only beginning to be marketed to commercial growers on an experimental basis.

Fruittree Leafroller
(*Archips argyrospilus*)

Damage: Caterpillars of the fruittree leafroller feed on the leaves of various fruit trees, shade trees, and shrubs. The caterpillars first tie the leaves together and then feed by skeletonizing the leaf, avoiding the larger veins. Leafroller outbreaks are rare but can result in large areas of temporary leaf loss. On fruit trees, the developing fruit may be enveloped within the tied leaves and chewed, later resulting in deep scarring.

Life History and Habits: The fruittree leafroller overwinters as eggs laid in masses on twigs and small branches. These eggs hatch shortly after buds open in the spring, and the young caterpillars migrate to the leaves. The caterpillars, which are pale green with a dark head, continue to feed and develop over a period of a month or more, then eventually crawl down the trunk or drop to the ground on silk strings. They pupate under bark flaps or other protected sites, forming a thin cocoon. The moths emerge in late spring and early summer, mate, and then lay eggs. There is one generation per year.

Natural and Biological Controls: Numerous parasites attack leafrollers, generally restricting populations below levels that are damaging to the plants. Leafroller infestations can become chronic in orchards when insecticides destroy their natural controls. Leafrollers are susceptible to *Bacillus thuringiensis*.

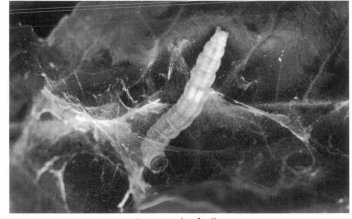
Fruittree leafroller

Chemical Controls: Several insecticides control leafrollers. But once the leaves are tightly rolled, insecticides often cannot reach the caterpillars. Systemic insecticides, which can kill the caterpillars, cannot be applied to fruit trees or other edible plants. However, dormant oil sprays can destroy many of the eggs that overwinter on twigs.

Miscellaneous Notes: Leafrolling with silk is not practiced by many other garden inhabitants. Spiders will tie leaves together when they produce an egg sac. A few other caterpillars, such as webworms, may produce some silk on leaves but do not tightly fold them. Tent caterpillars and fall webworms produce large amounts of silk and feed in groups, but do not roll leaves.

Diamondback moth

Diamondback Moth (Plutella xylostella)

Damage: Diamondback moth caterpillars feed on the leaves of cabbage and related plants. Although very common, the larvae are quite small and consume considerably less than other cabbageworms (imported cabbageworms, cabbage loopers, etc.)—about 3 percent as much as cabbage loopers, for example. However, populations can be high and cause serious injury.

Life History and Habits: The diamondback moth spends the winter in the adult stage. This small moth is one of the first insects to be active in the spring. Eggs are laid singly or in small groups on the leaves of various mustard family plants (Brassicaceae). The first, early-spring generation tends to reside on winter annual mustard plants. Larvae feed on the surface of the leaves and pupate in a loose cocoon attached to the plant. Generations are completed within approximately 4 to 6 weeks, with several occurring throughout the season.

Natural and Biological Controls: Parasitic wasps are the natural enemies of diamondback moth larvae. General insect predators (spiders, damsel bugs, etc.) are also contributing controls and the moths are susceptible to Bt.

Chemical Controls: Chemical controls are similar to those used for other cabbageworms. The habit of diamondback moth caterpillars to remain exposed on the plant simplifies application. However, in several areas of North America,

Diamondback moth larva

this insect has become highly resistant to insecticides and is extremely difficult to control once established.

Miscellaneous Notes: The caterpillar stage of the diamondback moth is hyperactive and wriggles vigorously when disturbed—an identifying characteristic singling it out from other cabbageworms. Caterpillars may also temporarily drop from the plant in response to a disturbance. They later climb back up the silken thread spun while dropping.

Western Grapeleaf Skeletonizer (Harrisina brillans)

Damage: A native insect originally associated with wild grapes, caterpillars of the western grapeleaf skeletonizer also feed on the leaves of cultivated grapes, Virginia creeper, and related ivies. Severe defoliation, though rare, can reduce subsequent yields and open canopies, resulting in sunburning of the fruit. The brightly colored caterpillars attract attention and some people become sensitized to the hairs of the insect. The western grapeleaf skeletonizer inhabits the southwestern United States and northern Mexico.

Life History and Habits: In a loose cocoon often under flaps of bark or other protective cover, the skeletonizer overwinters in the pupal stage. Adults emerge in the spring, a few weeks after the first signs of growth, and the females lay their eggs in masses on older, more shaded leaves. The newly emerged caterpillars eat ravenously, as a group, for the first couple of weeks, while older

Western grapeleaf skeletonizer

larvae disperse throughout the plant. Larvae of the first generation pupate in early summer and a second generation, produced later in the season, feeds in late August and September.

Natural and Biological Controls: Several parasitic wasps and a tachinid fly are native natural enemies of the western grapeleaf skeletonizer. Also, a virus disease is thought to make a significant contribution to regulating populations in wild grape. The caterpillars are vulnerable to *Bacillus thuringiensis*.

Cultural Controls: Check loose bark for pupae and destroy them before the adults emerge in the spring. To exclude migrant moths, establish plantings a good distance apart from wild grape and other hosts of this insect.

Chemical Controls: Western grapeleaf skeletonizers are easily controlled with sprays of most garden insecticides registered for use on grapes.

Peach Tree Borer (*Synanthedon exitiosa*)

Damage: These larvae tunnel under the bark of peach, plum, cherry, apricot, and other species of *Prunus*, usually near the base of the tree. The tunneling injuries subsequently weaken and often kill trees.

Life History and Habits: The adult moths emerge from mid-June through August. Females lay their eggs on lower trunks or in nearby soil cracks, particularly favoring previously wounded trees. The eggs hatch in 1 to 2 weeks, and the small larvae tunnel into the outer layers of bark. They continue to feed through late spring if temperatures allow, producing deep, gouging wounds that may devastate all of the lower bark. Pupation takes place in a silken cocoon, mixed with wood fragments, usually on the surface of the lower trunk.

Natural and Biological Controls: Experimental work suggests that drenching with insect-parasitic nematodes around the base of trees during late summer or early spring can kill some larvae be-

fore they cause serious damage. However, it is not known if this will also control larvae deep within masses of gum.

Cultural Controls: Egg laying is concentrated around wounds. Practices that prevent wounding and that control existing peach tree borer infestations can deter later infestations by the insect. White paint applied to the lower trunk can seal bark cracks often used by female moths for laying eggs.

Mechanical Controls: Individual larvae can be dug out or destroyed using a sharp wire. However, this needs to be done with care to avoid further tree damage.

Chemical Controls: Larvae cannot be controlled with insecticide sprays after tunneling has progressed. Preventive treatments of insecticides should be applied to the trunk while the moths are active and eggs are being laid, typically in early July and August. "Borer crystals" (paradichlorobenzene) can be used to fumigate larvae within the trunk. Apply crystals around the base of the trunk and temporarily mound with soil to retain the fumigant gas in the area of the borer infestation. The crystals should not directly touch the trunk. Application rates vary relative to trunk diameter and are indicated on label directions. Fumigation rescue treatments are best applied during warm periods in the fall, after harvest. However, future registration of paradichlorobenzene for use on fruit trees may become more restricted, so always check labels to ensure that they are registered for this use.

Miscellaneous Notes: Infestations of peach tree borers result in an accumulation of clear gum mixed with light brown wood fragments at wound areas. Almost all injuries occur at, or slightly below, the soil line, in contrast to other gumming on stone fruits caused by stress, mechanical injury, or infection with Cytospora fungi (see page 173). These latter problems are indicated by a clear, amber gum and can occur throughout the upper areas of the tree.

Belowground injury to plum caused by peach tree borer

Peach tree borer larva

Currant Borer
(Synanthedon tipuliformes)

Damage: The larvae of currant borers tunnel canes, particularly near the base of the plant. Leaves on the infested canes are small and yellow, and the canes often die back.

Life History and Habits: Currant borers spend the winter nearly full-grown in the base of the canes of currant, gooseberry, sumac, or black elder. They feed for a brief period in spring but cause little damage, then pupate, and later emerge as adults in late May or early June. The bluish-black adult clearwing borer moths resemble wasps and can be observed resting or mating on the leaves of the plants. Eggs are laid on the bark during June and early July, and the caterpillar stage larvae then bore into the plant. They move downward, tunneling the pith and wood. (Unlike the bronzed cane borer, they do not produce visible swellings on the cane surface.) These feeding injuries may girdle or weaken the plant, causing dieback of the canes in late summer.

Natural and Biological Controls: Insect-parasitic nematodes (species of *Steinernema*), applied as a drench to the crown area of the plants, control currant borer larvae that are tunneling canes.

Mechanical Controls: Cut out and discard all canes that show evidence of wilting and dieback in the spring, before the adult moths emerge.

Cultural Controls: Increasing plant vigor through proper culture minimizes the severity of infestations. Pruning overmature and damaged canes before insects emerge can also reduce problems.

Chemical Controls: Control of currant borers with insecticides has met with only marginal success. If attempted, treatments applied should coincide with periods when the moths are flying and laying eggs, typically early June. However, very few insecticides are registered that allow use on currants and gooseberries.

Associated Insects: The bronze cane borer (see page 96) is the borer most often associated with the canes of small fruit. The damaging stage is the flathead borer that develops in and girdles above ground parts of the cane.

Adult currant borer

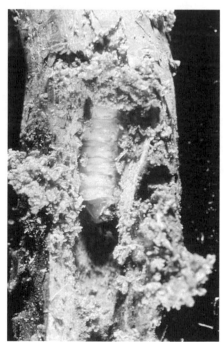

Raspberry crown borer larva and injury (Photo by John Capinera)

Raspberry Crown Borer
(Pennisetia marginata)

Damage: The larvae tunnel into the base (crown) of raspberry plants, which causes the entire cane to wilt and often kills the plants. The destruction is most severe in midsummer.

Life History and Habits: The life cycle of the raspberry crown borer takes 2 years to complete. Adult moths emerge from the base of infested plants from mid-July through August. After mating, the females lay their eggs around the canes. The eggs then hatch in 3 to 5 weeks, and the young borer larvae tunnel into the lower canes. The first winter is passed in a small chamber cut into the side of the lower canes. The larvae feed throughout much of the following season, eventually moving to the soft areas within the crown, where they overwinter a second season and resume feeding in spring. The majority of the damage is created by the larger, nearly full-grown larvae. During June and July, the larvae stop feeding, pupate, and later emerge as adult moths.

Natural and Biological Controls: Drenches of insect-parasitic nematodes (species of *Steinernema*) around the base of plants control larvae.

Mechanical Controls: Dig up and discard infested plants as soon as wilting is evident to kill the larvae before they emerge.

Chemical Controls: Applications of the insecticide diazinon, sprayed directly at the base of the plant during late summer, kills the moths along with the newly hatched larvae. Drenches of insecticides applied after harvest in early fall also destroy young larvae before they inflict serious injury. However, the registration of this treatment may be discontinued by the manufacturer. The raspberry crown borer has a life cycle that spans

2 years, so controls need to be sustained over a 2- to 3-year period during outbreaks.

Associated Insects: The bronze cane borer (see page 96) and stemboring sawfly (see page 116) are other regional insects that damage roses and raspberries.

Larvae of crown-boring moths also can affect strawberries. The strawberry crown moth, *Synanthedon bibionipennis,* is a clearwing borer originating from the Pacific Northwest. The strawberry crownminer, *Aristotelia fragariae*—the larva of a small moth—carves meandering tunnels throughout the crown.

Snailcase Bagworm (Apterona helix)

Damage: The larvae chew on the leaves of a wide variety of plants, including many garden flowers as well as weeds. Often little injury results, but sometimes these unusual insects instill a sense of panic as they attach themselves firmly to the undersides of fences, mailboxes, and building siding in preparation for the pupal stage. The snailcase bagworm is an introduced insect that has recently spread to many locations in western North America.

Life History and Habits: The snailcase bagworm derives its name from the coiled case it produces. This case is made out of silk but is also covered

Snailcase bagworm

with debris and the insect's fecal matter. Overwintering stages are as eggs, found within the sack. The tiny larvae are conveniently dispersed by winds as they emerge in spring. They soon produce the sack, which expands as they grow and feed during late spring and early July. When fully grown, they migrate and attach themselves to aboveground surfaces, and later pupate. The adult moth that subsequently develops never leaves the case and lays eggs within days. No males or winged stages ever exist. There is just one generation per year.

Natural and Biological Controls: *Bacillus thuringiensis,* applied to plants on which the young snailcase bagworms are feeding, should provide sufficient control.

Chemical Controls: No chemical control trials have ever been conducted with this insect. However, it can be expected that insecticides effective against most caterpillars (e.g., Sevin®, Orthene®, permethrin) would similarly be effective against this insect. Full-grown larvae wandering about in search of pupation sites are not susceptible to insecticides.

HYMENOPTERA (BEES, ANTS, SAWFLIES, ETC.)

Leafcutter Bees (species of Megachile)

Damage: Leafcutter bees cut distinctive semicircular notches out of leaves. Roses and ash trees are particularly favored by the bees. When leafcutter bees are very abundant, their damage can slightly reduce plant vigor and the quality of rose blossoming. Gardens established in desert areas often serve as welcome oases for leafcutter bees. In these instances, plantings can be devastated.

Life History and Habits: Adult leafcutter bees resemble small, dark bumblebees. They are solitary bees; each female individually rears her young. When rearing their young, the female bees cut leaves from roses, ash, and other plants. They work quickly and leaf cutting is very rapid,

Leafcutter bee

occurring in as little as 10 seconds. The bees then take the leaf disks to nest sites excavated out of rotten wood, pithy plants, or other hollows. The leaves are formed into thimble-shaped rearing cells, which are then packed with pollen on which the young are nourished.

Biological Controls: Leafcutter bees are attacked by many insects. Nests are frequently destroyed by blister beetles and velvet ants. Robber flies kill adult bees.

Cultural and Mechanical Controls: Usually, leafcutter damage to a rose plant is little more than a curiosity and does not require control. Insect populations are reduced by limiting breeding sites, such as the exposed pith of rose and caneberries, by sealing the openings with glue, shellac, or a tack. Where leafcutter bees are abundant, protecting susceptible plants with netting is the only effective control.

Chemical Controls: Many insecticides will immediately kill the adult bees, but they need to be reapplied frequently. Because of the beneficial habits of leafcutter bees as pollinators, insecticides should be considered only when very serious infestations threaten. Insecticides are not effective where very high leafcutter bee populations occur.

Miscellaneous Notes: Most leafcutter bees (unlike honeybees) are native insects that are useful pollinators of several native plants and alfalfa. Many do not cut leaves but instead make mud-lined nests such as the mason bees (*Osmia* species).

Gall Wasps
(species of Diplolepis)

Damage: Several species of gall wasps are associated with *Rosa* species, producing bizarre growths on the leaves and stems known as galls. These may take the form of balls, spikes or mossy growths. Species, rugosa, and old garden roses are most commonly galled. Little plant injury results from these galls; they are primarily a curiosity.

Life History and Habits: The biology of these insects is poorly understood. The common species that produce galls on stems overwinter in cells within the old galls, emerging during warm days in late winter. The adults are small, inconspicuous, dark wasps, and the females lay eggs in the dormant buds. The eggs hatch and the larvae feed on the buds as they begin to grow in the spring, inducing the distortion that ultimately produces the gall. Larvae live within the gall throughout their development, pupating the following winter. There is one generation per year. Species that produce leaf galls apparently lay eggs later in the season and may exhibit alternate forms during the season.

Mechanical Controls: Old galls can be handpicked and destroyed before the adult insects emerge in late winter.

Chemical Controls: None has been identified. Insecticides applied in midwinter as adults are laying eggs should be effective, but accurately timing such an application is difficult.

Stemboring Sawfly
(Hartigia trimaculata)

Damage: A cane borer that typically infests roses and raspberry plants is the stemboring sawfly. Damage is primarily caused by the larvae, which tunnel into the stem, often girdling it. The top of the plant, beyond the injury, wilts and dies. Canes break easily at the injury point. Rose plantings near wild roses are more likely to be infested, since the wild plants may be a reservoir of the insects.

Life History and Habits: The adult stage is an elongate, 1/2-inch, black and yellow wasp. Adults emerge in late April and May and insert eggs under the bark at the tips of current season canes. Upon hatching, the larvae enter the stems to feed. They feed in the pith, eventually forming a small chamber in the upper part of the stem during late June and July. There they pupate and a second

Stem gall of rose

Rose stem galls produced by gall wasps

generation of adult wasps gnaw their way out and emerge in late summer. These, too, lay eggs, which hatch into larvae that eventually tunnel downward, passing the winter near the base of the plant.

Natural and Biological Controls: Parasitic wasps commonly attack and kill full-grown sawfly larvae as they prepare to pupate.

Cultural Controls: Destroy the developing larvae by cutting and destroying the canes in which injury is first detected. Cut each affected cane below the wilted portion and examine the pith. Continue making short cuts until the pith is white.

Related Insects: Another stemboring sawfly, the raspberry horntail (*Hartigia cressoni*), attacks berry crops in the Pacific states.

Imported Currantworm (*Nematus ribesii*)

Damage: Currantworm larvae chew the leaves of currants and gooseberries, often defoliating the plants early in the season. Foliage in the interior of the bush is damaged first, but all the leaves may eventually be devoured. Both the yield and quality of the fruit may be adversely affected by this injury.

Life History and Habits: The imported currantworm spends the winter in a cocoon in the soil surrounding previously infested currants and gooseberries. The adult, a black and yellow wasp about 1/3 inch long, emerges early in the spring, usually by the first week of May. After mating, the female lays a series of white, oblong eggs in rows along the main veins of the leaf's underside. The larvae hatch about 7 to 10 days after the eggs are laid and initially feed in groups, chewing small holes in the interior of the leaves. Later they disperse throughout the plant and feed along the leaf margins, becoming fully grown in about 3 weeks. The young larvae are pale green, but develop distinctive dark spots as they grow and reach a size of about 3/4 inch. The full-grown larvae then drop to the ground

and fashion their cocoons. Some pupate and emerge in late June and July, producing a small second generation. However, the great majority of insects become dormant and emerge the following year, and rarely is there more than one period per year, in which the damage caused is severe.

Mechanical Controls: In small plantings, the larvae are controlled by simply handpicking or shaking. Careful examination of newly emerging leaves will reveal the eggs, which may then be crushed. Most eggs and larvae are found residing in the interior of the shrub. At the end of the season, rake and remove all debris from the base of the plants. Most of the overwintering cocoons are in this leaf litter and can be destroyed by this practice. A strong jet of water can also dislodge many larvae, few of which will be able to recolonize the plant.

Cultural Controls: This insect prefers damaging shrubs that are located in the shade. Planting in sun-exposed areas can reduce infestation.

Chemical Controls: Check plants for early signs of infestation. Egg laying is concentrated on the interior leaves and the newly hatched larvae create small "pinhole" chewing wounds in leaves.

Larvae can be controlled with sprays of diluted dishwashing detergent and insecticidal soaps. Other chemical control options are limited on currants and gooseberries with some formulations of pyrethrins and malathion being registered for the crops. However, most garden formulations of malathion do not permit use on these fruits. Sprays of irritants, such as soaps and wood ashes, have been reported to dislodge many of the larvae.

Miscellaneous Notes: The currant spanworm is another insect that often feeds on the leaves of currants and gooseberries. The larvae of this insect are also spotted, but are actually a type of inchworm with a distinctive looping walk. These are the immature stages of a small moth. The caterpillars of this insect, but not currantworms, are susceptible to Bt.

Stemboring sawfly larva in raspberry cane

Imported currantworm larva

Roseslug larva and injury

Pearslug larvae and injury

Rose/Caneberry Sawflies
Roseslug (*Endelomyia aethiops*)
Bristly roseslug
(*Cladius difformis*)
Raspberry sawfly
(*Monophadnoides geniculatus*)

Damage: Several sawflies feed on the leaves of roses and raspberries. The roseslug is a smooth, pale green worm that feeds on the undersides of rose leaves, producing characteristic "window pane" injuries that result from leaving the thin upper leaf surface intact. More elongated holes tend to be cut by the bristly roseslug. Under most conditions, defoliation caused by these insects is minor, but occasionally serious problems do occur.

Life History and Habits: Roseslug sawflies overwinter within a cocoon buried shallowly in the soil within the vicinity of previously infested plants. The adult stage is a small, thick-bodied wasp that emerges in May or June. Female wasps insert their eggs into the leaf, and about a week later the newly emerged larvae begin to feed. Feeding usually continues over a period of 2 to 3 weeks, and the fully grown larvae then drop to the ground, dig a small chamber in the soil, and prepare the cocoon for pupation. The roseslug propagates only a single generaton per year, but bristly roseslug injury to raspberries sometimes is the work of a small second generation.

Mechanical Controls: Hosing leaves with water readily dislodges most feeding larvae.

Chemical Controls: Significant injury by roseslugs is extremely rare and controls are often unnecessary. The roseslugs are also susceptible to essentially all garden insecticides, except *Bacillus thuringiensis*.

Pearslug (Pear Sawfly)
(*Caliroa cerasi*)

Damage: The sluglike larvae of the pearslug feed on the upper leaf surfaces of sweet cherry, plum, pear, and several ornamental shrubs such as cotoneaster. The injury is distinctive—a skeleton-izing defoliation in which the main veins and the lower leaf surfaces are not eaten. When abundant, pearslug injury can result in a reduction in fruit size and production the following season.

Life History and Habits: The pearslug passes the winter as a pupa in a small cocoon at the base of plants that were attacked the previous season. The adult emerges in late spring—a small, black, nonstinging wasp that is rarely observed. After mating, the female wasps insert their eggs into leaves, and the sluglike larvae hatch within 1 to 2 weeks. Young larvae are dark green, often turning more orange as they become nearly full-grown. They then drop from the plant and pupate in the soil. A second generation occurs in mid-August and September. The pearslug is also called the pear sawfly or cherry slug.

Mechanical Controls: Pearslug larvae can be simply washed off plants with a vigorous jet of water.

Chemical Controls: Dusting the plants with wood ashes controls pearslugs. The ashes stick readily to the body of the insect, and excess ashes can be removed immediately just by shaking the plant. This treatment works best during hot, dry weather. The pearslug is also very easy to control with many garden insecticides. Insecticidal soaps are effective but may cause leaf spotting damage on some plums and cherries.

Miscellaneous Notes: Because of their fondness for cherries, pearslugs are often called "cherry slugs." The closely related roseslug is a common pest of roses in the region. Neither of these insects is related to "true" slugs (see page 153), which are mollusks—a very different type of animal.

Western Yellowjacket
(*Vespula pensylvanica*)

Damage: Plant damage by the western yellowjacket is fairly minor and is restricted to that resulting from feeding on ripe fruit, particularly raspberries and peaches, in late summer. However, yellowjackets are the primary stinging insect in the region, typically accounting for at least

95 percent or more of the "bee stings" people report. As nests are usually located underground, their location is often not observed and most stings occur when nests are accidentally disturbed. Yellowjackets are notorious for disrupting outdoor meals and, late in the season, swarming over plants infested with honeydew-producing insects, such as aphids or soft scales. During very dry seasons, they may also become a nuisance around water sources.

Life History and Habits: The western yellowjacket comprises the majority of several types of yellowjackets found in western North America. During winter, only fertile mated "queens" survive, hidden under debris, clapboards of homes, or in other protected sites. In mid-spring the queens emerge from winter dormancy and seek desirable nesting sites. Their nests are almost always located underground, most often in abandoned rodent burrows or hollows under stones or slabs. Wall voids are sometimes inhabited as well. Nesting material is constructed of paper, produced from macerated bark and wood pulp. In design it is similar to the familiar hornet nests that hang from trees and eaves, consisting of layers of cells surrounded by a paper envelope.

Originally the nest is very small, since all the chores of the future colony are being performed by the single queen—nest building, foraging, egg laying, and rearing the young. As a result, the first yellowjackets produced tend to be small. These are infertile females known as workers. They assist with colony development and soon the original queen restricts her duties to those within the nest. Colony size increases almost exponentially during the summer, usually peaking in early September at which time there may be hundreds of individual yellowjackets. Those reared at the end of the summer have the benefit of increased attention from the larger colony of workers and some of these are fertile females, the potential queens of the next season. Some males are also produced, and they mate outside the colony with the queens. After mating the new queens leave the colony for winter shelter.

By early fall the old colony breaks up and all the workers and males die. The old colonies are abandoned and are not reused.

Yellowjackets feed on a wide variety of foods. When rearing young, protein-rich foods are sought. They feed on some live insects but primarily are scavengers, feeding on dead insects or worms, fresh garbage, and carrion. Sugar-rich foods, such as soft drinks and honeydew, are also sought, particularly late in the season.

Mechanical Controls: Yellowjackets can be trapped, using attractive lures. A typical trap consists of a cone-shaped entrance leading into the trap container, such as a fly trap. Fresh tuna fish, cat food, or canned fruit preserves make particularly good baits for yellowjackets, although the attractiveness fades after a couple of days. The western yellowjacket is also attracted to lures containing heptyl butyrate, which is provided with traps of some producers. It is best to use traps early in the season.

Plugging nest entrances may be a solution for nests located deep underground. The colony will immediately try to dig a new entrance and is often successful. *Nest entrances located in buildings should never be plugged* until the colony is destroyed. Often when exterior openings are plugged, the yellowjackets create a new entrance that opens into the building's interior.

Chemical Controls: If the colony location can be identified, it can usually be destroyed with a "wasp and hornet" type of spray. These products typically contain a combination of two insecticides—a fast-acting "knockdown" type, such as pyrethrins, along with some slower acting but more persistent insecticide. Widely available in supermarkets and nurseries, these sprays come in aerosol cans and usually

Western yellowjacket

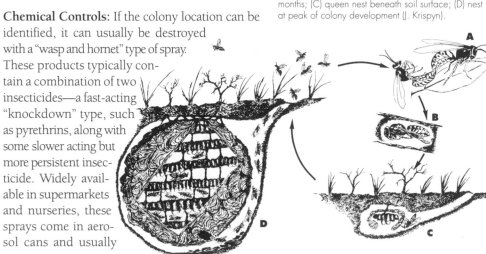

Yellowjacket life cycle *(Vespula pensylvanica):* (A) mating; (B) fertilized queen in diapause during winter months; (C) queen nest beneath soil surface; (D) nest at peak of colony development (J. Krispyn).

contain a propellant that allows one to be several feet away when treating the nest entrance. Spray the nests very late in the day or early in the morning, when yellowjackets are inactive. Because the entrance to the nest may meander, it is often necessary to treat it two or three times before the colony is killed. Colonies that are not in the way and don't pose a stinging risk can be left to die out on their own in the fall.

Field ants

Ants
Field Ants (species of Formica)
Cornfield Ants
(species of Lasius)
and other members of the
family Formicidae

Damage: Little direct damage is sustained by garden plants because of ants. Most problems result from ants protecting honeydew-producing insects, such as aphids and soft scales, or interfering with their biological control. Large ant nests around the root system of established plants can cause wilting, reduced growth and, in extreme cases, the death of plants. A few ants will also "clear" the area around nests, killing plants with their acidic excretions near the entrances.

Many ants also are at least partially predaceous on other insects. For example, fire ants, found in the most southern areas of the United States, are critical biological controls of many pest insects—unfortunately packing the sting that makes them significant pests.

Life History and Habits: All the ant species typically inhabiting gardens are social insects that produce a permanent colony and have different "castes" performing different colony functions.

The great majority of the colony consists of workers, which are wingless sterile females. In mature colonies, some reproductive forms are also produced that possess wings and consist of a large number of males and a lesser number of females. The latter are potential queens capable of establishing a new colony after mating.

"Swarms" of winged ants issue periodically from existing colonies. Typically, swarming behavior is brought on during a warm sunny day in summer that has followed some wet weather. After swarming, the males die and the mated females attempt to initiate new colonies, shedding their wings and sustaining themselves on the energy of their wing muscles. Those very few females that succeed in establishing a new colony are the queens that produce the eggs from which all the colony members originate.

Mechanical Controls: To prevent ants from tending aphid colonies and interfering with biological controls, apply an ant-proof barrier to plant stems, such as the sticky materials used in insect traps (e.g., Tanglefoot®).

Chemical Controls: Individual ant colonies are sometimes eradicated by treating the area around entrances with an insecticide (diazinon, chlorpyrifos). However, the most selective method for ant control is to incorporate a slow-acting insecticide into a bait that allows the toxicant to be moved back to the colony. Boric acid is most often recommended for this purpose. However, *boric acid is toxic to plants* and boron-containing materials should never be applied directly to garden beds.

To make an ant bait, it is first necessary to determine what foods they are actively foraging. Apple jelly, honey, and/or peanut butter are good choices to try as at least one will likely attract most ants. After finding a bait that is readily accepted, add a small amount of boric acid to it (about 1 part in 20, or 5 percent by volume) and let them continue to feed. Don't bother them with insecticide sprays or other disruptive practices! When baiting colonies, it may take a couple of weeks before there is a noticeable decline in ant numbers, but the method is usually more permanent than insecticide sprays that only kill foraging ants outside the colony.

DIPTERA (FLIES)

Seedcorn Maggot
(Delia platura)

Damage: Germinating seeds of beans, corn, squash, and most other garden vegetables can be destroyed or seriously scarred by maggots. Damage is particularly severe where large amounts of decaying organic matter are present and when seeds are planted in overly cool soils. Adult flies also can transmit the bacteria that causes soft rot of vegetables.

Life History and Habits: The seedcorn maggot spends the winter underground in the pupal stage. Adult flies emerge in early spring and lay their eggs in soils rich in organic matter. The newly hatched larvae feed on decaying plant matter, seeds, or seedlings. Their development is rapid and two to three generations may be completed by the time plantings are established in the spring. The flies become dormant during periods of high temperatures and cause little injury after late spring.

Natural and Biological Controls: Dry soil conditions do not favor the survival of eggs and larvae. These soil stages are preyed upon by rove beetles and other predators. Adult flies commonly die from a fungus, which causes them to become stuck to the tops of plants and other high objects. Insect parasitic nematodes (species of *Steinernema*) have been used to attempt to control root maggots but with little success.

Cultural Controls: Plant in a manner that facilitates rapid germination to avoid the effects of maggot feeding. In particular, this involves using an adequately warmed and well-prepared seedbed, and delaying planting of susceptible warm-season crops (beans, corn, squash) until soil temperatures are suitable. Apply only decayed organic matter, such as compost, to avoid attracting egg-laying flies. Till plant debris in the fall and moisten it to encourage some decay before spring.

Mechanical Controls: Yellow sticky traps capture adult flies and help suppress populations. Fine-meshed cloth (such as cheesecloth), row covers, or screening excludes flies from the planting.

Chemical Controls: Some insecticides (e.g., Diazinon®) provide control when applied to the seed (seed treatment) or when used as a band over the plants during seeding.

Related Species: The onion maggot (*Delia antiqua*) is a closely related fly that limits its at-tacks to onions and related plants (see following). The cabbage maggot (*Delia radicum*), which rarely occurs in this region, attacks radishes, turnips, and other mustard family plants. Controls are similar to those of the seedcorn maggot.

Summer-grown spinach and beets occasionally fall prey to the sugarbeet root maggot (*Tetanops myopaeformis*). Larvae tunnel the roots, enabling decay organisms to enter, causing wilting of the entire plant. Local populations can be reduced by pulling plants as soon as harvest is complete and tilling the crop debris to kill larvae that can overwinter. Fluorescent orange is highly attractive to these insects and can be used in traps to capture the adults, which fly during June and early July.

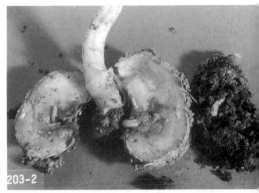
Seedcorn maggot larvae in bean seeds (Photo courtesy Oregon State University)

Onion Maggot
(*Delia antiqua*)

Damage: Onion maggot larvae tunnel into onion plants. Small plants may be killed and larger bulbs may suffer bulb rot due to the wounding. Related alliums (chives, scallions) are also at risk.

Life History and Habits: The onion maggot spends the winter underground in the pupal stage within the puparia—a stage that resembles a dark piece of grain. Adult flies emerge over a period of several weeks in late spring. The flies lay eggs in soil cracks around the base of onion plants. The maggot-stage larvae hatch and tunnel into the plants, feeding specifically around the base. After being sufficiently fed, they move a short distance from the plant and pupate. Two or three generations may occur during the growing season.

Cultural Controls: Dispose of old, infested onions before maggots emerge in the spring to limit overwinter populations. Alternatively, you may wish to plant some rotting onions as a trap crop for the adult onion maggots, which prefer the larger onions early in the season. However, using this technique necessitates that the trap crop onions be destroyed to kill developing maggots. High-moisture conditions favor survival of the

Onion maggot adult

eggs and maggots. Minimizing watering assists in onion maggot control.

Mechanical Controls: In small plantings, floating row covers are effective when combined with crop rotation. Adult flies can also be trapped on yellow sticky cards.

Biological Controls: Several predators of the onion maggot have been found in other areas of North America. In particular, the larvae of rove beetles are significant natural controls. Attempts to control onion maggots with insect-parasitic nematodes have been erratic; *Steinernema feltiae* is better adapted for control of fly larvae and is likely to be most effective.

Chemical Controls: Planting time treatments of Diazinon® controls root maggots in gardens.

Miscellaneous Notes: The seedcorn maggot often attacks onion bulbs that have been damaged by disease. Evidence shows that the seedcorn maggot does not usually damage healthy bulbs, as does the onion maggot.

Related Species: The seedcorn maggot (see page 120) is a close relative that damages germinating seeds and resides in decaying bulbs and tubers. The cabbage maggot, rarely found in this region, attacks radishes, turnips, and other mustard family plants. Cabbage maggot controls are similar to those for onion maggots.

Leafminers

Some of the most discriminating feeders among the insects are the leafminers. These insects tunnel between the upper and lower leaf surfaces, feeding on the soft inner tissue while avoiding the tough epidermis.

Many different types of insects share the leaf-mining habit, including the larvae of various flies, small moths, beetles, and sawfly wasps. However, they are often classified as a group, based on the pattern of the mines they create. *Blotch* leafminers carve irregular blotchy mines that are often black or brown. *Serpentine* leafminers make meandering mines that gradually become larger. The mines produced by *tentiform* leafminers pop up in the middle, like a pup tent.

Leafminer injury, particularly the blotch pattern type, is often easily confused with the leaf spotting caused by infection from various fungi. However, it can be accurately diagnosed by pulling apart the leaf at the injury. Leaves damaged by leafminers have a distinctly separate top and bottom leaf surface and often will contain the insect or its droppings. Leaves damaged by fungi have collapsed and compressed cells, which makes them difficult to separate.

Adult stages of leafminers insert eggs into the leaves or lay them on the lower leaf surface. The young insects tunnel into the leaf, where they develop for about 2 to 4 weeks. Often the insects cut their way out of the mine when they have finished feeding, dropping to the soil to pupate. Most leafminers produce about two generations in a season.

Because the mines are so conspicuous, they often attract attention. However, leafminers rarely cause serious, permanent injury to plants, since plants easily outgrow the damage. Leafminers suffer from many natural enemies, so ignore the problem and they will go away on their own. Spinach leafminers, common on beets, spinach, and chard, can sometimes leave these vegetables looking very unpalatable, however.

Leafminers are protected from most insecticides once they have entered the leaf. Only systemic insecticides are effective after the mining has begun. These include neem-derived insecticides, which have some systemic activity and are known to be particularly effective against leaf-mining flies, such as the vegetable leafminer. (Most systemic insecticides are *not* an option on food plants, although neem is registered for such use and has some systemic activity.) Nonsystemic insecticides are effective only if applied as eggs are laid, before tunneling occurs. Hand crushing eggs, picking infested leaves, and using row covers are other controls.

Blotch leafminers on columbine

TABLE 6-3: COMMONLY ENCOUNTERED LEAF-MINING INSECTS IN WESTERN GARDENS

Leafminer	Plants attacked	Description of mine
Spinach leafminer	Spinach, beets, lambs-quarters, chard	Dark blotch mine
Cottonwood blackmine beetle	Cottonwood, poplars	Dark blotch mine
Vegetable leafminer	Most vegetables (cabbage, melons, onions, celery, etc.), some flowers, weeds	Meandering serpentine mine
Lilac leafminer	Lilac	Light blotchy mine, with some leaf folding
Spotted tentiform leafminer	Apple	Light blotchy mine with raised center like a miniature pup tent; spotting on upper surface from sap feeding
Poplar tentiform leafminer	Cottonwood	Similar to above. Generally confined to lower third of cottonwood tree
Columbine leafminer	Columbine	Large blotch mine, usually with some dark areas
Grape leafminer	Grape, Virginia creeper	Very thin serpentine mine
Aspen/poplar leafminer	Aspen, cottonwood, poplar	Very thin serpentine mine

Spinach leafminer larvae exposed from mine

Spinach Leafminer (Pegomyia hyoscyami)

Damage: The immature maggot stage tunnels through older leaves of beets, Swiss chard, spinach, and related weeds such as lambsquarters. The large, dark blotchy mines that result destroy the leaves for use as greens, although the overall effects on plant growth appear to be minimal.

Life History and Habits: The insect overwinters in the soil as a pupa, emerging in mid-spring. The adult flies lay small masses of white eggs on the undersides of older leaves. Once hatched, the young maggots tunnel into the leaves, where they feed, typically for 2 to 3 weeks. Upon becoming full-grown, they cut through the leaf, drop to the ground, and pupate in the soil. Several generations may be completed during the season, but activity virtually ceases in midsummer with most of the damage taking place during the cooler sides of the growing season.

Mechanical and Physical Controls: Floating row covers, cheesecloth, or other screening excludes the adult flies and prevent egg laying. Regularly inspect leaves for newly laid egg masses on leaf undersides, which can then be crushed before tunneling begins. Infested leaves should be picked and destroyed to kill the larvae before they complete their development. These infested leaves need to be removed from the planting area, since the insects can continue to thrive in the picked leaf.

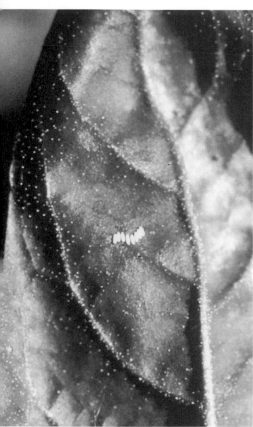

Spinach leafminer eggs on spinach leaf

Small fruit fly or vinegar fly (Photo courtesy of Oregon State University)

Cultural Controls: Fall plantings and very early spring plantings will most likely escape infestations.

Chemical Controls: Weekly applications of insecticides on the foliage destroy adult flies and small larvae before they enter the leaves. No registered insecticides are available that will kill maggots already residing within leaves. Sprays used on spinach usually require that 1 to 2 weeks elapse before it can be harvested.

Vinegar Flies (Fruit Flies) (Drosophila species)

Damage: Vinegar flies are attracted to wounds on fruits and vegetables and to overripe fruit. They do not injure growing plants but can become serious pests of harvested produce as tunneling by the tiny maggots hastens fruit rotting. The small flies also can be very annoying in kitchens and around compost piles and worm beds, where breeding conditions are favorable.

Life History and Habits: Vinegar flies are tiny flies, usually light brown with red eyes. They develop on the yeasts that grow on well-ripened fruit and around wounds of plants. Food residues in beverage containers or garbage cans also support the growth of yeasts and serve as breeding sites. Adults lay eggs in these areas and the young maggots reach maturity in less than a week. Prior to pupation, the larvae migrate away from the food source and attach themselves tightly to plant stems, walls of containers, or other dry areas. Individual adults live about 4 weeks, with females capable of laying a couple dozen eggs daily. Breeding is continuous throughout the warm season, and numerous generations are produced with populations peaking in late summer and early fall. Outdoors, they go into dormancy during the cool season; indoors, they may breed year-round.

Cultural Controls: The first step in managing fruit fly infestations is to eliminate all breeding sites. Susceptible fruits should be refrigerated or discarded. Compost piles should be well maintained to ensure that foods are rapidly buried and begin to decay. (Fruit flies are not attracted to decay produced by bacteria or fungi, which predominate in well-managed compost piles.) Residues in the base of garbage containers, bottles, and cans need to be washed out. Such sanitation practices must be continued for about a month before all the residual flies can be expected to have died out.

Mechanical Controls: Adult flies are attracted to traps baited with mashed banana sprinkled with a bit of yeast. Place a few ounces of the mixture in the bottom of a Mason-type jar and invert a paper funnel at the opening with a $1/2$-inch hole cut in the bottom. Large numbers of vinegar flies may be attracted to such a trap and will remain in it and begin to breed. The contents should be discarded at least every week to 10 days.

Chemical Controls: Pyrethrins sprays are sometimes effective near the harvest time of very susceptible fruits to reduce numbers of adult flies. Such treatments are also successful around garbage cans or other breeding areas during outbreaks. However, insecticides have little effect in a garden if the more fundamental step of reducing breeding material has not been taken.

Apple Maggot (Rhagoletis pomonella)

Damage: Most apple maggot damage results when the young larvae tunnel fruit, producing meandering brown trails that hasten rotting. Egg laying compels the adults to create small puncture wounds in the fruit's surface, which cause

Apple maggot injury to apple

dimplelike distortions. Apples are the primary fruit damaged by apple maggot, but large varieties of crabapple and occasionally European plum and cherries are also infested. Apple-damaging strains of this insect are only locally established, but their distribution is spreading. Native strains of apple maggot that restrict feeding to hawthorn and do not damage apple are widespread in the Rocky Mountain region.

Life History and Habits: The apple maggot is a "picture-winged fly," housefly-sized with dark patterned markings on its wings. During the winter, the apple maggot is in the pupal stage, buried shallowly in soil near previously infested trees. Adults emerge in early summer and the females initially feed on honeydew and other foods for about 2 weeks as their eggs mature. Eggs are inserted under the skin of the fruit and hatch within 1 week. Larvae feed within the fruit for 3 to 4 weeks before dropping to the soil to pupate. Peak egg laying tends to occur during mid to late July. One generation is produced per year.

Mechanical Controls: The apple maggot is one of the few insects that can be controlled by trapping. Newly emerged adults are highly attracted to yellow sticky traps. Females with matured eggs can be trapped using sticky red spheres—"super apples"—that are particularly attractive to them. In many cases using only a couple such traps per tree will adequately control this insect.

Cultural Controls: Apple maggots are more of a threat to soft, early-maturing varieties. Survival is reduced in firm-fleshed, late varieties. A cover of vegetation under the trees has been shown to reduce the survival of these insects as they move from the trees to pupate in the soil.

Chemical Controls: Cover sprays of several insecticides that are labeled for use on apples offer effective control. As with the codling moth, timing is critical and should coincide with peak periods of egg laying. Using yellow sticky cards makes it easier to determine when this occurs, the dark bands on the wings of the flies being distinctive.

Related Species: The walnut husk fly (*Rhagoletis completa*), is widespread in the West, where it feeds on walnuts. It also rarely develops in certain late varieties of peaches.

In some areas of the western United States, the western cherry fruit fly (*Rhagoletis cingulata*) is a serious pest of sweet cherries. Like the apple maggot, the adult female flies "sting" the fruit, producing small puncture wounds. The developing maggots then chew through the flesh of the fruit and infested berries are misshapen and undersized, and mature rapidly. In some regions (e.g., parts of Utah), strains have developed that attack and tunnel apples.

Rose Midge
(*Dasineura rhodophaga*)

Damage: The small maggot stage of the rose midge feeds by making small slashes in developing plant tissues in order to suck the sap. Developing flower buds usually die or are at least distorted by this injury. "Blind" shoots—where no flower buds appear to form—may also be the result of rose midge damage.

Life History and Habits: The rose midge overwinters in the pupal stage in the soil. The adult stage—an inconspicuous, small fly—emerges in late spring, sometimes after the first crop of blossoms. The adult stage lives only 1 or 2 days, but during this time the females lay numerous eggs under the sepals, in opening buds, and in elongating shoots. Hatching larvae slash plant tissues and feed on sap. Eggs hatch within a few days, and the larvae feed for about 1 week before dropping to the soil to pupate. The complete life cycle can take about 2 weeks, with numerous generations occurring during a growing season.

Cultural Control: To avoid introducing rose midge to the soil, purchase bare root roses or roses that were recently potted by local nurseries in the spring from bare root stock. Infested plantings should be examined every few days and all damaged buds trimmed and removed.

Apple maggot "super apple" sticky trap

Chemical Controls: The rose midge is difficult to control with insecticides. (Permethrin and Cygon® have proved effective against related insects, but have not been tested against rose midge.) Treating the soil at the base of the plant with insect-parasitic nematodes or soil insecticides such as Diazinon may reduce populations by killing the insect as it attempts to pupate.

Carrot Rust Fly
(Psila rosae)

Damage: Damage produced by the tiny maggot larvae as they tunnel the roots of carrots is the signature of the carrot rust fly. Meandering scars along the root are typical, and at wound sites the burrows often take on a rusty-red color. These injuries faciliatate the entry of rotting organisms and the invasion of secondary pests such as millipedes and sow bugs, which then cause further injury. Heavy infestations, which are extremely rare in this region, can thoroughly devastate the entire root. Although the carrot is the primary garden plant damaged, carrot rust fly is reported to attack celery, parsley, dill, coriander, celeriac, and fennel.

Life History and Habits: During the winter, carrot rust flies remain in the soil, usually as pupae but occasionally as larvae within roots. They emerge in mid-May, the adult form being a small green fly with a yellow head. Eggs are laid around the base of plants, hatching in 1 to 2 weeks, depending on temperatures. A cycle of feeding by larvae on the roots follows after which there is a second generation, with adults laying eggs in late July and August. A small, third, early-fall generation is also reported in some areas. Carrot rust fly is scattered throughout the region and its distribution is spreading.

Mechanical Controls: Row covers or similar fine mesh netting placed over plants in the spring can prevent egg laying by first-generation adults.

Cultural Controls: Harvest carrots in the fall to prevent remaining larvae from completing development. Similarly, pull other host plants, such as celery and parsley. Till the soil to mix in and bury overwintering larvae and pupae.

Chemical Controls: Planting-time treatments of diazinon mixed in the seed furrow can control the carrot rust fly.

Narcissus Bulb Fly
(Merodon equestris)

Damage: The narcissus bulb fly tunnels into the base of narcissus, daffodil, hyacinth, and many other bulbs during late spring and summer. Bulbs are either killed or are weakened and vulnerable to rot.

Life History and Habits: The insect spends the winter as a large maggot inside the bulb. It pupates the following spring, and the adult flies emerge around mid- to late May, shortly after blooms die back. The narcissus bulb fly is generally dark colored, primarily black with orange or yellow markings, and closely resembles a bumblebee. Female flies lay their eggs in soil cracks around the plant stems for 1 or 2 months after the flowers have withered. The newly hatched maggots crawl down along the plant stem and tunnel into the base of the bulb. They continue to feed throughout the summer, becoming full-grown in fall.

Cultural Controls: Carefully inspect all newly purchased bulbs and discard any that are soft and show signs of rot. Also inspect bulbs during fall digging and discard any that appear infested. Problems with this insect are report-

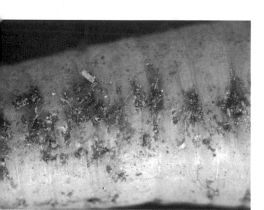

Carrot rust fly larva and injury

Narcissus bulb fly damage and larva

Narcissus bulb fly adult

edly less severe in windswept, as opposed to more protected, sites.

Chemical Controls: Insecticides applied around the base of plants during late spring kill the adult flies and newly hatched maggots. Egg laying, however, takes place over an extended period and necessitates multiple treatments.

Related Insects: The lesser bulb fly (*Emerus strigatus*) is a small fly that has been found in roots and bulbs of narcissus, hyacinth, onion, shallot, and iris. It is considered a secondary pest, rarely affecting bulbs that have not already been damaged or begun to decay.

THYSANOPTERA (THRIPS)

Onion Thrips
(Thrips tabaci)

Damage: Onion thrips feed on the foliage of a wide variety of plants and can be damaging to several vegetables, including onions, beans, and cabbage. Feeding injuries typically appear as silvery scarring wounds in the leaves resulting from the destruction of the upper cell layers. Seedlings sometimes are distorted from this injury, producing tightly curled leaves. As plants mature, sustained high numbers of thrips can reduce the vigor and yield of plants. Some varieties of cabbage react to injuries by producing warty growths, similar to edema, a physiological disorder related to moisture imbalance. (See section on edema on page 184.) Onion thrips are known to transmit tomato spotted wilt virus, but they are much less important vectors of the disease than western flower thrips.

Life History and Habits: Onion thrips overwinter in the adult stage throughout the region in protected sites and old plant materials. They may also be introduced into a field on infested transplants and are common on onion sets. Eggs are inserted into the leaves and stems. They hatch in about 1 week, and two feeding wingless stages (nymphs) develop on the plant, lasting about 2 weeks. These are followed by two nonfeeding stages (pre-pupa and pupa) that occur in the soil or in crevices on the plant. The winged adult stage commonly disperses throughout an area and can fly long distances aided by winds. Several generations occur annually, and all life stages may be present concurrently by early spring.

Natural and Biological Controls: Weather, notably rains that trap insects in the soil, are instrumental in limiting thrips populations. Serious thrips infestations are typically related to extended dry weather. Small predators, such as minute pirate bugs, predatory thrips, and predator mites, also feed on thrips. However, thrips are often well protected within the plant and many predators may be unable to reach them.

Mechanical Controls: Overhead irrigation, or directly hosing the plants, is destructive to thrips and will help provide control.

Cultural Controls: Onions' resistance to thrips is associated with their waxy leaves and a spreading habit of top growth. Cabbage varieties display a wide range of reactions to thrips feeding, with many varieties showing little effect from thrip injury.

Chemical Controls: Thrips exposed on leaves may easily be controlled with insecticidal soaps and many garden insecticides. However, thrips hidden within plant parts, such as the inner leaves of cabbage or onions, can successfully evade control.

Miscellaneous Notes: Onion thrips are commonly found on most produce, making them the most frequently eaten insect in North America.

Onion thrips

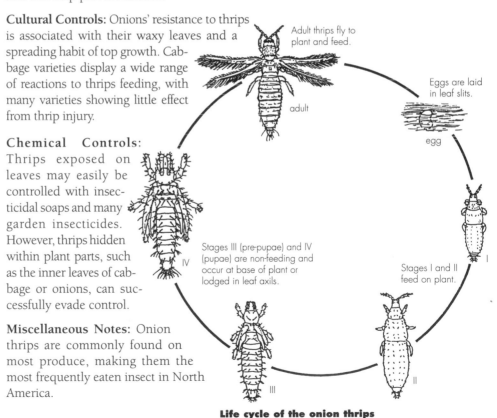

Adult thrips fly to plant and feed.

adult

Eggs are laid in leaf slits.

egg

Stages I and II feed on plant.

Stages III (pre-pupae) and IV (pupae) are non-feeding and occur at base of plant or lodged in leaf axils.

IV

III

II

I

Life cycle of the onion thrips

Flower thrips injury to carnation (Photo by John Capinera)

Gladiolus thrips injury

"Flower Thrips"
Western flower thrips
(Frankliniella occidentalis)
Tobacco thrips
(Frankliniella fusca)
Eastern flower thrips
(Frankliniella tritici) and others

Damage: Scarring injuries to flowers are of particular concern to gardeners. Injuries are usually minor, but occasionally may seriously blemish or distort the flower. Feeding injuries to vegetables are minor, at most only slight scarring. Cloudy "halo spots" may form on fruit around egg-laying puncture wounds. The role of flower thrips to vegetables has expanded in recent years because they are the number-one vector of tomato spotted wilt and impatiens necrotic spot viruses. (See discussion of tomato spotted wilt on page 161.) Tomatoes and peppers, as well as many greenhouse-grown flower crops, have sustained serious losses to this disease.

Life History and Habits: Flower thrips are thought to overwinter in much of the region in the adult stage. In addition, many also migrate, carried on winds from the South. The adults tend to seek out flowers for feeding and egg laying, although feeding sometimes targets on foliage. Eggs are laid into plant tissues and the nymphs feed on the flowers and developing fruit for about 1 1/2 weeks. Two non-feeding stages ("pre-pupa," "pupa") follow, which take place in the soil around the base of the plant or in crevices of the plant. Generations are produced throughout the growing season at approximately 3- to 4-week intervals.

Natural and Biological Controls: Heavy rains and crusting soils constitute abiotic controls of flower thrips. Predatory thrips and minute pirate bugs are natural enemies that reduce each other's overall populations. Releases of predatory mites (species of *Amblyseius*) have controlled flower thrips in greenhouses. Sprays of *Beauveria bassiana* can assist in control as well.

Mechanical Controls: Overhead irrigation decimates many thrips. Regularly "deadheading" flowers and discarding them will kill thrips developing in blossoms and reduce local population development. Yellow and, particularly, "baby blue"–colored sticky traps are very effective at capturing winged thrips. This technique is widely used in greenhouses, but its effectiveness for control of flower thrips outdoors is unproven and may be impractical due to the migratory behavior of the insects.

Cultural Controls: Dark flowers with blue coloration are more attractive to the adult thrips. The best way to prevent tomato spotted wilt is to make sure that only disease-free transplants are used. Although transmission of the disease between garden plants can occur, as it often does in warmer areas of the country, most spread of tomato spotted wilt in the West is usually limited to greenhouses. Diseased plants should be removed and promptly destroyed (to kill the thrips), particularly early in the season.

Chemical Controls: Controlling flower thrips with chemicals is difficult and seldom exceeds 50 percent. Organophosphate insecticides with some systemic activity, such as Orthene® and Dursban®, are currently the most effective.

Gladiolus Thrips
(Thrips simplex)

Damage: Gladiolus thrips are very small but they are also extremely destructive to gladiolus. Feeding by gladiolus thrips results in scarring injuries caused when the insect punctures cells and removes plant sap. Infested leaves appear silvery, later browning and dying. Thrips damage to developing flowers causes flecking and distortion. Heavy infestations will prevent flower production altogether. Gladiolus thrips also damage corms in storage, causing them to become sticky and dark from plant sap at wounds. Infested corms will produce poorly when replanted. Gladiolus thrips also feed on lily and iris, which are rarely seriously damaged.

Life History and Habits: In this region, gladiolus thrips cannot survive winters outdoors. Infestations are maintained by thrips that move to corms and hibernate on them in winter storage areas. When corms are replanted in the spring and temperatures rise above 60°F, the thrips begin to reproduce and infest the developing shoots. Several generations of gladiolus thrips occur during the growing season, each of which may be completed within a few weeks.

Mechanical and Physical Controls: Corms can be rid of thrips by dropping them in a hot water bath, between 112°F and 120°F, for 20 to 30 minutes. Spraying developing plants repeatedly with a vigorous jet of water kills exposed thrips, although many will remain protected in developing leaves.

Chemical Controls: Corms can be fumigated with naphthalene mothballs. The treatment requires exposure for 1 1/2 to 3 weeks at temperatures above 50°F. During the growing season, gladiolus thrips can be controlled with insecticides, particularly those that are systemic. However, because gladiolus thrips tend to hide in tightly curled new growth, it is difficult to achieve effective coverage, and repeated applications are required.

Orthoptera (Grasshoppers, Crickets, etc.)

Grasshoppers
Redlegged grasshopper
(Melanoplus femur-rubrum)
Differential grasshopper
(Melanoplus differentialis)
Twostriped grasshopper
(Melanoplus bivittatus)
Migratory grasshopper
(Melanoplus sanguinipes)
and others

Damage: During outbreak periods, grasshoppers are one of the premier destructive pests of vegetable crops, flowers, rangeland, and many field crops in the West. Pest species will chew on leaves and flowers, sometimes extensively defoliating and even killing the plants. Although some garden plants seem to be preferred (e.g., lettuce, beans, corn, most flowers), essentially all plants are potential food. When very high populations are present, twigs and stems of woody plants may also be chewed and girdled.

Life History and Habits: Most of the pest species of grasshoppers in the region spend the winter as eggs. These are laid underground in late summer or early fall in the form of elongate egg pods containing 20 to 120 eggs each. Egg laying is concentrated in dry, undisturbed areas, heavy along roadsides, in pasturelands, and on native prairie. Relatively little egg laying occurs in an irrigated yard or garden, and, if it does, is limited to small, dry areas in the yard, such as between sidewalk cracks. Eggs hatch in late May and June. The immature nymphs take 2 to 3 months to fully develop. Adults are present during August and remain until they are killed by a heavy frost. Grasshoppers feed during the day, resting on shrubbery, tall plants, or structures during the late afternoon and night. Their movement into yards accelerates as native vegetation becomes less available due to summer drying or defoliation. Light frosts that may kill many host plants in the fall further concentrate grasshoppers on the remaining plants.

Natural and Biological Controls: Grasshopper outbreaks tend to occur in cycles of roughly 11 years, with populations often lasting for 2 to 3 years. However, localized occurrences can be much more erratic. A large number of natural controls limit outbreaks. Cool, wet weather in the spring, particularly around the period of egg hatch, is one of the conditions most often associated with

Grasshopper ovipositing (Photographer unknown)

The Mystery of the Rocky Mountain Locust

One of the gravest threats to the early European settlers of western North America was the Rocky Mountain locust, *Melanoplus spretus*. Periodically, huge swarms of these migratory grasshoppers would take flight from their breeding areas in Colorado, Wyoming, Montana, and the prairie provinces and sweep across a broad area that could extend from eastern Washington to Minnesota and south to Texas and Louisiana. Swarms so dense that they literally blackened the sky were reported almost every year between 1860 and 1880. The intensity of the situation makes current grasshopper woes seem tame, as indicated in an account of an 1874 outbreak by Nebraska settler Everett Dick, in his book *The Sodhouse Frontier:*

> They came like driving snow in the winter, filling the air, covering the earth, the buildings, the shocks of grain, and everything. ... Their alighting on the roofs and sides of the houses sounded like a continuous hail storm. They alighted on trees in such great numbers that their weight broke off large limbs ... At times the insects were four to six inches deep on the ground and continued to alight for hours. Men were obliged to tie strings around their pant legs to keep the pests from crawling up their legs.

These flights of locusts have occurred for centuries, recorded in the famous Grasshopper Glacier near Granite Peak, Montana, where layers of grasshoppers have collected in bands. However, shortly after the new settlements began to spread and grow in earnest, the Rocky Mountain locust disappeared. No living specimen of this insect has been observed since 1902. Like the passenger pigeon, another animal that once was abundant beyond number, the Rocky Mountain locust appears to have become extinct!

What happened is one of the great mysteries of entomology. Some have speculated that the Rocky Mountain locust is still roaming in the guise of another grasshopper species that has retained a non-outbreak form. After all, the locusts of Northern Africa and the Mormon cricket of the western United States have "Dr. Jeckyl and Mr. Hyde" forms, with radical changes in appearance and habits between the outbreak and endemic stages. However, no one has ever been able to induce changes in any other grasshopper that would transform it into the Rocky Mountain locust of old.

The most likely explanation has to do with the environmental changes effected by ranching and farming. Although the Rocky Mountain locust ranged over a wide area, its egg beds were restricted to areas along streams and rivers. The elimination of the buffalo and its replacement with cattle could have been catastrophic to the insect, as cattle concentrated along these riparian habitats, destroying the habitat of egg beds. The extirpation of beaver may have contributed as well, since their damming of streams helped to modify stream flows and reduce flooding. And, of course, farmers settled extensively along river valleys, their cultivation of fields further destroying the eggs. Whatever the cause or causes, the Rocky Mountain locust remains the *only pest insect* that has ever been driven to extinction by human activity.

Rocky Mountain locust, laying eggs in the ground. (A) females with their abdomens in the ground; (B) an egg pod broken open; (C) scattered eggs; (D) egg packet in the ground.

declining grasshopper populations. Grasshoppers are also vulnerable to several diseases. The fungal disease *Entomophthora grylli* is very destructive to populations, although its spread is dependent on adequate moisture. A large nematode (*Mermis nigrescens*), several inches in length, also kills or sterilizes many grasshoppers. The microsporidian *Nosema locustae,* too, destroys or weakens grasshoppers. It is also manufactured and sold as a type of microbial insecticide under trade names such as Semaspore®, Grasshopper Spore®, and NoLo Bait®. It is most effective against young grasshoppers and will kill many of them under optimum conditions. Older grasshoppers are much less sensitive and rarely die, although they may lose vigor and lay fewer eggs the following season. Since *N. locustae* is slow acting, it is not recommended for use within the garden when grasshoppers are moving into the yard. Instead, it should be applied to breeding areas outside the yard before migrations occur.

Insects that feed on grasshoppers include the larvae of blister beetles (predators of the eggs), robber flies, and parasitic flies. Grasshoppers are also food for many birds such as the horned lark, American kestrel, and Swainson's hawk. Poultry, notably guinea hens and turkeys, eagerly devour grasshoppers and assist in controlling moderate grasshopper populations. Grasshoppers have even been used as a highly nutritious poultry feed.

Cultural Controls: Maintaining relatively lush areas of grass or other plants around the perimeter of a property can divert the feeding activities of many grasshoppers from the vegetable or flower garden. (This technique is further improved if this trap crop is treated with an insecticide.) Grasshoppers are excluded by floating row covers, although they can chew through lightweight fabrics and plastic screens. Tillage in the garden destroys most egg pods that are laid in these sites. During outbreaks, it becomes almost impossible to grow many of the plants favored by grasshoppers, so it is sometimes best to concentrate on growing early-maturing varieties and plants that are less appealing to grasshoppers, such as squash and tomatoes.

Chemical Controls: Since grasshoppers typically breed outside of the yard or garden, controlling grasshoppers in these areas is most productive. Sprays of several insecticides kill grasshoppers on rangeland and in pastures. In addition, various baits can be used (insecticide on a molasses-bran base) that facilitate selective application, harming fewer beneficial insects. As grasshoppers pour over the fence, insecticide treatments in the yard and garden are of little effect. The relatively short duration of the insecticides (usually only a couple of days), plus the continuous immigration of new grasshoppers, means that sprays must be reapplied frequently to have any effect.

Miscellaneous Notes: More than eighty species of grasshoppers are native to the High Plains and Rocky Mountain region. Most of these do not occur in large numbers though they are destructive pests. Many also have selective feeding habits and feed only on grasses or native shrubs (forbs) that keep them out of yards and gardens. The life cycles of various grasshoppers also vary, with many overwintering as nymphs or adults.

A perfect setting for grasshopper problems in the garden

DERMAPTERA (EARWIGS)

European Earwig (*Forficula auricularia*)

Damage: The European earwig is the earwig typically found within the High Plains and Rocky Mountain region, having migrated into the area during the 1940s and 1950s. Their appetites are capricious and they feed on several types of plant materials. Flower blossoms, corn silks (and some corn kernels), and tender vegetable seedlings comprise the earwigs' diet. Their habit of crawling into tight, dark places to spend the day accounts for their unwanted presence in harvested fruits, vegetables, and flowers. The European earwig also feeds on many insects and has even been used to control aphids in fruit trees. Soft-bodied insects, such as aphids, insect eggs, and young insect larvae, also satiate earwigs.

European earwig hiding in flower

European earwig (Female left; male right)

Earwigs

Few garden insects are so universally loathed as the earwig. Its prominent pincers (more correctly known as forceps or cerci) have inspired numerous folktales. Earwigs have the habit of seeking out dark (preferably humid), tight spots in which to spend the day. This means they can get into almost everything and are often encountered where we least expect them.

The most common earwig found in the region is the European earwig (*Forficula auricularia*). An introduced species, the European earwig spread into the Rocky Mountain area shortly after World War II. Although they have wings, they are not known to fly. Yet they have been readily distributed throughout the region by "piggybacking" along with human cargo.

Earwigs can cause damage in vegetable and flower gardens. Tight flower petals and corn silks are their favorite hiding sites. Soft plant materials, such as flower petals and seedling plants, may be destroyed. However, earwigs are often blamed for injuries caused by other insects. For example, tunneling wounds produced by codling moth caterpillars in fruit, or borers in vegetables, are often visited by earwigs seeking a daytime shelter. Although they did not cause the original injury, earwigs often show up at the "scene of the crime."

Conversely, earwigs also have several desirable habits that are often overlooked. Insects as well as plants are fed upon, and earwigs are significant predators of insects and insect eggs. Indeed, earwigs have even been successfully encouraged (by providing sheltering burlap bands) to control insect pests on fruit trees.

An exemplary model of parental care—for an insect—mother earwigs guard the eggs and tend their young for several weeks until they are able to forage on their own. From our perspective, this should compare very favorably with the "drop off the eggs and run" behavior of most insects. Although an unlikely candidate because of their disfavor by most humans, earwigs would actually be the perfect models for a "Family Week" promotion among insects.

Life History and Habits: Earwigs overwinter in the adult stage. They become active during warm days in late winter. Female earwigs build their nests within small holes dug underneath rocks or in other protected sites. A cluster of about 50 eggs are produced, which are tended by the mother and typically hatch in April. After the eggs hatch, the female continues to guard and care for the young earwigs for several weeks until they have molted and are ready to leave the nest. The young then forage on their own, becoming fully grown in about one month. Often the mother lays a second, smaller egg mass in May or June. There is only one generation per year, but developing earwigs are present throughout the growing season. Foraging occupies their nights, and they move to dark, sheltered areas during the day. As the season progresses they increasingly tend to aggregate in these shelters.

Although European earwigs possess wings, they do not fly.

Biological Control: A tachinid fly parasite of the European earwig, *Bigonicheta spinipennis,* has been introduced into North America and is now well established in the Pacific Northwest. A parasitic nematode (*Mermis micronigrescens*) and fungal diseases (*Metarhizium anisopliae*) are other natural enemies of this insect. Large fluctuations in earwig populations are reported, which may be related to the success of these natural enemies.

Mechanical Controls: The habit of earwigs to seek shelter during the day compels them to collect under boards, burlap, moistened newspapers, or similar objects. They are easily collected from these sites and destroyed. Mulching around plants may also limit earwigs' use of flowers for daytime shelter, thus reducing flower damage. Spring tillage will disturb earwigs that are developing nests in the garden. Baits that attract European earwigs include mixtures of bran with oily peanut butter or fish oil. These baits could be incorporated into traps and have also been used mixed with insecticides.

Chemical Controls: Insecticide-containing baits for earwigs are available from some nurseries. Sprays are also effective for earwig control. These treatments should be directed around the base of plants or under shelters where earwigs tend to concentrate their activity.

Miscellaneous Notes: Despite their appearance, earwigs are essentially harmless to humans. If handled or crushed, they can produce a moderately painful pinch from their jaws. The pincers, or cerci, which protrude off the hind end, are used during mating but exert little force and do not pinch. Males have more broadly bowed cerci; those of the females are slender and relatively straight.

HEMIPTERA (TRUE BUGS)

Squash Bug
(Anasa tristus)

Damage: Adults and nymphs feed on the foliage of vine crops, particularly winter squash and pumpkins. During feeding, squash bugs puncture cells and inject damaging saliva into the plant that cause areas of the stems and leaves to wilt and die off—plants may be dead by midsummer. Late in the season, squash bugs feed directly on fruits, producing wounds that offer entry to rotting organisms.

Life History and Habits: Squash bugs spend the winter in the adult stage in protected sites around previously infested plantings. They become active and first appear to feed in June, shortly after plant emergence. At this time they mate, and females lay masses of shiny brown eggs on leaf undersides and occasionally on stems. After hatching, the nymphs feed in groups, usually on the shaded undersides of the plant. The nymphs of the first generation mature by early July, followed by a second generation that is much more

numerous and destructive than the first. Adults that develop late in the season do not lay eggs and leave the fields for overwintering shelter. During warm seasons in southern areas, some of the second-generation adults may continue to develop and lay eggs, producing yet a third generation.

Biological Controls: A wasp parasite of the eggs and a tachinid fly parasite of the nymphs have been recorded. However, these do not usually provide adequate control in this region. Northern areas are rarely infested, probably due to erratic, killing spring frosts or other environmental conditions that limit squash bug development.

Cultural Controls: There are conflicting reports as to the feeding preferences of squash bugs on different types of squash. Early studies indicated that winter squash (*Cucurbita maxima*) was damaged more often than summer squash (*Cucurbita pepo*) and butternut squash (*Cucurbita moschata*). However, recent studies indicate that egg laying predominates on summer squash when the insect has a choice. Little egg laying and development occur on cucumber and melons. Trap crop planting of the more preferred species can be used to divert feeding from the less-favored cucurbits.

Mechanical and Physical Controls: Keep the area around the base of plants free of mulch and other covers that provide daytime shelter for squash bugs. For vining types, training plants to climb up a trellis will further expose the plant base, making it undesirable for squash bugs. However, newspaper, boards, or other sources of shelter can be placed near plants to concentrate squash bugs so that they can be collected and destroyed. Some protection early in the season is possible using floating row covers or other screening on small plantings. However, these covers must be removed prior to flowering to allow pollination. Egg masses of the squash bug, laid on the underside of leaves and on stems, are easy to spot during plant inspections and can be crushed. They have an appearance of small ball-bearings and are glued to the undersides of leaves and on stems.

Squash bug nymphs

Squash bug, mating pair

Harlequin bug, nymphs and damage

Twospotted stink bug feeding on potato beetles (Photo by John Capinera)

Chemical Controls: The squash bug has always been one of the more challenging garden pests to control, being inherently resistant to most insecticides, and because of coverage problems during insecticide applications on the large plants it infests. The best control is regularly checking plants to detect when egg masses are first laid. Applying insecticides (e.g., carbaryl, permethrin, sabadilla) at this time, followed by a second treatment approximately 2 weeks later, provides fair, season-long control. It is particularly important to treat the base of the plant, since squash bugs concentrate there during parts of the day, and fairly good control is achieved by just spot-treating the sites. Diatomaceous earth, applied around the base of the plant, is also effective.

Associated Insects: Another insect responsible for wilt of squash and pumpkin vines is the squash vine borer (*Melittia cucurbitae*). This is the larva of a clearwing borer moth that tunnels into the base of vines. Diagnosis is based on the presence of tunneling injuries and the existence of excrement in the damaged vines. This insect is very rare in the region, with some record of it extending along the Platte River Valley of eastern Colorado. In the southern areas of the region, other related borers are associated with native squash, such as buffalo gourd.

Harlequin Bug
(*Murgantia histrionica*)

Damage: Harlequin bugs feed on the sap of various mustard family plants (Brassicaceae). Areas around the feeding site typically turn cloudy. When young tissues are fed on, growth develops in a distorted manner and may turn brown and die. Severe winters typically limit harlequin bug population and subsequent damage in areas above about the fortieth parallel.

Life History and Habits: Hiding in protected sites, such as under older crop debris, harlequin bugs survive winters in northern regions only in the adult stage. The adults emerge from winter shelter in midspring, and primarily feed on wild mustards and other weed hosts. By June they may be found feeding on cabbage, radish, or other crucifers. The females then lay egg masses resembling rows of small, black- and white-banded barrels on the leaves of these plants. The immature nymphs usually develop in the same plants in which the eggs were laid and feed for about 2 months before becoming full-grown. If warm weather conditions occur, a second generation is produced. Otherwise, adults continue to feed without reproducing and move to winter cover at the end of the growing season.

Mechanical Controls: Individual bugs are hand collected and egg masses crushed. Harlequin bugs tend to seek more shaded areas on the plant and are most easily found early in the morning.

Cultural Controls: Some plants exhibiting a resistance to harlequin bugs have been identified. These include cabbage varieties Copenhagen Market 86, Headstart, Savoy Perfection Drumhead, and Early Jersey Wakefield; cauliflower varieties Early Snowball X and Snowball Y; and radish varieties White Icicle, Globemaster, Cherry Belle, Champion, Red Devil, and Red Prince. Infested plants should be removed and destroyed immediately after harvest, such as by composting. This kills stages of the insect that are developing and reduces local populations. In larger plantings, plowing or otherwise removing cover in the fall deprives overwintering bugs of shelter and limits their survival. Infestations of harlequin bugs are diverted from broccoli, cabbage, and cauliflower by planting more appealing crucifers such as mustards and radish (allowed to flower and seed).

Chemical Controls: Harlequin bugs are quite difficult to kill with insecticides. If needed, sprays should be applied when adults are observed, before many eggs are laid, or when the nymphs are small.

Related Insects: Harlequin bugs are frequently confused with another brightly colored stink bug, the two-spotted stink bug, *Perillus bioculatus* (see pages 92–93). However, the latter species is a predator of other insects, such as the Colorado potato beetle, and does not feed on plants.

False Chinch Bug
(Nysius raphanus)

Damage: False chinch bugs suck the sap from plants during feeding. The adults attack in tremendous numbers, causing plants to wilt and die rapidly. Outbreaks are sporadic but destroy plantings, particularly early in the year. Most garden plants are vulnerable during outbreaks, but beets or cruciferous plants such as radish and cabbage are preferred. Wild hosts include many weeds such as tansy mustard, kochia, Russian thistle, and sagebrush. This insect is sometimes a nuisance in homes and buildings in the summer when they migrate indoors.

Life History and Habits: False chinch bugs spend the winter as nymphs or adults under protective debris near annual winter mustards that serve as hosts. Some adults will also move to buildings or other sites outside of plantings to survive the winter. False chinch bugs become active in early spring and move to developing mustards to feed. Adults lay their eggs in loose soil or soil cracks around plants, and the eggs hatch in about 4 days. Under summer conditions, the wingless, gray nymphs feed for about 3 weeks, then reach the adult stage. The adults live for several weeks, flying readily and dispersing over a wide area. They tend to aggregate in

False chinch bugs

very large numbers on individual plants. About three generations are usually produced, with peak numbers often appearing in July and early August.

Mechanical Controls: The bugs can be brushed or swept off plants and collected in water pans.

Chemical Controls: There is little information on effective controls for false chinch bugs. Permethrin is the most effective garden insecticide for this insect.

Lygus Bugs
Tarnished plant bug
(Lygus lineolaris)
Pale legume bug (Lygus elisus)

Damage: Lygus bugs feed on developing leaves, fruits, and flowers, destroying the areas around the feeding site. This causes abortion of the young flowers, seeds, or buds. Older tissues may continue to grow but be deformed. Leaf curling and corky "catface" injuries to fruit are common distortions resulting from lygus bug feeding injuries. Peach, apricot, strawberry, and bean are the targeted garden plants. Some flower abortion of most plants is normal, and lygus bug feeding injuries have little effect on plant yields unless the insects are excessive. Lygus bugs also feed on aphids and other small, soft-bodied insects, effecting some beneficial biological control.

Life History and Habits: Lygus bugs spend the winter in the adult stage under the cover of piled leaves, bark cracks, or other shelter. They emerge in early spring and feed on new buds of trees and shrubs. Most then move to various weeds and other plants, where the females insert eggs into the stems, leaves and buds. The young hatch, feed, and develop on these plants, becoming fully grown in about a month. Several generations are produced during the year.

Cultural Controls: Legumes, particularly alfalfa, are important host plants for lygus bugs. If these plants exist around a garden, flowering stages should not be cut when fruits and vegetables are in critical stages, such as fruit set. Cutting will

Plant bugs and injury to young apple

Pale western legume bug, a common lygus bug

Catfacing injury to peach produced by lygus bug (Photo courtesy of USDA)

Leaf flecking by rose leafhopper

force migrations of lygus bugs to neighboring crops. Clean up weeds and other debris in orchards to restrict the overwintering shelter and survival of lygus bugs. However, most small yards offer plenty of sheltering sites.

Mechanical Controls: Lygus bugs can be trapped with sticky white cards. This is most useful for detecting when lygus bugs have moved into a planting, rather than for actual control.

Chemical Controls: Lygus bugs and most other true bugs are fairly difficult to control with insecticides. Since most injury occurs during early fruit development, insecticide sprays are best timed either immediately before flowering and/or immediately after petal fall. Insecticides should never be sprayed during flowering to avoid killing beneficial pollinating insects.

Miscellaneous Notes: In addition to lygus bugs, other plant bugs (such as the campylomma bug), stink bugs, and even boxelder bugs occasionally damage fruit in a similar manner.

HOMOPTERA (APHIDS, LEAFHOPPERS, WHITEFLIES, PSYLLIDS, ETC.)

White Apple Leafhopper (Typhlocyba pomaria)

Damage: The white apple leafhopper feeds on the leaves of apple trees, removing chlorophyll and sap. Feeding sites are white-flecked and heavily infested leaves look silvery. During early season outbreaks, the vigor and productivity of trees are reduced. The white apple leafhopper excretes tiny tobacco-juicelike droppings that cover fruit, making it unattractive. It also occasionally damages the leaves of roses, and peach, plum, and cherry trees.

Life History and Habits: The white apple leafhopper spends the winter in the egg stage, inserted under the bark of twigs and branches. Eggs hatch in the spring, generally when blooming begins. The developing nymphs crawl to feed on the undersides of older leaves. They attain full growth by early June, producing winged adult stages. These first-generation adults mate, and female leafhoppers lay eggs that produce a second generation. Adults emerging from this second cycle produce the overwintering eggs. Peak feeding injury occurs in late July and August. There are two generations per year. The insect is easily observed on leaf undersides and will dash away when disturbed. Even when it is no longer present on the leaf, the white flecking and old, shed skins serve to diagnose white apple leafhopper injury.

Natural and Biological Controls: Several general predators, such as green lacewings and damsel bugs, like to eat leafhoppers. Some hunting wasps specialize in gathering leafhopper prey to rear their young. Parasitic wasps and fungal diseases are other reported natural enemies of white apple leafhoppers. These biological controls usually keep leafhopper numbers low in unsprayed orchards.

Mechanical and Physical Controls: When possible, periodically hose off plants to dislodge many of the leafhoppers. Watering also softens the droppings that cover fruit, making them easier to wash off. However, hosing treatments or overhead watering should not be used if there is any possibility of spreading fire blight.

Cultural Controls: Pruning removes overwintered eggs under the bark.

Chemical Controls: Dormant season applications of horticultural oils may provide some extermination of overwintering eggs, although most are too well protected by bark to be killed by these treatments. Newly hatched nymphs are susceptible to many insecticides, including insecticidal soaps and carbaryl (Sevin®). However, insecticide-resistant strains have been reported in the eastern United States. Sprays should target leaf undersides where the nymphs feed.

Related Species: White flecking injuries on the leaves of garden plants are characteristically produced by many different leafhopper species that feed on the mesophyll cells of the leaf underside. One of the more common is the rose leafhopper,

Edwardsiana rosae, which feeds on roses. The life history and control of this species are similar to those of the white apple leafhopper, which it resembles. Also common are various leafhoppers in the *Erythoneura* genus. These include the grape leafhopper (described below), a pest of grapes in warmer areas of the West, and the "zic-zac" leafhopper, which plagues ivy and Virginia creeper. These spend the winter in the adult stage under loose bark and other protected sites. They are also attracted to lights and are an occasional nuisance.

Grape Leafhopper
(Erythroneura vulnerata)

Damage: Grape leafhoppers damage wine grapes, puncturing cells of the leaves as they feed and removing the sap. The damaged tissues around the feeding site turn white and later die. This loss of leaf area restricts photosynthesis. Fruit on heavily infested plants may have a lower sugar content and increased acids. Grape leafhoppers also excrete honeydew, which can stick to fruit, staining it and encouraging the development of sooty mold fungi.

Life History and Habits: The grape leafhopper feeds on a wide variety of plants, including Virginia creeper, maple, strawberry, burdock, and various mint family plants. When temperatures reach the mid-60s, the overwintering adult leafhoppers move to these plants to feed and lay eggs. As new growth is produced on the grapes, leafhoppers begin to migrate into the vineyard. Adult females prefer to lay eggs in newly matured leaves. Eggs are inserted into the grape leaf, and in about 1 to 2 weeks, the eggs hatch the immature nymphs. Grape leafhopper nymphs are pale-colored and highly active. They feed on the undersides of leaves, with populations higher on the lower leaves. They develop over the course of a month, molting five times before reaching the adult stage. The cycle is repeated, with probably two to three generations occurring during a growing season. At the end of the season, leafhoppers move to weedy areas to spend the winter.

Natural and Biological Controls: Cold and wet weather conditions in the spring and fall reduce populations of grape leafhoppers. The egg parasite of the grape leafhopper, *Anagrus epos*, is common west of the Rockies and is the control of choice where grape plantings are near other fruit crops. This is because these crops host alternate species of leafhoppers also consumed by *Anagrus epos*, allowing its populations to increase.

Cultural Controls: Maintaining a weed-free area in and around the vineyard reduces overwintering cover and grape leafhopper populations. Removing lower sucker canes in late June also eliminates many of the eggs.

Mechanical Controls: Adults can be trapped on sticky surfaces, such as a sheet covered with Tanglefoot® or Vaseline®. Hold the sticky cloth downwind of the vine and shake the vine. Winged leafhoppers dislodged by this activity can then be trapped.

Chemical Controls: The grape leafhopper is controlled by many insecticides, provided there is adequate coverage of the undersides of leaves. Sprays should be used only when sampling indicates a developing problem. Berry spotting rarely occurs unless leafhopper populations exceed an average of 15 per leaf. However, grape leafhoppers are distributed unequally on the vine, with the highest populations residing on the more shaded parts of the plant. When sampling populations, it is suggested that mid-shoot leaves from the north or east sides of the plant be collected, averaging a total of at least fifteen leaves.

Related Species: *Erythronueura zic-zac*, the zic-zac leafhopper, is also found on grape. However, Virginia creeper is the favored host of this insect, which produces white-flecked feeding wounds.

Beet Leafhopper
(Eutettix tenellus)

Damage: The beet leafhopper is the only insect capable of transmitting the virus that causes curly top disease. (See discussion of beet curly top

Grape leafhopper and injury

Beet leafhopper (Photo courtesy of Oregon State)

Aster leafhopper

disease on page 160.) Although feeding injury by the beet leafhopper is inconsequential, transmission of the virus can severely stunt or kill tomatoes, peppers, and beets. Curly top outbreaks tend to be very sporadic between seasons and correspond, in part, to the severity of winter temperatures and the amount of rainfall. However, outbreaks can be chronic in some areas.

Life History and Habits: The beet leafhopper overwinters in the region as an adult, feeding on wild host plants such as Russian thistle, wild mustards, and salt bush. In the early spring, eggs are laid and the first generation emerges. In late spring, large migrations are common, and the leafhoppers may fly for hundreds of miles. If migrating leafhoppers feed on plants infected with the curly top virus, they are capable of transmitting the disease for the remainder of their life, a period of several weeks.

Cultural Controls: The beet leafhopper thrives in open, arid areas and tends to avoid dense plantings. Higher plant populations and overhead irrigation reduce colonization of the plantings. Damage is also impeded by planting earlier, since older plants are less vulnerable to the disease.

Chemical Controls: Several insecticides kill beet leafhoppers. However, insecticides are ineffective for controlling the curly top virus because it can be transmitted before the insect is killed, and leafhoppers continually migrate into plantings.

Aster Leafhopper
(*Macrosteles quadrilineatus*)

Damage: The aster leafhopper (also known as the sixspotted leafhopper) transmits the phytoplasma responsible for aster yellows disease. (See discussion on aster yellows disease on page 181.) Aster yellows adversely affects more than forty families of plants, including many cultivated vegetables and flowers. Infections of carrots are marked by hairy roots and bushy, off-colored top growth.

Lettuce, particularly head lettuce, shows a distorted twisting of new growth. Several types of flowers (cosmos, marigold, petunia, zinnia, etc.) display distored flowering parts due to aster yellows. Feeding by leafhoppers that do not transmit the disease poses no serious problem. Infection of plants tends to appear in late July and early August, although may present earlier if large numbers of infected leafhoppers are blown into the region in late spring.

Life History and Habits: The aster leafhopper cannot survive the harsh winter temperatures of the West. It passes the cold season in the southern United States along the Gulf of Mexico. Winged stages of the leafhopper annually fly northward, aided by storm patterns and winds. Eggs are laid in the leaves and stems of plants. The immature nymphs take 3 to 4 weeks to complete development before becoming mature adults.

Two or three generations typically are produced during the growing season. Leafhoppers that feed on plants infected with aster yellows acquire the hytoplasma that spawns the disease. However, they cannot transmit the disease until the phytoplasma has circulated within the leafhopper and moved to its salivary glands, a process that typically takes 10 days to 3 weeks. Once this period has passed, they are capable of transmitting the disease organism for the rest of their lives. Typically, less than 3 percent of all leafhoppers carry the disease organism.

Cultural Controls: Carrot varieties exhibit a range of susceptibility to aster yellows infection. Royal Chantenay, Scarlet Nantes, Toudo, Hi Color, Amtou, Charger, El Presidente, Six Pak, and Gold King are some that possess the greatest tolerance. Head lettuce is much more susceptible to infection than are carrots, and no highly resistant varieties exist. However, damage from aster yellows is much less severe on leaf-type lettuce than on head types. Aster yellows resistance has not been developed for susceptible flowers. Planting early avoids the mid-summer period of peak infection.

Mechanical Controls: In small plantings, mulches of reflective aluminum or straw can repel leafhoppers and reduce infection.

Chemical Controls: When high numbers of infective leafhoppers are present, it is very difficult to control aster yellows infection. Under these conditions, leafhoppers continue to migrate into plantings, so repeated applications of insecticides, such as permethrin, are needed, often at short intervals, to maintain control.

Garden Leafhoppers (*Empoasca abrupta, Empoasca recurvata, and others*)

Damage: Several related leafhoppers (species of *Empoasca*) feed on the leaves of garden plants. Feeding injuries produced by the western potato leafhopper, *Empoasca abrupta,* on potatoes appear as white flecking. Another species, *Empoasca recurvata,* damages the leaves of pumpkin and squash, resulting in a "hopperburn" injury by which the leaves die back from the edge and appear scorched. Despite the appearance of these injuries, it is doubtful that they seriously affect yield.

Life History and Habits: *Empoasca* leafhoppers cannot survive in areas with extreme cold winter temperatures. Therefore, regional infestations originate with leafhoppers that fly northward, aided by winds, from more southern areas. Adult leafhoppers insert their eggs into leaf mid-ribs and petioles. The emerging nymphs feed on the plant, growing and molting several times before becoming full-grown. About two generations are produced annually in the West.

Chemical Controls: Controls are rarely needed, since damage tends to occur late in the season. Almost all garden insecticides, including insecticidal soaps, can control leafhoppers during serious outbreaks.

Related Species: A serious pest, the potato leafhopper, *Empoasca fabae,* causes "hopperburn"

injury to potatoes, beans, alfalfa, and many other plants. However, the potato leafhopper is almost always confined to the central and eastern regions of the United States and Canada. Rarely will small migrations enter the High Plains areas east of the Rockies.

Greenhouse Whitefly (*Trialeurodes vaporariorum*)

Damage: Nymphs and adults suck sap, weakening the plants. Honeydew is excreted during feeding, which contaminates fruit and vegetables.

Life History and Habits: The greenhouse whitefly originates from subtropical and tropical areas. In the northern United States and Canada, the greenhouse whitefly overwinters only indoors on houseplants and in greenhouses. The adult female whitefly lays eggs in a series of semicircles on the lower leaf surface. Eggs hatch in 1 to 3 weeks and immature nymphs emerge. The nymphs are pale yellow and difficult to detect. They rarely move, feeding for 3 to 5 weeks. After they have finished feeding, they change to a stage similar to the pupa stage, that is, a nonfeeding, immobile stage that lasts about 1 week. The adult whiteflies then emerge, and females may live for 4 to 6 weeks, laying up to 400 eggs each. Successive generations continue throughout the season so long as temperatures allow.

Natural and Biological Controls: The greenhouse whitefly cannot survive freezing temperatures and dies out in unprotected locations. In high-temperature greenhouses (average above 72°F), the parasitic wasp *Encarsia formosa* provides control. (See discussion of Biological Control Organisms in Chapter 2.)

Recently a second species of parasitic wasp was commercially developed that offers excellent control under greenhouse conditions. *Eretmocerus californicus* similarly develops on whitefly nymphs, but also the adult stages kill many of the nymphs when they sting them for a meal of blood. *E. californicus* is not widely available through garden catalogs but is usually carried by

"Hopperburn" injury to pumpkin

Garden leafhopper

suppliers that specialize in distributing biological control agents. (See Appendix I.)

The fungus *Beauveria bassiana* (e.g., Naturalis®, Botanigard®) will infect whiteflies, particularly under fairly high humidity conditions. Outbreaks of other fungus diseases of whiteflies also may spontaneously develop among high populations of whiteflies in high humidity.

Cultural Controls: Greenhouse whitefly is a subtropical species not adapted to winter survival in areas of annual killing freezes. As the nymphs do not move after settling to feed, they are killed when their host plant dies, and adult whiteflies will usually die within a few days if there are no food plants. An exposure of about five days to temperatures of 22°F, or two weeks at 27°F, is lethal to all stages. Therefore, taking care to avoid introducing the insect into a garden on infested transplants is an effective preventive practice. ("Just say no!") When starting plants indoors, a host-plant–free period of one to two weeks prior to seedling emergence will cause residual whiteflies to die out, breaking the life cycle.

Mechanical and Physical Controls: Yellow sticky traps can be used to capture adult whiteflies, and they are repelled by white or light-colored mulches.

Chemical Controls: Whiteflies are difficult to control. Most whitefly sprays sold to control adult stages contain pyrethrins or closely related insecticides (e.g., resmethrin, tetramethrin), but many of these are not permitted for use on edible vegetable crops. Sprays containing horticultural oils (e.g., Sunspray®) or neem are the most effective treatments for nymphs; insecticidal soaps also provide some control. Repeated applications are necessary, since egg and adult stages often elude these treatments and leaf undersides must receive thorough coverage to kill nymphs.

Related Species: In recent years, a new species of whitefly has become established in much of the southern United States and in greenhouses throughout North America. The sweet potato whitefly (*Bemisia tabaci*), sometimes known as the "silverleaf whitefly" has developed into a devastating pest of vegetables and certain ornamental crops in Florida and the southwestern United States. Feeding injuries alone produce growth irregularities in several plants, such as a silvery leaf condition of cucurbits, a blanching of broccoli stalks, and color mottling on tomato. In addition, the sweetpotato whitefly is a vector of many virus diseases, which the common greenhouse whitefly is not. Furthermore, *Encarsia formosa* is not a reliable natural enemy for this insect. (*Eretmocerus californicus* is better adapted to sweet potato whitefly and provides control under favorable conditions.)

Asparagus Aphid *(Brachycorynella asparagi)*

Damage: The asparagus aphid sucks the sap from asparagus plants. This distinctly deforms fern growth, producing stunting and bushiness. Continued feeding stimulates the premature release of dormant buds that are formed for the subsequent crop. Yields can be severely reduced and young plants killed by these injuries.

Life History and Habits: Asparagus aphids overwinter as eggs on and around the debris of asparagus plants. The eggs hatch in the spring and the aphids then move to the tips and bud scales of developing spears. There they reproduce, having several generations during the growing season. By late spring, some winged forms are pro-

Asparagus aphid

Greenhouse whitefly

duced that are able to infest new plantings. Mating occurs in late summer, and overwintering eggs are laid on lower areas of ferns, particularly on new growth produced from released dormant buds.

Natural and Biological Controls: Parasitic wasps and general aphid predators (lacewings, syrphids, lady beetles) provide some control. However, the asparagus aphid is an introduced insect that has only recently moved into the region, and effective biological controls are lacking.

Cultural Controls: Remove old ferns to eliminate overwintering eggs. Control is further improved by carefully tilling the soil over the dormant crowns in spring. Regular picking of asparagus shoots in spring removes many of the early-hatching aphids, although plants continue to be

Aphids

Aphids (Aphididae) are the most prolific family of insects found on plants in the West. Several hundred different species occur in this region, many as pests of vegetables, fruits, flowers, and other plants.

Aphids reproduce during the growing season without any males (asexually). The females are literally born pregnant and a newborn aphid may take only a week to mature. This extremely high rate of reproduction enables aphids to build up their numbers very rapidly. Large population "booms," usually followed shortly by equally spectacular "busts" as natural controls enter, are the hallmark of most aphid colonies.

During the spring and summer, developing females may produce either a winged or wingless adult female. Winged aphids tend to be produced more often when the plants on which they are feeding become overcrowded and decline in food quality, or when days become shorter. When conditions are favorable, wingless females predominate. These females have higher reproduction ability than the winged ones, which tend to disperse.

However, the life cycles of aphids are quite complex and involve numerous different stages throughout the year. For example, many common aphids alternate between annual plants, such as vegetables, during the summer and a perennial tree or shrub host in the winter. With these types of aphids, males are produced at the end of the summer. The males—and special reproductive stages of the females—meet on plants on which the insects overwinter. After mating, specialized, egg-laying daughter aphids are produced, which lay overwintering eggs that hatch in the spring. After a few generations, the aphids leave to search for summer plants.

Aphids feed by sucking and removing sap from plants. When aphids are abundant, this stresses the plant, rendering it less vigorous. Some aphids also produce a saliva that is somewhat toxic to the plants, causing discoloration or curling of the developing leaves during infestations.

Perhaps the greatest injury aphids cause is transmitting viral diseases. Dozens of viral diseases of vegetables, flowers, and berry crops are spread by aphids. Although the aphids themselves may cause little damage, the effects of the viral infections they spread can be devastating.

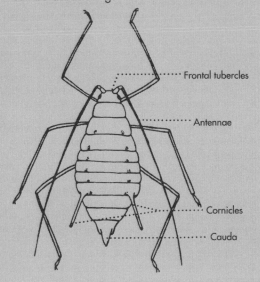

Frontal tubercles

Antennae

Cornicles

Cauda

Phil Cranshaw spring cleaning for aphid control in the flower garden

infested after harvest. Some varieties of asparagus exhibit a greater tolerance to injury, although no varieties are highly resistant.

Chemical Controls: Chemical control options for aphids are very limited on asparagus. Repeated applications of insecticidal soaps or malathion may provide some control during early stages of infestation. However, once dense fern growth has been produced, the aphids within are largely protected from insecticides.

Green Peach Aphid (*Myzus persicae*)

Damage: The green peach aphid feeds on more than 200 species of plants and is the most significant transmitter of viral diseases to vegetables. Diseases spread by the aphid include potato virus Y, potato leafroll, watermelon mosaic, and bean mosaic. Green peach aphids feed on many vegetables but rarely are abundant enough in gardens to cause serious injury by feeding injuries alone. On overwintering plants (peach, apricot, certain plums), green peach aphids produce leaf-curling injuries during early spring. Green peach aphids are also the most common aphid found in greenhouses or on houseplants. They are highly resistant to most insecticides, and problems with this insect have increased in greenhouse crops and certain vegetable crops.

Leaf curling produced by green peach aphid

Life History and Habits: Green peach aphids spend the winter in the egg stage around the buds of various species of *Prunus*—peach, apricot, and certain types of plum and cherry trees. Eggs hatch in April and May, and the aphids feed on developing leaves, often producing leaf-curling injuries. After 1 to 2 months, winged forms begin to develop that fly to summer host plants, including many vegetables and flowers. The developing nymphs can become full-grown in as little as 1 week and live for a month or more. Numerous generations occur on these summer hosts, which house both wingless and migratory winged forms. In the fall, they fly back to the overwintering plants, mate, and a special female form lays eggs.

Indoors, the green peach aphid reproduces continuously but does not produce special overwintering forms and eggs.

Natural and Biological Controls: Green peach aphids are preyed upon by many general aphid predators, including lady beetles, lacewings, syrphid flies, predator midges, minute pirate bugs, and damsel bugs. Various parasitic wasps also kill aphids. High populations of green peach aphids rarely persist on vegetables unless these biological controls are disturbed by pesticides or interference with ants. (See discussion on ants and aphids on page 22.)

Several natural enemies of the green peach aphid are also sold by suppliers of biological control agents. Green lacewings are most commonly available. The aphid predator midge, *Aphidoletes aphidiimyza*, is a tiny orange maggot that sucks the blood of many different aphids. A tiny parasitic wasp, *Aphidius matricariae*, develops within a green peach aphid, turning it into a hollowed "aphid mummy." All of these species occur naturally throughout the region, but supplemental releases of purchased insects assist in control by boosting beneficial populations. Effectiveness has been demonstrated in the control of aphids of greenhouse crops.

Cultural Controls: Most of the viral diseases spread by green peach aphids are carried for short distances. Therefore, remove all "off"-looking plants that may be infected with the virus to prevent further spread to healthy plants. Purchase

Green peach aphids

virus-free seed and transplants to limit later problems with virus spread by aphids. Flights of green peach aphids increase steadily through the summer. Planting early can avoid much of the infection of vegetables susceptible to viruses spread by aphids.

Mechanical and Physical Controls: Mulches made of reflective materials, such as aluminum foil or straw, repel winged aphids from plants. Sticky or slippery barriers that prevent access to the aphid colonies by ants are useful biological controls that ants may otherwise interfere with.

Chemical Controls: On the winter host plants (peach, plum, apricot, cherry), green peach aphids are controlled with dormant season applications of horticultural oils. Insecticides are ineffective in preventing the spread of aphid-transmitted viral diseases. The spread of most diseases occurs within a few seconds after landing on the plant, far more rapidly than insecticides work. Some studies have even shown increases in virus spread by aphids following the use of insecticides, since they increase aphid activity. Sprays of highly refined stylet oils and oil-containing materials such as milk prevent many aphid-transmitted viruses from getting to the plants.

Related Species: The black cherry aphid, *Myzus cerasi,* is active in late spring on the new growth of tart cherry. Leaves are not tightly curled by this insect, but when abundant they produce large amounts of honeydew and induce leaf shedding. Summer hosts are reported to be certain mustard family plants.

"Cabbage Aphids"
Cabbage Aphid
(*Brevicoryne brassicae*)
Turnip Aphid
(*Hyadaphis erysimi*)

Damage: Cabbage and turnip aphids feed on cabbage/mustard family (Cruciferae) plants, including cabbage, Brussels sprouts, and broccoli. The most serious injuries result from high populations of aphids feeding on and damaging developing cabbage heads, and causing permanent distortion. Cabbage aphids also can thrive during the fall on Brussels sprouts and contaminate them.

Life History and Habits: Cabbage and turnip aphids spend the winter as eggs on wild or cultivated cabbage/mustard family plants. The eggs hatch in early spring and development can span 2 to 6 weeks, depending on the temperature. Numerous generations are produced, and the aphids are active throughout the year. As with other common aphids, during most of the season, pure female populations are produced, with just one sexual generation (males and females) developing at the end of the season. Winged forms are occasionally produced, particularly following overcrowding, and these fly and colonize new plants. Cabbage aphids tend to build tight colonies on the new growth of the plant. Turnip aphids are more evenly distributed throughout the plant.

Natural and Biological Controls: Cabbage and turnip aphids are fed upon by most general aphid predators, such as syrphid flies and lady beetles. However, their waxy coating makes them less desirable to lady beetles than other aphids. Parasitic wasps are also available biological controls. Unfortunately, parasitized aphids often stick tightly to the foliage and increase contamination problems.

Cultural Controls: Before spring, destroy or remove mustard family plants in and around the garden to kill overwintering stages.

Chemical Controls: Several insecticides control cabbage aphids. However, because the plants and the aphids have a waxy covering, soap, detergent, or some other wetting agent should be used to provide better coverage. Control is problematic when infestations occur in protected areas within leaf curls, particularly with Brussels sprouts.

Associated Species: The green peach aphid (see preceding section) is also very commonly found on mustard family plants.

Cabbage aphids

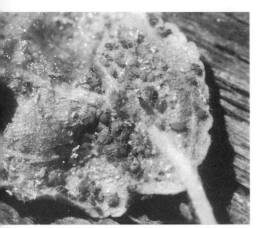

Rosy apple aphids

Rosy Apple Aphid
(*Dysaphis plantaginea*)

Damage: Large numbers of these aphids can develop on newly emergent apple leaves and young fruit. Leaf curling and stunting of new growth commonly results from these infestations. However, the most serious damage rosy apple aphids are responsible for is deformity of apple fruit.

Life History and Habits: Winter is spent as eggs near buds of apple, occasionally pear, and mountain-ash. The newly emergent nymphs travel to the buds and feed on the leaves, inducing leaf curls within which they live. Several generations are produced on the winter host plant during which time injury is also produced. By late spring, winged forms develop and disperse to their alternate summer host, narrow-leaved plantain. There they produce numerous generations, feeding on the stems and leaves. In late summer, separate winged stages are produced that include both sexual females and males. These rendezvous on apples, mate, and produce young that lay the overwintering eggs.

Cultural Controls: If possible, narrow-leaved plantain should be removed from the area of apple plantings damaged by this insect.

Chemical Controls: Dormant season applications of horticultural oils kill the majority of overwintering eggs.

"Rose Aphids"
Potato aphid
(*Macrosiphum euphorbiae*)
Rose aphid (*Macrosiphum rosae*)

Damage: Aphids are usually associated with roses, particularly late in the season. Infestations concentrate around new shoots and flower buds. During outbreaks these insects reduce flower size and may even kill buds. Aphids also feed on flower petals after bud break, causing losses in blossom quality.

Life History and Habits: Both rose aphid and potato aphid overwinter on rose canes as eggs laid near the buds. After hatching in spring, there are several generations produced on the emergent shoots. Both winged and the normal wingless forms are produced beginning in late spring.

Potato aphids disperse to other plants during the summer and may be found on a wide range of host plants during this period. Nightshade family hosts, such as tomatoes, are favored during this time, but potato aphids can be found feeding on most vegetables, a wide variety of flowers, on common weeds such as pigweed and sowthistle, and small fruits. Winged stages of the late summer generations disperse back to roses and reproduce, fueling late season outbreaks. Both pink and green forms of the potato aphid are common, and this insect may also be a serious greenhouse pest.

Rose aphids apparently restrict feeding to roses throughout the year. They also produce both pink and green forms, which may be winged or wingless, the latter dispersing to new plantings.

Natural and Biological Controls: General aphid predators, such as lady beetles and syrphid flies, as well as parasitic wasps, feed on rose aphids. These usually keep populations somewhat under control, although aphid outbreaks frequently occur during the spring and fall when biological controls are less active.

Rose aphids

Mechanical Controls: Rose aphids are quite delicate, so hosing plants with a strong jet of water (syringing) kills and dislodges them.

Cultural Controls: Pruning prior to bud break will remove many of the eggs that overwinter on canes.

Chemical Controls: Most general-use insecticides, including the "rose systemics" (Disyston®), are usually effective. Dilute sprays of insecticidal soaps or horticultural oils are also effective.

Root- and Bulb-Infesting Aphids
Sugarbeet root aphid
(Pemphigus populivenae)
Lettuce root aphid
(Pemphigus bursarius)
Western aster root aphid
(Aphis armoraciae)
Tulip bulb aphid
(Dysaphis tulipae)
and others

Damage: Several aphids spend at least part of their life cycle belowground on the roots and bulbs of various plants. When observed they may be surrounded by waxy threads and are sometimes mistaken for mealybugs. They feed on the sap of the plants and wilting or reduced growth results from their heavy infestations. Garden beets are the familiar host of the sugarbeet root aphid and lettuce for its close relative, the lettuce root aphid. Bulbs and roots of garden flowers such as gladiolus, iris, and tulips may host the tulip bulb aphid. Roots of asters—and dandelion—are usually infested by the aster root aphid.

Life History and Habits: The life history of some root infesting aphids includes the alternation of hosts. For example, aphids in the genus *Pemphigus* overwinter as eggs on cottonwood and poplar and form swellings (galls) in the leaves or petioles within which the spring generations are produced. These fly to summer hosts (e.g., beets, lettuce) in late spring to feed on roots, and late-summer generations produce winged forms that

emerge through soil cracks and return to cottonwood. Other species do not exhibit such defined host alternation but periodically produce winged forms that can colonize new plants.

Cultural Controls: Root aphids can be transported on bulbs and tubers, so plants should be carefully examined before planting to ensure that they are not infested. Root aphids are only able to colonize new plants by working their way through existing soil cracks. Any practices that reduce soil cracking, such as changing in soil tilth through organic amendments and regular watering, limit infestations. Root aphids are also impeded by mulching around the base of susceptible host plants.

Chemical Controls: No insecticides are available that effectively control root aphids. However, drenches of insecticidal soaps or other wetting agents can help control root aphids by destroying the waxy covering needed to protect them in the soil environment.

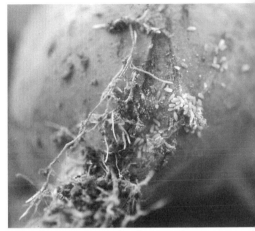

Sugarbeet root aphid colony on beet

Woolly Apple Aphid
(Eriosoma lanigerum)

Damage: The woolly apple aphid feeds on the bark of apple, crabapple, pear, mountain ash, and related plants. Large colonies of the wax-covered aphids may develop around tree wounds both above and below ground. The soft callous tissues of healing wounds are favored by the aphid. By repeatedly attacking these tissues, aphids prevent

Woolly apple aphid colony (Photo by Dave Leatherman)

TABLE 6-4: COMMONLY ENCOUNTERED APHIDS OF WESTERN GARDENS

Aphid	Host Plants
Asparagus aphid (*Brachycorynella asparagi*)	Asparagus*
Cabbage aphid (*Brevicoryne brassicae*)	Various wild and domestic mustard family plants (Brassicaceae)*
Turnip aphid (*Hyadaphis erysimi*)	Various wild and domestic mustard family plants (Brassicaceae)*
Green peach aphid (*Myzus persicae*)	Peppers, cabbage, many garden plants, peach,* plum,* apricot*
Currant aphid (*Cryptomyzus ribis*)	Currant,* motherwort, marsh betony
Black cherry aphid (*Myzus cerasi*)	Sweet cherry,* sour cherry, plum, wild mustards
Crescent-marked lily aphid (*Neomyzus circumflexus*)	Columbine, aster, lily, dock, violet
Artichoke aphid (*Capitophorus braggi*)	Russian olive,* globe artichoke, thistles
Rose aphid (*Macrosiphum rosae*)	Rose*
Potato aphid (*Macrosiphum euphorbiae*)	Rose,* potatoes, tomatoes, and many other garden plants
Rose grass aphid (*Metalophium dirhodum*)	Rose,* grasses, corn
English grain aphid (*Sitobium avenae*)	Apple,* grains
Corn leaf aphid (*Rhopalosiphum maidis*)	Corn, other grains
Pea aphid (*Acyrthosiphum pisum*)	Peas, beans, clover, alfalfa*
Lettuce aphid (*Acyrthosiphum lactucae*)	Lettuce
Rosy apple aphid (*Dysaphis plantaginea*)	Apple,* pear, plantain, mountain ash
Cotton/Melon aphid (*Aphis gossypii*)	Rose, melons, squash, many other garden plants
Bean aphid (*Aphis fabae*)	Euonymus,* viburnum,* beans, beets, cucumbers, carrots, lettuce, etc.
Apple aphid (*Aphis pomi*)	Apple,* pear, mountain ash, hawthorn
Western aster root aphid (*Aphis armoraciae*)	Aster, dandelion, milkweed, sagebrush, corn, dock, many garden flowers

Leafcurl plum aphid (*Brachydaudus helichrysi*)	Plum,* various sunflower family plants (Asteraceae), clover, vinca, thistle
Tulip bulb aphid (*Dysaphis tulipae*)	Celery, carrots, gladiolus, iris, tulips
Rusty plum aphid (*Hysteroneura setariae*)	Plum,* wheat, and other grasses
Sunflower aphid (*Aphis helianthi*)	Dogwood,* sunflower, pigweed, four-o'clock, ragweed, yucca, pigweed
Chrysanthemum aphid (*Macrosiphoniella sanborni*)	Chrysanthemum
(*Caveriella aegopodii*)	Carrots, parsley, dill, cilantro, willow*
Wild parsnip aphid (*Aphis heraclella*)	Carrots, celery, parsnip, cow parsnip
Sugarbeet root aphid (*Pemphigus populivenae*)	Beets, lambsquarters, many garden plants, narrow-leaf cottonwood*
Lettuce root aphid (*Pemphigus bursarius*)	Lettuce, carrots, dandelion, sow thistle, lambsquarters, cottonwood*
Woolly apple aphid (*Eriosoma lanigerum*)	Apple, crabapple, mountain ash, elm*

*Primary overwintering host plant from which populations disperse in spring. Where no plants are indicated, all listed plants may host the overwintering stages or the overwintering host plant in the region is unknown.

proper healing and cause knotlike growths to form at the sites. The cankers can then girdle, weaken, and ultimately kill heavily infested areas of the tree. Woolly apple aphids produce waxy threads that cover their body, and colonies display a conspicuous cottony appearance. On elms, their alternate host, the aphid causes a leaf-curling injury in late spring. These "elm" aphids are covered with powdery wax, although they do not produce the conspicuous threads.

Life History and Habits: The woolly apple aphid has an unusual life cycle, alternating between rose family plants (apple, pear, etc.) and elms. Most survive the winter as eggs on elm trees. Aphids emerging from these eggs feed on the developing leaves, causing a distinctive thickened folding. The aphids reproduce and often fill the leaf before they begin to produce winged forms that leave the tree. The winged aphids fly to and colonize the summer hosts, feeding in bark cracks and around old wounds. In early fall, many of them again produce winged stages, which move back to elms and later produce overwintering eggs. Some remain on the summer host and may survive the winter in protected areas, including the roots.

Natural and Biological Controls: During cold winters, the aphids are unable to survive the winter on apple trees. In these areas, infestations originate annually only from aphids that survived as eggs on elm trees and later flew to apple or other fruit trees. Parasitic wasps are the most effective biological control of the woolly apple aphid. The mummified aphids killed by these wasps are dark-colored with exit holes cut out of their backs.

Mechanical Controls: Woolly apple aphids concentrate around recent wounds and can easily be crushed in small plantings.

Chemical Controls: In areas where the aphids overwinter on apple and other fruit trees, dormant

San Jose scale on apple fruit (Photo by John Capinera)

Pear psylla nymph under honeydew droplet (Photo by Gene Nelson)

application of oil or lime sulfur before buds open controls colonies exposed on branches. Several insecticides applied directly to the bodies of aphids provide control as well, although the addition of soap to "wet" the insects is useful. Insecticidal soaps also control exposed aphids.

San Jose Scale
(Quadraspidiotus perniciosus)

Damage: San Jose scale feeds on the sap of apple, pear, currant, and many other fruit and shade trees. Heavy infestations weaken the branches and cause them to die back or yield poor fruit crops. During the growing season, some scales also infest the fruit, particularly around the stem and blossom ends. On fruit and twigs, the scales effect a small reddish spotting that gives it a mottled look. Infestations of San Jose scale are diagnosed by the small, circular wax coverings it produces. These are generally gray, with a lighter-colored central nipple. Old scale coverings remain on the bark for several years before weathering away.

Life History and Habits: San Jose scale spends the winter attached to bark as a dormant, partially grown nymph. As sap flow begins in spring, it resumes feeding and becomes full-grown around the time that apple trees bloom. The small male scales fly and mate with the stationary females, which shortly thereafter begin to produce eggs.

Eggs hatch over a period of weeks, after petal fall, producing tiny yellow *crawlers* (newly hatched scales). The crawlers move over the bark until they find a suitable site to feed, then they insert their mouthparts. Within a few days after settling, they molt their skin and start to secrete a waxy covering. San Jose scale repeats the life cycle throughout the growing season. Typically three to four generations are produced per growing season, the most of any scale insect within the region.

Natural and Biological Controls: San Jose scale is attacked by parasitic wasps. Some birds, such as nuthatches and brown creepers, also feed on scales.

Mechanical Controls: Infested twigs and branches should be pruned and removed.

Chemical Controls: Sprays of oils or lime sulfur before spring bud break are the most effective means of controlling San Jose scale. During the growing season, settled scales are not easily controlled by insecticides, since they are protected by their waxy covering. However, crawler stages are susceptible to most orchard sprays. Crawler treatments are most effectively applied during the two to four weeks the first generation is present. This tends to occur about one month after apples first bloom. Timing crawler emergence can best be determined by regularly shaking infested branches over a sheet of dark paper to collect the newly hatched crawlers.

Related Insects: The walnut scale, *Quadrispidiotus juglansregiae,* is a closely related scale of generally similar appearance. Walnut scale does not affect fruit trees, but is common on many shade trees including linden, silver maple, and nut trees. The life histories of the two species vary as well, with walnut scale producing only a single generation per season and overwintering in a slightly later stage of development.

Pear Psylla
(Psylla pyricola)

Damage: Pear psylla feed on the leaves of pear trees, excreting conspicuous droplets of honeydew. These droplets soil the leaves and fruit of the plant. Honeydew also facilitates the growth of sooty mold fungi, which discolors fruit. High numbers of psyllids on trees reduce plant vigor and adversely affect yield. Seriously affected trees sometimes go into "psylla shock" that may take several years to recover from. Pear psylla also transmit the bacteria (phytoplasma) that produce pear decline disease, a potentially lethal but rare disease in this region.

Life History and Habits: Pear psylla overwinter in the adult stage in protected areas (under bark, plant debris on soil, or other cover) in the vicinity of previously infested trees. They become active in late winter or early spring and move to pear trees, laying yellow-orange eggs as pear buds begin to swell. The emerging nymphs then travel to feed on the tender new growth.

As they feed, they are first covered with the honeydew droplets they produce. The final stage of the developing insect has conspicuous pads where wings are developing and does not live in the honeydew. They then molt to the adult stage. Later generations lay eggs on the new leaves, often concentrating on sucker sprouts late in the season. Two to three generations are normally produced during a season. At the end of the year, dark-colored winter adult forms move to shelter.

Natural and Biological Controls: During very dry weather, honeydew droplets covering the nymphs may dry and crust to kill the insects. Minute pirate bugs, predacious plant bugs, some lady beetles, and other general predators also feed on pear psylla. A chalcid wasp is a valuable parasite of the pear psylla in many areas. A predatory plant bug, *Deraeocoris brevis,* is offered by some biological control suppliers for pear psylla control, although effects of supplemental releases have not been evaluated.

Cultural Controls: Pear psylla thrive on tender new growth. Remove sucker shoots during midsummer to deprive the insects of their favored food sources after the main leaves have hardened.

Chemical Controls: Pear psylla are resistant to most insecticides and difficult to control. The best control is to treat for the insect two to three times before bloom, killing the overwintered adult stages before they have laid eggs. Oils are effective for this treatment, which is most effective if other pears in the area are also treated, limiting reinfestations.

Potato (Tomato) Psyllid (Paratrioza cockerelli)

Damage: Potato (tomato) psyllids inject saliva into plants during feeding that is damaging to tomatoes and potatoes. Damaged plants often stop growing and typically show leaf curling and color changes. The disease caused by potato psyllid injury is sometimes described as "psyllid yellows." Effects on potato tubers include reduced tuber size, premature sprouting, and rough skin. Tomatoes damaged by potato (tomato) psyllids produce small fruits that are soft and of poor quality. Yields of potatoes and tomatoes are reduced by potato (tomato) psyllid injuries. Infestations during the early stages of plant growth cause much greater injury than later infestations. Potato (tomato) psyllids infest a wide variety of other plants, including pepper, nightshade, morning glory, bindweed, and even beans. However, damage only affects tomatoes and potatoes. Potato (tomato) psyllid damage occurs throughout the western United States and parts of northern Mexico. Colorado, Wyoming, and Utah are the areas most often infested by psyllids. However, outbreaks have been recorded throughout all areas of the country, except the Pacific Northwest.

Life History and Habits: The potato (tomato) psyllid does not overwinter within this region, dying out after hard freezes. Annual infestations originate from populations that survive on native plants in the southern United States and northern Mexico. As temperatures in these areas rise in spring, the adult psyllids migrate north on winds. If food plants are available and temperatures are not excessively high, the psyllids may settle and lay eggs. Otherwise they may continue the northward migration. Females tend to lay eggs in groups, so the insects often are unevenly distributed on the plant. Eggs are small and yellow-orange. These hatch in about 5 days, producing a scalelike nymph stage. Nymphs are yellow when young and often turn light green as they become older. They move slowly and tend to concentrate on the undersides of leaves in more shaded areas of the plant. After 3 to 4 weeks, the adults emerge, repeating the cycle. During a season, three to four generations may be completed.

Natural and Biological Controls: High temperatures (at least 90°F) greatly reduce egg laying and survival and may also temporarily sterilize fe-

Potato/tomato psyllid nymphs and characteristic droppings

males. Predatory bugs, such as big-eyed bugs, minute pirate bugs, and damsel bugs, are some of the more common predators. Occasionally, parasitic wasps (*Tetrastichus triozae*) attack and kill nymphs of the potato (tomato) psyllid. However, none of these controls are reliable during outbreaks. The fungus *Beauveria bassiana* (Naturalis®, Botanigard®) can control potato/tomato psyllid, but complete leaf coverage is essential and humidity conditions should be relatively high during application.

Cultural Controls: Early plantings escape much injury. There is a range in susceptibility to the effects of psyllid injury among both potatoes and tomatoes, but this is still being researched. Peppers, although often infested, are not very susceptible to psyllid injury.

Chemical Controls: Infestations are usually irregular in occurrence and scouting can help to identify periods when plants might benefit from treatment. Check leaf undersides for nymphs or their characteristic droppings, which resemble granulated sugar or salt. Pepper, although not a plant that is damaged by the insect, is a good indicator plant of local psyllid populations early in the season. Sulfur and lime sulfur are highly effective for psyllid control. Some common garden insecticides, such as diazinon and permethrin, are also effective, but carbaryl is not. Insecticidal soaps and horticultural oils give some control when applied directly to the psyllids, although complete coverage is often difficult to attain.

Miscellaneous Notes: Potato (tomato) psyllids infest a wide variety of other plants, including peppers and eggplant. However, they do not seem to damage these. Psyllid injury on the leaves and growth of potatoes and tomatoes resembles that caused by infection with various viral diseases. However, the symptoms of reduced tomato fruit size, sprouting, and rough potato (tomato) skin are unique to psyllid yellows. Unlike many related insects that feed on plant sap and produce sticky honeydew, potato (tomato) psyllids excrete

a granular material known as psyllid sugar. This pelleted excrement resembles salt or sugar and fluoresces under ultraviolet light. The presence of psyllid sugar is a reliable indicator of infestation by potato (tomato) psyllids.

Arachnids (Spider Mites and Relatives)

Twospotted Spider Mite (*Tetranychus urticae*)

Damage: The twospotted spider mite pierces plant cells and feeds on the sap. Small, white flecking injuries are typical around feeding sites. More generalized discoloration, typically bronzing, occurs as infestations progress. The vigor of plants may be seriously reduced.

Premature leaf drop is a sign of heavily infested plants. Most garden plants are fed upon to some extent by twospotted spider mites. Bean, cucumber, raspberry, rose, and marigold are the plants that typically suffer the most damage. The twospotted spider mite is also the species usually responsible for greenhouse crop and interior plant damage.

Life History and Habits: Winter is spent as dormant females, which are orange-brown. They may be present around buds and under bark flaps of trees and shrubs but usually shelter under surface debris. Eggs hatch and the females resume activity in mid-spring with the return of sustained temperatures above about 50°F. Being arachnids, they have a life cycle substantially different from that of insects with life stages that include an egg, an early, six-legged immature stage (protonymph), eight-legged immature stages (deutonymph), and adult. Population buildup is rapid under the favorable conditions of warm temperature and low humidity. Generations are completed in as little as 10 days, and adult females typically lay up to five eggs per day over the course of 2 to 3 weeks. Populations peak during July and August, and at the end of the season, many of the mites go into a semi-dormant overwintering form, turning orange or orange-red. However, twospotted spider

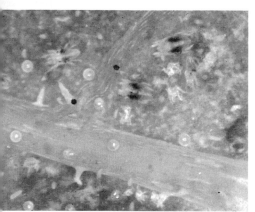

Twospotted spider mites and eggs

mites within greenhouses or other heated areas will reproduce continuously throughout the year.

Natural and Biological Controls: Several organisms prey on spider mites in field settings. Minute pirate bugs are usually the most aggressive natural enemies of mites on garden plants, and various predatory mites are extremely valuable on orchard crops. Banded-winged thrips and specialized lady beetles known as "spider mite destroyers" also control outbreaks. When high humidity prevails for extended periods, outbreaks of fungal diseases can occur.

Cultural Controls: Watering and water management are critical in controlling twospotted spider mites. Overhead watering—and the purposeful hosing of plants with water in a garden setting—dislodges and kills many spider mites. Providing adequate water for plant growth needs is also necessary for managing spider mites. Drought and fluctuating wet/dry soil conditions can stress plants, allowing spider mite populations to increase. Water also limits the rate at which mites feed, since they possess a limited ability to evaporate excess water. Higher humidity rates also decrease feeding by twospotted spider mites.

Chemical Controls: Spider mites are difficult to control with pesticides, and many commonly used insecticides (e.g., Sevin®) aggravate the problem by destroying their natural enemies. In addition, some miticides, such as malathion and Orthene®, are often ineffective because spider mites have developed resistance to them. Insecticidal soaps, horticultural oils, and sulfur dusts are useful miticides and are registered on most vegetable crops for spider mite control. Dicofol (Kelthane®) has long been a standard miticide for flowers and vegetable crops such as cucumbers, squash, and beans, but its availability is limited.

Related Species: Two other spider mites are sometimes problems on orchard crops. The McDaniel spider mite, *Tetranychus mcdanieli,* is closely related to the two-spotted spider mite and

has similar habits. In the past few decades, the European red mite, *Panonychus ulmi,* has emerged as a threat to commercial orchards, particularly where broad-spectrum insecticides are applied to control key pests such as codling moth. Habits of the European red mite that differ from the above are that they overwinter on the trees, rather than in ground cover vegetation, and tend to feed on the upper leaf surface during outbreaks.

The Banks grass mite, *Oligonychus pratensis,* is, as the name would imply, associated with grasses. Sweet corn is the only vegetable crop that is damaged by the Banks grass mite, which produces large populations on leaves and husks, bleaching and killing these tissues. Banks grass mites are also a significant pest of regional turfgrasses, injuring lawns in late spring, with outbreaks originating in droughty areas.

Eriophyid (Rust) Mites
Eriophyidae family

Damage: Eriophyid mites, commonly associated with most trees and shrubs, feed on leaves but rarely cause significant injury. Furthermore, their extremely small size, which makes a spider mite appear enormous in contrast, often causes them to be overlooked. "Leaf vagrant" forms on leaves can be detected with about 25X magnification and appear as tiny, pale-colored "walking carrots."

On some plants, high populations develop, causing the leaves or fruit to turn a rusty color. Within the region, lilac, honeylocust, and pear are the plants most often affected by this condition and, in the southwestern United States, the tomato russet mite inflicts similar injuries on tomatoes. Other eriophyid mites induce changes in the growth of plant parts, a condition known as a "gall." This takes the form of scabby patches on apple and pear leaves, elongate "fingergalls" on leaves of some stone fruits, and distortion of buds. These bizarre growths often are cause for concern, yet pose no serious threat to the health of plants.

Life History and Habits: Most eriophyid mites spend the winter as adults under the scales of buds or within previously produced galls. They

Appleleaf blister mite injury

Rust mites (Photo by Gene Nelson)

become active as new growth is produced in spring and are usually present in highest populations during late spring and early summer. Feeding by gall-producing species on the emergent growth induces the distortion within which they develop and reproduce. Multiple, overlapping generations are produced annually.

Biological Controls: Eriophyid mites are eaten by predatory mites, predatory thrips, minute pirate bugs, and most other small predators associated with garden plants.

Chemical Controls: Dormant season applications of horticultural oils control most overwintering eriophyid mites on trees and shrubs. Carbaryl (Sevin®) and permethrin are two of the most effective insecticide treatments.

ISOPODS (SOWBUGS AND PILLBUGS)

Sowbugs and Pillbugs ("Roly-polys")

Damage: Sowbugs and pillbugs have small mouthparts and feed on tender plant materials. Usually they feed only on decaying plant matter and fungi. However, tender seedlings of garden plants and plant roots may also be chewed. When abundant, they are a problem for newly seeded gardens. Sowbugs and pillbugs are classified as crustaceans, more closely related to lobsters, shrimp, and crayfish than to insects. Both are covered with a hard shell that enables them to live on land. However, they can be distinguished from each other by the pillbug's ability to curl protectively when disturbed. The dark gray, heavily armored pillbug, *Armadillidium vulgare,* also known as the "roly-poly," can roll into a hard, protective "pill" form; the sowbugs (species of *Porcellio*) cannot.

Life History and Habits: Sowbugs and pillbugs are rather long-lived,

Pillbug, or "roly-poly"

but slow-growing. Eggs and the newly hatched young remain inside the mother for several months, protected by her pouchlike marsupium. They then leave and undergo a series of molts as they develop. Young stages resemble the adults, except in size. They become full-grown after about 1 year. Most of the young fail to survive after leaving the mother, usually due to desiccation. However, the adults can live for 2 or more years. Pillbugs and sowbugs usually feed at night, spending the day under cover. They sometimes can be seen during the day, particularly after rains or during overcast conditions.

Natural and Biological Controls: Most sowbugs and pillbugs die from water-related problems—either too little or, less commonly, too much. They are also food for many animals, such as birds, ground beetles, and centipedes. Fungi, such as *Beauveria bassiana,* may infect many. One group of spiders (Gnaphosidae family) specialize in feeding on pillbugs, possessing large fangs that can penetrate the prey.

Cultural Controls: When growing susceptible plants, avoid the heavy use of organic mulches that provide favored shelter for sowbugs and pillbugs. Coarse mulches may be used if the site dries rapidly, and black plastic mulches on beds that receive a lot of direct sunlight in summer often are too hot for sowbugs and pillbugs. Elevating fruit above the soil surface prevents tunneling. Slug traps (beer, inverted fruit rinds) attract sowbugs and pillbugs and can concentrate them for collection.

Chemical Controls: Carbaryl-containing baits are available that control sowbugs, pillbugs, millipedes, and slugs. Barriers of diatomaceous earth repel sowbugs and pillbugs.

Miscellaneous Notes: Sowbugs and pillbugs are an occasional nuisance pest in homes in the West. Following periods of extended wet weather, they are often seen climbing walls and may accidentally enter homes. Once within a home, they rarely survive more than 1 to 2 days due to low humidity.

DIPLOPODS (MILLIPEDES)

Allajulus londinensis and other species

Damage: Millipedes feed on a wide variety of plant materials, but their small mouthparts usually limit them to decaying plant matter or material that is very soft. Strawberries ripening on the ground may be tunneled and destroyed by millipedes. Occasionally, millipedes damage tender vegetable seedlings and root crops such as carrots. The "small white worms" frequently found in such crops more often than not, upon close inspection, prove to be millipedes. Later stages are dark and wormlike and may collect around building foundations or enter basement areas during migrations.

Life History and Habits: Most millipedes spend the winter as adults or nearly full-grown nymphs. Eggs are laid in clusters in soil cracks or under moist, sheltering debris, usually between early spring and summer. These hatch in a few weeks, and the pale-colored, young millipedes move about and feed. They grow slowly, increasing in size and number of body segments with each molt. As they get older, they more closely resemble the adult form, becoming darker and thicker.

Cultural Controls: Millipedes are intolerant of dry conditions, so reducing moisture in a planting reduces the number of millipedes. Infestation is most severe in ripe or overripe fruit, so regular picking limits the problem. Surface-dry mulches that keep the berries off the ground reduce injury. Decaying vegetable and animal manures are particularly appealing to millipedes and should be reduced when millipedes are abundant.

Mechanical and Physical Controls: Millipedes, like slugs, concentrate on overripe fruits, under fruit rinds, or in moistened newspapers. Daily removal of millipedes from these sites reduces their populations.

Chemical Controls: Baits containing the insecticide carbaryl (Sevin®) controls millipedes, sowbugs, and pillbugs. Diatomaceous earth barriers prevent millipedes' access to plantings.

Miscellaneous Notes: Millipedes sometimes migrate en masse, when they congregate around the foundation of buildings. This typically occurs in early fall, particularly during cool, rainy weather.

GASTROPODS (SLUGS AND SNAILS)

Gray Garden Slug/Milky Slug (Agriolimax reticulatum)

Damage: Slugs chew on the foliage of many plants, preferring soft plant tissues such as strawberries, seedling lettuce, or beans, as well as many other garden plants. Young plants are killed or plantings are retarded by damage. Fruits and harvestable parts of leaf and tuber crops can be totally destroyed by slug feeding.

The worst culprit in this region is the gray garden slug, also sometimes known as the milky slug. Of European extraction, the gray garden slug is a pale gray color and reaches a size of about one to 1–1½ inches. Several larger slugs (notably species of *Limax*) also pose a threat, although the very large "banana slugs" found in the Pacific Northwest fail to thrive in this region and die out even though they are regularly reintroduced on plant materials.

Millipedes (Photographer unknown)

Slugs have a fondness for beer, which is detrimental to their health (Cartoon by Tess Henn)

Life History and Habits: The gray garden slug reproduces by laying masses of round, clear eggs in soil cracks and around the base of plants or other organic debris. The young slugs feed on organic matter, including soft plant parts, becoming full-grown in 3 to 6 months. Egg laying occurs during spring and fall, with development suspended during much of the hot season. Slugs feed at night or during heavily overcast periods, avoiding sunny, drying conditions. During the day, slugs migrate to sheltered areas under debris and in soil cracks. Occasionally, slugs are also active during rainy or overcast periods of the day. The gray garden slug may travel as far as 40 feet during an evening of foraging.

Natural and Biological Controls: Several organisms feed on slugs, including toads and garter snakes. Some of the better predators of slugs are larvae of certain fireflies. However, the common western species of fireflies do not exhibit the dramatic flashing characteristic of those found in eastern areas.

Gray garden slug

Cultural Controls: Slugs are highly sensitive to dry conditions, having a high water content and producing large amounts of protective mucous. Consequently, practices that reduce humidity within a garden planting are fundamental to limiting populations of slugs. To eliminate potential shelter for slugs, remove surface debris in and around the garden and avoid organic mulches such as straw and grass clippings. Also, increase air movement around plants and reduce high-moisture conditions with trellises and wider row spacing. Drip irrigation, soaker hoses, or other irrigation techniques that use limited amounts of water control slugs by decreasing the humidity. If overhead irrigation is used, it should be applied early in the day to allow more time for leaves and soil surfaces to dry before the slugs go out for their night on the town.

Mechanical Controls: Slugs are attracted to chemicals produced by many fermenting materials, and these make excellent bait for traps. For example, a shallow bowl of beer or of sugar water and yeast effectively attracts, traps, and drowns slugs. A single such baiting remains effective for several days, as long as it retains sufficient liquid. However, the attraction range of these traps is often only a few feet, so they must be placed strategically throughout a planting. Effectiveness of the traps is reduced if highly desirable plants are nearby. (*Note:* Alcohol is not an attractant to slugs or useful in capturing slugs.) Selective use of trap boards, moistened newspaper, or inverted fruit rinds placed on the soil surface can also be used to concentrate slugs as they seek shelter. These traps should be checked early every morning and any slugs collected destroyed. If traps cannot be regularly inspected, they should not be used, since they provide favorable shelter for the slugs to spend the day. Some plants are particularly attractive to slugs, such as lettuce, beans, hosta, calendula, and okra. Purposeful planting of these trap crops diverts some feeding by slugs on other garden plants.

Slugs often avoid traveling over materials that are highly acidic, alkaline, or abrasive. Diatomaceous earth sprinkled around plants can provide some protection, but loses its effectiveness quickly if it cakes as a result of exposure to moisture. Wood ashes also deter slugs due primarily to their high salt content. Similarly some soaps, which are chemically the salts of fatty acids, are also repellents with at least one (Slug-Out®) currently marketed as being a persistent repellent that will last a couple of weeks. Salt is toxic to slugs and direct application of table salt to a slug produces lethal—and dramatic—results. However, salt can only be applied sparingly in regional gardens since it aggravates existing salinity problems so common to area soils.

Alternately, salt-impregnated plastic strips are marketed to repel slugs. Also, copper strips are highly repellent to slugs, the metals ions apparently interacting with the moist slug to produce an electric charge—a "hot belly." Barriers of copper foil exclude slugs from greenhouse benches and from noninfested raised bed plantings, and are also used to prevent pest snails from climbing fruit trees. Other copper-based materials, such as copper sulfate, are also useful as slug repellents.

Chemical Controls: Household ammonia, diluted about 10:1, is an effective slug killer if directly applied to the slugs. Since slugs usually feed at night, this option is primarily limited to cool, overcast evenings following some rain, when slugs tend to emerge early for their nightly forays through the garden. More concentrated (2:1) dilutions of vinegar also offer some effectiveness as contact "slugicides."

Pesticides effective against slugs and snails are better known as molluscicides. These are typically very different types of chemicals than those used to control insects and other garden pests. Slugs are not susceptible to poisoning by most insecticides. Metaldehyde is the most commonly used molluscicide and is sold in a variety of bait or liquid formulations. Current labeling permits its use around fruit and vegetable crops. Metaldehyde kills slugs by dehydration resulting from the secretion of large amounts of mucous in response to this slug irritant. The success of metaldehyde for slug control requires care in application and favorable weather conditions. Slugs often recover from metaldehyde poisoning if high-moisture conditions occur. Also, control is reduced during very cool or very warm periods, since slugs are relatively inactive during these times. Metaldehyde is most effective if applied in the evening when warm, moist conditions that favor slug activity are then followed by drying weather. Metaldehyde breaks down when exposed to sunlight, so baits should be placed under leaves or in harborage areas used by the slugs.

(*Note:* Metaldehyde is attractive to and poses a significant poisoning risk to dogs. Make sure that boxes of metaldehyde baits are safely stored away so that dogs cannot reach them. Also, when applying baits for slug control, spread them in gardens so that they are not attractive to other animals.)

Bill hunting slugs with dilute ammonia

Related Species: Several other species of slugs, all introduced species, can wreak havoc in regional gardens. Particularly common are *Limax* species, including the great gray garden slug, which may reach 3 inches when fully extended. Although they do feed on plants, they are also predators of other slugs—including members of their own kind.

Snails are much less frequent visitors to our yards and gardens. Most are small and restrict their diet to decayed plant matter, not damaging garden plants. Occasionally large land snails, such as the brown garden snail (*Helix aspersa*), are introduced into the region, but do not thrive here, as they do along the Pacific Coast. This species is the one eaten as an "escargot" delicacy.

Chapter 7

Management of Common Plant Diseases

Conditions that disturb the normal, healthy growth of plants are said to produce plant disease. In the West, diseases very frequently stem from *abiotic* causes. These can be weather related such as desiccating winds, or the extremes of temperature and precipitation common to this region. Soil conditions are another major factor contributing to plant diseases. "Tight" heavy clay soils restrict root growth and drainage, suffocating the roots. Several nutrient imbalances are indicative of plants grown in alkaline, high pH soils, and soil salt levels, frequently excessive in western soils, damage plant growth. We may further aggravate these problems with our garden practices. Plant varieties poorly adapted to local conditions are doomed to struggle no matter how nice they look in a garden catalog. Overzealous garden-

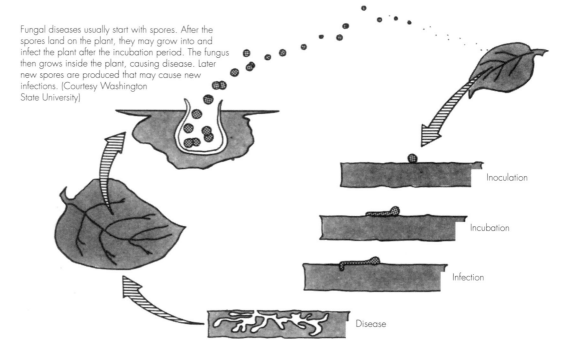

Fungal diseases usually start with spores. After the spores land on the plant, they may grow into and infect the plant after the incubation period. The fungus then grows inside the plant, causing disease. Later new spores are produced that may cause new infections. (Courtesy Washington State University)

Inoculation

Incubation

Infection

Disease

ing leads to problems such as overwatering, root pruning or herbicide injury while controlling weeds, and freeze damage.

However, often the cause of a plant disease is biological (biotic)—the result of infectious microorganisms, specifically a plant pathogen. Infection with various plant pathogenic fungi, bacteria, or viruses can be the root cause of many a malaise. Examples of these *biotic* diseases are powdery mildew, a common fungal disease of roses and melons, and fire blight, a devastating bacterial disease of apples and pears.

FUNGAL DISEASES

Fungi are the most important plant pathogens in the garden. Evidence of fungal disease includes rotting/decay of vegetables, powdery mildew on leaves, wilting, and leaf spotting.

Fungi spread primarily by *spores,* resistant stages broadcast by wind, rain, and human activity. Tremendous numbers of spores may be released by a fungus that is actively growing and fruiting. (For example, the fine dust released by a single mushroom consists of millions of spores, which are spread over large areas by wind and splashing.) When spores of fungi land on a susceptible plant, they may germinate if surface conditions are right. Crucial to germination of most spores is the presence of free moisture on the plant surface for a certain period of time. (Some fungi, such as the powdery mildews, germinate well when humidity is high but there is no free water.) After germination, the growing fungi penetrate the plant, either directly through the epidermis or through wounds and natural openings such as stomates. Once the fungus has successfully established itself, it can extend its threadlike structures (mycelia) throughout the host. As they develop, fungi form reproductive parts to produce the spores. The familiar mushroom exemplifies the spore-producing structure of some fungi, such as fairy ring in lawns. However, most fungi that attack garden plants, such as powdery mildew, produce less conspicuous structures that may appear as small dark dots or slightly fuzzy areas on the plant surface.

The overwintering stages of many plant pathogenic fungi are often capable of resisting environmental extremes, thus facilitating their long-term survival. In particular, many of the fungi that attack the roots of garden plants also produce resistant stages (sclerotia) that enable the fungus to remain alive for several years in the soil, making control particularly difficult.

Some fungi that cause plant disease can survive only on living plant tissues. Some of these rarely survive regional winters, but instead recolonize the area via wind-borne spores originating from more southerly areas. Other fungi thrive on dead plants and only rarely invade living tissues. These latter fungi are often called "weak" pathogens since they only injure plants that are already in a weakened condition.

BACTERIAL DISEASES

Very small, one-celled organisms, bacteria reproduce by dividing (binary fission) and are capable of rapidly increasing in number when conditions are favorable. Bacteria that cause plant disease dissolve plant tissues with enzymes, or plug the sap stream of the plant, causing it to wilt. Fire blight of apples and pears, soft rots, halo blight of beans, and crown gall are some common bacterial diseases.

Bacteria are limited in their ability to move by themselves. Typically, bacteria spread via splashing water or infected seed. Insects also transmit some bacterial diseases. High-moisture conditions are a critical requirement for the development of all bacterial diseases.

One special group of bacteria are known as *phytoplasmas* (often referred to in older books as *mycoplasmas* or mycoplasma-like organisms/ *MLOs*). The phytoplasmas infect cells of the sap stream (phloem) of plants and effect such symptoms as bushy or distorted new growth. Aster yellows, a significant phytoplasma disease in the West, affects many vegetable and flower crops. Pear decline and X-disease of peach trees are serious phytoplasma diseases that injure orchard crops. All phytoplasma diseases in this region are transmitted by leafhoppers or psyllids that feed on the plant.

VIRAL DISEASES

Viral infection is usually detected by symptoms such as leaf streaking, mosaic-patterned discoloration of leaves, yellowing of leaves, leaf curling or crinkling, and ring spots on leaves, blossoms, and fruit. Viruses do not reproduce like other plant disease agents, but instead multiply by causing the infected cells of their host plant to form virus particles. By changing the normal function of the plant cells, the plant is injured. Of all the plant disease-producing organisms, viruses are the most dependent on transmission by other organisms. Viruses, which are simply constructed, minute particles of protein-covered nucleic acid,

TABLE 7-1: COMMON VIRAL DISEASES OF WESTERN GARDENS AND AFFECTED PLANTS

Virus	Crop affected	Means of spread
Tobacco mosaic	Wide host range including peppers and tomatoes	Mechanical (hands, rubbing of leaves, cultivation), maintained on crop debris
Potato virus X	Primarily potatoes	Mechanical (hands, rubbing of leaves, cultivation)
Cucumber mosaic	Wide host range (34 plant families)	Mechanically transmitted (hands; cultivation, including cucurbits, beans, and tomatoes; machinery, etc.); aphid transmitted (green peach aphid, cotton aphid), maintained on seeds of some plants
Common bean mosaic	Beans	Aphid transmitted, mechanically transmitted
Watermelon mosaic	Cucurbits	Aphid transmitted only
Potato virus Y	Peppers, potatoes, tomatoes, and related plants	Aphid transmitted only
Potato leafroll	Potatoes, tomatoes	Aphid transmitted only
Beet western yellows	Lettuce, potatoes, and many vegetables	Aphid transmitted only
Corky ringspot (tobacco rattle)	Potatoes, many other plants	Nematode transmitted
Tomato spotted wilt/ Impatiens necrotic spot	Wide host range including tomatoes, peppers, lettuce, chrysanthemums, field bindweed, asters	Thrips transmitted (onion thrips, flower thrips), maintained on infected perennial plants and overwintered thrips, can be mechanically transmitted
Beet curly top	Tomatoes, beets, peppers	Beet leafhopper
Tobacco ringspot	Potatoes, peppers	Stubby root nematodes, through seed of some weeds (purslane, hairy nightshade, common cocklebur), seed potatoes

possess no means of movement on their own. They must be physically moved by other organisms into plant cells to cause an infection. Many viruses are also spread mechanically as plants rub together, or via hands and tools as gardeners move and work between diseased and healthy plants. Other viruses are spread only by certain insects, usually aphids or leafhoppers. A few viruses also rely on spread by mites, nematodes, and even fungi. Beet curly top, tomato spotted wilt, and the mosaic diseases of melons and cucumbers are some crippling viral diseases that are spread by insects.

PLANT PATHOGENIC NEMATODES

Nematodes are a type of animal sometimes known as a roundworm or eelworm. Most are microscopic in size and wormlike in general form. Thousands of different types of nematodes reside in healthy soils and water, and some of these play a major role in controlling pest insects. However, some species (e.g., root-knot nematodes, sting nematodes) are known to attack plants. Because of their small size, the plant injuries they cause are generally considered plant diseases.

On their own, nematodes can move only short distances in the soil. However, nematode problems may originate and become established in an area by human transmission of infested soil or plant materials. This is particularly common with nematodes that produce eggs inside a protective cyst (cyst nematodes) or a gelatinous sack (root-knot nematodes), which enables them to survive for several years.

Fortunately, serious problems with nematodes are uncommon in the West. Soil drying, dense clay soils, and severe winter temperatures are all unfavorable to most nematodes. Although a few species can affect regional agriculture, such as the sugarbeet cyst nematode and alfalfa stem nematode, problems are rare in yards and gardens.

COMMON VIRAL DISEASES

Cucumber Mosaic

Damage and Symptoms: Cucumber mosaic affects several garden vegetables but is particularly damaging to cucurbits (cucumbers, melons, squash) and lettuce. Common symptoms on cucurbits include a general stunting of plant growth, yellowing or mottling (mosaic) patterns, and wrinkling of the leaves. Fruit from infected plants may also show yellow mottling and a reduced size. A general yellowing, particularly of the older leaves, is typical of infected lettuce. Symptoms are most pronounced when the plants are infected during early growth. Effects of this disease are exacerbated by moisture stress.

Disease Cycle and Development: Cucumber mosaic is caused by infection of plants with the cucumber mosaic virus (CMV). Because it has an extremely wide range of hosts, overwintering sources often include weeds that are infected in the vicinity of the planting. A few plant species can allow the infection of CMV between generations through infected seeds. However, spread of the disease through seed occurs rarely. Cucumber mosaic virus is transmitted between plants either by feeding of aphids or by chewing insects such as the striped cucumber beetle, or mechanically, by practices such as handling infected plants and cultivating. Mechanical transmission is much less likely than with common mosaic, and aphid transmission is generally considered to be the most prevalent means of disease spread. Both of these methods of spread involve rapid infection (within minutes) after plant contact. The virus does not persist for long outside the plant host, but once inside the plant cell, the virus is reproduced at the expense of other plant growth processes.

Cultural Controls: Since infections can occur during greenhouse propagation, closely inspect and discard "off"-looking plants before purchase. During the growing season, remove and destroy plants that show suspicious symptoms of viral infection to reduce its spread. If potentially diseased plants are retained in the garden, they should be handled last, after working around other susceptible plants. Increasing plant populations is useful for reducing losses to cucumber mosaic—larger numbers of plants often results in a lower rate of infection. Infected plants should be removed as soon as possible. Light-colored mulches, particularly those that reflect light such as aluminum foil, effectively repel winged aphids, delaying the infection of plants until after they have overgrown the mulch. By this time, plants are much less vulnerable to the effects of the virus. Resistance to cucumber mosaic virus has been bred into some cucumber varieties, but these are not widely available to gardeners. Silver-leaved varieties also promise resistance because the aphids that spread the disease are less likely to land on them.

Chemical Controls: Cucumber mosaic virus is transmitted extremely rapidly (in seconds or minutes), usually by winged migrant aphids that rarely remain on the plant. Insecticides applied against the insect vector do not prevent the spread of this virus. Oil- or fat-containing sprays, including milk solutions, reduce transmission of the virus by aphids. However, these treatments have short-term effects and need to be reapplied at very short intervals (1 to 3 days), particularly when plants are growing vigorously.

Watermelon Mosaic

Damage and Symptoms: Watermelon mosaic infects all the cucurbit (squash family) plants. Most damaging to watermelon and winter and summer squash, a common symptom of this disease is a variable green mottling on the leaves. Blistered or puckered malformations may also be present. Fruit from infected plants may be abnormally shaped and colored, often with knobs or other outgrowths. Watermelon mosaic causes obvious stunting of watermelons and muskmelons, and the symptoms are most severe when plants are infected early. Watermelon mosaic may coexist in a plant with cucumber mosaic, causing a general loss of plant productivity.

Disease Cycle and Development: Watermelon mosaic results from infection with the watermelon mosaic virus (WMV). It is spread to new plants by winged aphids, which can acquire the virus from diseased plants and transmit it to healthy plants within a few seconds. The aphids that spread the disease are migrants that often do not remain on the plants for long and may or may not reproduce on it.

The virus is not transmitted to progeny via infected seed, nor is it mechanically transmitted by handling and wounding during the growing season. Overwintering sources of the virus in the region are not known, but in more southern regions, wild species of perennial cucurbits are hosts. New infestations may spread annually from aphids migrating from these southern areas. Once the disease has become established in the field, aphids can continue to spread it to new plants.

Cultural Controls: Light-colored mulches, particularly aluminum foil, prevent aphids from landing and retard watermelon mosaic infection. Intercropping of susceptible plants with nonhost plants (plants not related to squash and melons) also reduces disease incidence. Since the disease most seriously affects young plants, cultural practices that hasten plant development avoid loss. Obviously diseased plants should be removed and destroyed. Breeding to develop plant varieties that resist the effects of watermelon mosaic virus is being actively pursued, but no resistant varieties are yet available to gardeners.

Chemical Controls: Insecticides are ineffective for the control of watermelon mosaic virus, since the disease is spread so rapidly. However, special lightweight oil sprays that prevent aphids from transmitting the virus during feeding have been developed. These specialty products are not generally available to gardeners, but other oily materials (milk, horticultural oils, etc.) may be effective.

Beet Curly Top

Damage and Symptoms: The most typical symptom of beet curly top infection is dwarfing. On beans, leaves turn yellow, curl downward, and often become very brittle. Plants infected when young may die, while plants infected later show few symptoms. Beet curly top infects dozens of

Virus-infected pepper

plants, including tomato, pepper, beet, and bean. In addition, numerous weeds (Russian thistle, peppergrass, etc.) are hosts of this virus. The beet leafhopper, which transmits beet curly top (see page 137), is a desert species, native to the West. Both the leafhopper and the beet curly top virus it transmits inhabit dry regions during periods of high temperatures.

Disease Cycle and Development: Beet curly top is caused by infection with the virus of the same name. The virus is transmitted only by the beet leafhopper. Leafhoppers that have acquired the virus from infected plants can transmit it for the rest of their lives. Transmission to healthy plants is effected about 15 to 30 minutes after feeding.

Controls: See beet leafhopper (page 137).

Tomato Spotted Wilt/ Impatiens Necrotic Spot

Damage and Symptoms: Two closely related virus diseases, tomato spotted wilt (TSMV) and impatiens necrotic spot (INSV), emerged during the 1980s as extremely serious threats to greenhouse crops in North America. Since then this disease has frequently appeared in gardens, primarily via infected transplants. An extremely wide range of garden vegetables and flowering plants are hosts of these viruses, including over 500 species of plants comprising more than 50 plant families. Tomatoes, peppers, and lettuce are some of the vegetable crops commonly infected with tomato spotted wilt. Almost all flower crops are susceptible to either TSMV or INSV, with the notable exceptions of rose and poinsettia. Further complicating the management of these diseases is that many common weeds can be infected, such as field bindweed, nightshade, and pigweed, serving as disease sources that then spread to cultivated plants.

Symptoms of TSMV and INSV are similar but the host range varies slightly with tomato spotted wilt being more significant on vegetable crops. Characteristic symptoms of infection include concentric ring spots on the leaves and fruit, stunting and yellowing, and brown streaking or

spotting (cankers) on stems and leaf petioles, causing parts of the plant to wilt and die back. Positive confirmation of TSMV or INSV in plants suspected of the disease is possible through a laboratory test (ELISA—Enzyme Linked Immunosorbent Assay) that is available from most state university plant diagnostic facilities as well as several independent labs.

Disease Cycle and Development: Both tomato spotted wilt and impatiens necrotic spot result from plant infection with a virus. These viruses are spread by thrips, primarily the flower (species of *Frankliniella*) and onion thrips (*Thrips tabaci*). Young thrips developing on diseased plants acquire the virus during feeding, and later, during the adult stage, can transmit it to healthy plants. The virus typically requires 2 to 3 weeks of reproduction within the plant before it can be acquired by thrips and spread to new plants. No other insects are capable of transmitting the virus.

In greenhouses, the tomato spotted wilt and impatiens necrotic spot viruses spread by transplanting infected cuttings. On some plants (e.g., tomato, petunia), tomato spotted wilt virus also is known to be transmitted via infected seed. It may also be mechanically transmitted by wounding plants during gardening operations.

Cultural Controls: Carefully inspect all transplants for evidence of tomato spotted wilt symptoms, and discard and destroy all that are suspected of harboring the disease. If tomato spotted wilt becomes established in a greenhouse, a vigorous, sustained effort must be made to eradicate all plants with the disease. These sanitation efforts can be complemented with, but not replaced by, chemical control of the thrips.

Mechanical Controls: Very fine mesh screens exclude thrips from new plantings.

Chemical Controls: Control of the thrips vector sometimes reduces the spread of the disease, particularly when combined with sanitation efforts to eliminate disease sources. However, both flower thrips and onion thrips are resistant to most insecticides.

Tomato spotted wilt virus symptoms on tomato

Common Mosaic (Tobacco Mosaic Virus)

Damage and Symptoms: Common mosaic produces a broad spectrum of symptoms in susceptible garden plants. Leaves typically show some yellow and green mottling (mosaic), and new leaves may show puckering and distortions. Stunting and poor growth often result from common mosaic infection. The wide host range of common mosaic affects many vegetables (e.g., peppers, tomatoes, spinach, beets) and flowers (e.g., phlox, snapdragon, zinnia), as well as several weeds.

Disease Cycle and Development: Common mosaic results from the infection of plants with the tobacco mosaic virus (TMV). This is an extremely persistent virus that can remain on seeds, crop debris from infected plants, and even clothing for several months or even years. Typically, the virus is spread mechanically, entering plants through wounds that are inflicted during transplanting, pruning, or other handling. Roots growing through crop debris infected with the virus may also be infected. Transmission by chewing insects, such as grasshoppers, may take place but is insignificant. TMV is not spread by aphids, leafhoppers, or other insects that transmit many other plant viruses.

Cultural Controls: Carefully inspect all garden transplants before purchase and avoid those that appear diseased. Diseased plants observed in the garden should be discarded. If plants suspected of being infected are retained, the plants should be handled last to prevent subsequent spread. Most seeds are free of tobacco mosaic virus, although the virus can survive on plant tissues that remain on the seed. Therefore, avoid collecting seed from "off"-looking plants that may be TMV-infected. Breeding work has identified several sources of resistance to tobacco mosaic virus. TMV-resistant plants are most commonly available in some tomatoes and peppers (e.g., VFTN).

Chemical Controls: Tobacco mosaic is not spread by insects, so insecticides do not control

it. Spread of the virus can be minimized by spraying plants with skim or reconstituted milk. This treatment prevents new infections but does not affect the disease in plants that are already infected. Dipping hands in milk while handling plants also deters accidental transmission.

COMMON FUNGAL DISEASES

Phytophthora Blight (species of Phytophthora)

Damage and Symptoms: Phytophthora blight most often afflicts peppers, but can affect related plants such as eggplant and tomatoes as well as all the familiar cucurbits (squash, cucumbers, melons). Marigolds, too, are susceptible. Symptoms can extend to all parts of the plant. Infection of the stems results in wilting and death of the plant due to girdling. When infection contaminates leaves, an irregularly shaped spotting with a scalded appearance occurs. Fruits are infected from the stem end and consequently rot.

Disease Cycle and Development: Phytophthora blight is caused by fungi in the genus *Phytophthora* (usually *Phytophthora capsaci*) that survive on seed and in the soil. Conditions of high soil moisture enable the swimming spores to infect new plants. After plants become infected, other types of spores are produced that can be windblown for long distances. Warm, wet conditions are particularly accommodating to the infection of plants.

Cultural Controls: Crop rotations with non-susceptible plants are critical to reducing the survival of the organism in the soil. Also, improving drainage around plants prevents some of the original infections that are dependent on standing water. Later infections of leaves and fruit can be reduced by increasing air circulation around plants and watering in a manner that prevents the plant from remaining wet for long periods.

Chemical Controls: Repeated applications of copper-based fungicides or Bordeaux mixture

Bean common mosaic virus symptoms on leaf to the left

Phytophthora wilt (Photo by Howard Schwartz)

control infections of the leaves and fruit. However, these fungicides may damage plants, particularly cucurbits, when temperatures are high.

Related Species: *Phytophthora infestans*, or late blight, is a highly destructive disease of potatoes and related plants that caused the spectacular Irish potato famines in the mid-1800s. To date, late blight has rarely been a problem in the arid West because the pathogen requires extended periods of rain or fog to successfully infect plants and spread. However, new strains have evolved that are highly resistant to fungicides, and as a result, the incidence of the disease has increased significantly through North America in recent years.

Verticillium Wilt (*Verticillium albo-atrum, V. dahliae*)

Damage and Symptoms: Plants infected with verticillium wilt first show a yellowing of leaves, with leaves dying progressively from the margins in. Foliar symptoms often show a V-shape of yellowing or necrosis that is widest along the leaf margin. Overall stunting of infected plants may occur but, since the disease affects the vascular system, symptoms may be restricted to one side of the plant or even one side of the leaf. On established plants, the disease progresses upward, first affecting the older leaves. Infections on new canes of raspberry, rose, or other perennial plants may show the reverse, with dieback occurring first at the tip. Symptoms on all plants emerge rapidly following periods when plants are under stress from drought or heat. Dark streaking of the vascular system (xylem) is often a symptom of infection with verticillium wilt. These symptoms are similar to those of fusarium wilt, and the two diseases often cannot be separated except through laboratory culture, although streaking of the vascular system by fusarium often extends higher up on the plant. Potato, eggplant, and other nightshade family plants, strawberry, raspberry, most stone fruits (species of *Prunus*), and several flowers and weeds are the most common hosts of

verticillium. Of the two species found in the region, *Verticillium dahliae* tends to be found in warmer regions whereas *V. albo-atrum* thrives in cooler soils.

Disease Cycle and Development: Verticillium wilt results from infection of plants by fungi, either *Verticillium albo-atrum* or *V. dahliae*. The fungus survives in the soil and infects plant roots that contact various stages of the fungus, generally entering through wounds. The fungus then grows within the root, destroying the vascular system. As the infected roots die, the fungus reproduces by forming spores. Verticillium wilt infection is widespread with hosts comprising various flowers, trees, fruit crops, and most vegetables. Grasses and sweet corn are not hosts of the disease-producing organism.

Cultural Controls: Verticillium wilt is introduced into gardens on infected plants or soil, materials that should not be brought into a garden unless the source is free of the disease. Many plant varieties are resistant to verticillium wilt. In particular, resistant tomato varieties are widely available, as indicated by the "V" in VFN (or VFTN, etc.) designation on seed packs or labels. Crop rotation encompassing a cycle of three to four years or more aids in limiting the disease. In the vegetable garden, these rotations should include nonsusceptible plants, such as sweet corn, as well as plants that are rarely infected such as onions, spinach, most mustard family plants, beans, and peas. In areas of high summer temperatures and sunlight, soil solarization kills many of the surviving stages of verticillium wilt fungus in soil. This method should be coordinated with other cultural controls, such as crop rotation, for best effect. Infected plants should be removed and destroyed by disposal. Composting or tillage often does not kill the more

Late blight symptoms on leaf (Photo by Howard Schwartz)

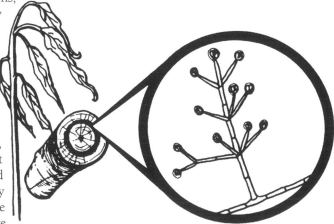

resistant stages of the fungus. Providing favorable growing conditions of adequate soil moisture, moderate temperatures, and nutrients limits the effects of infection. It is particularly important to avoid overwatering early in the season.

Fusarium Wilt of Tomato (*Fusarium oxysporum, lycopersici strain*)

Damage and Symptoms: Fusarium wilt attacks the root system of plants, causing wilting of the top growth. The first symptoms often include yellowing of lower leaves followed by general wilting. Sometimes the leaves will die without wilting symptoms, and the effects of the disease may be confined to only one branch of the plant. Brown streaking of the interior of stems and leaf petioles is characteristic. Fusarium wilt of tomato infects tomatoes, eggplant, and several weeds such as pigweed.

A closely related pathogen, *Fusarium oxysporum* F. sp. *radicis-lycopersicia,* produces a crown rot of tomatoes and wilting of the top growth. In this disease, the streaking of the vascular system only extends about 6 inches from the roots to the crown of the plant.

Disease Cycle and Development: Fusarium wilt is caused by infection with a fungus, *Fusarium oxysporum, lycopersici* strain. Spores of the fungus enter a garden on infested seeds, soil, or decaying plant parts. The spores germinate when susceptible plants grow roots adjacent to them. The germinated fungus invades the plant root system, often through wounds. Once inside the roots, the fungus grows through the xylem of the plant. On susceptible plants, it may grow up the stem and even into the petioles of the leaves. In some resistant plants, infections are restricted to the roots. Growth of the fungus is favored by temperatures of about 80°F and declines in very cool or very warm soils. The disease can progress rapidly in actively growing, succulent plants.

Cultural Controls: Using resistant varieties is fundamental to managing fusarium wilt of to-

Fusarium wilt symptoms on eggplant

mato. Resistant varieties are indicated in descriptions of plant characteristics and can include resistance to both Race 1 (VFN) and Race 2 (VFTN) of the fungus. Several soil and growing condition retard development of the disease. Near-neutral soil pH (6.0–7.2) reduces disease incidence. Fertilization should also be moderate, since high nitrogen (particularly ammonium nitrogen) favors the disease. Cultivation around plants should be minimized to prevent root wounding. Crop rotation is of minimal value, since the spores are so tenacious. Consequently, extra effort should be made to prevent introducing the disease on infested soil and plants. In areas with high summer temperatures and sunlight, soil solarization kills many surviving stages of the fusarium wilt fungus in the soil. This method should be coordinated with other cultural controls, such as crop rotation and resistant varieties, for best results.

Biological Controls: Mycostop®, the K61 strain of the bacteria, *Streptomyces griseoviridis,* help prevent Fusarium infections on greenhouse-grown tomatoes. Research with this organism on field-grown tomatoes is lacking. Methods of application include dipping transplants prior to planting or formulating an in-furrow drench.

Miscellaneous Notes: Several different species and strains of the fusarium wilt fungus reside in garden soils. Most are weak pathogens that damage primarily young plants grown under stressful conditions. Species of *Fusarium* also cause problems with seed piece decay of potatoes and storage rot of onions.

Anthracnose of Cucurbits (*Colletotrichum orbiculare*)

Damage and Symptoms: Anthracnose is a common disease of most cucurbits, particularly cucumbers, muskmelons, and watermelons. The first symptoms of this disease are small, yellow leaf spots that later turn brown-black. These irregular spots of dead tissue often drop out, leaving holes. The spotting can also spread, killing leaves, stems, and developing fruit. Anthracnose

symptoms also ravage fruit. Dark, sunken spots pit the skin of infected fruit, and small, dark spots, the fruiting bodies of the fungus, may be observed within the affected area of tissue. Although anthracnose does not penetrate into the fruit flesh, other rotting organisms can enter the plant through anthracnose-damaged tissues, causing further fruit injury.

Disease Cycle and Development: Anthracnose of cucurbits results from infection with the fungus *Colletotrichum orbiculare*. This fungus survives on nondecomposed plant debris and on seed from infected plants. Spores are splashed or mechanically moved about by insects or during handling. Once on the plant, spores germinate following a favorable period of high humidity and then en-ter the plant cells. External symptoms may appear in about a week. The fungus continues to grow within the plant, periodically producing new spores that spread the infection. Plants may be infected at any stage of growth, including after harvest.

Cultural Controls: Because the fungus survives on old debris of infected plants, plants and old fruit should be destroyed by tilling or composting. Crop rotation of cucurbits of three or more years is also of benefit, although this option is less useful in small garden plantings than in commercial fields. Since high humidity and water splashing facilitate disease spread, trickle or furrow irrigation reduces disease incidence. If gardens are watered with sprinklers, watering should be done

Rose anthracnose

Early blight

early in the day to allow leaves to dry rapidly. Several cucumber varieties are resistant to strains of anthracnose, including Dasher II, Slicemaster, and Pixie. Resistant varieties of watermelon include Allsweet, Crimson Sweet, Jubilee, Sugarlee, and Triple Sweet.

Chemical Controls: Fungicides used preventively control infection. Treatments should be applied during periods when leaf wetting favors the disease. (*Note:* Sulfur fungicides should not be used since they burn leaves of "sulfur-shy" plants such as cucurbits.)

Related Diseases: Anthracnose is a description applied to many different plant diseases. Angularly shaped leaf spots, usually surrounded by a discolored area, are typical of leaf infections. In addition to certain vegetables, anthracnose infections can develop in gardens on hosta, phlox, penstemon, verbena, and other ornamental plants as well as on some trees (ash, sycamore). For example, on rose leaves infections of spot anthracnose, caused by the fungus *Sphaceloma rosarum,* often follow periods of wet weather. It generally produces a rusty brown, angular leaf spot with a dark margin. Most of the nightshade family vegetables are also vulnerable to various species of *Colletotrichum.* The primary damage is the production of small, dark sunken spots on fruit of crops such as eggplant, tomato, and pepper. The management of these diseases is similar to that for anthracnose on cucurbits.

Early Blight
(*Alternaria solani*)

Damage and Symptoms: Early blight primarily causes a leaf spotting characterized by a series of dark, concentric rings often surrounded by a slight yellow area. As the disease spreads, the entire leaf may die and drop from the plant. Older leaves are most susceptible and the disease typically progresses upward in the plant. Infections also invade the calyx end of fruit. These appear as dark spots that radiate from the stem. Often the fruit spots form a distinctive concentric ring

pattern. Infections on potato tubers appear as dark spotting on the surface. Early blight infects tomatoes, potatoes, eggplant, and several weeds in the nightshade family.

Disease Cycle and Development: Early blight follows infection with the fungus *Alternaria solani,* which survives on old plant debris in the soil or on the soil surface. When conditions are favorable, the fungus continues to grow on these plant parts, producing spores that are spread by wind, rain, and insects. Injuries by flea beetles also serve as sites of infection. The fungus spores germinate after a few hours at very high humidity. They then enter the plant through natural openings or penetrate directly through the plant cuticle if the surface remains wet for several hours. Symptoms of spotting appear 2 to 3 days after infection and grow rapidly for about a week. As the fungus continues to grow, it periodically produces spores capable of causing new infections.

Cultural Controls: Vigorously growing plants naturally resist infection by early blight. Older plants, or plants carrying heavy fruit loads, tend to succumb to the disease. Cultural conditions that provide optimal fertilization, watering, and temperatures greatly retard development of the disease. Infected plant remains should be handled in a way that hastens decomposition, since the fungus requires plant parts to survive. Composting or rototilling into the soil reduces the amount of fungus that will survive into the following season. Crop rotation helps as well, particularly in larger gardens. Watering should minimize the length of time that leaves are wet. Trickle types of irrigation decrease ambient humidity, which favors infection. When overhead irrigation is the only option, it should be applied during periods when leaves will dry quickly.

Chemical Controls: Protectant fungicides such as sulfur prevent spores from infecting plants.

Related Diseases: Several species of *Alternaria* fungi occur on vegetable crops, including alternaria leaf spot/blight of cucumbers and other squash family plants (*A. cucumerina*), purple blotch of onion (*A. porri*), and alternaria leaf spot/black spot of cabbage (*A. brassicae*). Cultural controls for these diseases are similar to those for early blight.

Botrytis Blight/Gray Mold
(Botrytis cinerea)

Damage and Symptoms: Botrytis, a common disease of vegetables, grapes, and many flowers, attacks various plant parts. On roses and peonies, botrytis produces a fuzzy, gray mold that kills flower blossoms. Damage to grapes takes the form of bunch rot of the developing fruit. Leaf blight symptoms result from Botrytis infection of lettuce, tomatoes, and onions. Botrytis also causes a common gray mold on the fruit of tomatoes, peppers, carrots, raspberries, and other fruits and vegetables kept in storage.

Disease Cycle and Development: Botrytis blight, also known as gray mold, is caused by infection with the fungus *Botrytis cinerea*. Spores survive the winter on previously infected plant parts around the garden. In addition, Botrytis is an extremely common organism and is annually transported long distances as windblown spores. Infections often originate on dead or damaged tissues before invading healthy parts of the plant. Conditions conducive to germination of the spores are extended periods of very high humidity (90–100 percent) and temperatures of 68°F–76°F. However, the disease can infect stored vegetables at much lower temperatures.

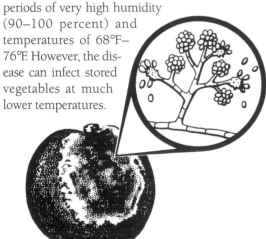

Cultural Controls: Since high humidity is almost a prerequisite for infection with botrytis, susceptible plants need good air circulation to encourage leaf drying. If possible, watering should be done in a manner that does not allow leaf wetting or prolonged high humidity around the plants. Where botrytis occurs as a leaf disease, cultural conditions that encourage vigorous plant growth reduce susceptibility. Also, because botrytis typically enters wounds, use care when working around plants when infection is likely. This disease organism is so common and spreads so easily that crop rotations are not very effective for control.

Chemical Controls: Several fungicides are available that help control botrytis on many garden plants.

Related Species: *Botrytis squamosa* produces leaf blighting and dieback of onion leaves, a much more severe injury to this plant than is produced by *B. cinerea*. *Botrytis fragariae* can be a common problem on strawberries, giving them a moldy taste.

Powdery Mildew of Cucurbits
(Erysiphe cichoracearum,
Sphaerotheca fulginea)

Damage and Symptoms: A fine, powdery growth forms on the leaves, often starting on the more shaded areas of the plant. The growth may spread and cover much of the leaf surface of the plant. Affected leaves often shrivel, dry, and die, exposing the fruit to sunburn. Although fruits are rarely infected directly, damage to the leaves can cause small fruit size, reduce sugars that develop fruit flavor, and produce fruit of poor texture. Problems usually harass squash and pumpkins, since resistant varieties of cucumbers and muskmelons are currently available.

Erysiphe cichoracearum has one of the widest host ranges of any of the powdery mildews. In addition to cucurbits, other hosts include various composites such as zinnia, dahlia, phlox, begonia, chrysanthemum, and sunflower.

Powdery mildew on squash

Disease Cycle and Development: Powdery mildew of curcurbits is a by-product of infection with either of two species of fungi, *Erysiphe cichoracearum* or *Sphaerotheca fulginea*. The fungus requires a living plant for its development, and dies out annually after frost kills the plants. However, the spores are produced in enormous numbers and, surviving in more southern regions, they are easily dispersed northward with the winds. When conditions allow, the spores can germinate and infect leaves. Unlike other fungi, very high humidity is not needed to infect plants—infection has occurred at a relative humidity as low as 46 percent. Optimal temperatures for infection are around 80°F. Leaves are most susceptible 2 to 3 weeks after unfolding.

Cultural Controls: Developing plants that are resistant to powdery mildew has been the most effective control. Breeding has been most successful with cucumbers and muskmelons, but has lagged with pumpkins and squash.

Biological Controls: Several fungi have been identified that invade and parasitize powdery mildew fungi. At least one of these, *Ampelomyces*

Powdery mildew on chokecherry

Powdery Mildew

Powdery mildew is a familiar type of fungal disease in the western yard and garden. It primarily affects the new growth; infected leaves often curl and fail to fully grow. Most characteristic is a powdery covering of the leaves, which consists primarily of threadlike chains of spores. The effects of powdery mildew infection commonly include reduced growth and the death of leaves and buds. Although fruit are rarely infected, sugar and flavor can be affected and sometimes weblike russeting will scar the fruit skin. Among the plants usually damaged are rose, cucurbits (squash, cucumbers, melons), apple, grape, and various flowers such as zinnias and asters. Many grasses, including Kentucky bluegrass, also are susceptible to powdery mildews.

Although powdery mildew produces generally similar symptoms among all these plants, a wide variety of different species of fungi are responsible. For example, the fungus that produces powdery mildew infection of roses is a different species than what infects cucumbers, as that of bluegrass differs from powdery mildew of peas.

Powdery mildew thrives during the summer and early fall, provided temperatures are moderate and there is a bit of shade from intense sunlight. Unlike most other fungal pathogens of plants, germination of powdery mildew spores does not mandate that the leaves be wet for several hours, and very wet conditions can even harm delicate germinating spores. Instead, powdery mildew infections can take place when the relative humidity on the leaf surface is high, about 70 percent RH being a lower limit. Although humidity in this region averages far below that, a period of cool, overcast weather following a rain or increased nighttime humidity associated with temperature drops can provide the ideal environment. Therefore, increasing air circulation around plants to lower these humidity peaks is necessary for powdery mildew control. Resistance to powdery mildew has long been a focus of plant breeders, and resistant varieties of many cultivated plants are now available (see Table 7-2).

Powdery mildews should not be confused with downy mildews (species of *Peronospora*). The latter are uncommon in the region because of their need for sustained damp conditions. Outbreaks of downy mildew (page 174) on plants such as onion, spinach, and mustard family plants require unusually wet, cool weather. The primary symptom of downy mildew infection is typically a dark leaf spotting, and the furry mildew growth is only visible when plants are damp.

quisqualis (AQ10® Biofungide®), is currently marketed for control of powdery mildew on cucurbits, as well as some fruit crops and ornamentals. Application instructions indicate that it should be applied with oil in the initial stages of powdery mildew infection with a follow-up treatment. This fungus is not compatible with most chemical fungicides.

Chemical Controls: Some fungicides are useful for the control of powdery mildew. Copper-based fungicides are probably the most widely available for garden use at present. Sulfur, and sulfur combinations such as lime sulfur, should not be used since cucurbits are notoriously "sulfur-shy" and are readily burned by these treatments.

TABLE 7-2: SOME CUCURBIT VARIETIES RESISTANT TO POWDERY MILDEW

Cucumbers

Ashley	Atlantic	Belle Aire
Bravo	Burpless F1 Hybrid	Burpless Green King
Burpless Tasty Green	Cherokee	Commanche
Dasher	Early Set	Early Triumph
Gemini 7	Marketmore 76	Pickmore
Pixie	Poinsett	Polaris
Quick Set	Shamrock	Slicemaster
Sprint 440 II	Supersett	Sweet Slice
Tablegreen 65	Tex Long	Victory

Muskmelons (Cantaloupe)

Ambrosia	Classic	Dixie Jumbo
Gold Star	Gulfstream	Imperial 4-50
Luscious	Magnum .45	Mainstream
Planters Jumbo	PMR 45	Saticoy
TAM Uvalde		

Winter Squash

Table King

Powdery Mildew of Rose (*Sphaerotheca pannosa*)

Damage and Symptoms: Powdery mildew of rose often first develops on young stem tissues, later spreading to the leaves and flower buds. Infections restrict plant photosynthesis, resulting in reduced growth, and the overall appearance of plants and flower quality are damaged. Apricots, peaches, and plums (all members of the rose family) are also attacked by this fungus.

Disease Cycle and Development: Powdery mildew of rose overwinters on canes, often behind bud scales, and in other protected sites. During this period, powdery mildew produces winter-resistant forms that appear pepperlike on the canes. In the spring, the fungus resumes growth and produces spores when warm temperatures return. These spores are windblown or splashed onto leaves or other parts of the plant and will germinate if conditions are favorable. Optimal temperatures for spore germination are similar to those of many fungi that infect the leaves of garden plants, between 65°F and 80°F. However, the moisture requirements are unusual since germination is inhibited by leaf wetting. Instead, high humidity around the range of 70–99 RH is preferred. The germinated spores then create a penetration tube that forces the fungus into the upper cell (epidermis) of the plant, initiating infection. After growing within the plant cells for a few days, the fungus begins to grow along the leaf surface and invade new cells. Periodically, the mass of powdery mildew on the leaf surface produces and releases new spores (conidia), which further spread the infection. Infections most often impair newer growth, since powdery mildew cannot infect old growth. During periods when new growth increases, such as after flowering, infections increase as well.

Cultural Controls: Since the germination of powdery mildew spores requires high humidity, planting in locations with open air circulation reduces humidity and, hence, infections. Air circulation can also be improved by using raised beds and reducing the density of plantings. Interestingly, powdery mildew of rose does not need wet leaves to allow spores to germinate and infect the plant. This was demonstrated during the late 1930s and early 1940s when frequent water sprays were used as the primary means of spider mite control. Under these conditions, problems with powdery mildew declined, since the fungus is delicate and easily damaged by these water sprays (although other fungal diseases do increase with watering). Because the fungus overwinters on shoots, pruning and removing infected shoots helps provide control. It is also useful to remove fallen leaves, which under some conditions allow the fungus to survive. Resistance to powdery mildew varies among the several types of roses. Hybrid teas and climbers are generally highly susceptible, whereas wichurianans and all shrub roses are more resistant. Although many new varieties are resistant to powdery mildew, this resistance often breaks down as new races of powdery mildew develop.

Mechanical Controls: As mentioned above, powdery mildew is a delicate fungus adversely affected by water films. Regularly hosing the plants suppresses infections, both by washing off spores and by breaking the germination tubes of recently germinated spores. These water washes are of particular benefit when conducted during periods when both the temperature and humidity favor infection. Also, they should concentrate on the new growth as mature tissues are no longer susceptible to infection. Since other rose diseases are encouraged by leaf wetting, water washing should be done during the day to allow rapid drying.

Chemical Controls: Several sprays are useful in the control of powdery mildew. Protectant fungicides, such as sulfur and triforine, can prevent new powdery mildew infections. (*Note:* Sulfur will injure plants when temperatures are above 90°F.) It is critical to control the disease at the times when the disease spreads most rapidly. Sprays should be applied to protect the newly produced tissues, which are susceptible to infection. Sprays of dilute (about 1 percent) horticultural oils and neem oils can be very effective for powdery mildew, and the addition of a small amount of baking soda is reported to improve control of oil sprays. In addition, antitranspirants (e.g., Wilt-Prufe®), which are sometimes used to retard water loss during transplanting or over winter, may also reduce the spread of powdery mildew. This action results from physically thickening the leaf surface, inhibiting infection.

Related Species: On apple and pear, another species of powdery mildew, *Podosphaera leucotricha,* may cause injury. Symptoms of infection on shoots are similar to those of rose. Weblike russeting of fruit may also result from this disease. Additionally, peach and nectarine are susceptible to *P. leucotricha,* which produces a "rusty spot" symptom on the maturing fruit. Pruning infested shoots during the dormant season and spring fungicide treatments applied just prior to flower bud break can manage problems with this disease. Red and Golden Delicious varieties of apple are fairly resistant to powdery mildew. Redhaven, Redglobe, July Elberta, Reliance, and Blake are among the peach varieties most resistant to rusty spot.

Powdery Mildew of Grape
(Uncinula necator)

Damage and Symptoms: New plant tissues are infected and produce a powdery covering when powdery mildew attacks grape. Infected leaves may be distorted and stunted, fruit clusters may exhibit poor fruit set, and infected berries are discolored and often split. Wines produced by the infected berries have off flavors. The disease takes more of a toll on the European wine grapes, *Vinis vinifera,* than on the species native to North America. Ivy and Virginia creeper are additional hosts.

Disease Cycle and Development: Powdery mildew of grape is caused by the fungus *Uncinula necator.* In areas of cold winter temperatures, the fungus survives between seasons in a protected stage (cleistothecia) in bark cracks. In spring, spores are produced, which may blow or splash onto developing grapes.

When environmental conditions permit, the spores germinate and infect the plant. The fungus grows into the epidermis of the plant and spreads along the surface. Spores may be produced a week after infection, allowing further spread of the disease. Temperatures ranging from 68°F to 77°F are optimal, although the fungus develops in a wide range of conditions. Relative humidity from 40 to 100 percent is needed for spore germination, but free water, such as rainfall, is damaging to the spores. The fungus also favors shading from direct sunlight. Infections occur only on new tissues. Grape berries are vulnerable only until they reach a sugar level of about 8 percent.

Cultural Controls: Most grape varieties claiming parentage of the native grapes of North America, *Vinis labrusca,* are resistant to powdery mildew. These include Concord, Freedonia, Valiant, and many of the more commonly grown grapes in the West.

Biological Controls: Several fungi have been identified that invade and parasitize powdery mildew fungi. At least one of these, *Ampelomyces quisqualis* (AQ10 Biofungicide®), is currently marketed for control of powdery mildew on grapes, apples, strawberries, and ornamentals. Application instructions indicate that it should be applied with oil at the initial stages of powdery mildew infection with a follow-up treatment. This fungus is not compatible with most chemical fungicides.

Chemical Controls: Several fungicides control powdery mildew of grape. These are best applied early in the season to protect the plant when sensitive new growth is being abundantly produced. Early treatment also prevents the production of new spores, which can cause damaging outbreaks. Sulfur is often used for powdery mildew control. However, some grape varieties, such as Concord, are damaged by sulfur. On wine grapes, sulfur should not be used late in the season to avoid producing hydrogen sulfide during fermentation.

Infected buds give rise to young shoots completely covered by fungus

Fungus sporulates on surface of green shoots and leaves

Common Smut
(Ustilago maydis)

Damage and Symptoms: Common smut infects any of the aboveground tissues of corn and is particularly noticeable when ears are involved. Attacked cells become greatly enlarged and fill with the fungus, forming very conspicuous spongy swellings with a thin gray cover. As the fungus matures, it turns black with the formation of huge numbers of spores.

Disease Cycle and Development: Common smut is produced by the fungus *Ustilago maydis.* Spores of this fungus overwinter in the soil, on seed, and on infected plant debris that has not decomposed. Splashed by rain or blown by wind, these overwintering spores (teliospores) contaminate developing corn and germinate to form a new stage (sporidia) that is capable of infecting plants. Corn smut usually invades the plant through wounds, although it can also penetrate the stomates. Corn is particularly susceptible to corn smut infection when it is only a couple of feet tall and before the tassels form (whorl stage). Some moisture is necessary for the spores to germinate and infect the plant.

Corn smut

Cooking up the corn smut

"Shothole" symptoms from Coryneum infection

Cultural Controls: Crop rotation and tilling decrease the amount of surviving corn smut spores in the area of the planting and reduce subsequent infections. However, wounding during the early stages of growth, either by windblown sand or cultivation injuries, can facilitate increased infections. Corn plants are also less likely to be infected if conditions favor steady, normal growth; excessive use of nitrogen should be avoided.

Miscellaneous Notes: The young stages of the fungus, before the dark spores are produced, are edible and considered by many to be a delicacy. They are popular in cooking in Mexico and Latin America. In these areas, corn smut is sometimes purposely cultured by wounding young plants and exposing them to spores.

Apple Scab
(*Venturia inaequalis*)

Damage and Symptoms: Symptoms of apple scab on the leaves include scabby spotting and leaf puckering. Less common but more severe injuries produced by apple scab are those affecting apple fruit. Scabby patches develop on the fruit surface that are slightly sunken and light brown, often with visible, dark spores developing around the margin. Affected fruit is often distorted by infections. Heavily infected leaves may drop prematurely. Crabapple, hawthorn, pyracantha, and mountain ash serve as other apple scab hosts. Crabapple, particularly a few varieties such as Radiant, are habitual victims. Apple scab is rare in this region since the required high moisture is infrequent.

Disease Cycle and Development: Apple scab overwinters as spores on previously infected leaves and fruit. Splashing rain and wind carry the spores to new hosts in the spring, and germination occurs following periods of continuous wetting lasting at least 12 hours. Optimal temperatures for infection are in the range of 55°F to 75°F. New spores begin to be released from infected tissues after about 2 weeks with infections progressing as favorable conditions persist.

Cultural Controls: Apple scab can be well controlled in backyard orchards through sanitation. Infected leaves should be raked and removed along with dropped fruit. (These materials should be composted or buried to promote decomposition, which kills overwintering spores.) Sprinklers should be set to avoid wetting leaves or should take place early in the day to allow drying. Some apple scab resistant varieties have recently been developed (e.g., Liberty, Prima).

Chemical Controls: If necessary, apple scab can be controlled with timely applications of fungicides. The period between bud growth and when fruit is about ½ inch in diameter is particularly critical for the application of fungicides, especially if conditions of extended wetting exist.

Coryneum Blight/
Shothole Fungus
(*Wilsonomyces carpophilus*)

Damage and Symptoms: Coryneum blight primarily infects peaches, apricots, and nectarines; sweet cherry, several wild cherries, and plum serve as occasional hosts. On the leaves, small red-purple spots develop, which later drop out of the leaf, producing a characteristic shothole injury, similar to flea beetle damage to vegetables and flowers. More serious damage results from the infection of the fruit. Early infections leave rough, scablike spots on the fruit and induces distorted growth. Late-season infections produce slightly sunken, grayish areas on the fruit.

Disease Cycle and Development: Infection with the fungus *Wilsonomyces carpophilus* (=*Coryneum beijerinckii*) results in coryneum blight. The fungus overwinters on buds of dormant leaves and flower buds or in infections on twigs. Spores produced during wet periods and are splashed by rain or blown by wind. Sustained wet conditions are necessary for the spores to successfully germinate and infect new plant parts. Once infections occur, the fungus reproduces and new infective spores are released. Infection is most rapid under optimal temperatures of 70°F to 80°F;

however, germination can also take place at very low temperatures. Once established in an orchard, coryneum blight is difficult to eliminate.

Cultural Controls: Early identification and control of infestation limits the need for other control practices. To eliminate overwintering spores, prune to remove infected twigs, buds, and blossoms. Also pick up infected fruit and rake up infected leaves. Most damage occurs on lower leaves that remain wet longer. Improved aeration reduces infections as well.

Chemical Controls: Several fungicides help control coryneum blight. Treatments are most critical when early-season wet weather favors outbreaks of the disease. During outbreaks, on peach and apricot it is recommended that fungicides be applied after the leaves have dropped in the fall to prevent overwintering bud and twig infections.

Cytospora Canker (Gummosis) (*Cytospora leucostoma*)

Damage and Symptoms: A very common disease of stone fruit, cytospora canker kills areas underneath the bark (cankers) of peach, cherry, plum, and apricot trees. This injury weakens the trees and branches often die. Newly transplanted trees are at greater risk of infection, particularly if planted in an area of existing infections or if the plant is wounded during transport and planting. External symptoms of the disease are production of amber gum oozing through the bark around infected areas (gummosis).

Disease Cycle and Development: Cytospora canker is produced by infection with the fungus *Cytospora leucostoma*. Spores of the fungus are widely distributed by wind and air and can be found on the bark of trees year-round. The spores need a wound in the bark through which to enter the tree, with colonized wounds typically being the result of freeze damage, pruning, hail or lawnmower injuries, and borers. The fungus then grows under the bark, killing the wood and producing the canker symptoms. Within a month of infection, spores begin to form around the can-

kered area, which can then be spread by insects, splashing rain, and on pruning tools. Growth of the fungus is maximized in spring as temperatures first warm. During periods of active tree growth, fungus growth is temporarily inhibited by the tree's natural defenses. Spores capable of initiating new infections may be found on bark year-round, but are produced in greatest number from July through September.

Cultural Controls: Because Cytospora is a wound parasite, cultural practices that avoid stress and injury are essential in managing the disease. These include proper fertilization and watering so that trees grow vigorously in late spring and early summer but become suitably hardened off to survive fall freezes. Pruning wounds and borer injuries should be minimized to avoid infection at these sites.

Mechanical Controls: Infected branches can be pruned. Pruning conducted during late winter and early spring is recommended since the production of new spores is minimal at this time. In areas of intense sun, use white reflective paint on trunks to reduce sunscald injuries, thus avoiding later problems with cytospora canker.

Chemical Controls: Protectant fungicides reduce infection probability if applied immediately after wounding by pruning or hail injury.

Miscellaneous Notes: Cytospora canker and other stresses impel stone fruit trees to ooze amber gum. Damage by the peach tree borer also causes gumming, but the gum is characteristically mixed with bark fragments chewed from the trunk. Clear gum is often a response to freeze injuries.

Damping-off (species of Pythium, Rhizoctonia, and other fungi)

Damage and Symptoms: Seeds may decay before they emerge and the tender stems of seedlings that sprout from the soil may be infected, causing the plants to fall over and die. Surviving plants may show darkened depressions on the stems associ-

Oozing ("gummosis") associated with Cytospora

ated with a reduction in growth—a condition commonly described as a type of "crown rot."

Disease Cycle and Development: Seed decay and damping-off are caused by infection with various fungi, primarily a species of *Pythium*. Common in garden soils, these fungi generally survive in decaying plant debris. They also survive on seeds, although most commercial seed is treated to be disease-free. However, when conditions of moisture and temperature are suitable, fungi can successfully invade and reproduce within seeds and tender seedling tissues.

Cultural Controls: Seeds should be planted under conditions that favor rapid seed germination and seedling development, since older plants are more able to resist infection. However, excessive moisture greatly favors the disease. Watering should be done carefully to avoid prolonged soil wetting, such as in early morning, and to allow thorough sun drying. Maximizing air circulation also reduces humidity near the soil surface. Excessively heavy seeding rates increase the spread of the disease, although some increase in seeding can compensate for lost plants. This recommendation is typically included in seed package instructions that suggest seeding at a high rate and later thinning. When growing seedlings in a cold frame or greenhouse, damping-off can be avoided by using disease-free soil. Some, but not all, artificial potting mixtures do not contain damping-off fungi. When garden soil is used to grow seedlings, it should be treated with high temperatures to kill the fungus spores.

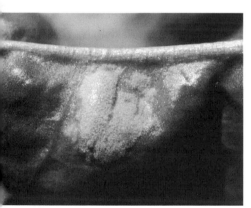
Blue mold, downy mildew on spinach

Biological Controls: At least three microbial controls of damping-off fungi have recently been marketed. Mycostop®, the K61 strain of the bacteria *Streptomyces griseoviridis,* is primarily sold for control of damping-off in greenhouse/nursery container-grown stock, applied as either a dust to seed or as a soil drench. *Burkholderia cepacia* (type Wisconsin), sold as Deny®, may be used similarly at the planting time of seedling transplants. (Deny also claims control of many common nematodes.) The use of these products in field situations must still be considered experimental. SoilGard®, containing a fungus, *Gliocladium virens* (GL-21 strain), that is antagonistic to Pythium and Rhizoctonia, is sold to mix in the soil prior to seeding.

Chemical Controls: Several fungicide seed treatments (e.g., thiram, captan) are available to control damping-off. Many seed suppliers routinely offer seed that is already treated with these fungicides, or they may be purchased separately if desired.

Downy Mildew/Blue Mold (*Peronospora effusa*)

Damage and Symptoms: Blue mold can be the most important disease of spinach in this region. Infections appear as yellowish patches on the leaves, which later turn black and die. Late in the season, infected spinach may survive, but the leaves become yellow and the plants are stunted. During periods of wet weather, which favors the fungus that produces the disease, leaves rot rapidly and plants may die or are severely weakened.

Disease Cycle and Development: Downy mildew of spinach, also known as "blue mold," is caused by infection with the fungus *Peronospora effusa*. It survives winters on living spinach plants, in the soil or on the seeds. New spores that infect plants are first produced in spring. The germination of these spores requires free water on the leaves for several hours, provided by sources such as dew, rain, or overhead irrigation. This is a cool-weather fungus (optimum around 46°F).

Cultural Controls: Since leaf wetting is required for infection with the blue mold fungus, watering should be done in a manner that does not prolong leaf wetting or high humidity around the plants. If possible, plantings should increase air circulation by using raised beds. The life cycle of the fungus can be broken by crop rotations. In a garden, eliminating spinach for a year usually is a sufficient amount of time for the disease to die out. Growing winter crops of spinach, which enables the fungus to survive the following season, increases problems with blue mold. After harvest, spinach plants should be removed or spaded into the soil as soon as possible. Downy mildew reproduces well on dying spinach leaves and survives on the seeds. Blue mold has several different races, and resistant plants have been developed for some of the most common ones. Some of the spinach varieties resistant to the common races of blue mold are Melody, Norgreen, Marathon, Bonus, Duet, Mount St. Helens, Highpak, and Badger Savoy. However, new races of the fungus that can damage these varieties have already evolved in this region.

Related Species: Although the generally arid climate of the region does not favor infection with any downy mildew fungus, some plant damage is possible. The most likely culprit is *Peronospora destructor,* which sometimes damages the leaves of onions and related crops during seasons with cool, wet weather. Downy mildew also threatens lettuce (caused by the fungus *Bremia lactucae*) and some mustard family plants (caused by the fungus *Peronospora parasitica*).

Rhizoctonia
(Rhizoctonia solani)

Damage and Symptoms: Rhizoctonia encompasses a wide variety of disease symptoms in various vegetable crops. It is a member of the damping-off gang that causes seedlings to collapse and die. Surviving plants affected by the disease may be weakened and grow poorly because of wirestem (the destruction of much of the plant's stem). Petunias and other annual flowers may sustain a dark, charcoal black rot of the roots, which usually results in the death of the plant. On lettuce and other leafy vegetables, the disease produces a "bottom rot," usually initiated around leaf mid-ribs touching the soil and later progressing through the lower head. Infected tissues subsequently are often invaded by secondary organisms, which produce a slimy rot. On potatoes, the most common symptom of the disease is black scurf, sometimes described as "the dirt that won't wash off." Rhizoctonia also creates small, dark-ened areas on the stem (cankers). If much of the stem area is damaged, aboveground (aerial) tubers may form.

Associated Organisms: Black or charcoal-colored root rots can also be caused by several other fungi. *Thielaviopsis basicola* is particularly prevalent in flower gardens. Occasionally *Phytophthora* fungi will produce root rots, usually on vegetables. Typical symptoms include a watery decay of roots and sometimes a purplish discoloration along the edges of the more affected leaves.

Disease Cycle and Development: The fungus *Rhizoctonia solani* produces various Rhizoctonia diseases. Several strains of the fungus are known, each attacking separate types of plants. Rhizoctonia is easily transported on infected soils and plants and typically resides in garden soils. It can persist for very long periods in its resistant sclerotia form (e.g., the black scurf on potatoes). When susceptible plants are grown, the fungus is also stimulated to grow and infect crops. Although wet soil is needed for infections, favorable temperatures vary. For example, the strain of Rhizoctonia that causes black scurf on potatoes prefers an optimum temperature of about 54°F; the optimum for bottom rot on lettuce is about 78°F.

Cultural Controls: High humidity favors disease. Increasing air circulation around the plants to avoid prolonged wetting of the base of the plant deters some infection of lettuce. Growing on mulches that prevent soil/leaf contact also limits this problem. Rhizoctonia prefers dead plant materials and, when soils are rich in organic matter, gradually show reduced ability to infect healthy plants. Increasing soil humus reduces disease caused by the fungus. Obviously diseased plants should be removed and discarded to prevent further development of the fungus. Crop rotations reduce the incidence of some strains, such as the one that infects potatoes, although most forms of Rhizoctonia are too persistent to be significantly affected by garden rotations. Crop rotations involving nonsusceptible plants, such as sweet corn and beans, must be of several years' duration to eliminate the disease. The black scurf condition of potatoes develops rapidly in cool, wet soils, so prompt harvesting reduces this problem.

Hollyhock Rust
(*Puccinia malvacearum*)

Damage and Symptoms: The leaves, stems, and vigor of hollyhock are the targets of hollyhock rust. Common mallow (cheeseweed) and okra are also susceptible. The first symptoms to appear are yellow-orange spots on the upper leaf surface. These expand and ultimately form rusty-brown swellings (pustules) on the underside of the leaves.

Hollyhock rust on mallow

Disease Cycle and Development: Hollyhock rust results from infection by the fungus *Puccinia malvacearum,* which survives on old plant debris infected the previous year. It resurges in spring, producing spores that infect the plant. Following exposure to leaf wetting for several hours, the spores germinate and grow. The fungus grows into the plant, ultimately producing the rusty-brown pustules on leaves, which are packed with summer-stage spores (urediospores). These produce infections later in the growing season. More resistant overwintering stages of the fungus are formed in late summer.

Cultural Controls: Old plant parts should be removed and destroyed to alleviate overwintering

Rust Fungi

The rust fungi are some of the most notorious plant diseases, periodically devastating wheat, coffee, and other crops worldwide. They usually attack leaves and stems, and the germinating spores directly penetrate the leaf surface or move through natural plant openings such as stomates. Infected areas die or function poorly, and plants may yield poorly. Fruits and berries of some crops are also infected. In the course of infection, most rusts produce yellow, white, or, more commonly, rusty red or orange spots—each packed with spores (urediospores).

One unusual characteristic of the rust fungi is that many require two different types of host plants to complete their development. For example, juniper-hawthorn rust alternates between juniper and hawthorn. It spends the winter on juniper, producing a jellylike, horned growth that forms following wet weather in the spring. Infections caused by the spores from this growth occur during the summer on hawthorn, where rust-colored growths collects on the leaf underside. Cedar-apple rust (cedar/apple), wheat stem rust (wheat/barberry), and white pine blister rust (white pine/currants or gooseberries) are other examples of these synergistic two-host rusts. In the absence of both hosts, the disease wanes, being dependent on the spread of spores for long distances by winds. (White pine blister rust is such a significant disease of white pine in the Northeast that culture of its alternate host—currants and gooseberries—is restricted in some areas.)

Much work on the control of rust fungi has involved breeding resistant plants. However, the rusts have shown a tremendous ability to overcome these defenses as new races of the fungi overcome plant defenses. For serious rust diseases, such as wheat stem rust, ongoing sophisticated programs detect new races early and immediately breed resistant varieties.

Rust fungi is also controlled by many fungicides, including triforine (Funginex®), copper fungicides, and maneb-type fungicides.

stages of the fungus. During the growing season, leaves showing symptoms of infection should be promptly picked and removed to prevent spread. A new cover of mulch placed around the base of the plant further prevents the spread of overwintered stages of the fungus. Planting in sites with open air circulation reduces infection by hollyhock rust.

Chemical Controls: Applying sulfur or other preventive fungicides prevents spores from infecting plants. These are most effective during periods of high humidity.

Leaf pustules of bean rust

Rose Rust
(species of *Phragmidium*)

Damage and Symptoms: Rose rust infects the leaves and occasionally the young stems and sepals of roses, and is most noticeable when orange or red-orange spots (pustules of aeciospores) form on the underside of the leaf. As the spots enlarge, brown spots may be observed on the upper leaf surface. Infected leaves are less vigorous and sometimes will drop in response to infection.

Disease Cycle and Development: Caused by infection with *Phragmidium* fungi, nine different species of rose rust fungus have been found on roses. Spores of rose rust blow in the air and infect leaves through natural openings, such as stomates. Continuous moisture for 2 to 4 hours and favorable temperatures (65°F to 72°F is optimal) are needed for successful infection. Hot, dry conditions limit the disease. The fungus grows through the leaf tissues, and later produces clumps of spores in characteristic pustules on the leaf underside. The orange or orange-red urediospores that result cause new infections throughout the growing season. At the end of the year, the fungus forms black, resistant spores (teliospores) that survive the winter on fallen leaves and stems. The following spring, these subsequent stages of the fungus renew growth and produce spores that repeat the cycle.

Cultural Controls: Reducing periods of leaf wetting, particularly when temperatures are favorable for infection, is fundamental to managing rust on roses. Water early in the day so leaves dry quickly. Plantings pruned to increase air circulation also aid drying and reduce infection. Old leaves and other plant debris should be removed from the rose beds in the fall, and mulching further inhibits rust spores that remain from overwintering around the soil surface. Rose varieties vary greatly in their susceptibility to rose rust. Many are quite resistant; others are highly susceptible.

Chemical Controls: Several fungicides are effective for control of rose rust. These are most effective when applied during periods when environmental conditions favor infections (e.g., moderate temperatures combined with leaf wetting).

COMMON BACTERIAL DISEASES

Angular Leaf Spot of Cucumber
(*Pseudomonas syringae*, *lachrymans* strain)

Damage and Symptoms: Infestations on leaves of cucumber plants appear as dark, angular spots bordered by leaf veins. During moist conditions, tearlike droplets of bacteria may ooze from the infested tissues. As the leaf dries and shrinks, irregular tears in the leaf are formed. Similar symptoms occur on squash and watermelon, although infested areas are typically surrounded by a small,

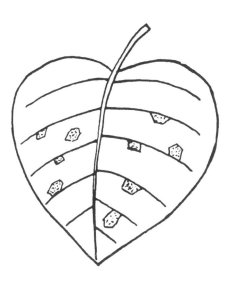

yellow halo on these plants. Fruit may also be infested, resulting in circular spotting. This is usually confined to the surface of the fruit but can allow soft rotting bacteria to enter.

Note: "Scorch" symptoms on cucurbits are very common and often are due to fluctuations in environmental conditions during growth. High salts and irregular moisture during growth cause the dieback seen on the leaves.

Disease Cycle and Development: Angular leaf spot is caused by the bacteria *Pseudomonas syringae, lachrymans* strain. They overwinter within the garden on old, infected plant debris. Movement into plants is through wounds or natural openings (stomates). Since the bacteria require water to move and persist, wet conditions in early morning, when stomates are open, can be pivotal to infection. Once the disease has started to develop, it can spread easily on tools, clothing, and hands during routine gardening operations.

Cultural Controls: Since the bacteria survive for only a limited period, crop rotation can be beneficial. Tillage or the removal of overwintering plant debris further decreases the surviving bacteria. Leaf wetting affects the spread of the disease. Furrow or drip irrigation significantly retards the disease, in contrast to sprinkler watering. Take care to water in a way that allows the leaves to dry during the early part of the day. Nitrogen fertilizers should be used moderately, since excessive nitrogen tends to increase the severity of the disease. Some cucumber varieties have been developed that demonstrate a resistance or tolerance to the disease, including Stokes Early Hybrid, Bounty, Carolina, Score, and Liberty Hybrid.

Chemical Controls: Copper-based bactericides can protect the plants, and several are registered for use on cucumbers, melons, and squash. However, frequent application of these materials can damage cucurbits, particularly in high temperatures.

Miscellaneous Notes: One of the related bacteria, *Pseudomonas syringae, phaseolicola* strain, infects beans, causing a disease known as "halo

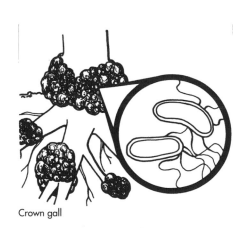

Crown gall

blight." Controls are similar to those for angular leaf blight.

Crown Gall (*Agrobacterium tumefaciens*)

Damage and Symptoms: Infections with crown gall cause warty, tumorlike growths to develop on stems and roots. These growths, called galls, are generally rounded with a rough surface. At first, the growth may be soft and light-colored, but it becomes woody and darkens with age. Crown gall infects a wide range of plants, including rose, apple, raspberry, cherry, plum, peach, and walnut. Several garden flowers, such as chrysanthemum, daisy, and aster, also may be infected. Most plants exhibit some stunting or slowed growth due to infection with crown gall. However, the response to infection is variable, with some plants showing little damage while others may stop producing altogether.

Disease Cycle and Development: Crown gall infections are the work of the bacteria *Agrobacterium tumefaciens,* which enter the bark through wounds caused by pruning, grafts, cultivation injury, or natural causes such as frost heaving. Once inside the plant, the bacteria transform some of the cells into tumor-producing cells. These transformed cells continue to grow without the bacteria. Meanwhile the bacteria develop between the tumor cells at or near the surface of the gall. As the gall breaks down, or is cut during gardening work, the bacteria are released and are free to spread to new plants.

Cultural Controls: New plants should be carefully examined before purchase and planting so that infected plants are not introduced into a yard. Diseased plants should be removed immediately. If possible, the soil surrounding the plant should also be removed or sterilized, since the bacteria can reside in the soil for up to two years.

Biological Controls: Treating plants with the K84 strain of the bacteria, *Agrobacterium radiobacter,* inhibits growth and the establishment of *A. tumefaciens* and prevents crown gall. Sold under such trade names as Galltrol-A® or Norbac-84®, this was the first commercially developed biological control of a plant disease. However, these products are not distributed through popular garden catalogs and their use has been limited to nurseries and some orchards during propagation and planting.

Chemical Controls: Gallex® is a kerosene-based paint that controls existing galls by drying them out. It is not widely distributed and is marketed only through some specialty suppliers of the nursery industry.

Miscellaneous Notes: Because of the tumor growth crown gall infection produces in plants, this disease was studied extensively in developing early cancer research models. More recently, *Agrobacterium tumefaciens* has proved to be extremely useful in the development of transgenic plants.

Fire Blight
(*Erwinia amylovora*)

Damage and Symptoms: Areas of inner bark are destroyed by this disease, producing a canker. Branches, twigs, leaves, and fruit often die back rapidly beyond the cankers, appearing dried and blackened as if scorched by fire. In severe infections, entire trees are killed. Many plants of the rose family are susceptible, including crabapple, apple, pear, cotoneaster, hawthorn pyracantha, serviceberry, and mountain ash. Some of the most susceptible fruit varieties are Bosc and Bartlett pears; Rome, Lodi, and Jonathan apples; and Bechtal crabapples. Stone fruits (*Prunus* species) are not susceptible to fire blight.

Disease Cycle and Development: Infection with the bacteria *Erwinia amylovora* results in fire blight. Infected areas of bark produce bacteria-rich ooze during favorable periods of growth. The bacteria are most often splashed by rain and enter the plant through wounds or natural openings such as blossoms. Dispersion of the disease by insects, including pollinators such as honeybees, is also common. The probability of fire blight infection increases dramatically if cool temperatures extend blossoming time. The bacteria then move into the inner bark and multiply. They kill the infected areas, producing a canker injury, which weakens or girdles the branch or twig. In response, the plant dies back to the area where girdling cankers have formed. The bacteria continue to grow and spread during favorable conditions, moving to progressively larger areas of the tree, and growing most rapidly in temperatures of 70°F to 81°F. Very little growth is sustained when temperatures drop below 65°F or exceed 90°F. Rainfall or high humidity also favor bacteria growth and enable increased infection.

Cultural Controls: Some varieties are partially resistant to infection, including apple varieties Red Delicious, Winesap, and Haralson; pear varieties Magness, Moonglow, and Starking Delicious; and crabapple varieties Vanguard and Red Vein Russian. Trees should not be excessively fertilized with nitrogen, since succulent growth is susceptible to infection. Watering and fertilizing just enough to sustain growth keeps fire blight infection in check.

Mechanical and Physical Controls: Pruning infected branches prevents the spread of fire blight. However, several precautions should be taken when pruning, since this disease is highly infectious. Prune during dry periods in winter, when the trees are dormant. Cuts should be clean—at least 12 inches below visible infections in twigs, 6 inches in branches. If wood is darkened at the cutting site, cut farther back. When multiple, new blossom infections occur, pruning may not be feasible without destroying the tree. In these cases, it is advisable to hold off on some pruning until the following season to determine if the infection is spreading. Many blossom infections die out during the winter. Throughout all pruning, tools should be continuously sterilized to avoid transferring bacteria to new wounds. Sterilize with a disinfectant (either bleach at 1:4 dilution with water or 70 percent alcohol) after each cut. (Lysol® spray is an alternative disinfectant.) Allow

Oozing from fire blight canker

Terminal wilting caused by fire blight

at least 30 seconds to adequately disinfect. Avoid any additional tree wounding, since this supplies new sites for infection. It is possible, though somewhat difficult, to prune individual canker wounds on larger limbs. The bark of infected areas can be scraped out during periods of warm, dry weather. All the outer bark and cambium should be removed at the darkened canker and at least 1 inch beyond the infected area. All prunings should be removed from the vicinity of the host plant since it continues to be a source of the pathogen.

Biological Controls: A recently introduced biological control for fire blight is a strain of the common bacteria *Pseudomonas fluorescens,* sold under the trade name Blight Ban®. When sprayed onto the tree, this bacteria secretes antibiotic substances that inhibit the growth of fire blight bacteria. (This bacterial strain is also reported to suppress the development of bacteria that are involved in nucleation of frost, thus helping to prevent freeze injury.) Good control has been reported from application of the bacteria alone and excellent control when it is combined with applications of agrimycin. Applications are not compatible with copper-based bactericides.

Chemical Controls: Blossoms are most likely to succumb to infection if conditions are conducive—18 or more hours during which temperatures remain between 65°F and 90°F and relative humidity is above 65 percent. Applications of the antibiotic streptomycin or copper sprays during these high-risk periods can prevent new infections. Rotating streptomycin with copper sprays retards the development of fire blight bacterial strains that are resistant to these pesticides. Sprays typically provide protection for about 5 days.

Bacterial Soft Rot
(*Erwinia caratovora, Erwinia chrysanthemi*)

Damage and Symptoms: Bacterial soft rot can be blamed for a broad spectrum of symptoms on garden vegetables. It is reputed to be one of the most common causes of decay of root crops (carrots, onions, potatoes) both during the growing season and after harvest. The bacteria also infect leafy vegetables, such as lettuce. Usual symptoms include a slimy gray or brown rot, with the outer layer of the plant remaining intact. Often other organisms subsequently invade the wound, producing a foul-smelling decay. Bacterial soft rot is also responsible for the decay of potato seed pieces, along with the effects of certain *Fusarium* fungi.

Disease Cycle and Development: Bacterial soft rot follows infection with a strain of the bacteria *Erwinia caratovora* or a related species, *Erwinia chrysanthemi*. These bacteria are widespread in soils and survive on crop debris, and they multiply on the roots of crop plants and weeds. The bacteria must enter through wounds in the plant. Sunscald, wind or hail damage, wounding during cultivation, and insect injuries create vulnerable points in a plant where the bacteria enter. Bacteria spread primarily by splashing or moving water but can also be spread by certain insects, such as sap beetles and root maggots. The root maggots (seedcorn maggot, onion maggot, and cabbage maggot) are particularly to blame, since they physically wound the plant as well as carry the bacteria on their body.

Cultural Controls: Because soft rotting bacteria enter through wounds, avoid bruising or injuring plants during garden cultivation and harvest. Use special care when pulling plants with foliage (e.g., "greentop" carrots) or with thin skins (e.g., "new" potatoes), since these are especially susceptible to infection. Since the bacteria that cause bacterial soft rot commonly reside in soils, crop rotation is of limited benefit. Some of the plants preferred for rotations to reduce this problem are beans, peas, spinach, beets, and sweet corn. Populations of bacteria that survive on discarded plant materials can be reduced by promoting rapid decomposition through fall tillage or composting. To alleviate seed piece decay of potatoes, make sure that the cut surfaces of seed potatoes have healed (suberized) before planting. Planting in warm (above 50°F), moist soil further speeds wound healing and reduces decay. To avoid infections in stored vegetables after harvest, keep temperatures just above freezing (32°F) and relative humidity below 90 percent.

Chemical Controls: No effective bactericides are available to control bacterial soft rot in gardens, though insecticide seed treatments kill root maggot flies that spread the disease to some plants, such as seed potatoes and germinating beans.

Related Strains: A strain of *Erwinia caratovora* commonly infects potatoes, producing a disease known as blackleg. Symptoms of this disease include a black discoloration and wilting of the shoots. The best way to prevent blackleg in a garden is to buy certified seed potatoes.

Aster Yellows

Damage and Symptoms: Aster yellows is produced by infection with a phytoplasma, and it has one of the widest host ranges of any plant pathogen, capable of infecting at least 300 species of plants in 48 plant families. The most common garden hosts are members of the sunflower family (Asteraceae) and include lettuce, carrots, aster, cosmos, marigold, and zinnia. However, species in many other plant families can be infected, such as petunia, beets, and onions, as well as several common weeds. Two strains of the disease exist, with the only difference being that the western strain (celery aster yellows strain) is more infectious on celery. Typical symptoms include yellowing and bronzing of foliage. New growth is often twisted or consists of an overabundance of small shoots—a "witches broom." On head lettuce, in addition to a twisting of the new leaves, dark latex spots appear on the stems. Top growth of carrots becomes very bushy and roots produce numerous hairy roots at the expense of tap root growth. Symptoms on flowers vary but usually involve the disruption of normal petal growth, which inhibits flower formation or causes them to revert to a leaflike condition (phyllody).

A gradation of symptoms depends on the time of infection, ranging from mild symptoms to plant death.

Disease Cycle and Development: Aster yellows is transmitted only by the feeding activities of certain species of leafhoppers that have acquired the disease from infected plants. Within this region, the aster (six-spotted) leafhopper, *Macrosteles quadrilineatus* (see pages 138–139), is the primary vector of the disease, although some 16 species of leafhoppers are capable of acquiring and transmitting the aster yellows phytoplasma. In the Far West, the carrot leafhopper (*Aphrodes bicinctus*) assumes a major role in the spread of the celery/western strain of aster yellows.

Aster leafhopper vectors are restricted to the Gulf of Mexico area during winter. In late spring and early summer, the leafhoppers fly and disperse throughout most of the United States and southern Canada. Aster leafhoppers acquire the aster yellows phytoplasma while feeding on an infected plant. A period of approximately 2 weeks must pass before the insect is capable of transmitting the disease to new plants. Symptoms of infection initially appear about 3 weeks after the disease organism is transmitted and progress with time. Peak infection, paralleling the peak activity of infective leafhoppers, typically occurs in late July and early August.

Infected perennial plants almost always die following infection. However, purple coneflower (Echinacea) and some other plants may survive winters following infection, and then provide a source of aster yellows phytoplasma that affects plantings the subsequent year. In general, the incidence of aster yellows in the region is independent of what transpired during the previous year as infections result primarily from leafhoppers carrying the pathogen during annual migrations.

Cultural Controls: Aster leafhopper, the vector of aster yellows, thrives in areas of low, sparse vegetation around humid sites. Infection is reduced in open, windy areas with dense

Twisting of lettuce head by aster yellows infection

Flower distortion (phyllody) of cosmos produced by aster yellows infection

TABLE 7-3: SUSCEPTIBILITY OF CARROT CULTIVARS TO ASTER YELLOWS

Cultivars Most Susceptible to Aster Yellows

Bonanza	Candy Pak	Caromba	Carona
Clairion	Dandy	Danvers 126	Flakkese
Giganta	Goldpak	Lucky's Gold	Nantes
Nantes ST	Nantes Superior	Orlando Gold	Red Cored Chanentay
Spartan Bonus	Super Sprite	Sytan	Touche

Cultivars of Intermediate Susceptibility

Casey	Goldpak	Goldpak G	Long Imperator
Midas Touch	Nanco	Pakmore	Spartan Fancy
Triple Gold	Trophy 301		

Cultivars Most Resistant to Aster Yellows

Amtou	Charger	El Presidente	Gold King
GT Dicer	Impak	Nanton	Royal Chantenay
Scarlet Nantes	Six Pack	Toudo	W465

Source: University of Wisconsin

Hairy root symptom of carrot (on left) produced by aster yellows infection

growth. Planting very early can often avoid infection by maturing before the main flights of infective leafhoppers arrive in late spring or early summer. Carrots encompass a considerable range in susceptibility (see box), although none can completely resist infection during outbreaks.

Chemical Controls: There are no effective controls for the pathogen; chemical controls are directed toward the leafhopper vectors. Since the aster leafhopper is highly migratory, control with insecticides is very difficult. Pyrethroids, such as permethrin, have been most effective on commercial vegetable crops and provide about a week of plant protection. Carbaryl (Sevin®) and malathion are also used but demonstrate less residual action. On flowers, planting time soil treatments of the systemic Disyston® have been recommended, but since this provides only about a month of protection, it will likely offer little defense against midsummer flights of leafhoppers. Because symptoms of infection typically take 2 to 3 weeks to develop, treatments can be safely discontinued as harvest approaches.

X-Disease of Stone Fruits (Other Names: Western X-Diseases, Peach X-Diseases, Yellow Leaf Rot)

Damage and Symptoms: X-disease infects all stone fruits but is particularly damaging to sweet cherries, peaches, and nectarines. The most severe response is rapid wilting and death of the tree, usually following high temperatures before harvest. Sometimes a zipperlike, irregularly darkened area is noticeable at the graft union. Irregular fruit ripening, gradual decline, and dieback are symptoms on other varieties. Red spotting on leaves and a yellowing similar to iron chlorosis are additional leaf symptoms. Fruit often drop prematurely and peaches may swell at the flower end. Increased susceptibility to winter kill is also associated with X-disease infection. At present, the incidence of X-disease in this region is limited to areas west of the Rockies.

Disease Cycle and Development: Infection with a bacteria, similar to a phytoplasma, produces X-disease. This disease is spread by several species of leafhoppers, including the mountain leafhopper, *Collandonus montanus.* Leafhoppers acquire the X-disease phytoplasma when feeding on an infected plant. It moves into the blood of the leafhopper and multiplies in the insect vector. After a 6- to 8-week latent period, the leafhopper is capable of transmitting the disease organism to healthy plants for the remainder of its life. Among infected trees, the course of the disease varies. For example, sweet cherry on Mahealeb rootstock often collapses suddenly due to rejection reactions at the graft union; on sweet cherry on Mazzard rootstock and on tart cherry the decline is gradual.

Mechanical Controls: No cure for X-disease is known. Since infected trees can be sources of additional infection, trees should be promptly destroyed.

Chemical Controls: The disease is spread by leafhoppers, so effective control of the leafhopper vectors theoretically should control transmission to new trees. However, the species of leafhoppers that are responsible for X-disease spread are poorly known, and effective insecticide treatments have not been identified. Regardless, in the absence of strict sanitation practices that remove infected trees, any chemical controls are likely to be only minimally effective. Sprays of iron chelate fertilizers can extend the life of producing trees infected with X-disease.

COMMON ENVIRONMENTAL DISORDERS

Tipburn

Damage and Symptoms: Edges of the internal leaves brown on cabbage, Brussels sprouts, and lettuce. Symptoms often are not visible from the outside. Soft-rotting bacteria invades the damaged tissues, causing the heads to decay.

Disease Development: A deficiency of calcium in the growing plant induces tipburn symptoms. This often results from nutrient imbalances that occur during periods of high temperature when soils contain excess nitrogen. Excessive soil salt concentrations and fluctuating water and humidity levels also aggravate the problem.

Cultural Controls: Applying moderate rates of nitrogen fertilizers and watering practices that avoid periodic water stress reduce the incidence of tipburn. Susceptibility to tipburn is also related to varietal differences.

Blossom-End Rot

Damage and Symptoms: Beginning as a small watery bruise on the blossom end of tomatoes and peppers, blossom-end rot spots enlarge, darken, and become depressed as the fruit grows. Fruits damaged by blossom-end rot often ripen earlier. Blossom-end rot is differentiated from sunscald and fungal infections on tomato by its restriction to the blossom end of the fruit. Flat tomato varieties tend to be most susceptible.

Disease Development: Blossom-end rot results from a deficiency of calcium in the developing fruit. This causes actively growing cells to leak water and nutrients and, consequently, die. Calcium deficiencies can be induced by deficient soil calcium levels, imbalances of magnesium or nitrogen, excess soil moisture, compacted soils, or other fluctuating conditions during plant growth. Excess levels of salts in the root zone also contribute to blossom-end rot. Planting in cold soils, poor drainage, and high temperatures increase problems as well. The earliest fruit set most often exhibits blossom-end rot symptoms due to the fluctuating conditions of watering, temperature, and transplanting.

Cultural Controls: Blossom-end rot can be reduced if garden culture allows for moderate, steady growing conditions. This includes providing adequate water and avoiding root injury by hoeing. Few soils in the region are deficient in calcium. However, calcium may not be readily available to plants if soil imbalances (nutrients, pH, salts, water) occur. Sprays of calcium chloride or calcium nitrate have reduced symptoms of blossom-end rot. Some tomato varieties are less susceptible to blossom-end rot.

Edema

Damage and Symptoms: Edema results in wartlike outgrowths on the undersides of leaves. Geranium is one of the most common plants on which edema occurs. Many succulent vegetables can be affected, such as potatoes, tomatoes, muskmelons, cauliflower, and beans, but it is most common on cabbage. As the outer layer of cells bursts, the damaged area becomes brown and corky.

Disease Development: A water imbalance in the plant created when water is taken up by the roots faster than it is lost through transpiration is the cause of edema. This typically occurs during periods when cool nights follow warm, humid days, and soil moisture is high. The engorged cells burst from the water pressure.

Cultural Controls: During periods of weather that favor edema, watering should be reduced and air circulation around the plants should be increased. There is also a range of resistance to edema, so susceptible varieties should be replaced in future plantings where edema is a problem.

Miscellaneous Notes: On some cabbage varieties, feeding by onion thrips (see page 127) can cause a reaction similar to edema.

Sunscald

Damage and Symptoms: Sunscald causes large, pale-colored, wrinkled, or sunken areas, most noticeable on fruit, but also occurring on trunks, stems, and leaves. Damaged areas often become papery as they dry out. On raspberry plants, sunscald (solar injury) appears as white areas on the fruit. Sunscald injuries are limited to areas of the plant that receive the most intense sun exposure.

Disease Development: Exposure to direct sunlight, particularly during conditions of high temperature, fuels sunscald. Previously shaded plant parts that suddenly become exposed are particularly susceptible to injury. In addition to direct injury caused by high temperature, several insects, fungi, and bacteria can enter the damaged areas.

Sunscald of tomato with secondary infections beginning

Cultural Controls: Plants that produce sufficient foliage to shade fruit and other susceptible tissues limit sunscald injuries. Also, varieties with fruit that grows downward and underneath foliage are less likely to be injured by sunscald. When harvesting and working around plants, avoid breaking branches or otherwise exposing fruits. Controlling diseases that kill leaves prevents sunscald injuries as well. Shading cloths can be used to protect some fruits and vegetables. The trunks of susceptible fruit trees can be protected by using reflectant paint applied to the south and west sides. White latex paint diluted 1:4 with water is commonly used to protect the trunk. Older trees that have thicker bark and bark that is protected by shading show less damage.

Cold Injury

Damage and Symptoms: Cold temperatures precipitate many different types of plant disorders, including:

- Cessation of plant growth and seed germination
- Death of leaves, plants, blossoms, shoots, and developing fruit
- Prevention of pollen production
- Prevention of pollinator activity
- Catfacing of fruit (e.g., strawberries, tomatoes)
- Blistering of leaves and fruit
- Shrinking and pitting of fruit
- Production of "off" tastes
- Development of nutrient deficiencies, particularly those asociated with phosphorus deficiency
- Skin russeting (sheet pitting) of fruits and vegetables
- Cracking of sun-exposed bark in winter

Exposure to cold temperatures also affects the growth response of transplants, causing them to flower prematurely (bolt). Many garden vegetables (onions, cabbage, broccoli, etc.) are biennial plants, which require 2 years to complete their development by producing flowers and seeds. Normally these crops are harvested the first season, before flowering occurs. However, cold temperatures after transplanting stimulate a signal to the plant that the first season is over, initiating flowering.

In addition, cold damage indirectly causes wounds or damaged tissues to form, which facilitate the invasion of disease organisms. The reduced vigor of plants resulting from prolonged exposure to cold also favors damage by insects and diseases that are well adapted to cold conditions, such as seed-corn maggots and damping-off fungi.

Disease Development: Cool temperatures slow the growth rate of all plants. The effect is greatest on warm-season plants, such as muskmelons and peppers, which stop growing and ripening when temperatures drop below 60°F. More cold-hardy plants, such as onions, spinach, and lettuce, may not cease growing until temperatures have dropped below 35°F.

Even temperatures above freezing can wreak havoc with some cold-sensitive plants. Pitting can occur in beans, melons, and cucumbers when temperatures reach 45°F; a more generalized russeting of skin (sometimes called "sheet pitting") occurs on peppers and eggplant. Temperatures at which many fruits and vegetables suffer bursting of cells and cell death are usually slightly below freezing, around 30°F. Fruit blossoms are somewhat more tolerant, requiring a hard freeze of approximately 28°F. These effects can be further dependent on hardening, or previous exposure to cool temperatures, so the timing of cold exposure is often more important than the temperature in determining plant injury.

Cultural Controls: Several different types of cultural practices help to limit garden freeze injuries:

- Plant cold-resistant varieties that can tolerate freezing injury.
- Plant cold-dodging varieties of perennial plants that emerge late and escape damage by spring frosts.
- Plant bulbs deep to avoid early emergence in spring.

- Plant vulnerable perennials in shaded areas, such as north-facing slopes, to prevent premature emergence in spring.
- Refrain from planting susceptible plants in low, sheltered areas where cool air settles. Orchards are often best located on slopes.
- Mulch perennial plants after the ground has frozen to retard emergence in spring.
- Harden off seedlings in spring before transplanting by gradually exposing them to outdoor conditions.
- Protect seedlings with row covers, hotcaps, or other protectant screens to retain heat.
- Cover susceptible vegetables and flowers during early freezing periods in fall.
- Do not apply nitrogen fertilizer to perennial plants late in the season so that plants can harden off for winter protection.
- During late summer, reduce watering of peaches, grapes, and other sensitive woody perennials so that they can harden off.
- Provide water to perennial plants in fall to reduce damage by winter drying. This should be done after sensitive species have hardened off.
- Do not handle frozen plants until they have thawed.

Biological Controls: Freeze injuries occur at higher temperatures if certain bacteria are present on the plant. These "ice-nucleating bacteria" produce proteins on their surface that promote ice crystal formation, allowing frost to develop and extend into cells, causing cell death. However, other bacteria (sometimes known as "ice minus" bacteria) do not produce these proteins so that frost is not promoted. One naturally occurring strain of these bacteria is *Pseudomonas fluorescens* strain A506. Sold under the trade name BlightBan®, sprays of this bacterial strain enable it to colonize the plant, displacing ice-nucleating bacteria that promote freezing and thus lowering the temperature at which frost injury occurs to the plant. *P. fluorescens* A506 has been tested experimentally with success in some locations but has just recently begun to be marketed and used under a wider range of conditions. This bacteria is also used to help control fire blight.

TABLE 7-4: SUSCEPTIBILITY OF GARDEN PLANTS TO COLD INJURY

Most Susceptible

Apricots	Asparagus	Basil	Beans
Cosmos	Cucumbers	Eggplant	Grapes (wine)
Morning glory	Nectarines	Okra	Peaches
Peppers	Petunia	Potatoes	Summer squash
Sweet cherries	Sweetpotatoes	Tomatoes	Zinnia

Moderately Susceptible

Ageratum	Broccoli	Carrots	Cauliflower
Celery	Cosmos	Geranium	Grapes (native)
Lettuce	Marigold	Onions	Pears
Peas	Plums	Radishes	Raspberries
Rosemary	Strawberries	Tart cherries (summer-bearing)	Winter squash

Least Susceptible

Apples	Beets	Brussels sprouts	Cabbage
Currants	Garlic	Gooseberries	Kale
Kohlrabi	Oregano	Parsley	Raspberries
Rutabagas	Sage	Spinach (fall-bearing)	Turnips

Pollination Problems

Damage and Symptoms: Pollination is required for the successful production of almost all fruits and fruiting vegetables. Unsuccessful pollination prevents seed production. For crops in which the seed is the edible part of the plant, there are direct losses, such as poor kernel fill of sweet corn or pod fill of peas and beans at stake. Incomplete pollination of fruits and vegetables in which the flesh of the fruiting structure is eaten (e.g., apples, peaches, strawberries, tomatoes, melons, and squash) often results in reduced fruit size or its distortion. In some plants, such as tomatoes, "puffy," poor-textured fruit indicates incomplete pollination. When pollination success is minimal or prevented completely, fruit usually aborts.

Disease Development: There are many factors contributing to poor pollination, including:

1) **Cold weather.** Low temperatures can prevent the germination of pollen grains. The activity of insect pollinators is inhibited by cooler weather with hardly any activity occurring below 50°F. Extreme cold kills pollen grains and windy conditions aggravate injuries.

2) **Rainfall and humidity.** Rainfall during pollen production adversely affects the shed and dispersal of windblown pollen. High humidity also interferes with pollen shed. The combination of high temperature, humidity, and light decreases the viability of pollen. Conversely, low humidity dries out the stigmas of flowers. Insect pollinators cease their activity with sustained rain, but not with intermittent showers.

3) **Poor pollen viability.** The pollen of some fruit varieties is not highly viable. This is particularly true when the chromosome number is abnormal, for example, with triploid apples such as Baldwin, Winesap, Jonagold, Mutsu, Stark, and Stayman.

4) **Pollen incompatibility.** Many plants produce pollen that is incapable of successfully fertilizing its own fruit, the fruit of plants of the same variety, or of closely related varieties. Such plants are described as being *self-sterile* or *self-unfruitful* and include varieties of apples, pears, some types of plums, and sweet cherries (see Table 7-6). Gradations of pollen incompatibility occur, with some varieties being *partially self-sterile,* capable of setting some seeds but not as much as when pollinated with more compatible pollen. Successful cross-pollination requires pollen from a compatible variety, known as a *pollinizer.*

5) **Insect injuries.** Although not strictly affecting pollination success, insect feeding on flowers, seeds, and developing fruit often induces abortion. Many "true bugs," such as plant bugs, seed bugs, and some stink bugs, tend to feed on flower buds and young fruit, killing the tissues at their feeding site. Certain weevils and caterpillars may chew buds and young

TABLE 7-5: APPROXIMATE TEMPERATURE (°F) REQUIRED* TO PRODUCE 10 PERCENT AND 90 PERCENT FLOWER BUD KILL OF TREE FRUITS

	Bud Development Stage (Stage #)			
Crop and percent expected bud death	Buds beginning to swell (1)	Pink/white just showing (4)	Just prior to flower (7)	First flowering bud break (6)
Apples				
10% bud kill	13–15	24–27	25–28	25–28
90% bud kill	0–2	19–21	23–25	23–25
Pears				
10% bud kill	15	24	25	27
90% bud kill	0	19	22	23
Peaches				
10% bud kill	18	25	26	27
90% bud kill	1	14	19	22
Apricots				
10% bud kill	15	25	26	27
90% bud kill	—	14	19	22
Sweet cherries				
10% bud kill	15–17	24–26	25–27	28
90% bud kill	3–5	15–17	22–24	25

*Approximate lethal temperatures from 30-minute exposure.
Source: Washington State University

fruit. These injuries may kill developing seeds or induce buds to abscise and drop prematurely.

6) **Absence of pollinating insects.** Many flowers, including almost all with a showy appearance, require pollination by insects. (Plants producing inconspicuous flowers, such as corn or grape, are usually wind-pollinated or self-pollinated.) A great many insects that visit flowers can act as pollinators but some, notably the bees, are exceptionally efficient and effective in this process. When effective pollinators are not present during pollen shed, the seed set of insect-pollinated plants will be poor with fruit production reduced or even prevented entirely. For example, many areas have experienced problems with fruit pollination in recent years because honeybee populations have been reduced dramatically following the introduction of tracheal mites and varroa mites, two new parasites of honeybees in North America.

Controls: Problems with self-unfruitful varieties that produce incompatible or nonviable pollen are solved by providing a compatible pollinizer *that will have overlapping bloom.* Usually almost any other variety of the same species can serve as a pollinizer. In fact, sometimes other closely related species may adequately pollinate a flower, such as crabapples serving as pollinizers for apples. Most nurseries can provide information on bloom time and the pollination compatibility of different tree fruit varieties.

There is little that gardeners can do to prevent weather-related pollination snafus. Plants can be sited in more shaded areas to delay blossoming and thus avoid some cold-related problems during pollination. Flowers may also be hand-pollinated if pollen shed is inhibited by the weather or absence of effective insect pollinators.

TABLE 7-6: POLLINATION REQUIREMENTS OF COMMONLY GROWN FRUIT CROPS

Crop*	Method of Pollination	Pollen Compatibility
Apples	Insect-pollinated	Most varieties are partially self-unfruitful and benefit from cross-pollination with a different variety. Pollen of a few varieties is nonviable; hence these are not effective pollinizers. Many crabapples can also serve as pollinizers, provided there is an overlap of bloom.
Pear	Insect-pollinated; under unusual circumstances of warm weather (70–85°F) through bloom, some parthenocarpic (seedless) fruit may be produced.	Most varieties are self-unfruitful. With some exceptions (e.g., Bartlett and Seckel), other varieties are acceptable pollinizers if blooming dates are synchronized.
Sweet Cherry	Insect-pollinated	Most varieties are self-unfruitful and require a pollinizer for fruit production. Several cross-incompatible groups exist among sweet cherries among which pollen is not cross-compatible (e.g., Black Tartrian and Bing).

Tart Cherry	Insect-pollinated	Tart cherry varieties are self-fruitful and do not need a pollinizer.
Plums	Insect-pollinated	Pollen campatibility varies. Among European plum varieties some are self-fruitful while others are nearly self-unfruitful and require a pollinizer. Japanese plums are also self-unfruitful. American species of plums and hybrid plums are usually self-unfruitful and many of the latter produce nonviable pollen.
Apricot	Insect-pollinated	With few exceptions (e.g., Riland, Perfection), apricots produce self-fertile pollen and are self-fruitful.
Peach	Insect-pollinated	With few exceptions (e.g., J. H. Hale, Marsun, Candoka, Halberta, June Elberta, Alamar), peaches produce self-fertile pollen and are self-fruitful.
Strawberry	Insect- and wind-pollinated	Strawberries are self-fruitful.
Raspberry, Blackberry	Raspberry is insect-pollinated; blackberry is self-pollinated	Raspberries and blackberries are self-fertile and self-fruitful.
Currant, Gooseberry	Insect-pollinated	Currants and gooseberries produce pollen that is self-fertile.
Grape	Self-pollinated	Pollen is self-fertile and plants are self-fruitful.

*Pollination of all flowers is not necessary for a full crop. For example, with apples, peaches, and pears, about 10 to 15 percent of the flowers successfully setting fruit is optimal. Excessive fruit set on these plants can lead to reduced fruit size and biennial bearing—cycles of large crops being followed by small crops. High levels of fruit set, 50 percent or more, are necessary for superior cherry production.

Where insect pollinators are absent a couple steps can be taken: Create a diverse habitat that can support increased numbers of flies, native bees, and other flower-visiting insects that can pollinate flowers. Many bees, such as leafcutter bees or digger bees, can be further encouraged by providing favorable nesting areas (see pages 115–116). Maintain nearby hives of honeybees, or develop a cooperative arrangement with a local beekeeper, to ensure adequate numbers of these valuable pollinators.

Herbicide Injuries

Damage and Symptoms: 2,4-D and the other growth regulator herbicides produce characteristic symptoms, such as twisting of the plant stems and leaf petioles. Developing leaves do not expand normally and show crinkled or highly elongated growth. Leaves may curl upward (cup) as effects of some herbicides. Leaf veins are prominent and light colored. If herbicide exposure is severe, plants may die. Most garden vegetables are susceptible to 2,4-D injury. There is a range in susceptibility, however, with beans, grapes, tomatoes, cucumbers, and squash being among the most sensitive. Some of the effects of herbicide injury are similar to those of other types of garden afflictions, including infection with viral diseases, aster yellows, or potato psyllids. These can be distinguished from other injuries by looking at the pattern of symptoms. Herbicide injury is generally spread among many

2,4-D injury to tomato

2,4-D injury symptom

different garden plants. Other diseases are typically limited to a single type of plant.

Herbicides that inhibit production of certain amino acids (glyphosate, glufinosate) produce different symptoms. With glyphosate (Roundup®, Kleenup®) growth is slowed and chlorosis develops within a week, usually on the younger foliage and around the growing point. (A reddish-purpling discoloration develops on some plants.) Perennial plants, including young trees and shrubs, may produce leaves with whitish markings or sometimes multiple shoots that form small "witches broom."

Effects from exposure to glufinosate (Finale*) develop more rapidly than those from glyphosate. Chlorosis often appears within 3 to 5 days, with symptoms most intense under conditions of bright sunlight. Wilting and leaf necrosis also can occur.

Disease Development: 2,4-D and the other growth-regulating herbicides (e.g., MCPP, dicamba, mecoprop) are popular on lawns and other areas for weed control. Most are selective herbicides that have little effect on grasses. However, many garden and flower crops are broadleaf plants that are very susceptible to injury. Herbicide injury typically results from drift of the herbicide onto desirable plants, which can occur while applying sprays in windy conditions. These herbicides may also convert to the gas form (volatilize) during very warm weather and move to garden plants. Herbicide-treated grass clippings used as garden mulch are a source of herbicide residues. Accidental garden injury is also a consequence of using lawn fertilizers that contain herbicides.

Glyphosate and glufosinate are nonselective herbicides best used as general vegetation killers. Typically, accidental injury occurs through drift or misapplication when spot treating weeds around desirable plants. Unlike 2,4-D, neither are highly volatile and both demonstrate negligible persistence and activity when applied to the soil.

Controls: Using 2,4-D around gardens should be avoided whenever possible. Sprays of any herbicide should never be applied during windy conditions. If herbicides are employed, a coarse setting spray should be used to avoid producing fine droplets, which drift much more easily in the wind than larger droplets. Treatments should also not be made during periods of very high temperature (above 90°F) as some herbicides readily volatilize, converting to a gas that drifts and harms other plants in the area. Grass clippings suspected of containing residues of growth-regulating herbicides should not be applied directly to the garden. If used, they should first be composted thoroughly to allow decomposition of the herbicide. These precautions are probably unnecessary for glyphosate- and glufosinate-treated plants as these herbicides readily degrade through microbial action.

Nitrogen Deficiency

Damage and Symptoms: Nitrogen deficiencies take the form of a general yellowing (chlorosis) of the entire plant, with symptoms particularly evident on older leaves. If the chlorosis is severe, the older leaves die and drop from the plant. Deficient plants are stunted and yield poorly. An excess of nitrogen results from overfertilization. High levels of nitrogen stimulate top growth at the expense of balancing root growth. Treated plants exhibit a delay in flowering and are more susceptible to many diseases.

Disease Development: Nitrogen is a basic element of proteins and amino acids that is used throughout the plant. It is also used within the chlorophyll molecule, which captures energy from the sun for use by the plant. Nitrogen is constantly being recycled within the plant for various growth needs and is concentrated in the newer growth. Nitrogen deficiencies are common, and are aggravated by repeatedly removing plant matter and not fertilizing. Temporary deficiencies accompany cold soils, which slow the activity of soil microbes that release nitrogen. The addition of carbon-rich plant matter, such as straw or sawdust, also increases deficiencies as the microbes remove nitrogen for decomposition. Since soil nitrogen is water-soluble and moves readily in the soil, it is easily leached if excess water is applied. Recently there has been increased attention focused on ground-water pollution by the nitrate form of nitrogen.

Controls: Nitrogen is continuously being lost from soils because of plant removal and the natural activities of soil bacteria. Adding nitrogen is necessary to maintain the productivity of a garden. Many nitrogen-containing chemical fertilizers are readily available. Nitrogen is also available in most organic materials, being particularly abundant in most dried animal manures. These organic sources are more slowly released, since they require the activity of microbes to release nitrogen to the plant. Some plants "fix" nitrogen from the air through special nitrogen-fixing bacteria on the plant roots. This ability is common to all the legumes (beans, peas, etc.), which can then be planted to increase the amount of nitrogen in the soil. However, since these plants move almost all of the nitrogen to their seeds, a greater nitrogen benefit is realized if legumes are tilled into the soil without harvesting.

Iron Deficiency

Damage and Symptoms: Iron deficiencies are indicated by a general yellowing of leaves, accompanied by dark green veins (interveinal chlorosis). Because iron does not move in plants, the symptoms are most pronounced on the new leaves. Iron-deficient plants are stunted and grow poorly. When deficiencies are moderate, plants may recover later in the season. However, seedlings are particularly vulnerable to iron deficiency and plant yields may later be decreased following short periods of seedling deficiency. Iron deficiencies may also vary during the season, being most severe in cool, damp springs. Peach, corn, bean, potato, petunia, and dahlia are among the garden plants that are especially sensitive to iron deficiencies. Different rootstocks or plant varieties that determine the chemical environment around the roots subsequently effect iron deficiencies.

Disease Development: Soils that have high pH or excess calcium carbonate which can produce chemical reactions that inhibit the availability of iron to the plant roots are most often deficient in iron. Since iron is absorbed in the area immediately behind the growing root tip, cultural conditions that slow root growth also contribute to iron deficiency. Compaction, excess water, or other soil conditions that cause oxygen starvation of the root zone further deplete iron reserves.

Controls: Because iron deficiencies are aggravated by high pH or high levels of calcium carbonate, correcting these soil conditions is the best long-term solution. Adding sulfur or amending with manure or sewage sludge improves iron availability. Inorganic sources of iron, such as iron sulfate, applied to the soil will not correct deficiencies in soils that are excessively alkaline or high in calcium carbonate. Only the iron chelate EDDHA (Sequestrene 138 Fe) remains in a usable form in alkaline soils (pH above 7.0). Where soil conditions cannot be adequately altered, less susceptible plants should be considered. Improving the soil structure alleviates iron deficiency by providing better conditions for root growth. Sprays of iron chelates or iron sulphate on leaves restore green color to plants and temporarily correct iron deficiencies. However, if soil sources remain deficient, reapplication is required.

Iron chlorosis

Zinc Deficiency

Damage and Symptoms: Visible symptoms of zinc deficiency vary among different plants. Zinc-deficient plants tend to be stunted. The upper leaves of some plants, such as beans, may be yellow, while the lower leaves show bronzing. A soil test is needed to confirm zinc deficiencies.

Disease Development: Zinc deficiency is most common in soils that are alkaline and low in organic matter, most likely where topsoil has been removed. Excessive levels of phosphorus may also decrease zinc. The symptoms of zinc deficiency usually are present following cold and wet periods during spring growth.

Controls: Several types of zinc-containing fertilizers effectively correct zinc deficiencies, such as animal manure, zinc chelates, or zinc sulphate.

Chapter 8

Weed Control
in Flower and Vegetable Gardens

Sometimes a gardener's green thumb gets a little out of hand as plants we don't consciously plant start to grow. These unwanted plants, or weeds, can do more than merely upset our aesthetic sense. Perhaps most important is that they compete with vegetables or flowers for light, nutrients, and water. Some weeds, such as quackgrass, also produce chemicals from their roots that inhibit the growth of nearby plants.

You may work hard to grow Kentucky bluegrass in your lawn. But if it creeps into your garden, it becomes a weed. Even things we intentionally plant in the garden, such as horseradish, Jerusalem artichokes, and many flowers, become weeds when they spread to areas where they aren't welcome. On the other hand, plants that are widely recognized as weeds can be beneficial at some sites. For example, quackgrass growing on a steep bank prevents erosion, and thistles are food for butterflies and birds.

CHARACTERISTICS OF WEEDS

Weeds can be classified in several ways, but most commonly they are described by the length of their life cycle. Using this method, weeds can be *annuals* (1-year life cycle), *biennials* (2-year life cycle), or *perennials* (multiyear life cycle).

Annual weeds are plants that germinate from seed, grow, flower, and produce new seed, all in less than a twelve-month period. However, among the annual weeds there are further varieties of life cycles. *Spring* or *summer annuals* are plants that germinate in the spring or early summer, flower and produce seed during the summer, and then die in the summer or fall. Many of the most common yard and garden weeds are spring or summer annuals, such as lambsquarters, pigweed, crabgrass, and purslane. *Winter annuals* are less common in gardens. These are plants that germinate in the fall or early winter, survive the winter as low-growing plants, and then resume growth and flower in the spring. Common winter annual weeds are mustards, such as flixweed, blue mustard, and sheperdspurse.

Biennial weeds produce a compact cluster (rosette) of leaves the first year. Biennials survive the winter as a rosette, resuming growth the following spring, and then bolt, flower, and die during this second season. Biennial weeds (e.g., mullein, musk thistle) do not typically inhabit gardens, but are usually found along roadsides and in pastures. However, many of our garden plants (carrots, cabbage, onions, Brussels sprouts, etc.) are biennial plants that we simply harvest the first season.

Perennial weeds live for several years and are the most difficult weeds to control. Bindweed, quackgrass, dandelion, and Canada thistle are examples of common perennial weeds. Many perennial weeds produce extensive root systems that enable the plants to resist destruction by practices that kill only the aboveground parts of the plants. Perennial weeds reproduce by seeds, and most infestations originate in this manner. However, once established, many perennial weeds can spread by underground structures such as runners (spreading roots, stolons, or rhizomes), bulbs, and tubers.

Weeds are particularly damaging to garden crops early in the season. When plants are small, they are easily displaced by crowding, and a tender-spirited seedling may never fully recover from the trauma of being pushed aside by a bullying weed.

The effect of weeds as competitors is best represented with plants that root and grow in the same area of the soil. Several garden weeds are close cousins of plants we now choose to grow in the garden and compete strongly with them (e.g., pigweed and spinach). Garden weeds also affect other pest management practices. Attempts to maintain a garden rotation plan can be upset by weeds that support the fungus we are trying so hard to squeeze out. Thick weed cover is a favored egg-laying environment for cutworm moths in late summer.

Other gardening efforts determine the status of weeds in a garden. Since weeds compete for water, light, and nutrients, vigorously growing garden plants may outgrow the competition with little effect. Fertility and water conditions in the garden that provide enough for all further narrow the competitive margin.

Weeds in the garden often boast a more offbeat lineage than weeds in typical agricultural settings. Kentucky bluegrass creeps beyond the boundaries set for the lawn and over the edges of flower beds. Seeding trees, such as Siberian elm, constitute a major garden headache as the seeds blow into the garden and sprout. Another primary source of garden weeds is often those we planted earlier that have since "gone wild" and naturalized.

WAYS WEEDS SPREAD

More than any other type of garden pest, common garden weeds are the result of accidental, and sometimes purposeful, introduction by humans. Almost all garden weeds (as well as our cultivated garden plants) are not native to North America. More than 700 different species of plants now considered to be weeds were introduced to North America from Europe and Eurasia. A considerably smaller number of plants that have become garden weeds originated from Asia or tropical America, or actually happen to be native to the region.

Gardeners further distribute weeds by moving soil or other materials infested with weed seeds or viable plant parts. Frequently seeds move into a yard via straw, hay, or animal manures brought into the garden. These typical garden materials are often infested with weed seeds, so it is important for the gardener to know their source. Hay or straw mulches grown in areas with serious weed problems, or manure from animals fed weed-infested grain, should not be directly introduced into the garden until it has been composted at high temperatures.

Windblown weeds, such as dandelions and sowthistle, are more difficult to eradicate. If possible, try to prevent seeds from forming on plants in and around the garden by mowing or removing the weeds before they flower. Periodically check the garden and destroy and discard germinating weeds to control the occasional migrants.

One of the positive aspects of weed control is that a gardener really can enjoy obvious progress against this type of pest. If weed control practices kill off existing weeds and preventive efforts restrict unwanted migrants, problems with weed infestation gradually decline.

WEED CONTROLS

Mulches

Mulches solve many garden weed problems. Properly placed, mulches exclude light and smother seedlings. Although they are considerably less effective against established perennial weeds such as bindweed, mulches render these weeds easier to pull and further deter their regrowth.

Mulches further affect the garden environment. Moisture conditions around the plants are

TABLE 8-1: ORIGIN OF COMMON GARDEN WEEDS OF THE WEST

No garden pests are more cosmopolitan in origin than weeds. Very few are native to North America, the majority having been brought from abroad, often as stowaways in seed and other plant products.

Weed	Introduced from/Area of Origin
Crabgrass	Europe
Green/Yellow foxtail	Eurasia
Annual bluegrass	Europe
Barnyardgrass	Europe
Quackgrass	Mediterranean region
Redroot pigweed	Tropical America
Lambsquarters	Europe
Wild buckwheat	Europe
Purslane	Eurasia
Wild mustard	Europe
Shepardspurse	Europe
Flixweed/Pinnate tansymustard	Europe
Creeping woodsorrel	Europe
Hairy nightshade	South America
Common ragweed	Native (North America)
Sunflower	Native (North America)
Prickly lettuce	Europe
Annual sowthistle	Europe
Dandelion	Europe
Common mallow	Europe
Russian thistle	Central Asia
Leafy spurge	Eurasia
Prostrate knotweed	Central Asia
Kochia	Asia native, introduced from Europe
Field bindweed	Europe
Canada thistle	Southeastern Eurasia

However, some weeds have become established following their purposeful introduction by gardeners and horticulturists. Some of the most serious noxious weeds originally were grown as garden plants, only to "escape" and spread naturally. Perhaps the best current example is purple loosestrife, a very attractive flowering plant—sometimes still available for sale—that aggressively invades wetland areas. Salt cedar (tamarisk) has similarly colonized vast areas of the West along rivers and ditches, profoundly changing the natural ecosystems. Some of the more serious weed pests that originated from garden plantings are:

Purple loosestrife	*Lythrum salicaria*
Oxeye daisy	*Chrysanthemum leucanthemum*
Yellow toadflax	*Linaria vulgaris* (Butter-and-eggs)
Dalmation toadflax	*Linaria genistifolia ssp. damatatica*
Saltcedar/Tamarisk	*Tamarix ramosissima*
Russian olive	*Eleagnus angustifolia*
Mediterranean sage	*Salvia argentia*

notably altered by mulches that reduce evaporation from the soil. (Some mulches may also prevent water from moving into the soil.) This stabilizes fluctuating soil moisture and facilitates more even growth of the plants.

On the other hand, increased soil moisture sometimes creates new garden problems. Moisture-loving garden pests, such as slugs, thrive in a well-mulched garden. Mulches also restrict air circulation in a planting, contributing to some disease problems.

Changes in garden temperatures can be effected by mulching. Most organic mulches, such as grass clippings, straw, or sawdust, are light colored and reflect heat. This may have a cooling effect on the soil. Dark-colored plastic mulches have the reverse effect—heating the soil. As a result, mulches are sometimes used to accelerate the growth of warm-season plants such as peppers and melons. (The effects of specific mulches follow.)

Grass Clippings

Grass clippings are a readily available source of mulch. Used in the compost or garden, they eliminate a major source of landfill trash and recycle nutrients. Grass clippings form a dense mulch that will smother seedlings of most weeds and conserve soil moisture. They decompose more quickly than most organic mulches, primarily because of their small size. However, grass clippings have a tendency to mat, which prevents water percolation. Regular stirring of the clippings can limit matting. Occasionally, grass clippings are contaminated with herbicides. Several herbicides used in lawn care, such as 2,4-D and dicamba, can adhere to grass clippings for several days or even weeks after an application and can subsequently injure susceptible garden plants. Where herbicide contamination is suspected, compost the grass clippings first to decompose the herbicide or try to find a clean source.

Hay or Straw

Hay or straw is often cheap source of mulching material, particularly when spoiled bales are used. However, these mulches are coarse, so it is challenging to achieve a uniform smothering effect when thinly applied. (On the other hand, this same quality is what makes these mulches excellent for protecting garden plants from winter injury.) The main drawback of hay and straw is that they may inadvertently be a source of weed seeds in a garden. The thick mulches created by these materials decrease air circulation around the plants and increase some disease problems. This can be avoided, in part, by keeping the mulch away from the base of garden plants. As hay and straw decompose, soil nitrogen may be temporarily drawn from the soil. This is most likely to occur with more nitrogen-poor materials such as straw. Alfalfa hay is fairly high in nitrogen and usually decomposes without drawing deeply from soil nitrogen sources. One other concern involves barley straw as a mulch. When decayed it may release chemicals that can disrupt growth of plants, and thus its use is not recommended for mulching garden beds.

Leaves

Leaves literally fall from the sky in the fall. They are cheap, weed-free, and provide an effective mulch for smothering annual weeds. However, using leaves often creates problems with matting, which prevents water movement into the soil. Because of their high carbon content, decomposing leaves may temporarily remove nitrogen, so it is best to compost leaves before using them in the garden.

Sawdust

Sawdust in areas near sawmills or other woodworking operations is potentially very beneficial mulching material, but it can also cause garden problems. Sawdust mulches applied directly to the garden require additional nitrogen to prevent soil deficiencies as the sawdust decays. Fresh sawdust can injure plants by acids produced during decomposition. Where large amounts of sawdust are used, they should be well aged and largely decomposed before being introduced to the garden.

Compost

Well-decomposed compost constitutes a superior mulch in a garden. However, if improperly prepared so that high-temperature decomposition does not occur, compost may be a treasure trove of viable weed seeds. This problem is avoided by using only composting materials that are free of weed seed, either by using only weed-free source materials or by carefully composting to ensure high temperature inactivation.

Black Plastic

Dark plastic mulches are among the most effective garden mulches—and they are weed-free. A thick plastic mulch that is impermeable to light can even challenge the livelihood of a persistent perennial weed such as bindweed. Black plastic mulch warms the soil, which encourages the growth of peppers, melons, and other warm-season plants that may need some extra help to make it through the gardening season. The plastic barrier further prevents direct contact of fruit with the soil, reducing problems with fruit-rotting organisms. However, because black plastic mulch is so effective at blocking water out of the soil, it can also be too effective at preventing water movement *into* the soil. Where sprinklers are used, plastic mulches need to be punctured to facili-

tate watering, although this consequently reduces their effectiveness by permitting light to penetrate. Drip systems placed under the plastic alleviate this problem. Although well-maintained plastic mulches can often be used for several years, they eventually must be discarded. This end use of the plastic is the main reason many gardeners opt for a more biodegradable mulching material. Recently, thick, dark-colored paper mulches have been marketed that can be tilled into the garden at the end of the year to decompose.

Landscape Mulches

In recent years, several fabric weed barriers have appeared on the market for use around landscape plants. These are constructed so as to prevent light penetration while allowing water to percolate. Typically, they are covered with an organic mulch, such as wood chips or bark. Landscape fabrics are rather expensive but very durable. When properly placed, they can suppress weeds for several years so long as the fabric remains intact. To use them in flower gardens, small planting holes must be cut. They are not appropriate for most berry or vegetable gardens where plants spread or are rotated to new areas each year.

Miscellaneous Mulches

For the creative gardener, mulching materials may be found in many forms. For example, old newspapers or discarded carpet laid between rows can give the garden that casual, "lived-in" look, while also diligently suppressing weeds.

Hoeing and Pulling

Battling garden weed problems typically translates "one-on-one" handpulling or hoeing. Although this activity enables the gardener to become intimately familiar with the garden environment, it is generally not well liked.

The primary aims of hand hoeing and pulling are fairly brutal: (1) kill the weeds, and (2) kill all their progeny (seeds, rhizomes, etc). Ideally, the weeds will ultimately be banished from the garden—and this is not entirely unrealistic.

Although there will always be some windblown weed seed landing in the garden, the weeds themselves don't move about and most drop their seeds on top of the soil. Unlike the more mobile insects and diseases that can continually reinvade, populations of most weed seeds steadily decline in a garden following a sustained effort to control them. Your good efforts in weed control *will* be rewarded by reduced weed populations in the future.

Plants vary in their vulnerability to hoeing—environmental conditions can help or hinder their recovery. To begin with, try to control weeds when they are young. Seedlings have poorly developed root systems and few energy reserves that would allow regrowth. For example, the annual weed purslane cannot regrow from the roots until the plants are at least 3 to 5 inches tall. Even seedlings of the persistent perennial field bindweed need 10 to 15 weeks of growth (about the 5-leaf stage) before their roots have developed sufficiently to bounce back from a hoeing attack. A single cultivation usually means the end of these young upstarts.

With established perennial weeds (e.g., quackgrass, field bindweed, Canada thistle), weed control is substantially more difficult. Since food reserves exist in the roots of the plants, the aim is to prevent any food manufacture by the plant. This is achieved by constantly (at approximately 2- to 3-week intervals) forcing the weed to regrow, speeding consumption of its food stores.

Hoeing, handpulling, or tillage breaks off the terminal buds of these plants—an exercise similar to pinching back plants to make them bushier. As a result, numerous side shoots form. This regrowth causes the plant to temporarily use more energy producing the new leaves than it receives from photosynthesis.

Typically, this regrowth process requires 2 to 3 weeks, after which time the plants once again begin to replenish root reserves. Therefore, repeated, frequent attacks on the plants yield the best results. Since regrowth is usually more rapid early in the season, focusing on perennial weeds is particularly important at this time.

Principles of Effective Hoeing

Plants should be hoed or pulled during conditions that hasten their demise. Early morning hoeing is often best, since it allows the heat of the day to finish off the uprooted weeds. This is critical for killing rhizomes and roots brought to the surface during hoeing or pulling. Delaying irrigation for a day or so after hoeing further prevents rerooting by a particularly hardy survivor.

Seedlings are also extremely susceptible to hoeing or rototilling. Garden beds should always be tilled shortly before seeding to kill any germinating weed seeds. Furthermore, between plantings one can make a particularly good dent in the "seed bank" by actually trying to stimulate the weed seeds to grow. Such a program might involve the following steps: (1) rototill or hoe the garden bed; (2) wait for the tilled weed seedlings to die; (3) water the bed to stimulate new seedling growth; (4) wait about a week before seeding your main crop; (5) rototill/hoe the emerged seedling weeds; (6) plant.

The depth of hoeing is not a significant factor in weed control. Most annual weeds can be killed by cutting them at the soil line. However, deep-rooted perennial weeds, such as Canada thistle and field bindweed, can recover rapidly from cuts that occur several inches belowground. Deep cultivation provides better control of some shallow-rooted perennials (e.g., quackgrass) by bringing the rhizomes near the surface. This should then be followed by a shallow hoeing of sprouts as they emerge.

However, deep hoeing or tillage is not recommended for weed control purposes. The deep burial of surface layers during spading or rototilling merely prolongs weed problems by delaying germination. Many weed seeds survive for years in a dormant state underground, germinating when favorable conditions of warmth and light occur as they are returned to the surface. A shallow cut of the hoe that barely disturbs the soil surface is usually the best technique.

Each gardener has his or her own favorite gadgets for hoeing weeds. Almost any hoe does the job—so long as the gardener maintains the interest to work it. (My personal favorite is Glide n' Groom®, which slides just under the soil surface and cuts the plants.) Regardless of type, hoes should be kept sharp to ease cutting and reduce the effort.

But even hoes effect serious damage to the garden if wielded inexpertly. The blade can cut both crops and weeds with equal ease, with selectivity subject to the hands of the gardener. (A parallel situation, known as "cultivator blight," is a well-recognized phenomenon of mechanized agriculture.) More subtly, overzealous hoeing may prune the roots of plants, retard their growth, and reduce their resistance to plant pests.

A sustained, season-long weed control effort is particularly appropriate in light of the need to prevent reproduction. A temporary lapse, particularly late in the season, will surrender the garden to rapid repopulation in following years by young "garden urchins." And don't be misled by the size of the plants. Many weeds produce hundreds of seeds when only a few weeks old and a few inches in size if conditions are favorable to flowering (e.g., short and declining day length). Remove plants that have begun to flower and set seed.

Since weeds also originate from our cultivated plants, remove spent flowers before they reproduce. This often has the additional benefit of stimulating renewed flowering.

Herbicides

Using herbicides in and around vegetable and flower gardens poses special difficulties, since they must be handled with extreme care to avoid damaging desirable plants. Because of these potential problems or because of a wish to avoid pesticides in general, many gardeners opt not to use herbicides and limit weed control to mechanical practices such as hoeing. Also, there are few herbicides that are registered for use in gardens compared with those available for lawns or agricultural crops. However, they should be discussed, since in some instances herbicides can be used effectively in the garden to reduce weed problems and gardening effort.

The effective use of herbicides dictates that the gardener learn how they act to kill or suppress unwanted plants. Herbicides work in many different ways. (See Table 8-2.) Several types, the *preemergent herbicides,* work by killing newly germinated seedlings. On the other hand, *postemergent herbicides* are applied to plants after they have emerged, and some do not affect later germination of seeds.

These effects determine the *selectivity* of the herbicide. Most herbicides can harm many desirable plants as well as weeds. How these products are applied determines how effective they will be. For example, most preemergent herbicides are fairly selective in that only seedlings are affected. Using preemergent herbicides around transplants or established plants allows them to work selectively on the germinating weeds. However, if the vegetable garden is to be seeded, the herbicides may also kill the vegetable plants.

Most postemergent herbicides are selective as to what types of plants they affect. The selective grass killers, such as fluazifop-butyl (Grass-B-Gon®), are only active against grasses and can sometimes be used to remove grass from around certain flowers or perennial plants. Other herbicides, such as 2,4-D (not a garden herbicide), tend to have the opposite effect and are mostly used to kill broadleaf plants. However, even these selective herbicides can cause unwanted injury if they are used in too high a concentration or drift onto desirable plants.

Some commonly used nonselective herbicides are glyphosate (Roundup®, Kleenup®) and glufinosate (Finale®, Liberty®), which kill most plants to which they are applied. Selective use of these materials requires very careful application, as spot treatments, to prevent injury to adjacent garden plants. Shielding desirable plants and painting the herbicide onto the weeds are methods used to avoid contaminating and damaging desirable plants. Neither glyphosate or glufosinate should used in or around edible plants. (Characteristics of specific herbicides are also discussed in Appendix IV.)

TABLE 8-2: COMMON GARDEN HERBICIDES

Herbicide	Pathway into the Plant	Activity in the Plant
DPCA (Dacthal®)	Absorbed only through the roots and shoots of seedlings.	Unknown.
trifluralin (Treflan®)	Absorbed only through the roots and growing shoots of seedlings before soil emergence.	Inhibits cell division in growing cells.
fluazifop-butyl (Grass-B-Gon®)	Absorbed through leaves of actively growing grasses.	Interferes with the production of lipids necessary for cell membrane function.
2,4-D	Primarily absorbed through leaves and green stems of established plants but has some residual effect in soil.	Acts as a plant hormone and interferes with many plant actions; most obvious is an overstimulation of growing cells, producing distorted growth and starving roots. Broadleaf plants are much more susceptible than grasses.
glufosinate (Finale®, Liberty®)	Absorbed through leaves.	Very little residual effect in soil and little movement in xylem or phloem. Inhibits production of glutamine and causes lethal levels of ammonia to develop in cells.
glyphosate (Kleenup®, Roundup®)	Absorbed through leaves or green stems of established plants.	Immobilized rapidly in soil and has no soil activity. Disrupts the production of certain amino acids (tyrosine, tryptophan, phenylalanine) used by plants.
herbicidal soaps (Sharpshooter®)	Contact action on cells of leaves and stems.	Causes cells to leak ions used in normal function and subsequently die.
corn gluten meal (WOW®, others)	General inhibitor of germinating seeds' growth.	Unknown.

COMMON WEEDS IN FLOWER AND VEGETABLE GARDENS

(*Note:* The following includes a discussion of a few of the more common weeds found in gardens. However, for an outstanding identification guide to essentially all the weeds found in this region, there is no better reference than *Weeds of the West*. This book is primarily distributed through the Extension Bulletin Room of the Land Grant University in each state [listed in Appendix VII] and is also carried by some bookstores. It can also be ordered through the Western Society of Weed Science, P.O. Box 963, Newark, CA 94560.)

Quackgrass (*Agropyron repens*)

Weed Description and Growth Pattern: Quackgrass is a perennial grass that reproduces by seeds

and creeping rhizomes. It grows vigorously during the cool weather of early spring and fall. Flowers are produced throughout most of the growing season. Seeds can remain dormant for many years. Quackgrass roots produce toxic chemicals that inhibit the growth of surrounding vegetation. The pointed rhizomes can penetrate most soft plant tissues and damage root crops.

Mechanical Controls: Quackgrass germinating from pieces of rhizomes takes about sixteen weeks to regrow roots and produce new rhizomes, so young plants are the easiest to control. Established plants should be tilled or raked to expose the shallow roots to kill rhizomes and root fragments. Repeated cultivation at short intervals is particularly effective, since it can fragment the roots and rhizomes, causing the plant to use up stored energy to produce leaves.

Chemical Controls: In flower gardens, quackgrass can be stopped dead by the selective herbicide fluazifop-butyl (Grass-B-Gon®). The nonselective herbicides glyphosate (Roundup®, Kleenup®) and glufosinate (Finale®, Liberty®) can systemically move in the plant and kill roots, although desirable plants can also be easily damaged by this herbicide.

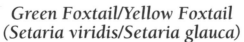

Green Foxtail/Yellow Foxtail
(Setaria viridis/Setaria glauca)

Weed Description and Growth Pattern: Green and yellow foxtails are summer-annual grasses that reproduce by seeds. They are marked by the dense, bushy spike the plants produce. Flowering begins in June, and seeds may be produced continuously throughout the summer and early fall. Foxtail seeds are less persistent than those of other weeds. Most seeds germinate the season following production.

Mechanical Controls: Young plants are very susceptible to hoeing. Older plants can easily reroot, so the root system must be thoroughly disrupted.

Mulching effectively controls foxtail in a garden. Since most seeds germinate the following season, a sustained weed-control effort eliminates most foxtail problems in one to two years.

Chemical Controls: The preemergent herbicides DCPA (Dacthal®) and trifluralin (Treflan®) can control plants if applied in spring before foxtail seeds germinate. In flower gardens, the selective postemergent grass killer fluazifop-butyl (Grass-B-Gon®) kills younger seedlings.

Crabgrass
(species of Digitaria)

Weed Description and Growth Pattern: Crabgrass is a summer-annual, grassy weed most often plaguing lawns. It thrives in hot, dry weather and may invade flower and vegetable gardens. Although its ground-hugging growth does not compete for light, crabgrass can spread rapidly, consuming the water and nutrients needed by other plants. Most seeds germinate during the early part of the growing season. Areas of warmer soils may begin to produce seedlings by mid-spring. However, some seeds continue to germinate through August, particularly when watered after a dry spell. Flowers and seeds are produced on spikelets from July through October. With cold weather, crabgrass turns purplish, dying after hard frosts. Two species of crabgrass are found in the West. Smooth crabgrass (*Digitaria ischaemum*) tends to occur in more northern areas; large crabgrass (*Digitaria sanguinalis*) is a southern species. However, both occur throughout much of the region, and controls are similar.

Crabgrass

Foxtails

Mechanical Controls: Germinating seeds and small seedlings are easily controlled with a mulch. Hoeing or cultivating also kills small seedlings. This method is particularly effective on low-growing weeds, such as crabgrass. However, larger plants often reroot unless the root system is exposed to drying conditions.

Chemical Controls: Preemergent herbicides that prevent seed germination, such as DCPA (Dacthal®), trifluralin (Treflan®), and corn gluten meal, can control crabgrass. But garden use is generally impractical because of the timing of crabgrass germination. Very early-season treatments necessary to control early crabgrass do not persist in controlling later-germinating seeds. The selective grass killer fluazifop-butyl (Grass-B-Gon®) can be used to spot-treat smaller crabgrass plants around some flowers and ornamentals. Nonselective herbicides, such as herbicidal soaps (Sharpshooter®), glufosinate (Finale®, Liberty®), and glyphosate (Kleenup®, Roundup®), kill crabgrass but must be used carefully to prevent injury to desirable plants. Cultivation is usually far simpler and safer for crabgrass control in established gardens.

Lambsquarters
(Chenopodium album)

Weed Description and Growth Pattern: Lambsquarters is a spring-annual broadleaf plant that reproduces by seeds. Leaves are generally light green and covered with a white powder; stems are often marked with red and green streaks. Under favorable conditions, lambsquarters may grow several feet in height. Lambsquarters seed germinates early in the season. Plants grow rapidly and easily outgrow other garden seedlings. The plant produces flowers in ball-like clusters from June through October. The small, black seeds are formed continuously, beginning in early summer.

Mechanical Controls: Lambsquarters is susceptible to hoeing, although very large plants may require handpulling. Thick mulches prevent seedling establishment.

Biological Controls: Lambsquarters is fed on by many of the same insects that attack spinach and beets, including spinach leafminer, leafhoppers, and cutworms.

Chemical Controls: Lambsquarters is susceptible to preemergent herbicides such as corn gluten meal, DCPA (Dacthal®), and trifluralin (Treflan®). However, these need to be applied very early in the season to kill early-germinating seeds and are considered impractical and undesirable for gardening.

Harvest Controls: When picked young, lambsquarters is an edible green similar in taste to spinach.

Redroot Pigweed
(Amaranthus retroflexus)

Weed Description and Growth Pattern: A spring-annual broadleaf plant, redroot pigweed is marked by a distinctly red root. It produces oval to lance-shaped, light green leaves and may reach several feet in height under favorable conditions. Redroot pigweed is a vigorously growing weed that is highly competitive with other plants. Flowers are produced in bristly, irregular clusters at the top of the plant. Seeds are produced continually once flowering starts.

Mechanical Controls: Though redroot pigweed is very susceptible to hoeing during early stages of growth, older plants are more fibrous and can regrow from roots. Since redroot pigweed can begin flowering when only a few inches tall, it should be controlled early.

Chemical Controls: Susceptible to the preemergent herbicides DCPA (Dacthal®), corn gluten meal, and trifluralin (Treflan®). Emerging redroot pigweed can also be spot treated with herbicidal soaps (e.g., Sharpshooter®).

Miscellaneous Notes: Redroot pigweed is a close relative of the cultivated amaranth.

Spurge
(species of Euphorbia)

Weed Description and Growth Pattern: Prostrate spurge (*Euphorbia supina*) and spotted spurge

Lambsquarters

Redroot pigweed

Prostrate spurge

Purslane

(*Euphorbia maculata*) are relative newcomers to much of the West. They are annual broadleaf weeds with a low, spreading growth habit. Like other members of the plant family Euphorbiaceae, they produce a characteristic milky sap. They are related to leafy spurge (*Euphorbia esula*), which is an extremely aggressive perennial weed of pastures that has overrun the region. The plants are highly tolerant of drought and poor soil, which has enabled them to thrive in the cracks of driveways and sidewalks, as well as in gardens and lawns. Seeds begin to germinate in late spring as soil temperatures rise above 55°F, and germination may continue over several months. The plants accelerate in warm weather and produce small flowers, usually at the base of leaves. Seeds are shed from early July until the plants are killed by frost.

Mechanical Controls: The seeds of spurge are small and the subsequent seedlings are easy to smother with mulches and hoeing. Older plants, which are easily hand pulled or hoed, should be removed before they produce seeds.

Chemical Controls: Spurges resist most herbicides. The preemergent herbicide DCPA (Dacthal®) is probably one of the most effective treatments but may need to be reapplied due to the length of the period during which spurge seeds germinate. Spurges are also quite tolerant of contact herbicides such as glyphosate (Roundup®, Kleenup®), herbicidal soaps (Sharpshooter®), and 2,4-D.

Purslane
(*Portulaca oleracea*)

Weed Description and Growth Pattern: An annual broadleaf weed that reproduces by seeds, spurge has succulent leaves and a low-growing, spreading growth habit, and is related to the garden flower known as portulaca or moss rose. It thrives in moist soils but the seeds require fairly warm soil temperatures to germinate. Flowers appear in mid to late summer and seeds are produced continuously after this point. Because of its low-growing habit, purslane does not com-

pete for light with garden plants as much as other common weeds. However, it uses a lot of water during growth and can form a mat that inhibits small plants.

Mechanical Controls: Hoeing is most effective on smaller plants, since purslane can regrow from the roots once it reaches 3 to 5 inches. Because of the succulent growth, pulled plants may reroot if the soil remains moist, so irrigation should be suspended for several days after cultivation. As flowers begin to form, purslane should be removed from the garden, since seeds can mature on drying plants. Because of its low-growing habit, purslane is easy to control with mulch. However, the seeds are extremely persistent and are among the few that are little affected by soil solarization.

Chemical Controls: DCPA (Dacthal®) and trifluralin (Treflan®) control germinating purslane. However, because seed germination is rather late, applications of these herbicides early in the season to control other weeds may no longer be effective against later-germinating purslane. Also, seeds persist for several years. Purslane is one of the weeds most resistant to glyphosate.

Harvest Controls: An edible plant, cultivated varieties of purslane are grown in many areas of the world. It was originally introduced into North America as a vegetable crop. The younger leaves have a tart, acidic taste.

Dandelion
(*Taraxacum officianale*)

Weed Description and Growth Pattern: Dandelion, one of the most cosmopolitan of all weeds, has, since its introduction into North America, spread widely throughout much of the continent. Presently, it is one of the most conspicuous weeds in lawns because of its contrasting, bright yellow flowers. Dandelion also inhabits pastures, mountain meadows, roadsides, and gardens, since the wind-borne seeds grow rapidly after landing on any moist, bare soil. Dandelion is a perennial and produces a long taproot that can measure 1 to 2 feet in depth. The leaves are flattened and often grow close to the soil. Because of this low-growing habit, dandelions generally do not compete with garden plants for sunlight and are not aggressive garden weeds. However, they remove nutrients and water from garden soils and may crowd out some garden plants. Most flowers are produced in early spring and fall but dandelions flower nearly nine months of the year. Plants reproduce both by seed and by producing new shoots from the taproot.

Mechanical Controls: Although seedling plants are easily pulled, established plants resist cutting or pulling. Unless the taproot is completely removed, which is sometimes possible in very loose soils, the plants may regrow, requiring repeated hoeing until the root reserves are depleted. Since the plant also regrows from root fragments, rototilling may spread dandelions throughout a garden. Because of its low-growing habit, dandelions are more easily controlled with mulches than are other more aggressive perennials, such as field bindweed.

Chemical Controls: During early spring (before flowering) and fall, dandelions are most susceptible to the herbicides such as 2,4-D. Unfortunately, these herbicides can injure most garden plants, so chemical control of dandelions is often undesirable. Spot treatment with nonselective systemic herbicides such as glyphosate or glufosinate can help if applied with utmost care

Dandelion seed head

so as not to damage desirable plants. Best results from these latter herbicides are usually obtained when they are applied during flowering.

Harvest Controls: Dandelions were deliberately introduced into North America and are cultivated as food. All parts of the plant are edible, and it is a good source of a number of vitamins (A and C) and minerals (iron, copper, and potassium).

Field Bindweed/ Wild Morning Glory (*Convolvulus arvensis*)

Weed Description and Growth Pattern: Field bindweed, also known as morning glory or creeping jenny, is one of the most persistent and difficult weeds to control. Once established, field bindweed produces roots that may penetrate 15 to 30 feet or more, and it tenaciously regrows after hoeing. Field bindweed produces a vine that may climb or spread across the garden. From June through September, the plant produces showy white or pink flowers, miniatures of the cultivated morning glory. The flowers only last a short while (typically 1 day), and field bindweed doggedly produces its prolific seeds throughout the growing season. Field bindweed also reproduces and spreads by underground roots.

Mechanical Controls: Seedling plants (before the 5-leaf stage) can be killed by hoeing a single time. After this point, the plants regrow from the root system. Regrowth from established plants starts about two weeks after cutting, before the leaves begin to send food back to the roots. By cutting at 14- to 18-day intervals, the plants are gradually starved. Individual plants in a garden can be "canned and smothered" by inverting a large can over plants that emerge following hoeing. Soil solarization also kill plants during periods of high temperature and light intensity.

Biological Controls: No biological controls appear to greatly affect field bindweed. Among the more conspicuous insects associated with the plant are the brightly colored "golden tortoise beetles," which

Field bindweed

Gold in the Garden—Life of the Tortoise Beetles

Late in the summer as you work the plants, a glint of gold strikes your eye. Peering closer, you espy what appears to be a bright gold lady beetle. It is, however, a "golden tortoise beetle."

The tortoise beetles are leaf beetles, relatives of the Colorado potato beetle, striped cucumber beetle, and the various flea beetles. They feed on leaves, yet their favorite host in the West is field bindweed, a plant that is little mourned. (Sweetpotato and morning glory are alternate hosts, but suffer little damage.) Small, nearly circular holes in the leaves of bindweed advertise their presence. The most common species in this region is *Deloyala guttata*, which can range from a bright gold to a burnished coppery color.

The tortoise beetles spend the winter under debris in the vicinity of the garden, returning in late spring to lay their eggs on morning glory and other host plants. Thorny spines cover the body of the young grubs, which feed inconspicuously on the underside of the leaves. Further contributing to their cryptic habit is that they pack old shed skins and excrement on their back; they're often called "peddlers" as a result.

The gold pigment of these insects is an ephemeral gift, lost quickly after they die.

chew holes in the leaves (see above). An eriophyid mite is currently under development by the USDA as a potential future control.

Chemical Controls: Field bindweed is quite resistant to control with herbicides. Although several herbicides can kill the top growth, the extensive root system often remains, allowing the plant to regrow. Treatments of glyphosate (Roundup®, Kleenup®) and glufosinate (Finale®, Liberty®) are most effective when applied during periods of peak flowering. Combining the herbicide treatment with regular hoeing and rotating with highly competitive plants, such as squash, improves control.

Miscellaneous Notes: Field bindweed is often confused with annual buckwheat, a weed with lancelike leaves and a similar vining habit. Annual buckwheat does not produce the showy flowers of bindweed and it is not perennial.

Canada Thistle
(*Cirsium arvense*)

Weed Description and Growth Pattern: Along with field bindweed, Canada thistle is a challenging garden weed to control. Once established in the garden, this deep-rooted perennial spreads rapidly by creeping roots and rhizomes. Eradication is not only a long-term project, but touching the spiny leaves with an ungloved hand only adds insult to injury. Initial infestations originate with windblown seed, although fertile seeds are rarely shed in the thistledown. However, the plants easily regrow from roots, which may remain dormant for several years if buried deeply. The plants tend to die back after flowering, regrowing in late summer and early fall.

Mechanical Controls: Root reserves of plants can be exhausted by repeated hoeing. Hoeing should be done at least every 2 weeks to prevent plants from recovering energy reserves. Because new plants can sprout from small root pieces, deep cultivation, including rototilling, actually spreads them.

Biological Controls: Several insects feed on Canada thistle, most prominently the thistle caterpillar, alter ego of the painted lady butterfly. Aphids, lacebugs, and planthoppers occasionally suck sap from plants. Rust disease can individually destroy susceptible plants. Unfortunately, these natural controls appear to have little permanent effect on Canada thistle. The USDA, in conjunction with some state agencies, is currently releas-

Canada thistle

ing new species of insects developed specifically for the biological control of Canada thistle.

Chemical Controls: Canada thistle is most susceptible to herbicides when plants are small or have been stressed by repeated pulling and hoeing. Periodically disrupting the root system by tilling the soil, which inhibits the production of lateral roots, eases control. Plants in the early bud stage are most susceptible to the herbicide 2,4-D. Applying immediately after bloom is recommended for the application of systemic, nonselective herbicides such as glyphosate (Roundup®, Kleenup®) and glufosinate (Finale®, Liberty®). However, since these herbicides also kill or damage many garden plants and cannot be employed around food crops, they must be used with extreme care. Selectively brushing or painting with the herbicide is a solution.

Common Mallow/Cheeseweed (*Malva neglecta*)

Weed Description and Growth Pattern: Common mallow (cheeseweed) is a broadleaf plant with a spreading habit of growth. It often invades lawns and gardens and, although not highly aggressive, can be difficult to eradicate. Highly variable in growth, common mallow may occur as a leafy annual, biennial, or even perennial weed, depending on growing conditions. The plant produces pale-colored, 5-petal flowers, and the time of flowering depends on the age of the plant but usually lasts throughout the growing season. Common mallow later forms a sectioned ("cheesewheel") seed pod that scatters seeds as it dries. Seeds most often germinate in late spring, but germination continues throughout much of the summer.

Mechanical Controls: Seedlings and young plants can be controlled easily with hoeing. However, if common mallow has already been growing for several months, it has produced a deep taproot that makes it difficult to kill. These taproots must be pulled or cut well below the underground crown area to prevent rapid regrowth. Mulches prevent seedling emergence, and are effective for preventing regrowth following pulling and hoeing.

Chemical Controls: No effective chemical controls are available for use in vegetable plantings. Spot treatment with glyphosate (Roundup®, Kleenup®) provides control in flowers and around fruit trees. Glufosinate (Finale®, Liberty®) also can be used in flower gardens.

Common mallow

Chapter 9

Managing Garden Problems
with Mammals and Birds

Peter Rabbit is only one of the uninvited vertebrate pests that may visit a garden patch. Deer and elk can demolish a vegetable garden in short order, favoring the tender shoots or most succulent parts of the vegetables. Coyotes may arrive late in the summer to feast on melons, for which they show a decided preference. Ripening fruit is also devoured by raccoons, robins, and blackbirds. Sometimes even neighborhood pets wreak havoc digging around the plants.

Special circumstances arise when controlling vertebrate pests. They are highly mobile and intelligent and can be difficult to exclude from a garden. Lethal controls—shooting, poisoning, and even trapping—are often strictly limited by game laws, city ordinances, and concerns of possible injury to pets, desirable wildlife, or children.

MAMMALS

Voles
(species of Microtus)

Damage: Voles (also called "meadow mice") injure fruit and ornamental trees and shrubs by gnawing on the bark. Extensive injury produces girdling wounds that kill smaller plants. The small size (about 1/8 inch wide) of the chewing wounds differs from that of other gnawing animals, such as jackrabbits. Vole damage to tree bark (juni-

pers are a favorite) is most frequent during the winter and greatest injury occurs in years of heavy snowfall. Voles will eat almost anything green, including grasses, tubers, bulbs, and garden plants, and often damage lawns by clipping the grass while making surface runways.

Life History and Habits: Voles are rodents, related to the white-footed and deer mice that sometimes invade homes. There are several species of voles in this region, including the pine vole, prairie vole, long-tailed vole, montane vole, and meadow vole. The pine vole has been particularly damaging to orchards. Voles actively feed and reproduce throughout the year. Breeding peaks during spring and summer. About three to six young are produced in each litter. They develop rapidly and become full grown in about 45 days. Their life span is fairly short, averaging less than one year. Population numbers fluctuate dramatically, with peak injury to trees and shrubs paralleling periodic outbreaks. Voles produce and maintain runways and shallow tunnels that cross the soil surface. These burrow systems may support several voles. The home range area used by voles varies during the year.

Biological Controls: Natural predators of voles include large snakes, owls, and weasels, which normally will not be found in yards. However, cats rarely pass up an opportunity to feed on voles.

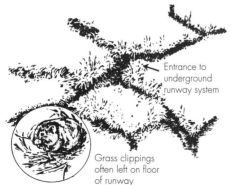

Entrance to underground runway system

Grass clippings often left on floor of runway

Surface runway system of the prairie vole

Cultural Controls: To thrive and increase their numbers, voles require cover and ready access to food. Mowing lawns and weedy areas, and periodically spading or tilling a garden, reduces the available cover favored by voles. Mulches, which also provide cover, should be cleared away at least 3 feet from the base of susceptible trees and shrubs to impede bark feeding. If vole injury is serious to overwintered perennials, such as strawberries, mulching should be delayed until after the ground has frozen.

Mechanical Controls: Individual trees and shrubs can be protected from vole injury by tree guards or wire mesh screening, 1/4 inch or less in diameter. Because voles can tunnel, the barriers should be buried at least 6 inches. Placing small, sharp pebbles in planting holes for bulbs also deters voles. During the winter, compacting the snow around trees and shrubs serves as a barrier to vole tunneling. Mouse traps, placed with the trigger along the runways, can be used to kill voles. Baiting is not necessary if traps are properly placed in the runway.

Chemical Controls: Hot pepper mixtures and thiram-based repellents have been registered for control of meadow voles, though their effectiveness is considered questionable.

Eastern Fox Squirrel (Sciurus niger)

Damage: The eastern fox squirrel hangs out in yards and gardens east of the Rockies. Active throughout the year, it is an interesting and valued member of backyard wildlife. But raids of gardens, trees, and bird feeders sometimes cause people to have second thoughts about squirrels. Fox squirrels prefer to feed on nuts and fruits, which can include the plums and cherries that were planted for another purpose. More significant, they chew tree bark and buds, particularly during fall and early spring, causing dieback of branches. Squirrels occasionally also feed on sweet corn in the vegetable garden.

Nesting squirrels periodically cause some injury to ornamental plants. Trees and shrubs that produce long strips of loose bark, such as honeysuckle and Russian olive, may be patronized by squirrels searching for material to line their nests.

Life History and Habits: Fox squirrels reproduce rapidly. There are two breeding seasons (December to January and June) during which the male squirrels noisily chase females and each other around the yard. The young are born about 45 days later. Nesting may occur in leaf nests lined with bark and other plant materials. However, fox squirrels prefer to nest in a cavity, such as a tree hollow or even an attic. Litters average about three young squirrels, which are weaned in 2 1/2 to 3 months. Fox squirrels can be highly migratory and will travel for miles if food is scarce. They do not hibernate and are active all year.

Legal Status: Fox squirrels are considered to be game animals under some state wildlife laws. Check local regulations if squirrels are to be trapped or killed.

Biological Controls: Although squirrels may live up to ten years in captivity, about half of all squirrels typically die from natural causes each year. Insect and mite parasites are very common. Predators such as hawks, owls, and domestic and feral cats take many squirrels as well, although they are not considered to be instrumental in regulating populations. House cats discourage squirrels from nesting in attics and other areas of a home.

Cultural Controls: If the squirrel population is high and threatens to cause bark-chewing injuries, providing supplemental food is a reasonable defense.

Mechanical Controls: Squirrels can be excluded from individual trees by metal collars. These should be 2 feet wide and placed high on the trunk—preferably at least 6 feet aboveground. However, fox squirrels are excellent jumpers and all other access must be eliminated (e.g., fences, nearby trees, roofs). Squirrels nesting in homes can be kept out by 1/2-inch mesh hardware cloth. They are also easily trapped in box or cage live traps. Nuts, seeds, apples, and peanut butter are

Fox squirrel

good attractants. However, trapping generally has little effect on populations, since new squirrels migrate readily and reproduction is rapid. When siting traps, place them near existing trails commonly used by the squirrels and direct them into the traps with fencing.

Repellents: Moth repellents containing naphthalene or paradichlorobenzene can repel squirrels from nesting in attics. However, the value of these fumigant-type materials outdoors is questionable. Thiram-based animal repellents may prevent gnawing damage to fruit trees when applied in the dormant season. However, registrations and product availability are limited.

Miscellaneous Notes: Several types of ground-dwelling squirrels, such as the Richardson ground squirrel (*Spermophilus richardsoni*) and thirteen-lined ground squirrel (*S. tridecemlineatus*), are common in this region. They feed on crop seedings and damage pastureland in less developed areas, but rarely occur in high numbers around yards and gardens. Unlike fox squirrels, ground squirrels hibernate during the winter. Ground squirrels are usually controlled by trapping using poison baits. They are not generally protected by law, although local wildlife agencies should be consulted before employing these methods.

Raccoon
(*Procyon lotor*)

Damage: Raccoons feed on a wide variety of plant and animal foods, including fruits and vegetables. Sweet corn and grapes are their favorites. Plants are knocked over and ears partially eaten just as they begin to ripen. Raccoon damage to sweet corn is characterized by husks that have been pulled back. Raccoons will also eat melons, digging a small hole in the rind and scooping out the contents. Some tree fruits, such as cherries and berries, are relished by raccoons as well. In addition, raccoons kill young birds, including poultry, and they also feed on insects, often tearing up lawns in search of white grubs, cutworms, or other large insects.

Life History and Habits: Raccoons exist throughout the West and have thrived with human perturbation, but they are most common near wooded cover and water. They are active at night and may roam half a mile or more from their dens. Adult males, which remain solitary, maintain the largest ranges. Raccoons usually give birth in April or May, occasionally later. Litter size is typically three to five, and the young often stay with their mother for the first year, separating the following spring. In winter, raccoons do not hibernate, but remain inactive in their dens during unfavorable weather.

Legal Status: Raccoons are classified as protected furbearers in most states. Individual raccoons that are causing damage can be killed or trapped only with permission from state wildlife agencies.

Mechanical Controls: Fencing excludes raccoons. Electric fences are very effective for protecting sweet corn and other garden vegetables. Fence wires should be 6 inches high, with a second lower wire to increase effectiveness. Wire mesh is also exclusive. However, raccoons are excellent climbers. Mesh screening should incorporate an overhang or be left unattached (floppy wire fence) to deter climbing.

Frightening devices sometimes provide temporary control of raccoons, but rarely offer long-term control. These include radios, dogs, wind chimes, and other noise-making devices. Similarly, nighttime lighting deters raccoons, but they will begin to revisit the site once they adapt to the change.

Repellents: Repellents offer little benefit for the control of raccoons in open-air settings, such as gardens. Moth crystals (paradichlorobenzene) hung around plants is reported to be partially effective as a raccoon deterrent.

Traps: Raccoons are best trapped using cage- or box-type live traps. Traps used for capturing raccoons need to be large (at least 10 by 12 by 32 inches) and of strong construction. Baits of fish-flavored cat food, chicken, or fish are attractive.

However, trapping is rarely recommended since there is little if any suitable area for their release that is not already colonized by raccoons and transporting them may transmit diseases such as distemper and mange.

Cottontail Rabbit
(species of Sylvilagus)

Damage: Rabbits feed on and destroy many different garden plants. Despite their reputation for carrots (promoted largely by Bugs Bunny), other vegetables, such as beans and peas, appear to be more preferred and root crops are often little damaged. During winter, cottontails will gnaw fruit tree bark, raspberries, and many ornamental plants. (Evergreens are particular favorites.) Succulent shoots of young trees are also browsed by rabbits, clipped at snow height. Rabbit damage is characterized by a sharp, clean, 45-degree-angle feeding cut. When rabbits are abundant, other signs, including round droppings and footprints, can be used to distinguish rabbit injury from that of other gnawing mammals, such as voles and squirrels. Several species of cottontail rabbits reside in this region. The eastern cottontail (*Sylvilagus floridanus*) is generally most abundant east of the Rockies, although several other species occur in the West. Cottontail rabbits prefer to nest in areas offering brush or other cover, and landscaped areas of developed neighborhoods is ideal for this activity. Cottontails are rarely found in dense forests or open rangeland. In open areas of the plains, jackrabbits (species of *Lepus*) may predominate. These rabbit relatives (actually classified as hares) are especially disruptive when drought or overgrazing forces them into yards and gardens.

Some of the plants most frequently damaged by rabbits are tulips, carrots, peas, beans, beets, most rose family plants (including apple, raspberries, cherry, plum, mountain ash), basswood, red maple, honeylocust, oak, willow, sumac, and dogwood. Garden plants least favored by rabbits include corn, squash, cucumbers, tomatoes, potatoes, and peppers.

Life History and Habits: Despite the well-known exploits of Peter Cottontail (actually a European hare), cottontail rabbits do not dig underground nests. During warmer months, they form shallow hollows in dense vegetation for cover; for winter protection, natural cavities or burrows are used. Rabbits breed like—rabbits. Cottontails typically produce two to three litters per year and each litter contains about three to five young. The young rabbits leave the nest about three weeks after birth and are sexually mature within a few months. Populations increase rapidly when food is abundant. Cottontails do not hibernate and are active throughout the winter, walking on snow and feeding on plants at whatever level the snow cover allows.

Legal Status: In most of this region, cottontail rabbits are classified as a game animal. As such, they fall under the regulations of state wildlife agencies, which generally restrict hunting and trapping to specific seasons, and require a license. However, exemptions may be granted by these state agencies for rabbits that are damaging property.

Biological Controls: Rabbits suffer predation by many animals in the wild, including owls, foxes, snakes, and hawks. Rabbits also succumb to various diseases. Cottontail rabbits rarely live for more than 15 months under natural conditions. In areas of dense human habitation, domestic and feral cats are important predators, feeding on young rabbits in nests. Dogs also restrict rabbits from roaming in yards, although they rarely kill them.

Cultural Controls: Rabbits tend to avoid open areas where they are particularly vulnerable to predators. Keeping areas mowed and landscaping to provide open areas will deter rabbits. Removing brush piles and other dense, protective cover eliminates sites where rabbits hide and nest.

Mechanical Controls: Rabbits can simply be excluded from gardens with fencing. A 2-foot-high chicken wire fencing, buried shallowly in the soil, prevents most rabbits from entering gardens during the summer. Plastic tree wraps are also available

Rabbit injury (Photo by David Leatherman)

Cottontail rabbit (Photo by David Leatherman)

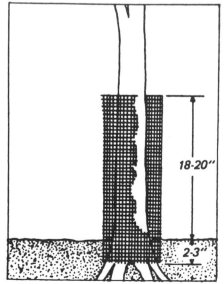

Rabbit barrier

18-20"

2-3"

that will generally provide control for 3 to 5 years. Alternately, flexible polypropylene netting, galvanized poultry wire, and even aluminum foil serve as barriers to rabbit feeding on trees and shrubs. Such barriers are best constructed 1 to 2 feet above snow line. Holes in fencing should not be larger than 1/2 inch to exclude small rabbits.

Repellents: Various types of odor repellents marketed as animal repellents, such as naphthalene mothballs, are not effective for rabbit control outdoors. Taste repellents, usually involving the fungicide repellent thiram, do prevent rabbit feeding. However, thiram is a toxic material to other mammals, such as humans, and cannot be applied to food crops.

Traps: Box live traps baited with apples, carrots, ears of corn, or cabbage facilitate rabbit trapping. Traps should be placed close to areas of cover used by rabbits.

Mule Deer
(Odocoileus hemionus)

Damage: Throughout much of the region, no pest deserves the destructive-and-difficult-to-manage label more than the mule deer. In spite of the residual "Bambi syndrome," most gardeners change their tune after losing a vegetable or flower garden to deer. (The white-tailed deer, *Odocoileus virginianus,* is also found in much of the region and causes similar plant injury.) Deer feed on a very wide variety of plants, depending on the season and the availability of alternative foods. Many vegetable crops may be browsed by deer feeding; chewing of sweet corn ear tips and nipping the center from heads of broccoli and cauliflower are examples. Deer also chew on twigs of fruit and ornamental trees, sometimes causing severe damage to younger trees. Feeding damage by deer is characterized by ragged wounds. Deer (and elk) lack upper incisor teeth, which account for the clean cuts of other gnawing animals, such as rabbits.

Deer also damage trees by battering them with antlers during late summer and fall. Young trees are a common victim of this sparring practice.

Life History and Habits: Deer prefer areas of mixed vegetation and have been described as creatures of the forest edge. The ideal habitat for deer comprises areas near shrubby plants that provide year-round food of leaves, twigs, and buds and where denser growth is also available for cover. This mix is sometimes achieved with landscaping, which can attract deer into neighborhoods. Where deer have lost their fear of humans, they may prefer the plantings found in yards and become a costly nuisance. Most deer feed during dusk and dawn. They may wander half a mile or more from resting areas to search for food. In the more northern areas, deer often gather under dense cover for winter protection. Deer breed during late fall and bear their young about 202 days later; birth numbers peak during May and June. Twin births are the norm. The young fawns develop rapidly and some does are capable of reproducing when only six months old. Their reproduction is very dependent on the amount of available food. Deer are long-lived, with some individuals living almost twenty years. Hunting is the primary mitigating factor in deer life expectancy in most areas.

Legal Status: Deer are protected animals and killing them is only allowed during specified hunting periods and then, only with a license. Deer

Mule deer (Photo by David Leatherman)

hunting in many communities is further restricted by local ordinances. In some cases, special permits may be issued by state wildlife agencies to farmers suffering from specific deer problems.

Mechanical Controls (Exclusion): In areas where deer damage is severe, fencing provides the only satisfactory control. However, deer are excellent jumpers and can easily clean a typical 6-foot yard fence. They can also climb through or under fence openings that are less than a foot wide. Constructing a truly deer-proof fence constitutes a substantial project. Various designs are offered as follows:

Basic deer fence. A properly constructed fence at least 8 feet tall will exclude deer. A thick wire mesh is highly durable and ideal for this purpose. Lighter mesh materials (chicken wire, plastic netting) can also be used, but these degrade rapidly. Unless well marked, the light mesh may not be seen by the deer, and, consequently, it may push through accidentally. The fence should reach to the soil line to prevent deer from crawling under it. Solid wood or brick fences, through which the deer cannot see, can be somewhat lower (6 to 8 feet) and still deter deer from jumping into the yard.

Slant fence. An outward-slanting fence can be more simply and cheaply constructed than an 8-foot vertical fence. For example, a 7-foot fence angled at 45 degrees usually deters deer, as they tend to approach desiring to travel under the fence, and are then unable to jump through it.

Electric fence. A variety of effective electric fence designs have been proposed for excluding deer. Although not generally appropriate for most yards, these are much cheaper and easier to construct than fences built to physically exclude the deer. Deer will generally try to go under or through a fence, even if they could easily jump over it. Most electric fence designs encourage this habit so that the deer will touch the fence. After this "shocking experience," deer will often learn to avoid the fence and stay several feet away. Since they usually jump from a point very close to the fence, their avoidance of the fence vicinity reduces

their inclination to jump relatively low fences. A typical electric fence design would be about 5 feet in height with wires placed at 8- to 12-inch spacings. Usually wire spacing is tighter at the lower end of the fence. Alternatively, two shorter electrified fences, spaced 3 feet apart, can be used to exclude deer.

Repellents: Many different repellents have been touted as deer deterrents. Some of these are contact repellents, which mediate taste. Contact deer repellents include hot pepper sauce (commercially available as well as home brews) and thiram (a fungicide and animal repellent). An important limitation of these contact repellents is their inability to protect the favored new growth that emerges after treatment. To make some of the less residual sprays, such as hot pepper, last longer during rainy periods, it is recommended that they be mixed with additives that reduce evaporation (e.g., Vapor-Guard®, Wilt-Pruf®). The commercially available contact repellents cannot be applied directly to food crops.

Area repellents that protect plants mediate odor, and dozens of materials have been proffered. For example, human hair or blood meal are often suggested as repellents, although the general consensus of the seriously deer-plagued is that these are marginally effective at best. Bags of some brands of deodorant soaps are known to repel. Also the manure and urine of large cats (provided by your obliging neighborhood cougar) or coyotes are more widely recognized as being fairly good repellents against deer.

Some commercial repellents appear to be the most promising. These include fermented egg solids (Deer-Away®, MGK-BGR®, Big Game Repellent®) or ammonium soaps produced from certain fatty acids (Hinder®). The latter is one of the few repellents that can be applied directly to plants that are to be eaten. A highly effective homemade repellent is a mixture of eggs blended with water.

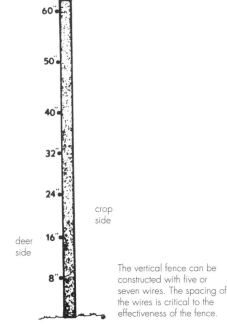

crop side

deer side

The vertical fence can be constructed with five or seven wires. The spacing of the wires is critical to the effectiveness of the fence.

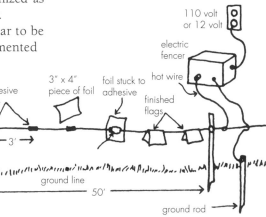

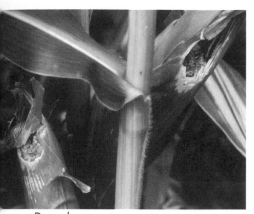

Deer damage to sweet corn

Crack the eggs and remove the small, white membranous allantois, which tends to clog the sprayer. Blend in a 1:4 egg/water ratio and use this for a plant spray.

Dogs kept around garden areas will repel deer. However, unrestricted dogs are often not allowed in many residential areas, since they also may threaten livestock and other wildlife.

House finch injury to seedling peas

TABLE 9-1: SOME YARD AND GARDEN PLANTS THAT ARE LEAST LIKELY TO BE BROWSED BY DEER

Trees and Shrubs

Barberry	Redosier dogwood	Forsythia
Honeylocust	Beautybush	Norway spruce
White spruce	Colorado spruce	Mugho pine
Austrian pine	Scotch pine	Common lilac
Southern sage	Four-winged saltbush	Quince
Rabbitbrush	Fernbush	Winged euonymus
Rose of Sharon	Vanhoutte spirea	Tatarian honeysuckle
Mountain ninebark	Potentilla	Wild plum
Nanking cherry	Gambel's oak	Fragrant sumac
Common hackberry	Hancock coralberry	Silver buffaloberry
Snowberry	Concolor fir	Common juniper
Mahonia	Pyracantha	Alpine currant

Herbs and Flowers

Eupohorbias	Feverfew	Dusty miller
Salvias	Helianthemum	Penstemons
Snow-in-summer	Yarrow	Lavender
Oregano	Thyme	Catmint
Zinnia	Lupine	Peonies
Chives	Black-eyed Susan	Coreopsis
Bleeding heart	Iris	Columbine
Leadplant	Clematis	Marjoram
Rhubarb	Shasta daisy	Goldenrod
Prickly pear	Golden banner	Delphinium
Daylily	Cowania	Mertensias
Saponaria	English ivy	Purple coneflower
Chocolate flower	Lily of the valley	Echinops
Snowdrop	Dotted gayfeather	Poker plant

BIRDS

Damage: Several types of birds feed on ripening fruits. Cherries and berries are particularly favored and the fruits may be entirely eaten or merely pecked, a common habit of robins. Such injuries spoil the appearance of fruit and allow entry of rotting organisms. Birds also feed on seeds with sunflowers topping the list.

Special problems accompany particular birds, primarily house finches and occasionally starlings, chickadees, or house sparrows, that feed on developing seedlings. The tender growth of these plants may be clipped severely, retarding development, and injuries at the base of low-growing flowers cause wilting. Birds have also been observed pulling out entire seedlings. Crows are notorious for digging up large seeds such as corn after planting.

Life History and Habits: Some of the most damaging birds to fruit crops are robins, starlings, and the various blackbirds. All of these typically nest in and around yards and gardens. Although more protein-rich foods (worms, insects) are usually eaten while raising young in late spring, many birds will switch to ripening fruit as it becomes available. Late in the season, flocking birds abound, ravaging ripening crops such as sunflowers.

Legal Status: With the exception of the starling, pigeon, and English sparrow (the latter two are not garden pests), all birds commonly found around yards are protected by the Federal Migratory Bird Treaty Act and should not be trapped or harmed. Where serious damage is threatened, local wildlife agencies may sanction limited trapping.

Cultural Controls: Injury to fruit crops may be reduced by offering alternative foods for fruit-feeding birds such as elderberry, mulberry, hawthorn, and mountain ash.

Mechanical Controls: Several bird-repellent devices are sold through garden catalogs, including "scare-eyes," owl replicas, and vibrating wires. Typically these provide only short-term protection because the birds readily adapt to their presence. The most effective control is netting to exclude birds from fruit trees and berries. The netting must completely enclose the plant, since the birds seek out any openings. It should also extend a few inches beyond the plant to prevent birds perched on the netting from reaching the fruit. Mesh bird netting, as well as cheesecloth or shade cloth, will do the trick.

Robin (Photo by David Leatherman)

"Scare-eye" balloon used to deter bird damage

Bird netting

Appendix I
Sources of Biological Control Organisms

LADY BEETLE

When sold as "lady beetles" or "ladybugs," the species referred to is the convergent lady beetle, *Hippodamia convergens*, a native lady beetle found throughout most of North America. Purchased lady beetles are all field-collected insects, captured in the high-elevation areas of California where they periodically immigrate and mass aggregate, facilitating easy collection. The ability of the collected lady beetles to reproduce is suspended (they are in "reproductive diapause"), so eggs are not produced for several weeks after release. (Prefeeding lady beetles prior to release can allow some egg maturation to start and a few companies provide such "preconditioned" lady beetles.) Lady beetles tend to readily disperse from the area of release. Since they store well, lady beetles are available most of the year, although supplies are often limited by midsummer.

Sources: 2, 5, 6, 8, 9, 10, 12, 13, 14, 15, 16, 17, 19, 20, 21

GREEN LACEWING

Chrysoperla carnea and *Chrysoperla rufilabris* are green lacewings that are commonly reared in insectaries and distributed by suppliers of biological control organisms. They are usually sold as eggs, most often mixed with a carrier such as rice hulls to be sprinkled around plants. Some suppliers apply the eggs to cards that can be hung on plants. Shipped insects should be released soon after receipt as the larvae are cannibalistic, and eggs should not be chilled. Ants are predators of the eggs and may disrupt the effectiveness of a release if abundant.

Sources: 2, 3, 4, 5, 6, 7, 8, 9, 10, 12, 13, 14, 15, 16, 17, 18, 19, 20, 21

(PRAYING) MANTIDS

The Chinese mantid, *Tenodera aridifolia sinensis*, is the species of commercial trade. The are sold as egg cases (oothecae), each containing about 200 eggs. Adult Chinese mantids reach a size of about 4 inches and are the largest mantids found in North America. They are poorly adapted to surviving winter conditions common to much of the region, although other species of mantids do overwinter successfully. Mantid egg cases are usually available only during spring through early summer.

Sources: 2, 5, 8, 9, 16, 17, 18, 19, 20

APHID PREDATOR MIDGE

Larvae of a tiny fly, *Aphidoletes aphidimyza*, develop as predator of aphids. It is a native insect of the region, found most commonly in late summer within aphid colonies. *A. aphidimyza* is sold for use in greenhouses, supplied as pupae that disperse after they transform to the adult stage.

When used during winter, supplemental lighting must be provided to maintain a minimum of 12 hours of daylight or the predators become dormant.

Sources: 1, 2, 7, 9, 10, 12, 13, 14, 15, 16, 18, 19, 20, 21

PREDATORY MITES

Over half a dozen species of predatory mites (Phytoseiidae family) are insectary-produced and commercially available. Most are advertised to control spider mites, but *Amblyseius cucumeris, A. degenerans,* and *A. fallacis* are marketed for control of thrips. There is also a soil-dwelling predatory mite, *Hypoapsis miles,* that is used to help control fungus gnat larvae and thrips pupae. Temperature and humidity requirements for the different predatory mites vary greatly and it is important to match the species with the conditions at the release site. Predatory mites have been used almost exclusively in greenhouses, although there have been applications in control of certain mites damaging to fruit crops.

Sources (*Neoseiulus californicus*): 2, 3, 9, 10, 12, 13, 14, 16, 17, 18, 19, 21
Sources (*Phytoseiulus persimilis*): 1, 2, 3, 5, 7, 9, 10, 12, 13, 14, 15, 16, 17, 18, 19, 20
Sources (*Mesoseiulus longipes*): 2, 3, 5, 9, 10, 12, 14, 16, 18, 19, 21
Sources (*Galendromus occidentalis*): 2, 3, 4, 9, 12, 14, 16, 17, 19, 21
Sources (*Amblyseius degenerans*): 13, 17, 21
Sources (*Amblyseius cucumeris*): 10, 12, 13, 14, 15, 16, 19, 20, 21
Sources (*Amblyseius fallacis*): 1, 7, 14, 16, 19, 21
Sources (*Hypoaspis miles*): 1, 2, 9, 12, 14, 15, 16, 19, 21

MINUTE PIRATE BUG

The tiny predatory bug *Orius insidiosus* is an important predator of spider mites, thrips, and other small insects in western North America. Commercially available, it is primarily sold for release in greenhouses.

Sources: 2, 5, 9, 10, 12, 13, 14, 15, 16, 18, 19, 20

DERAEOCORIS BREVIS

This predatory species of plant bug, *D. brevis,* native to much of North America, is sold to assist in control of both outdoor (e.g., pear psylla on pears, lygus bugs) and greenhouse pests (e.g., whiteflies, thrips, aphids). Light is critical to their activity with the insect going into dormancy when day length drops to less than 16 hours.

Sources: 1, 12, 16, 21

TRICHOGRAMMA WASP

Trichogramma wasps develop as parasites of eggs of caterpillars. They have been used primarily for control of corn earworm, but have the potential to manage several other garden pests such as tobacco budworm, loopers, codling moths, cabbageworms, and certain cutworms. Trichogramma wasps are supplied on cards containing parasitized eggs from which the adult wasps will emerge. Several different species of trichogramma wasps are produced—*T. minutum, T. planteri, T. evanescens, T. pretiosum*—each with unique habits that are crop-specific.

Sources: 2, 3, 4, 5, 7, 8, 9, 12, 13, 14, 15, 16, 17, 18, 19, 20, 21

APHID PARASITE

Several wasp parasites of aphids (species of *Aphidius*) are commercially available, primarily for greenhouse use. These predators are generalists, capable of attacking many species of aphids, and are native in gardens throughout much of the region.

Sources of *Aphidius matricariae:* 1, 2, 5, 10, 12, 14, 15, 16, 21
Sources of *Aphidius colemani:* 9, 16, 21
Source of *Aphidius ervi:* 16

WHITEFLY PARASITE

A small wasp, *Encarsia formosa,* attacks and develops within immature whitefly nymphs. Introduction of this parasitic wasp has proven effective for whitefly management in warm greenhouses (average temperatures above 72°F). The whitefly parasite is supplied on cards, as developing wasps within whitefly nymphs. The latter turn black when hosting this parasite.

Sources: 1, 2, 6, 7, 9 10, 12, 13, 14, 15, 16, 17, 18, 19, 20, 21

ERETMOCERUS CALIFORNICUS

Another parasite of whiteflies is *Eretmocerus californicus*. Originally developed to help manage sweetpotato whitefly, it also is an effective natural enemy of greenhouse whitefly. Adult stages may kill many developing whiteflies by stinging them and then blood feeding. Whitefly nymphs parasitized by this insect turn a golden color.

Sources: 5, 13, 14, 15, 16, 21

MEXICAN BEAN BEETLE PARASITE

Pediobius foveolatus is a small, parasitic wasp that develops within immature stages of the Mexican bean beetle. Releases should be made shortly after bean beetle eggs are first detected. This insect does not survive the winters in this region.

Source: 2

FLY PARASITES

Several species of parasitic wasps attack the pupae of house flies and other manure- and garbage-breeding flies. Suppliers generally provide a mixture of two or more species and recommend releases at about 2-week intervals. Although marketed primarily for the control of flies associated with horses and livestock, the mixture may control some of the larger flies associated with decaying plant matter.

Sources: 4, 5, 7, 8, 9, 12, 15, 16, 17, 18, 19, 21, 22

BACILLUS THURINGIENSIS

Bacillus thuringiensis (Bt) is a bacterial disease organism that has been formulated into a number of microbial insecticides. Several strains of Bt exist, each effective against specific insect pest groups. Most common is the "kurstaki" strain, useful for control of leaf-feeding caterpillars, such

as cabbageworms, leaf rollers, and hornworms. The "israelensis" strain is effective against larvae of certain flies and midges and is used to control mosquitoes, blackflies, and fungus gnats. The "tenebrionis" (or "San Diego") strain is effective against leaf beetle larvae, such as Colorado potato beetle and elm leaf beetle.

Sources (Lepidoptera larvae): 2, 5, 6, 8, 9, 12, 16, 19, 20, and most local nurseries
Sources (mosquito, fungus gnat larvae): 2, 6, 9, 12, 16, 19, 20, and some local nurseries
Sources (Colorado potato beetle, elm leaf beetle): 2, 6, 12, 20

BEAUVERIA BASSIANA

A common fungal disease of many insects, two commercial strains of *Beauveria bassiana* (Naturalis®, Botanigard®) are currently on the market, primarily to control whiteflies and aphids. Moderately high humidities are necessary to achieve the successful infection of insects.

Sources: 9, 10, 13

NOSEMA LOCUSTAE

Nosema locustae is a protozoan parasite of many grasshoppers. It is most effective against younger stages of grasshoppers and is used to control grasshoppers in breeding areas, rather than to kill migrating stages actively damaging crops and gardens. Commercial formulations (NoLo Bait®, Semaspore®) are mixed with a bran-based bait carrier designed to be broadcast. *Nosema locustae* baits are fairly perishable, so they should not be stored for long periods or their effectiveness will be compromised.

Sources: 2, 5, 9, 10, 12, 13, 15, 19, 20

PARASITIC (PREDATORY) NEMATODES

Several nematodes develop as parasites of insects. Two genera have been developed and are sold for control of a broad range of insects that develop or live in the soil—cutworms, white grubs, root weevils, webworms, and fungus gnats. *Steinernema* species are widely available, as they have the advantages of being fairly easily (and cheaply) reared, they store well, and there are strains that can be active in relatively (50–60°F) cool soils. *Heterorhabitis* species are capable of infecting a wider range of insect hosts (e.g., white grubs, root weevil larvae) since they are able to penetrate directly through susceptible insects, rather than being limited to entry through natural openings. Mixtures of both genera are sold (e.g., Guardian®). Insect-parasitic nematodes are sold in moist pelleted or semiliquid formulations designed to be mixed with water and applied as a drench or spray.

Sources (species of *Steinernema*): 2, 5, 7, 9, 10, 11, 12, 13, 14, 15, 16, 18, 19, 20, 21
Sources (species of *Heterorhabditis*): 2, 5, 6, 7, 8, 9, 10, 11, 12, 13, 15, 16, 18, 19, 21

"BIOFUNGICIDES"

Several bacteria and fungi that are antagonistic to the fungi that produce plant diseases have recently been commercially developed. Most are designed for use in greenhouses or nurseries to manage soil disease. Examples include Soilgard® (*Glioclidium virens* GL-21), Mycostop® (*Streptomyces griseoviridis* strain K61), and Deny® (*Burkholdia cepacia*), which are labeled for use as soil drenches or amendments to potting soil. AQ10® is a fungus (*Ampelomyces quisqualis*) that is applied as a foliar spray to manage powdery mildew.

Sources (Soilgard): 9, 13
Sources (Mycostop): 9, 10, 19, 21
Sources (AQ10): 9, 19
Source (Deny): 19

BLIGHT BAN

A naturally occurring strain of *Pseudomonas fluorescens* can help reduce fire blight by displacing the latter on plant surfaces. This "ice-minus" strain does not induce ice crystal formation and also may outcompete bacteria responsible for freeze injuries.

Source: 19

SUPPLIERS OF BIOLOGICAL CONTROL ORGANISMS

The following list includes several suppliers of biological control organisms. Many of these businesses are producers of these organisms; others are merely distributors. Prices range considerably. When purchasing large numbers of these organisms, it is often desirable to make prior arrangements with a producer to get the most timely service at the most favorable price.

1. Applied Bionomics
   8801 East Saanich Road
   Sidney, British Columbia
   Canada V8L 1H1
   (250) 656-2123
   e-mail: bug@islandnet.com

2. ARBICO
   P.O. Box 4247
   Tuscon, AZ 85738-1247
   (800) 305-2847

3. Beneficial Insectary
   14751 Oak Run Road
   Oak Run, CA 96060
   (800) 477-3715

4. Bowen Biosystems
   2982 "G" Street, Suite A
   Merced, CA 95340
   (800) 900-0246

5. The Bug Store
   113 West Argonne
   St. Louis, MO 63122-1104
   (800) 455-2847
   website: www.bugstore.com

6. Gardens Alive!
   5100 Schenley Place
   Lawrenceburg, IN 47025
   (812) 537-8651
   e-mail: gardener@gardens-alive.com

7. Great Lakes IPM
   10220 Church Road, N.E.
   Vestaburg, MI 48891
   (517) 268-5693
   e-mail: glipm@nethawk.com

8. Gurney Seed and Nursery
   110 Capital Street
   Yankton, SD 57079
   (605) 665-1671

9. Harmony Farm Supply
   P.O. Box 460
   Grafton, CA 95444
   (707) 823-9125

10. Hydro-Gardens
    P.O. Box 9707
    Colorado Springs, CO 80932
    (800) 634-6362

11. Integrated BioControl Systems, Inc.
    P.O. Box 96
    Aurora, IN 47001-0096
    (812) 537-8673

12. Integrated Fertility Management
    333-B Ohme Gardens Road
    Wenatchee, WA 98801
    (800) 332-3179

13. International Technology Services, Inc.
    P.O. Box 19227
    Boulder, CO 80308
    (303) 473-9141

14. IPM Labs, Inc.
    Main Street
    Locke, NY 13092
    (315) 497-2063

15. M & R Durango, Inc.
    P.O. Box 886
    Bayfield, CO 81122
    (800) 526-4075

16. Natural Insect Control (NIC)
    RR#2
    Stevensville, Ontario
    Canada L0S 1S0
    (905) 382-2904
    e-mail: nic@niagara.com

17. Natural Pest Controls
    8864 Little Creek Drive
    Orangevale, CA 95662
    (916) 726-0855
    website: http://www.natural-pest-controls.com

18. Nature's Control
    P.O. Box 35
    Medford, OR 97501
    (541) 899-8318

19. Peaceful Valley Farm Supply
    P.O. Box 2209
    Grass Valley, CA 95945
    (530) 272-4769
    website: http://www.groworganic.com

20. Planet Natural
    1612 Gold Avenue
    P.O. Box 3146
    Bozeman, MT 59772
    (800) 289-6656

21. Rincon Vitova Insectaries, Inc.
    P.O. Box 1555
    Ventura, CA 93022
    (805) 643-5407

22. Spaulding Laboratories
    760 Printz Road
    Arroyo Grande, CA 93420
    (800) 845-2847

Appendix II

Butterfly Gardening
in the Rocky Mountain Region

We garden for many reasons: to provide fresh produce, to make landscapes more attractive, and to attract wildlife. One form of wildlife that is quite easily persuaded into a yard is butterflies. In recent years, butterfly gardening has become an increasingly popular form of landscaping in the United States, following a long history in England and other areas of Europe.

At its core, the principles of butterfly gardening are simple—purposeful plantings to attract and retain local species of butterflies to the site. This is achieved by providing for the basic needs of the insects—foods used by both the adult and caterpillar stages of the butterflies, as well as attention to shelter requirements.

Shelter needs are easy to accommodate in most yards. Garden sites chosen for a butterfly garden should provide some protection from the strong winds common to this region. A hedge or windbreak of some sort may be necessary for butterfly gardens established in exposed locations. In residential neighborhoods, protection is afforded by the buildings and landscaping already in place.

The most obvious prerequisite of a butterfly garden are nectar-bearing flowering plants. Plants favored by butterflies are those that provide the sugary nectar used by many species as an energy source. There are many types of flowers that span the range of butterfly appeal, and many commonly used bedding plants such as geraniums and petunias are rarely visited by butterflies, although the latter may be visited at dusk by the large "hummingbird moths," which are the adult stage of hornworm caterpillars.

However, many butterflies are not nectar feeders, particularly many of the early season species. For example, the Nymphalidae, which include such attractive species as the Weidemeyers admiral, mourning cloak, and hackberry butterfly, typically feed on sap flows, rotting fruit, and even animal dung. Periodically placing cut fruit around the garden or providing fruit-bearing trees may attract these species. Also, the oozing wound from a tree that you may have considered cutting might be useful to attract some butterflies.

Males of some butterflies also visit damp areas, sometimes collecting in large groups. The purpose of these "mud puddle clubs" is unclear, but it is thought that dissolved minerals are useful nutrients for the butterflies. A small pool or area of moistened soil can provide for the needs of these butterflies.

When designing a butterfly garden, attempt to make mass plantings of butterfly food plants, which are more attractive than are scattered plantings. Also, give consideration to providing a sequence of desirable flowers and plants throughout the season. Although some butterflies may be present during the entire growing sea-

Tiger swallowtail visiting larkspur

Massed plantings are most attractive to butterflies

TABLE A-1: SOME NECTAR-BEARING FLOWERING PLANTS PREFERRED BY BUTTERFLIES

Asters	Bee balm (*Monarda*)
Bush cinquefolia (*Potentilla fruticosa*)	Butterfly bush (*Buddleia davidi*)
Butterfly plant (*Asclepias tuberosa*)	Cosmos (*Cosmos* spp.)
Gaillardia	Larkspur
Lilac (*Syringa vulgaris*)	Marigolds
Rabbitbrush (*Chrysothamnus nauseosus*)	Sunflower (*Helianthus*)
Sweet pea	Thistle
Verbena	Zinnia

son, butterfly visits typically peak during mid to late summer, so it is particularly critical to provide nectar and other adult food sources at this time of the year.

Also crucial in a butterfly garden are food plants used by the caterpillar stage of the butterflies. These plants are actively sought by the female butterflies for egg laying, and the presence of caterpillar foods facilitates the establishment of a "native" population of butterflies. Furthermore, the caterpillar stages are often unusual in form or color and are particularly interesting to observe. Cultivating caterpillar food plants enables one to observe all the stages of butterfly development (eggs, caterpillars, chrysalis, adult), increasing the overall enjoyment of the butterfly garden.

TABLE A-2: PLANTS USED BY THE CATERPILLAR STAGE OF SEVERAL REGIONAL BUTTERFLIES

Butterfly	Caterpillar food plants
Twotailed Swallowtail	Green ash, chokecherry
Western Tiger Swallowtail	Willow, cottonwood, chokecherry
Black Swallowtail	Dill, parsley, carrot, fennel
Monarch	Milkweed
Weidemeyer's Admiral	Willow, aspen, cottonwood
Hackberry Butterfly	Hackberry
Painted Lady	Thistle, sunflower, hollyhock
Mourning Cloak	Willow, aspen, elm, cottonwood
Wood Nymph	Grasses
European Cabbage Butterfly	Mustards (including broccoli, cabbage)
Checkered White	Tumble mustard, other mustards
Clouded Sulfur	Alfalfa, clover
Orange Sulfur	Alfalfa, vetch, pea
Melissa Blue	Wild licorice, alfalfa, other plants
Milbert's Tortoiseshell	Nettles
Variegated Fritillary	Pansy, many other plants
Edwards Fritillary	Nuttall's violet
Gorgone's Checkerspot	Sunflower
Checkered Skipper	Mallow, hollyhock
Silverspotted Skipper	Wild licorice, locust, others

There *are* some conflicts that arise with butterfly gardening, as with all other landscaping designed to attract wildlife. Most obvious are the caterpillar feeding habits, which involve eating some of the plant leaves. Although caterpillars of most butterflies never occur at levels that seriously damage plants, there are a few that can be considered "pests" in some settings. A primary culprit is the European cabbage butterfly, the common "cabbageworm" of home gardens. Unfortunately the caterpillars of this insect all too often spoil a head of cabbage or broccoli and may need to be controlled on these plants.

A few other caterpillars may also feed on some garden plants. The strikingly colored caterpillar of the Black Swallowtail butterfly, the parsleyworm, is a caterpillar familiar to gardeners who make plantings of parsley, fennel, or dill. In addition, the caterpillar of the Variegated Fritillary often resides in a patch of pansies and may nibble a few leaves. However, in larger plantings designed for ornamental purposes the feeding by these insects will rarely be noticeable.

Butterfly gardens tend to look a little more wild than formal garden designs. Some of the best plants for attracting butterflies do not have a compact growth habit, and some of the plants preferred by caterpillars and butterflies are actually considered weeds in some settings. Careful landscape design can minimize this problem.

Finally, most insecticides are contraindicated in a butterfly garden. Caterpillars are very susceptible to most insecticides, including *Bacillus thuringiensis* (Dipel®, Thuricide®). Adult butterflies are less sensitive to insecticides, but still can be killed or repelled by some ingredients. However, most fungicides, selective miticides, and insecticidal soaps *can* be safely used on plants frequented by butterflies or caterpillars. A conscious decision must be made to not treat the butterfly garden plantings, a decision eased by selecting plants less prone to pest problems.

Western tiger swallowtail on zinnia

Painted lady on cosmos

Appendix III

Attracting Insectivorous Birds to the Yard and Garden

Many people wish to encourage birds to nest and feed in their yard and neighborhood because birds are a source of enjoyment. They may also wish to benefit from birds' insect-eating habits so that pest problems can be reduced. Many common species of birds offer such an accommodation. Insectivorous (insect-feeding) birds that are easy to attract to the yard include the house wren, American robin, blue jay, northern flicker, and European starling.

The percentage of insects comprising the diet of birds varies greatly. Some birds feed almost exclusively on insects; others have vegetarian and seed-feeding habits. However, even many seed feeders will feed high-protein insect foods to their young.

The nesting requirements of most birds are quite specific, but a few common species, such as robins, chickadees, and house wrens, are fairly adaptable. These can be found in a variety of rural and urban habitats. Other birds may have more discriminating needs that will limit their desire to nest in a backyard or neighborhood. However, catering to the environmental needs of a bird species increases its nesting incidence in an area.

NESTING NEEDS OF BIRDS

Like all other wildlife, birds have three basic requirements: adequate food, water, and cover. This is true for nesting birds as well as for birds that are transients or seasonal residents. Favorable cover for birds includes nesting habitat, a means of escape from danger, and protection from the weather. Weather cover is best achieved with clumped plantings of vegetation that buffer wind and rain. Conifers such as juniper, spruce, and pine are ideal for these plantings.

Requirements for nesting cover vary among different bird species. For example, a dense thicket of alder or willow might be ideal for a flycatcher, vireo, or warbler, but will not attract cavity nesters such as chickadees or flickers. If the bird species is a cavity nester, artificial nest boxes or birdhouses are an acceptable alternative to trees with natural holes. Often the size of the birdhouse cavity and entrance hole will determine its suitability for a particular species of nesting bird. Consideration should also be given to making hole sizes small enough to exclude aggressive and less desirable species such as starlings. Birdhouses should be located high above the ground (10 to 20 feet for most species) with open access for easy exit. Other birds, such as robins, barn swallows, and phoebes, prefer an open nesting shelf.

Certain insectivorous bird species, such as the barn swallow and cliff swallow, actually prefer manufactured structures for nesting. Other birds that use buildings for nesting are the western flycatcher and Say's phoebe. Minor glitches, such as infestations of barn swallow bugs and mites, may afflict birds nesting on buildings, but these are infrequent and easily managed. Occasional problems also result from woodpeckers damaging trees and manufactured structures.

Suitable escape cover allows birds to more readily escape attacks from other birds and mammals. Usually this takes the form of a mixture of shrubs or brush into which the birds can easily flee when threatened. Escape cover also provides a quiet place for resting, preening, and molting.

WATER AND FOOD REQUIREMENTS

Another important feature to provide throughout the year is water. Birdbaths and/or small ponds can attract many species and demand little maintainance during warm weather. Overwintering birds also need drinking water; and immersion heaters keep containerized water from freezing. This, along with supplemental feeding, encourages those species that are marginally adapted to regional winters to live here year-round. Consult with a local birding group before purchasing a heater, as certain brands are safer than others.

Many birds supplement insect food with fruit and seeds. (And some, such as robins, may damage garden crops in the process!) The actual type of food consumed usually varies according to local availability of different insects and other foods. The use of alternate foods is particularly critical in winter when even primarily insectivorous species of birds feed on vegetarian foods. These food needs are met by planting a mixture of fruiting trees and shrubs and supplementing them with seeds. By closely observing the feeding preferences of birds in a yard, one can obtain the means to attract and retain birds in the area.

SOME COMMON CONFLICTS

Some practices are incompatible with attracting birds to a yard. Allowing cats to roam freely in the yard discourages birds since cats prey upon them. In addition, the careless use of insecticides reduces bird populations. Insecticide treatments not only reduce the insects on which birds feed, but some are also directly toxic to birds that may inadvertently contact the residue. (Diazinon®, used widely in lawn care, is one of the most toxic insecticides to birds.) A tolerance of some insects and weeds may be essential in order to attract and maintain the birds that value them for food.

Some birds may be considered undesirable because they drive off other species of birds. Starlings, house sparrows, and blackbirds can occasionally become overbearing in some situations and dominate more desirable species of birds. Blackbirds, robins, and starlings may damage ripening fruit, such as cherries. Although undesirable species of birds cannot be entirely eliminated from the yard, providing shelter specific to the more desirable bird species will limit their establishment. (*Note:* The temporary presence of large numbers of starlings or blackbirds feeding on lawns is typically due to their habit of feeding on turf-feeding insects, such as sod webworms and cutworms. This activity is highly beneficial to the management of these turf insect pests, which are common in this region.)

TABLE A-3: INSECTIVOROUS BIRDS AND THEIR NESTING REQUIREMENTS

Bird species	Nesting requirements	Part of diet composed of insects	Other food resources; remarks on nesting
American Kestrel	Prefers natural cavities, holes excavated by flickers, or manufactured nest boxes. Requires 30-inch-diameter entrance.	Large insects like grasshoppers are commonly a major part of diet.	Reptiles, small birds, and mammals are also taken.
Eastern and Western Screech Owls	Use natural cavities in hardwoods or old flicker holes in cottonwoods and pines. Nest primarily in heavily wooded areas and are rare in urban areas.	More than one-third of diet is insects, including night-flying moths and beetles.	Small birds, mammals, and reptiles are a major part of diet.
Chimney Swift	Constructs a nest of twigs and saliva in chimney or barn silo.	Almost entire diet is made up of day-flying insects; occasionally will feed upon caterpillars in trees and shrubs.	Avoid cleaning chimney between May and August if nesting occurs.
Downy Woodpecker	Excavates cavities in dead trees. Nest boxes should have entrance diameter of $1^1/_2$ inches.	About three-quarters of diet is insects, including bark beetles, borers, larvae, ants, caterpillars, and weevils. Also feeds on berries, acorns, and tree sap.	A year-round resident, easily attracted to wooded areas. Suet and fruits are winter food supplements.
Northern Flicker	Nests in cavities of decayed wood between 10 and 30 feet above ground.	Primarily ants.	A common year-round resident. Grains, fruits, and seeds are occasionally eaten.
Flycatchers, including Eastern and Western Kingbirds	Construct twig and fiber nests in deciduous trees, commonly in elms and cottonwoods. Sometimes old hawk nests are used.	Diet is almost exclusively winged insects caught as they pass perching area.	Berries and seeds rarely eaten in nesting season but fruit is eaten in overwintering grounds.
Barn Swallow	Builds mud nests under eaves and bridges and on sides of walls.	Entire diet comprises flying insects.	A nearby source of mud and straw is needed for nest construction.
Blue Jay, Steller's Jay	Nests in trees, preferably conifers, approximately 20 feet above ground.	About one-quarter of diet is insects.	A year-round resident. May harass other nesting birds. Nuts, fruits, and grains are primary foods.
Black-Capped and Mountain Chickadees	Use cavities in trees with partially decayed cores but firm shells. Often excavate their own holes or may use old woodpecker holes.	Predominantly insects are eaten, including many insect eggs, scale insects, aphids, and small caterpillars.	Common year-round residents that are easy to attract. Fruit, suet, and seeds are desirable in winter diet.

Bird species	Nesting requirements	Part of diet composed of insects	Other food resources; remarks on nesting
White- and Red-Breasted Nuthatches	Use cavities in living trees or abandoned woodpecker holes. Prefer birdhouses with entrance diameter of 1¼ inches.	In summer, feed exclusively on insects found on tree bark and shrubs, including caterpillars and borers.	Year-round residents that feed upon nuts, suet, and sunflower seeds in winter.
Brown Creeper	Prefers dense, wooded areas and is often associated with chickadees and kinglets.	Feeds primarily upon small insects it finds while searching bark.	Suet and seeds are supplemental foods.
House Wren	Prefers cavities but will nest in just about any hole, tin cans, and hoods of cars. Uses small (1¼-inch) openings in birdhouses.	Feeds almost exclusively on a wide variety of insects, including grasshoppers, beetles, and caterpillars.	Easily attracted to brushy areas. Will destroy eggs of other birds nesting nearby.
European Starling	A cavity nester but highly adaptable and will nest almost anywhere. Can be excluded from cavities with entrance diameter less than 2 inches.	Adult food is almost one-half insects; nesting food entirely insects. Valuable in control of caterpillar insect pests on lawns.	Fruits, grains, and seeds comprise remainder of adult diet. May drive off or out-compete other birds attempting to nest in area. Starlings are year-round residents in some western regions.
Red-Eyed and Warbling Vireos	Prefer upper foliage of willow and other shade trees.	Most of diet is small insects.	Fruits and berries are also eaten.
Northern and Orchard Orioles	Build large pendant nest of straw, string, and yarn high in trees. Often will return to same nest site.	Much of diet is larger insects, such as caterpillars.	Fruit, berries, and nectar are supplemental foods.
American Robin	Nests in crotches of trees and shrubs. May use artificial shelves for nesting. Needs nearby source of mud for nest construction. Some robins are present year-round.	Feeds primarily on earthworms but will feed on various insects such as caterpillars.	Fruits and berries are common supplemental foods. Can be very damaging to cherries.

Appendix IV

Characteristics
of Common Garden Pesticides

A large number of different pesticides are in use in agriculture. A considerably smaller number of these are registered for use around yards and gardens. These yard and garden pesticides comprise a wide range of uses, chemistries, and biological effects. A discussion of all the different pesticides used in yards and gardens is beyond the scope of this publication, but a brief summary is included.

GARDEN PESTICIDES

This section is organized using the common names of *active ingredients,* arranged in alphabetical order. Each active ingredient is discussed as listed below.

Common Name: The accepted common name of the active ingredient of the pesticide. (For some older pesticides, this is the same as the trade name.)
Trade Names: The names of products sold containing the active ingredient.
Scientific Name: The complete chemical name, included on the label in small print as an active ingredient.
Pesticide Class: The chemical class of the active ingredient, if any.
Toxicity: Primarily the acute toxicity of the compound, based on laboratory animal studies testing effects of exposure following ingestion or skin exposure. (Toxicity and the hazards associated

with use of a particular product are also reflected on label instructions. Highly hazardous products have the signal words *Danger—Poison* and are now almost never found on garden center shelves. Moderately hazardous products have the signal word *Warning,* while products of lowest hazard use the signal word *Caution.* All pesticides must carry some warning label statement.)
Uses: Uses of the product in formulations sold for yard and garden use. (Agricultural or commercial uses of the same active ingredient may be different.)
Notes: General comments as to specific properties or cautions associated with the pesticide.

Acephate (Orthene®)

Trade Names: Orthene®, Isotox® (various formulas), Orthenex®
Scientific Name: O,S-Dimethyl acetyl phosphoramidothioate
Pesticide Class: Organophosphate insecticide
Toxicity: Moderate to low, although some breakdown products are highly toxic.
Uses: Control of aphids, caterpillars, thrips, and other insects on ornamentals. Control of sod webworms in turf. Grasshopper control in noncrop areas. (*Note: Home use formulations are not labeled for use on food crops.* Certain commercial formulations are labeled for use on head lettuce, beans, and some cole crops.)

Notes: Acephate has systemic activity when applied to leaves, making it highly effective against concealed insects such as leafminers and leaf-curling aphids. When applied to the soil, it has some systemic activity but is not currently registered for this use. The environmental persistence of acephate and its breakdown products is longer than with most insecticides, with preharvest intervals of 7 to 21 days for vegetables. *Note: Acephate is not labeled for any garden food crop (fruit, vegetable, herb) uses.* Lack of registration on food crops has caused frequent problems with accidental drift into gardens. Acephate may injure poplar, cottonwood, willow, American elm, redbud, and sugar maple trees. A primary breakdown product of acephate, methamidophos, is highly toxic to mammals.

Bacillus thuringiensis (Bt)

Trade/Scientific Names: *kurstaki* strain: Dipel®, Caterpillar Attack®, Thuricide®, MVP®; *israelensis* strain: Mosquito Attack®, Vectobac®, Gnatrol®, Bactimos®; *tenebrionis* (aka *san diego* strain): Foil®, M-Trak®, Colorado Potato Beetle Beater®
Pesticide Class: Microbial insecticide
Toxicity: Considered essentially nontoxic and can be used on most food crops up to harvest.
Uses: Control of leaf-feeding caterpillars on vegetables and fruit (*kurstaki* strain). Control of Colorado potato beetles and elm leaf beetles (*san diego* and *tenebrionis* strains). *Israelensis* strain used for control of mosquitoes and blackflies in water and fungus gnats in greenhouses.
Notes: A naturally occurring bacterial disease, *Bacillus thuringiensis* is produced by several manufacturers for use as a microbial insecticide. It must be eaten to be effective (stomach poison) and is highly selective in its activity. (Selectivity differs according to various strains.) Affected insects stop feeding within hours after ingesting but may not die for 2 to 3 days. Persistence on foliage less than 1 week if exposed to sunlight. Its selective activity allows it to conserve the natural enemies of insects and integrate with existing biological controls. Bt is more perishable than most pesticides but will remain effective for at least 2 years if kept dry and out of direct sunlight.

A toxic protein crystal produced by *Bacillus thuringiensis* is responsible for its insecticidal activity. Genes responsible for production of this protein have been inserted into certain agricultural plants (e.g., tobacco, cotton, corn) and into a bacterium that is better adapted to surviving on leaf surfaces (*Pseudomonas fluorescens*). Some Bt insecticides currently contain genetically-altered *P. flourescens* that have the genes to produce the protein that is toxic to insects.

Bordeaux Mixture

Trade Names: Bordeaux mixture, Bor-Dox®, Bordeaux powder
Scientific Name: A mixture of hydrated lime and copper sulfate
Pesticide Class: Inorganic fungicide
Toxicity: Low mammalian toxicity but may be irritating to skin.
Uses: Primarily used to control fungal diseases on fruits, particularly in combination with dormant oil sprays. Registered crops include tomatoes, strawberries, apples, peaches, and grapes.
Notes: Bordeaux mixture is one of the oldest known fungicides, discovered over 100 years ago. In cool, damp weather it may cause plant injury. It has a long persistence but acts only as a preventive fungicide, so it must be applied before infection. It is also repellent and insecticidal to some insect species. Young leaves of apple and peach trees may be injured by sprays.

Carbaryl (Sevin)

Trade Names: Sevin®, Sevimol®, many garden dusts and baits
Scientific Name: 1-Naphthyl N-methyl carbamate
Pesticide Class: Carbamate insecticide
Toxicity: Low toxicity to mammals and birds. Highly toxic to honeybees and earthworms.
Uses: Carbaryl has registrations on most vegetable and fruit crops as well as flowers, turf, and shade trees. Carbaryl is generally effective against most chewing insects, such as caterpillars, sawflies,

beetles, grasshoppers, and earwigs. It has some activity against slugs and snails.

Notes: Carbaryl is mostly active as a stomach poison. It is generally ineffective against most sucking insects and may aggravate problems with certain aphids and spider mites. Not systemic. The environmental persistence is fairly short, with typical preharvest intervals of 1 to 3 days (14 days on leaf lettuce). Carbaryl can be very hazardous to honeybees and should not be applied to blooming flowers or weeds. Carbaryl can cause excessive blossom shed of apple trees and is used to thin them. It can also injure certain vines (Virginia creeper, clematis, etc.).

Chlorothalonil

Trade Names: Daconil 2787®, Bravo®
Scientific Name: Tetrachloroisophalonitrile
Pesticide Class: Unclassified fungicide
Toxicity: Very low toxicity to mammals but can cause eye irritation.
Uses: Broadly labeled for use on vegetables, fruits, turf, and ornamentals, chlorothalonil controls a wide variety of leaf-spotting fungi, some rusts, and Botrytis.
Notes: Chlorothalonil is the most widely used fungicide in commercial vegetable production and is commonly available in yard and garden products. Its use is likely to increase with recent restrictions on the EBDC fungicides, such as maneb. Chlorothalonil is not systemic in its action and is most effective when applied as a protectant before disease develops. Most food crops have preharvest intervals of 0 to 14 days.

Chlorpyrifos

Trade Names: Dursban®, Lawn and Garden Insect Control®, Kill-a-Bug Granules®, many other formulations
Scientific Name: O,O-Diethyl O-(3,5,6-trichloro-2-pyridinyl) phosphorothioate
Pesticide Class: Organophosphate insecticide
Toxicity: Moderate to high toxicity to mammals, birds, and earthworms
Uses: Chlorpyrifos is the most widely used insecticide in the world. It is contained in numer-ous home use products for control of household insects, surface-feeding turf insects, borers in shade trees, and many insects of ornamental plants. Over-the-counter formulations do not allow use on food crops.
Notes: Chlorpyrifos is fairly persistent and over the past decade has largely replaced lindane for control of shade tree borers and diazinon for household pest control uses. However, recent attention has focused on chlorpyrifos due largely to provisions in the Food Quality Protection Act. As a result, it is anticipated that many current uses will be dropped as a means to reduce overall potential exposure to this insecticide.

Coppers, Fixed

Trade Names: Microcop®, Tri-basic copper, Kocide 101®, included in Fertilome Triple Action® and other garden mixtures
Scientific Name: Metallic copper, copper oleate
Pesticide Class: Inorganic fungicide, bactericide
Toxicity: Low mammalian toxicity and exempted from food crop tolerance requirements.
Uses: Controls a wide variety of fungi and bacteria on fruits and vegetables. Has some bactericidal activity.
Notes: Copper-based pesticides can cause plant injury, such as burning of leaf edges, and should not be used on cabbage family plants. Should not be mixed with any other pesticides or plant injury may result. Federal agencies have exempted copper compounds from tolerance requirements, so they can be used up to harvest. The compounds are often accepted for use in "certified organic" production.

Corn Gluten Meal

Trade Names: WOW®, Concern Weed Prevention Plus, others
Scientific Name: Corn gluten meal
Pesticide Class: Botanical herbicide
Toxicity: Essentially nontoxic.
Uses: Corn gluten meal contains compounds that are general inhibitors of seed germination. It is sold as a preemergent herbicide for use in lawns and gardens. As it will also inhibit the germina-

tion of garden plants, it is used after garden plants have emerged or around perennial plants (e.g., Kentucky bluegrass, shrubs, perennial flowers).

Notes: Effects of corn gluten meal as a germination inhibitor are fairly short-lived and it must be applied repeatedly during the season to maintain weed control. It also has considerable fertilizer value. However, large amounts are needed and some odor problems have been reported as it decomposes.

DCPA (Dacthal)

Trade Names: Garden Weed Preventer®, Dacthal®
Scientific Name: Dimethyl tetrachlorterephthalate
Pesticide Class: Chlorinated benzoic acid herbicide
Toxicity: DCPA is considered to have very low acute toxicity to mammals and is nonirritating. However, in its registration review, several problems were identified, including a tendency to leach to groundwater and the presence of some contaminants during manufacture. As a result, production has been discontinued, although existing products can be sold and used.
Uses: DCPA is used to control germinating weeds in flower gardens and around some fruit and vegetable crops.
Notes: DCPA acts by inhibiting cell division of root tips. It has little effect on established plants. It has occurred as a groundwater contaminant in several surveys. It should not be used in areas (e.g., high water table, sandy soils) where groundwater contamination is likely. Future uses may be restricted because of environmental concerns.

Diatomaceous Earth

Trade Names: Perma-Guard®, Organic Crawling Insect Killer®, others
Scientific Name: Mined deposits of diatoms
Pesticide Class: Inorganic dessicant dust
Toxicity: Essentially nontoxic by ingestion. Inhalation may cause irritation.
Uses: Diatomaceous earth is sold for control of crawling insects and other arthropods (millipedes, pillbugs). It has repellent activity against a broad spectrum of garden insects.

Notes: Diatomaceous earth primarily kills insects by absorbing waxes on their exoskeleton, producing excessive water loss. It is used as a dry powder, caking readily and losing effectiveness under moist conditions. Label directions of most formulations are a bit unclear as to legality for use around garden plants. Some formulations that combine diatomaceous earth with pyrethrins (e.g., Dri-Die) are clearly labeled for used on a broad number of garden plants.

Diazinon

Trade Names: Diazinon®, Spectracide®, Knox-out PT-265®, Bug-B-Gon®, others
Scientific Name: O,O-Diethyl O-(2-isopropyl-4-methyl-7-pyrimidinyl) phosphorothioate
Pesticide Class: Organophosphate insecticide
Toxicity: Moderate toxicity to mammals; extremely toxic to birds.
Uses: Diazinon is most widely used for control of soil insects on turf and many vegetables. It has broad spectrum activity as a foliar spray against exposed sucking and chewing insects on fruits, ornamentals, and some vegetables.
Notes: Diazinon is a contact and stomach poison without systemic activity in plants. Persistence in the environment is moderately long with typical preharvest intervals of 7 days for vegetables (longer on root crops) and 10 days for fruit. Toxicity of diazinon to birds is approximately 100 times greater than to mammals, and its uses have recently been restricted or canceled for many sites where bird injury is likely. Because of costs associated with re-registering diazinon, the primary manufacturer has decided to cancel many minor uses of this insecticide.

Dicofol

Trade Names: Kelthane®, Red Spider and Mite Spray®
Scientific Name: 4,4-Dichlor-alpha-trichloromethylbenzhydrol/1,1-bis(chlorophenyl)-2,2,2-trichloroethanol
Pesticide Class: Chlorinated hydrocarbon insecticide
Toxicity: Moderate to low.

Uses: Spider mite control on ornamental plants, some vegetables, and fruits.

Notes: Dicofol is a selective miticide that has little effect on most insects. It has moderate persistence on plants, with preharvest intervals on registered food crops ranging from 2 to 30 days. It is very closely related chemically to DDT, but has very different effects on pests (it is a miticide, not an insecticide) and does not persist and accumulate in tissues as DDT does.

Disulfoton

Trade Names: DiSyston®, Systemic Insecticide Granules®, Systemic Insecticide Bug Dart®, Systemic Rose and Flower Care®, others

Scientific Name: O,O-Diethyl S-((2-(ethylthio) ethyl)) phosphorodithioate

Pesticide Class: Organophosphate insecticide

Toxicity: Disulfoton is highly toxic to mammals and is the most toxic insecticide available to the general public.

Uses: Disulfoton for gardens is sold as a soil-applied granule or plant stake, often formulated with fertilizer. Almost all products containing disulfoton limit use to ornamental plants, including roses. However, some disulfoton granules (1 to 2 percent) continue to be sold for control of some vegetable insects as well as for ornamental plants.

Notes: Disulfoton is a systemic insecticide that is picked up by plant roots and translocated to leaves and other actively growing plant tissues. It is generally effective against most leaf-feeding insects and mites but less effective against borers and scale insects. Home use formulations are in the form of low-percentage granules or stakes that reduce hazard. *Note: Despite these safeguards, this product should be used with extra caution because of the high toxicity of the active ingredient.* Disulfoton is highly water-soluble, so use with house plants should be avoided if watering allows leaching out of pots.

Egg Solids, Putrescent Whole

Trade Names: Deer-Away®, Big Game Repellent®, MGK BGR®

Pesticide Class: Unclassified, produced from putrefying egg solids

Toxicity: Very low.

Uses: Animal repellent for ornamental trees and shrubs, nonbearing fruit trees, and bearing fruit trees when fruit is not present.

Notes: This group of animal repellents is sold as a two-part concentrate designed to be mixed and sprayed. To humans it has a slight odor of fermented eggs but is a strong odor repellent to deer and other animals. It cannot be used on fruit trees when flowers or harvestable fruit are on the tree. Homemade mixtures of eggs diluted in water (1:4 egg/water dilution) have also shown repellency to mule deer.

Fluazifop-Butyl

Trade Names: Grass-B-Gon®, Over-The-Top-Grass Killer®, Fusilade®

Scientific Name: RS butyl 2-[4-(5-trifluoromethyl-2-pyridol oxy) phenoxy] propinoate

Pesticide Class: Postemergent herbicide

Toxicity: Low toxicity to mammals but has irritant properties.

Uses: Control of grass around ornamental plants. Some agricultural formulations but no yard and garden formulations allow use for grass control around strawberries and raspberries.

Notes: Fluazifop-butyl is a selective herbicide affecting grasses that acts systemically. Because of its selective action, it can be used over the top of broadleaf plants. It is most effective when applied on young, actively growing plants. Typical symptoms following treatment include slowing of growth, yellowing, and death of plants after 1 to 4 weeks. Plants should not be cut or tilled after treatment. Fluazifop-butyl is water-soluble and should not be applied in light soils where contamination of groundwater is likely.

Glufosinate-Ammonium

Trade Names: Finale®, Liberty®, Rely®

Scientific Name: DL-homoalanine-4-yl-(methyl) phosphinate

Pesticide Class: Unspecified class, systemic herbicide

Toxicity: Low toxicity to mammals, birds, and fish.

Uses: Glufosinate-ammonium is a nonselective herbicide with systemic activity. Chemically related to glyphosate, it is somewhat faster acting with rapid "burn-down" action on some plants. Labeled uses currently allow for spot treatment of weeds around ornamental shade trees, shrubs, and flowers, but *does not* permit use around edible garden plants.

Notes: A contact herbicide with no soil activity. Glufinosate breaks down rapidly in soil through microbial action and does not affect seed germination or root growth of plants not directly contacted with spray. Maximum uptake in plants necessitates at least a 6-hour period that is rain-free after application.

Glyphosate

Trade Names: Roundup®, Kleenup®, Knockout®, many other trade names

Scientific Name: N-(phosphonomethyl) glycine

Pesticide Class: Unspecified class, systemic herbicide

Toxicity: Low toxicity to mammals, birds, and fish.

Uses: Glyphosate is a nonselective, broad-spectrum systemic herbicide. It is used in spot treatment or directed treatment in noncrop areas. Labeled uses do allow application around the base of fruit trees, but not in other food crops.

Notes: The systemic activity of glyphosate allows control of several perennial broadleaf and grassy weeds. It does not have soil activity (e.g., root uptake), is strongly adsorbed to soil particles, and rapidly degrades in soils due to microbial action. Drift onto desirable plants is a common problem and can injure woody plants if immature bark or foliage is treated. Glyphosate is not volatile, but droplets can easily drift by wind action during application. Best control of perennial broadleaf plants occurs with applications made during flowering; grasses are most effectively controlled when succulent and before woody stems have been produced.

Lime Sulfur (Calcium polysulfides)

Trade Names: Polysul®, Dormant spray, Dormant disease control

Scientific Name: Calcium polysulfides

Pesticide Class: Inorganic fungicide/miticide

Toxicity: Highly corrosive to eyes and harmful if swallowed or absorbed through skin. If mixed with acids, can cause release of toxic hydrogen sulfide gas.

Uses: Lime sulfur is primarily used as a dormant application to control fungal diseases on fruit trees, raspberries, and roses. Some insects and mites that overwinter on the plants are also controlled by these applications. Lime sulfur is sometimes used as foliar or summer applications, although this use is limited because of the potential to cause plant injury.

Notes: One of the oldest fungicides, lime sulfur is produced by boiling sulfur and lime in water. Previously very popular, current availability is quite limited. It offers some control of mites and scale insects that may overwinter on plants, but its corrosive activity can damage painted surfaces. To reduce chance of injury to any crop, do not apply if temperatures are expected to exceed 80°F within at least the following 24 hours. Lime sulfur has a strong odor, similar to that of rotten eggs.

Malathion

Trade Name: Malathion, found in many combination pesticides

Scientific Name: O,O-Dimethyl dithiophosphate of diethyl mercaptosuccinate/O,O-Dimethyl phosphorodithioate of diethyl mercaptosuccinate

Pesticide Class: Organophosphate insecticide

Toxicity: Low to moderate to mammals; higher to birds.

Uses: Broadly labeled for insect control on vegetables, fruits, and ornamentals. Primary target insects are aphids and mites, but has broad spectrum activity against most chewing insects. Still frequently used to kill adult mosquitoes.

Notes: Malathion has more labeled uses than any insecticide other than carbaryl (Sevin®). Persistence is short, with typical preharvest intervals of 1 to 3 days. Despite label claims, its effectiveness against most spider mites is marginal, since resistant strains proliferate. Because of existing gaps in safety data, registrations of malathion are currently under review by the Environmental Protection Agency. Registered uses of malathion will be more limited in the near future. Malathion has a strong, unpleasant odor. It is not systemic. Liquid formulations may injure aspen, viburnum, and some varieties of juniper. Some formulations (notably the ultra-low-volume formulations sprayed by aircraft) injure paint finishes.

Metaldehyde

Trade Names: Bug-geta Snail and Slug Bait®, Deadline®, Corry's Snail and Slug Death®, Eliminate®, others

Pesticide Class: Unclassified, molluscicide

Toxicity: Low toxicity to humans and other mammals. Metaldehyde is attractive to dogs and should be stored carefully to prevent access. Dispersed applications in a garden pose little risk to pets. Accidental poisoning of pets usually results in a temporary stupefaction, resembling drunkenness.

Uses: Slug control around food crops and vegetables.

Notes: Metaldehyde is the most commonly used slug bait. Common formulations include mixtures with bran- or apple-pomace–based baits or as a gel. Metaldehyde kills slugs by causing irritation and dehydration. Baits become attractive after wetting, but effectiveness is reduced if wet conditions persist after application. Metaldehyde breaks down rapidly in sunlight and should be applied late in the day.

Neem Extract

Trade Names: Bio-Neem®, Azatin®, Neemazad®, Neemix®, etc.

Scientific Name: Extract of the seeds of the neem tree; primary active ingredient is azadirachtin but oils of the neem seed also possess pesticidal activity.

Pesticide Class: Botanical insecticide (extracted from seeds of the tree *Azadirachta indica*)

Toxicity: Neem extracts appear to have very low toxicity to mammals. Neem has several pharmaceutical uses (e.g., ingredient in certain toothpaste products, burn oinments).

Uses: Broad labeling of neem-derived insecticides now includes essentially all ornamental and food

crops. Individual products specify the plants on which they may be used. Products containing primarily the oil of neem seed extracts have activity as a fungicide and can deter feeding of some insects.

Notes: Neem extracts can affect insects both by deterring feeding and by disrupting the hormones that regulate normal growth and development. Typically, neem extracts have fairly slow-acting effects, since sensitive insects are killed as they attempt to molt or at some other change in stage. Treated leaf surfaces are often simply avoided.

Oils, Horticultural

Trade Names: Sunspray®, Dormant Oil Spray®, Volck Oil®, Scalecide®, many other products

Scientific Name: Refined petroleum for horticultural use. Horticultural oils typically have a low percentage of aromatic compounds and distill at fairly low temperatures (ca 412–450°F).

Pesticide Class: Oils

Toxicity: Low.

Uses: Primarily used as an insecticide for application during the dormant season to control insect eggs and overwintering insect and mite stages on woody plants. Some oils are sufficiently refined to allow "summer" use on plants with foliage to control mites, whiteflies, and other soft-bodied arthropods. Horticultural oils can also assist in control of powdery mildew.

Permethrin

Trade Names: Intercept Insect Control®, Bug Stop Concentrate®

Scientific Name: (3-phenoxyphenyl)Methyl$\pm$ *cis-trans*3-(2,2-dichloroethenyl)-2,2-dimethyl-cyclopropanecarboxylate

Pesticide Class: Pyrethroid insecticide

Toxicity: Low toxicity to mammals and birds. Very high toxicity to fish and aquatic organisms.

Uses: A general use insecticide with specific activity against beetle larvae and caterpillars. Not generally effective against aphids and may aggravate problems with spider mites. Newly registered products allow use on many vegetables and fruits as well as ornamental plants.

Pyrethrins, Pyrethrum

Trade Names: A variety of flying insect aerosols, some vegetable crop sprays, Pyrenone®, etc.; sometimes combined with other insecticides

Scientific Name: Pyrethrins

Pesticide Class: Botanical insecticide (derived from flowers of *Chrysanthemum cinaeriofolium*)

Toxicity: Pyrethrins have very low toxicity to most mammals, making them among the safest insecticides in use. Asthmatic-like reactions have been reported from individuals with broad allergic backgrounds. Some breeds of cats are sensitive to pyrethrins.

Uses: The fast degradation and safety of pyrethrins facilitate their use for agricultural purposes more than any other insecticide. Pyrethrins can be used legally in the production of almost all food crops as well as on ornamentals. They are among the only insecticides labeled for use as a postharvest treatment on fruits and vegetables. Pyrethrins are also labeled for use in food handling establishments and other indoor areas. Pyrethrins, or related compounds (see tetramethrin, resmethrin, sumithrin), are extremely fast-acting, "knockdown" insecticides for flying insects and irritant flushing agents for cockroaches. Some formulations are available for vegetable insect control. Indoor fogging formulations are also available.

Notes: Pyrethrins are naturally derived insecticides extracted from flowers of the pyrethrum daisy, which thrives as a cultivated plant in many parts of the region. Pyrethrins have some unusual activities as insecticides. Most insects are highly susceptible to pyrethrins at very low concentrations. Perhaps most desirable is the rapid knockdown effect, which causes most flying insects to drop almost immediately upon exposure. Pyrethrins are also highly irritating to insects, allowing their use as a flushing agent. Because of their high cost, pyrethrins are almost always formulated with the synergist piperonyl butoxide, which greatly increases insecticidal action. Pyrethrins rapidly break down in light, so persistence is less than 1 day in most circumstances. Pyrethrum (powdered formulations of the flower) or extracted pyrethrins can be used in "certified organic" production in many areas, if synergists are not added.

Ro-Pel®

Trade Name: Ro-Pel®

Scientific Name: A mixture of benzyldiethyl [(2, 6-xylyl carbomoyl) methyl] ammonium saccarhide and thymol

Pesticide Class: Unclassified animal repellent

Toxicity: Low.

Uses: Animal feeding repellent for use on ornamental plants.

Notes: Ro-Pel® is an extremely bitter material. Use is not permitted on edible plants, indoor plants, or seeds of edible plants.

Rotenone

Trade Names: Rotenone, sometimes found in mixtures with other garden pesticides such as pyrethrins (e.g., Red Arrow®)

Scientific Name: Rotenone and other cube resins (rotenoids)

Pesticide Class: Botanical insecticide

Toxicity: Rotenone is moderately toxic to most mammals but exhibits a wide range of animal sensitivity. Some animals, notably swine, are very susceptible. Rotenone is an extremely potent fish poison and is generally used to poison "trash" fish during restocking projects.

Uses: Most use of rotenone is for control of various leaf-feeding caterpillars and beetles, such as cabbageworms and Colorado potato beetles, on vegetables. Some insects with sucking mouthparts, such as aphids, are also susceptible to rotenone. Thrips are also often listed as insects that can be controlled with rotenone. Rotenone has been used to control external parasites of cattle. It is fairly slow-acting, often requiring several days to kill most susceptible insects. However, insects stop feeding shortly after exposure.

Notes: Rotenone manufacture for use in the United States has been discontinued due to problems identified during its reregistration review. Using previously manufactured products is legal if used according to labeled directions.

Sabadilla

Trade Names: Sabadilla Dust®, Sabadilla Pest Control®
Scientific Name: Ground seeds of a South and Central American plant, sabadilla (*Schoenocaulon officinale*), which contain veratrine alkaloids
Pesticide Class: Botanical insecticide
Toxicity: Generally considered to have low toxicity but highly abrasive to mucous membranes of the nose and throat, inducing a sneezing reaction. Active ingredient is a powerful suppressor of blood pressure.
Uses: Used to control caterpillars, thrips, and bugs on certain vegetables, including squash, cucumbers, melons, beans, turnips, mustard, collards, cabbage, peanuts, and potatoes.
Notes: Since the 1940s and early 1950s, little research on the control of insects has been conducted on sabadilla dust. It is both a contact and a stomach poison and has shown promise against several of the true bugs (Hemiptera), such as squash bugs, chinch bugs, harlequin bugs, and stink bugs.

Effectiveness against leaf-feeding caterpillars, Mexican bean beetles, and thrips has also been demonstrated. The toxins in sabadilla are rapidly destroyed by light, although storing in dry, dark conditions for an extended period reportedly does not reduce its insecticidal activity. Uses on food crops are poorly specified but appear to require that a 24-hour interval elapse between treatment and harvest on registered crops.

Soap, Ammonium

Trade Name: Hinder®
Scientific Name: Ammonium soaps of higher fatty acids
Pesticide Class: Fatty acid salt (soap)
Toxicity: Very low.
Uses: Deer and rabbit repellent on fruit trees, ornamental plants, vegetables, and field crops.
Notes: Hinder® is designed to be sprayed or painted on plants. It is the only animal repellent currently registered to be applied directly to food crops.

Soap, Herbicidal

Trade Name: Sharpshooter®
Scientific Name: Potassium salts of saturated fatty acids
Pesticide Class: Fatty acid salt (soap)
Toxicity: Very low.
Uses: A nonselective, contact herbicide allowed for use around food crops as well as ornamental plantings.
Notes: Herbicidal soaps are nonselective and will injure the foliage of desirable plants that are treated or are exposed to drift. Activity of herbicidal soaps is most rapid during warm, dry weather. They rapidly (within hours) burn foliage of many treated plants but do not move systemically to kill plant roots. Several grasses, including Kentucky bluegrass and quackgrass, do not appear to be very susceptible. Soaps leave a visible, but temporary, white residue on concrete or asphalt when used to kill weeds in cracks.

Soap, Insecticidal

Trade Names: Safer Insecticidal Soap®, Insecticidal Soap Concentrate®, M-Pede®, others
Scientific Name: Various potassium salts of fatty acids
Pesticide Class: Fatty acid salt (soap)
Toxicity: Essentially nontoxic to humans. Can damage some plants.
Uses: Control of small, soft-bodied insects and mites on trees, shrubs, flowers, vegetables, and fruits. Also controls moss and algae in greenhouses.
Notes: Their high degree of safety to applicators has recently made use of insecticidal soaps more popular. They act strictly as a contact insecticide with no residual activity, so thorough application is essential. Since they react with minerals in hard water, they are more effective when used with soft water. Additionally, they can be used on food crops. Insecticidal soaps work best if applied when environmental conditions favor slow drying. Several plants are injured by soap sprays, so always test a small area before treatment. Nasturtiums, sweet peas, gardenias, certain zinnias, eu-

phorbias, horse chestnut, coleus, certain maples, and mountain ash are some of the plants that are vulnerable to injury. Several liquid dishwashing detergents are almost equally effective for insect control. Insecticidal soaps are usually acceptable for use in "certified organic" production.

Streptomycin

Trade Names: Streptomycin, Streptomycin sulfate
Pesticide Class: Antibiotic bactericide
Toxicity: Low toxicity to mammals but may cause allergic skin reaction. Toxic to fish.
Uses: Control of fire blight in apples and pears; crown gall control of roses.
Notes: Use directions do not allow application when fruit is present. Many bacteria have developed resistance to streptomycin where use has been frequent. Rotating with alternative bactericides, such as copper-based products, is recommended.

Sulfur

Trade Names: Sulfur, Flowable Sulfur, Wettable Sulfur
Scientific Name: Sulfur
Pesticide Class: Inorganic fungicide and miticide
Toxicity: Essentially nontoxic but highly irritating to skin and eyes.
Uses: Sulfur is used primarily to control powdery mildew, rust, brown rot, and other fungal diseases on fruits, vegetables, roses, and ornamentals. It is also effective and labeled for use against spider and rust (eriophyid) mites on several crops. Sulfur dusts are highly effective for control of potato (tomato) psyllids.
Notes: Sulfur is the oldest pesticide, having a recorded use of over 2,000 years. It can cause plant injury, particularly if applied during very high temperatures. (Labels vary, suggesting treatments be avoided during temperatures in the range of 85°F to 95°F or above.). Sulfur reacts with oils to cause plant injury on many fruit crops. Labels recommend that sulfur not be applied for 2 to 4 weeks after oils have been applied. Several plants are sulfur-shy and can be injured by sulfur. These

include cucurbits (melons, cucumbers, etc.), nut trees, viburnum, spinach, and apricots. Since residual sulfur affects processed fruits and vegetables (e.g., canned tomatoes, wine grapes), use should be discontinued for 2 or more weeks before processing. Due to its abrasive properties, applications of sulfur currently require a 24-hour waiting period (reentry interval) before gardeners can return to treated areas of the yard and garden.

Thiram

Trade Name: Thiram
Scientific Name: Tetramethyl thiuram disulfide
Pesticide Class: Organo-sulfur fungicide; animal feeding repellent
Toxicity: Thiram has moderately low toxicity to mammals but is irritating to the skin. Thiram is chemically similar to the drug Antabuse, used in the treatment of chronic alcoholism. Ingestion of alcohol after exposure to thiram will similarly produce sickness. Thiram is an older fungicide, and several safety studies are considered deficient based on current registration standards.
Uses: Fungicide seed protectant. Animal taste repellent for use on trees, shrubs, and dormant fruit crops.
Notes: On fruit trees, thiram may be applied only during the dormant season. Thiram is generally used as a deer repellent, applied in a dilute spray. If rainfall is frequent, the addition of a latex sticker or the specialty nursery protectant Wilt-Pruf® will increase the retention of thiram on twigs. However, adding wetting agents may result in severe plant injury.

Trifluralin

Trade Name: Treflan®
Scientific Name: a,a,a-Trifluoro-2,6-dinitro-N,N-dipropyl-p-toluidine
Pesticide Class: Dinitroaniline herbicide
Toxicity: Trifluralin has very low acute toxicity to mammals. However, some studies have raised concerns about possible carcinogenicity and mutagenicity, apparently because of impurities produced during manufacture. Trifluralin is

highly toxic to earthworms and fish. It is considered nontoxic to most other animals.

Uses: A preemergent herbicide used to control newly germinated garden weeds, widely used in agriculture. Trifluralin can be used for weed control in and around seeded carrots, okra, beans, and southern peas. Other permitted uses include transplanted (but not seeded) broccoli, tomatoes, Brussels sprouts, cabbage, cauliflower, peppers, and potatoes. Trifluralin may also be used for weed control around many seeded and most transplanted garden flowers.

Notes: Trifluralin inhibits the germination of seeds. Existing weeds are not controlled and must first be removed. Trifluralin is not water-soluble and does not move well in soil. Effective use requires that the herbicide be mixed with the upper soil during application. It can persist in the soil for several months before decomposing.

Triforine

Trade Names: Funginex®, Orthenex® (combined with acephate)
Scientific Name: N,N-1,4-piperazinediylbis [2,2,2-trichloro-ethylidene]-bis-(formamide)
Pesticide Class: Unclassified systemic fungicide

Toxicity: Active ingredient has low toxicity to mammals, but Funginex® label indicates moderate to high hazard (*Warning, Danger* signal statements).

Uses: Controls black spot, powdery mildew, and rust on roses and many other flowering plants.

Notes: Triforine moves systemically a short distance within the plant. It has both eradicant and protectant activity.

Zinc Phosphide

Trade Names: Mole and Gopher Bait
Pesticide Class: Inorganic rodenticide
Toxicity: Highly toxic to mammals, although most formulations sold as baits have a low percentage of the active ingredient.

Uses: Used as a pelleted bait to control moles and other ground-burrowing rodents to protect bulbs and other plants.

Notes: Not for use in vegetable gardens or other areas where food plants may be contaminated. Dead animals should be collected and buried after treatment. Zinc phosphide can react with acids to form a highly toxic phosphine gas. Many formulations are "Restricted Use Pesticides," which require licensing by users.

Appendix V

*Dilution Rates
for Small-Quantity Sprayers*

Many pest management products sold in small quantities (e.g., insecticidal soaps, horticultural oils) often state use rates as a percentage dilution or dilution ratio with water. This is often not clear to many users. For the nonmetric world, the following table has been prepared to assist in computing the approximate amount to add for gallon, quart, or pint quantities of spray.

TABLE A-4: DILUTION RATIO APPROXIMATIONS

Dilution ratio (Ingredient to water)	Percent dilution	Approximate amount to add to water volume: gallon	quart	pint
1:99	1	2¹/₂ Tbsp (−)	2 tsp (+)	1 tsp (+)
1:49	2	5 Tbsp (−)	4 tsp (+)	2 tsp (+)
1:32	3	8 Tbsp (+)	2 Tbsp (+)	1 Tbsp (+)
1:24	4	10 Tbsp (−)	2¹/₂ Tbsp (+)	4 tsp (+)
1:19	5	13 Tbsp (+)	3 Tbsp (−)	5 tsp (−)

+ = Will produce a solution of a slightly higher concentration than indicated.
− = Will produce a solution of a slightly lower concentration than indicated.

60 drops = 1 teaspoon (tsp)
3 teaspoons = 1 tablespoon (Tbsp)
2 tablespoons = 1 fl. oz. = 6 tsp
4 tablespoons = ¹/₄ cup = 2 fl. oz. = 12 tsp
8 tablespoons = ¹/₂ cup (teacup) = 4 fl. oz. = 24 tsp
16 tablespoons = 1 cup = 8 fl. oz. = 48 tsp
1 cup = 8 fl. oz. = 16 Tbsp = 48 tsp
2 cups = 1 pt. = 16 fl. oz. = 32 Tbsp = 96 tsp
2 pints = 1 qt. = 32 fl. oz. = 64 Tbsp = 192 tsp
4 quarts = 1 gal. = 128 fl. oz. = 256 Tbsp = 768 tsp

Appendix VI

Sources of Insect Traps and Other Pest Management Products

The following companies are involved in the manufacture or distribution of insect traps or other pest management supplies. Prices vary, and minimum orders are required by some distributors.

ARBICO
P.O. Box 4247
Tucson, AZ 85738-1247
(800) 827-2847
Carries some pheromone traps and most types of insect traps commonly used in gardens.

Consep Membranes
213 S.W. Columbia
P.O. Box 6059
Bend, OR 97708
(503) 388-3705
Producer of BioLure® line of pheromone traps and CheckMate® line of insect mating disruptants.

Gardens Alive!
5100 Schenley Place
Lawrenceburg, IN 47025
(812) 537-8651
e-mail: gardener@gardens-alive.com
Primarily markets to home gardeners, most commonly used traps are carried.

Gempler's
211 Blue Mounds Road
P.O. Box 270
Mt. Horeb, WI 53572
(800) 332-6744
IPM Buyer's Catalog offers widest range of traps and insect sampling equipment of any U.S. supplier.

Great Lakes IPM
10220 Church Road, N.E.
Vestaburg, MI 48891
(517) 268-5693
Distributor of several lines of pheromone traps, visual traps, and other pest management supplies.

Harmony Farm Supply
P.O. Box 460
Grafton, CA 95444
(707) 823-9125
Wide variety of traps, including some pheromone traps for fruit insects and codling moth mating disruption.

Integrated Fertility Management (IFM)
333-B Ohme Garden Road
Wenatchee, WA 98801
(800) 332-3179
Carries most commonly used insect traps and the BioLure® pheromone lures. Distributor of the Isomate line of pheromones used for mating disruption.

IPM Technologies, Inc.
P.O. Box 511
Kingsburg, CA 93631
(209) 897-0891
Supplier and developer of pheromone traps and lures for a wide variety of agricultural and forestry insect pests.

Iselin and Associates, Inc.
4520 S. Juniper
Tempe, AZ 85282
(602) 897-2051
Carries a wide variety of pheromone traps and mating disruption products.

Natural Insect Control (NIC)
RR #2
Stevensville, Ontario
Canada L0S 1S0
(905) 382-2904
e-mail: nic@niagara.com
Carries most common traps used around gardens and several pheromone traps.

Olson Products, Inc.
P.O. Box 1043
Medina, OH 44258
(216) 723-3210
Producer of sticky tape and sticky card traps for control of whiteflies and thrips in greenhouses.

Peaceful Valley Farm Supply
P.O. Box 2209
Grass Valley, CA 95945
(916) 272-4769
website: http://www.groworganic.com
Primarily markets to commercial organic growers. A very extensive line of insect traps is carried, including most pheromone traps and pheromone confusion systems.

Planet Natural
1612 Gold Avenue
P.O. Box 3146
Bozeman, MT 59772
(800) 289-6656
Carries some pheromones and most of the traps commonly used in gardens.

Appendix VII

State Extension Media Resource Centers for Information on Plant Pest Problems in the Western United States

ARIZONA

University of Arizona
Publications Distribution Center
4042 N. Campbell Avenue
Tuscon, AZ 85719
(520) 621-1713

COLORADO

Cooperative Extension Resource Center (CERC)
115 General Services Building
Colorado State University
Fort Collins, CO 80523
(970) 491-6198
website: http://www.colostate.edu/Depts/CoopExt

IDAHO

Ag Communications
University of Idaho
Ag Sciences Building
Moscow, ID 83844
(208) 885-2332
website: http://info.ag.uidaho.edu

KANSAS

Distribution Manager
Production Services
Umberger Hall, Room 16
Kansas State University
Manhattan, KS 66506
(785) 532-5830
e-mail: lheller@oz.oznet.ksu.edu

MONTANA

Extension Bulletin Room
118 Culbertson Hall
Montana State University
Bozeman, MT 59717
(406) 994-3273

NEBRASKA

Extension Media Distribution Center
105 Ag Communications Building
University of Nebraska
Lincoln, NE 68583-0918
(402) 472-9712
website: http://www.ianr.unl.edu/pubs

NEW MEXICO

Extension Bulletin Office
New Mexico State University
P.O. Box 30003, Dept. 3AI
Las Cruces, NM 88003
(505) 646-3228

OKLAHOMA

University Mailing Services
Oklahoma State University
115 Printing Building
Stillwater, OK 74078
(405) 744-5385

OREGON

Publications Orders
422 Kerr Administration
Oregon State University
Covallis, OR 97331-2119
(541) 737-2513
e-mail: puborder@ccmail.orst.edu

TEXAS

Publication and Supply Distribution
Texas Agricultural Extension Service
P.O. Box 1209
Bryan, TX 77806-1209
(409) 845-6571
website (entomology): entowww.tamu.edu

UTAH

Extension Bulletin Room
Utah State University
Logan, UT 84322-8960
(435) 797-2251
e-mail: krelw@ext.usus.edu

WASHINGTON

Bulletin Office
Cooper Publications Building
Washington State University
P.O. Box 645912
Pullman, WA 99164-5912
(509) 335-2857

WYOMING

Bulletin Room
P.O. Box 3313
University of Wyoming
Laramie, WY 82017
(307) 766-2115

Index

Fusarium, 27, 31, 34

Gall wasps, 116
Garden leafhoppers, 13, 139
Garlic, 33, 43, 60–61, 186
Geranium budworm (*see* Tobacco budworm)
Gladiolus thrips, 128–129
Gliocladium virens, 27, 174, 217
Glusinofate (Finale), 48, 51, 190, 198–200, 204–205, 230–231
Glyphosate (Round-Up), 46, 47, 48, 51, 190, 198–200, 204–205, 231
Golden tortoise beetle, 204
Gooseberries, 32, 72–73, 186, 189
Grape leafhopper, 137
Grapes, 6, 73, 186, 189
Grasshopper spore (*see* Nosema locustae)
Grasshoppers, 129–131
Gray garden slug, 86, 153–155
Gray mold, 167
Green foxtail/Yellow foxtail, 200
Green lacewings, 14, 23, 137, 141–144, 214
Green peach aphid, 40, 142–143
Greenhouse whitefly, 31, 139–140
Ground beetles, 14, 104
Gummosis (*see* Cytospora canker)
Gypsum, 3, 7

Handpicking, for pest management, 37–38, 87, 94–95, 99, 104–105, 114, 116–117, 124, 131, 196–198
Harlequin bug, 134
Herbs, diagnosis of common problems, 78–79, 186

Herbicides, 42, 46, 47–51, 198
    Injuries to plants, 189–190
Heterorhabditis spp., 28, 46, 217
Hoeing (*see* Tillage)
Hollyhock rust, 176–177
Hollyhock weevil, 95
Honeybees, 25
Hornworms, 104–106
Horticultural oils (*see* Oils, for pest management)
"Hummingbird" moths, 104–105

Ichneumonid wasps (*see* Wasps, parasitic)
Impatiens necrotic spot virus, 161
Imported cabbageworm, 40, 99–100
Imported currantworm, 40, 76, 117
Insecticides, 42–47
Insects
    characteristics of, 84–86
    common pest species, 87–150
Integrated Pest management (IPM), 48–49
Iris, diagnosis of common problems, 79
Iron, 4, 7, 191
Irrigation (*see* Watering)

Kale, 55–56

Lacewings (Green lacewings), 14, 23, 137, 141–144, 214
Lady beetles (Lady bugs), 14, 23, 87, 92, 141–144, 151, 214
Lambsquarters, 201
Leafcutter bees, 115–116
Leafhoppers, 136–139
Leafminers, 122–123 (*see also* Spinach leafminer)

Leafroller (*see* Fruittree leafroller)
Leeks, 33, 60–61
Lettuce, 4, 6, 33, 59, 186
Lettuce root aphid, 145
Lime sulfur, 231
Lygus bugs, 134–135

Magnesium, 4, 6
Malathion, 231–232
Mallow (Common mallow), 206
Manganese, 4, 7
Mantids, 24, 214
Metaldehyde, 155, 232
Mexican bean beetle, 87
Mexican bean beetle parasite, 27, 87, 216
Microbial insecticides, 46 (*see also Bacillus thuringiensis*)
Miller moth (*see* Army cutworm)
Millipedes, 86, 154
Milky slug (*see* Gray garden slug)
Minute pirate bug, 17, 104, 127–128, 151, 215
Mites
    eriophyid mites, 151–152
    predatory mites, 18, 25–26, 127–128, 215
    spider mites, 48, 150–151
Molybdenum, 4, 7
Mulches, 36–37, 48, 131, 139, 143, 160, 175, 185, 193, 195, 200–201
Mule deer, 42, 210–212
Muskmelon (Cantaloupe), 4, 5, 33, 59–60
Mycoplasma-like organisms/ MLOs (*see* Phytoplasmas)

Naphthalene, 208, 209
Narcissus bulb fly, 31, 126–127
Neem, 42, 43, 88, 232